REAL WORLD

MICRO

EDITED BY ROB LARSON, BRYAN SNYDER, CHRIS STURR,

AND THE *DOLLARS & SENSE* COLLECTIVE

REAL WORLD MICRO, TWENTY-FIFTH EDITION

Published by:
Economic Affairs Bureau, Inc. d/b/a *Dollars & Sense*
89 South St., Suite LL02, Boston, MA 02111
617-447-2177; dollars@dollarsandsense.org.
For order information, contact Economic Affairs Bureau or visit: www.dollarsandsense.org.

Real World Micro is edited by the *Dollars & Sense* Collective, which also publishes *Dollars & Sense* magazine and the classroom books *Real World Macro, Current Economic Issues, Real World Globalization, Labor and the Global Economy, Real World Latin America, Real World Labor, Real World Banking and Finance, The Wealth Inequality Reader, The Economics of the Environment, Introduction to Political Economy, Unlevel Playing Fields: Understanding Wage Inequality and Discrimination,* and *Our Economic Well-Being.*

The 2018 *Dollars & Sense* Collective:
Betsy Aron, Will Beaman, Autumn Beaudoin, Sarah Canon, Peter Kolozi, Tom Louie, John Miller, Jawied Nawabi, Zoe Sherman, Nick Serpe, Bryan Snyder, Chris Sturr, De'En Tarkpor, Cadwell Turnbull, and Jeanne Winner.

Co-editors of this volume: Rob Larson, Bryan Snyder, and Chris Sturr
Design and layout: Chris Sturr.

Printed in U.S.A

CONTENTS

CHAPTER 5 • MARKET FAILURE I: MARKET POWER

CHAPTER 6 • MARKET FAILURE II: EXTERNALITIES

CHAPTER 7 • LABOR MARKETS

CHAPTER 8 • THE DISTRIBUTION OF INCOME AND WEALTH

CHAPTER 9 • TAXATION

CHAPTER 10 • TRADE AND DEVELOPMENT

CHAPTER 11 • POLICY SPOTLIGHT: DEINDUSTRIALIZATION

INTRODUCTION

It sometimes seems that the United States has not one, but two economies. The first economy exists in economics textbooks and in the minds of many elected officials. It is a free-market economy, a system of promise and plenty, a cornucopia of consumer goods. In this economy, people are free and roughly equal, and each individual carefully looks after him- or herself, making uncoerced choices to advance his or her economic interests. Government is but an afterthought in this world, since almost everything that people need can be provided by the free market, itself guided by the reassuring "invisible hand."

The second economy is described in the writings of progressives, environmentalists, union supporters, and consumer advocates as well as honest business writers who recognize that real-world markets do not always conform to textbook models. This second economy features vast disparities of income, wealth, and power manifested in a system of class. It is an economy where employers have power over employees, where large firms have the power to shape markets, and where large corporate lobbies have the power to shape public policies. In this second economy, government sometimes adopts policies that ameliorate the abuses of capitalism and other times does just the opposite, but it is always an active and essential participant in economic life.

If you are reading this introduction, you are probably a student in an introductory college course in microeconomics. Your textbook will introduce you to the first economy, the harmonious world of free markets. *Real World Micro* will introduce you to the second.

Why "Real World" Micro?

A standard economics textbook is full of powerful concepts. It is also, by its nature, a limited window on the economy. What is taught in most introductory economics courses today is in fact just one strand of economic thought—neoclassical economics. Fifty years ago, many more strands were part of the introductory economics curriculum, and the contraction of the field has imposed limits on the study of economics that can confuse and frustrate students. This is particularly true in the study of microeconomics, which looks at markets for individual goods or services.

Real World Micro is designed as a supplement to a standard neoclassical textbook. Its articles provide vivid, real-world illustrations of economic concepts. But beyond that, our mission is to address two major sources of confusion in the study of economics at the introductory level.

The first source of confusion is the striking simplification of the world found in orthodox microeconomics. Standard textbooks describe stylized economic

1

interactions between idealized buyers and sellers that bear scant resemblance to the messy realities of the actual economic activity that we see around us. There is nothing wrong with simplifying. In fact, every social science must develop simplified models; precisely because reality is so complex, we must look at it a little bit at a time in order to understand it. Still, these simplifications mystify and misrepresent actual capitalist social relations and excise questions of race, gender, and class from the analysis.

Mainstream economic analysis calls to mind the story of the tipsy partygoer whose friend finds him on his hands and knees under a streetlight. "What are you doing?" asks the friend. "I dropped my car keys across the street, and I'm looking for them," the man replies. "But if you lost them across the street, how come you're looking over here?" "Well, the light's better here." In the interest of greater clarity, economics often imposes similar limits on its areas of inquiry.

As the title *Real World Micro* implies, one of our goals is to confront mainstream microeconomic theory with a more complex reality to direct attention to the areas not illuminated by the streetlight, and particularly to examine how inequality, power, and environmental imbalance change the picture. The idea is not to prove the standard theory "wrong," but to challenge you to think about where the theory is more and less useful, and why markets may not operate as expected.

This focus on real-world counterpoints to mainstream economic theory connects to the second issue we aim to clarify. Most economics texts uncritically present key assumptions and propositions that form the core of standard economic theory. They offer much less exploration of a set of related questions: What are alternative propositions about the economy? Under what circumstances will these alternatives more accurately describe the economy? What differences do such propositions make? Our approach is not to spell out an alternative theory in detail, but to raise questions and present real-life examples that bring these questions to life. For example, textbooks carefully lay out "consumer sovereignty," the notion that consumers' wishes ultimately determine what the economy will produce. But can we reconcile consumer sovereignty with an economy where one of the main products in industries such as soft drinks, cars, and music is consumer desire itself? We think it is valuable to see ideas like consumer sovereignty as debatable propositions and that requires hearing other views in the debate.

In short, our goal in this book is to use real-world examples from today's economy to raise questions, stimulate debate, and dare you to think critically about the models in your textbook.

What's in This Book

Real World Micro is organized to follow the outline of a standard microeconomics text. Each chapter leads off with a brief introduction, including study questions for the entire chapter, and then provides several short articles from *Dollars & Sense* magazine and other sources that illustrate the chapter's key concepts.

Here is a quick overview:

Chapter 1, Perspectives on Microeconomic Theory, starts off the volume by taking a hard look at the strengths and weaknesses of actual markets, with special attention to weaknesses that standard textbooks tend to underemphasize.

Chapter 2, Supply and Demand, presents real-world examples of supply and demand in action. *Dollars & Sense* authors question the conventional wisdom on topics such as price volatility, affordability of essential goods like food (and issues of hunger), and price regulations like the minimum wage and rent control.

Chapter 3, Consumers, raises provocative questions about utility theory and individual consumer choice. What happens when marketers shape buyers' tastes? What happens when important information is hidden from consumers? How can consumer decisions include broader considerations like environmental sustainability or labor conditions? What roles should government play in consumer protection?

Chapter 4, Firms, Production, and Profit Maximization, illustrates how business strategies to maximize profits may come at the expense of the social good, and challenges students to think about different ways of organizing firms. The chapter considers issues like executive compensation, and the relation between the profit motive and essential goods like food and healthcare.

Chapter 5, Market Failure I: Market Power, explores market power and monopoly, just one example of the unequal power relationships that pervade our economic system. The chapter critiques market power in such industries as pharmaceuticals, banking, and agriculture, but also questions whether small business prevalence would be an improvement.

Chapter 6, Market Failure II: Externalities, addresses cases where processes of production, exchange, and consumption affect not only the parties to those transactions, but also third parties (especially negatively). It considers how public policy should address cases where such spillover effects create a divergence between private and social costs and benefits.

Chapter 7, Labor Markets, examines the ways in which labor-market outcomes can be affected by unionization, globalization, and a host of other factors largely left out of the standard supply-and-demand models. Among the issues discussed are the reasons for union decline, the causes of slow growth in wages today, the rise of "contingent" labor arrangements, and possible ways to improve labor conditions domestically and internationally.

Chapter 8, The Distribution of Income and Wealth, discusses the causes and consequences of inequality, countering the mainstream view that inequality is good for growth. The chapter examines the contours of inequality, with particular attention to race and gender. It questions conventional views attributing rising inequality to technological change and globalization, and considers the impact of a changing balance of power between workers and employers. And it deals with issues of wealth and poverty, both domestic and global.

Chapter 9, Taxation, explores issues of incomes, wealth, and taxation, including who actually pays taxes and at what rates. It also explores whether changes in taxes lead to changes in economic behavior and outcomes. This proposition is explored in the areas of taxes on high-income individuals and their effects on savings and investment, as well as taxes on financial transactions and effects on speculative activity. Finally, it discusses new controversies over growing inequality and the possibility of international taxation on accumulated wealth.

Chapter 10, Trade and Development, covers key issues in trade policy and the world economy. The chapter's articles question the value of free trade and foreign investment for development, consider the role of currency markets in global trade outcomes, address the impacts of globalization on workers (in both high-income and low-income countries), and discuss issues of development and environmental protection.

Chapter 11, Policy Spotlight: Deindustrialization, explores the possible causes of job losses in manufacturing in the United States, including the roles played by automation, trade deficits and trade policy, financialization, monetary policy, and asset bubbles. ❑

Chapter 1

PERPECTIVES ON
MICROECONOMIC THEORY

INTRODUCTION

Economics is all about tradeoffs. The concept of "opportunity cost" reminds us that in order to make a purchase, or even to make use of a resource that you control (such as your time), you must give up other possible purchases or other possible uses of that resource. Markets broaden the range of possible tradeoffs by facilitating exchange between people who do not know each other, and in many cases never meet at all. Think of buying a pair of athletic shoes in Atlanta from a company based in Los Angeles that manufactures shoes in Malaysia and has stockholders all over the world. As the idea of gains from trade suggests, markets allow many exchanges that make both parties better off.

But markets have severe limitations as well. The economic crisis that began in 2008 has made those limitations all too clear. Even lifelong free-marketeers such as former Federal Reserve chair Alan Greenspan have been forced to question their belief in the "invisible hand."

In this chapter's first article, economist Marty Wolfson critiques a mainstream "free-market" ideology that views markets as delivering to each person their just rewards, based on their talent or effort. In fact, he argues, markets are often structured in ways that stack the deck in favor of the wealthy and powerful (Article 1.1).

Markets and price determination, in neoclassical economics, have been idealized into elegant, utility-maximizing perfection. Chris Tilly, in "Shaking the Invisible Hand" (Article 1.2), uncovers the curious assumptions necessary to allow for the market mechanism to be the most efficient allocator of scarce resources. He provides us with eight "Tilly Assumptions" underlying perfectly functioning markets. If any of these assumptions is violated, then there is a possibility of "market failure," or less-than-optimal economic results.

In "Pursuing Profits—Or Power?" (Article 1.3), James K. Boyce questions the assumption that the firm seeks to maximize profits alone. In Boyce's view, a great deal of business behavior (especially political behavior) suggests that corporate decision-makers often put the pursuit of power above profits.

Alejandro Reuss provides us with a clear discussion of the idealized neoclassical view of exchange, with a particular focus on labor markets, in "Freedom, Equity,

5

and Efficiency" (Article 1.4). Ideal neoclassical markets offer the promise of freedom of choice, equity (fairness), and efficiency, but often fail to deliver on all three counts. Reuss walks us through these neoclassical standards and contrasts them to the not-so-rosy reality of unrestrained labor-market competition.

In "Whatever Happened to the Working Class?" (Article 1.5), Martin Oppenheimer breaks down our vague ideas of the "middle class" into more realistic categories, based not only on incomes but on work roles. Taking a focused view allows us to consider the different kinds of work done by these workers and smaller business owners, and to see surprises in their conflicting and shared interests.

Finally, in "Sharing the Wealth of the Commons" (Article 1.6), Peter Barnes focuses our attention on the oft-ignored forms of wealth that we do not own privately, but are held in various "commons." He challenges the way that conventional economists view the environment and other goods that are shared by many people.

Discussion Questions

1. (General) What things should not be for sale? Beyond everyday goods and services, think about human bodies, votes, small countries, and other things that might be bought and sold. How do you draw the line between what should be bought and sold and what should not?

2. (General) If not markets, then what? What are other ways to organize economic activity? Which ways are most likely to resolve the problems brought up in this chapter?

3. (Article 1.1) Wolfson argues that markets, far from being "free," are often rigged in favor of the wealthy and powerful. What are some examples?

4. (Article 1.2) Write out the eight "Tilly Assumptions" and corresponding realities using Tilly's exact terms for the assumptions. Are these assumptions reasonable?

5. (Article 1.2) For each of the eight "Tilly Assumptions," explain how the market mechanism would fail if the assumption were violated.

6. (Article 1.3) Boyce argues that firms frequently put power before profits. If greater power goes hand in hand with higher profits, how can we tell what aim firms are actually pursuing?

7. (Article 1.4) According to neoclassical theory, how do markets deliver "efficient" results if all "barriers" to exchange are removed? In what sense are these results "efficient"?

8. (Article 1.4) How is the word "freedom" defined by neoclassical economists? What freedoms do they argue workers lose under regulated labor markets? How does this compare to your view of what kinds of freedoms are valuable?

9. (Article 1.4) Does the unfettered operation of the market mechanism deliver "equity" to society? In your view, what would fair labor-market processes or outcomes look like?

10. (Article 1.5) Martin Oppenheimer finds that incomes alone aren't enough for us to make analytical distinctions among social classes. What other issues does he suggest are relevant?

11. (Article 1.5) Describe the concept of the "new middle" or "managerial" class. In your opinion, is this social category worth its own distinct label as a social or economic class, or is another concept more useful?

12. (Article 1.6) Barnes says that we take for granted an enormous number of resources—including the natural environment, but also the laws and institutions that make economic activity possible. Is his point the same as saying that there are market failures, such as pollution externalities, that prevent markets from taking into account the full value of the environment?

Article 1.1

"FREE MARKET" OUTCOMES ARE NOT FAIR—AND NOT FREE

BY MARTY WOLFSON

November/December 2012

"Since 1980, the U.S. government has reduced its intervention in the U.S. economy, which has become much more of a free market. Conservatives applaud this development because they think that free-market outcomes reward talent and hard work; progressives object to the income inequality of free-market outcomes and want to use government tax and transfer policy to reduce inequality."

Most people, whether conservative or progressive, would probably agree with this statement. This framing of the issue, however, plays into a right-wing story in which conservatives are the defenders of (free) market outcomes, including the success of the rich who have made it "on their own"; meanwhile, the "dependent poor" look to the government for handouts. This has been a basic element of the right-wing playbook for a long time. Then-presidential candidate Mitt Romney was drawing on this narrative when he complained about the 47% of the U.S. population "who are dependent upon government ... who believe that government has a responsibility to care for them."

This view has two main themes: 1) Because the U.S. free-market economy rewards talent and hard work, the middle class should emulate the wealthy for their success, not vilify them; and 2) those who have been failures in the market want the government to take care of them by redistributing income from those who have been successful. We can see these themes play out on all sorts of political issues. They form, for example, the basis for the attacks on the Affordable Health Care Act (or "Obamacare"). Middle-class Americans, in the conservative view, are being taxed—forced to pay—to provide health insurance for those "unsuccessful" elements of the population who have not earned it themselves.

The conservative argument assumes that the outcomes we observe are the result of a free-market economy. However, the right-wing objective has not been to create a free market; it has been to rig government policy and the market so as to redistribute income towards large corporations and the wealthy.

For example, conservatives themselves want to use government policy to bring about a different distribution of income from what we have now—a distribution that is more favorable to corporations and the very rich. A central policy objective for conservatives, ever since the Reagan Administration, has been to cut taxes on the wealthy. And by cutting government revenue, they have been able to make the argument that government programs for the poor and the middle class need to be cut in order to balance the budget.

Also, conservatives have eliminated restrictions on corporations and protections for workers, consumers, and the environment. They have attacked barriers to international capital mobility, deregulated industries, and reduced government regulations aimed at ensuring a safe workplace and a healthy environment.

Because conservative policies have often taken the form of reducing government programs and regulations, the ideology of a free market has been useful in rationalizing them. Other conservative interventions, however, have been less able to fit into the free-market mold, and therefore are especially revealing of conservatives' genuine aims.

When the financial crisis of 2008 threatened the survival of the large banks, they were quick to ask for the government to intervene with a large bailout. The "right-to-work" law recently passed in Indiana, designed to deprive unions of financial resources, is an explicit rejection of a market outcome—the private agreement between management and union to require all workers to pay their "fair share" of the costs of union representation. "Free-trade" agreements, ostensibly designed to eliminate restrictions on the movement of goods and capital, have nonetheless continued to restrict the free movement of people. Even the repeal of financial regulations in the 1980s and 1990s, ostensibly a free-market endeavor, created the anti-competitive giant financial firms that demanded to be bailed out in 2008.

The realization that the economy is rigged to benefit the rich and large corporations takes away the force of the right-wing argument that progressives want to use government to "vilify" the "successful" and reward the "slothful and incompetent." When the game has been rigged, it is wrong to say that the market simply rewards talent and hard work, and the outcomes that result can hardly be called fair. When the market outcomes that we observe are unfair, we need to both change the rules for how the economy works and use the government to restore fairness. ❏

Sources: Dean Baker, *The End of Loser Liberalism: Making Markets Progressive* (2011); Transcript of Mitt Romney video, *Mother Jones*, September 17, 2012 (motherjones.com).

Article 1.2

SHAKING THE INVISIBLE HAND
The Uncertain Foundations of Free-Market Economics

BY CHRIS TILLY
November 1989; updated March 2011

> It is not from the benevolence of the butcher, the brewer or the baker that we
> expect our dinner, but from their regard to their own interest... [No individ-
> ual] intends to promote the public interest... [rather, he is] led by an invisible
> hand to promote an end which was no part of his intention.
>
> —*Adam Smith,* The Wealth of Nations, *1776*

Seen the Invisible Hand lately? It's all around us these days, propping up conservative arguments in favor of free trade, deregulation, and tax-cutting.

Today's advocates for "free," competitive markets echo Adam Smith's claim
that unfettered markets translate the selfish pursuit of individual gain into the greatest benefit for all. They trumpet the superiority of capitalist free enterprise over
socialist efforts to supplant the market with a planned economy, and even decry liberal attempts to moderate the market. Anything short of competitive markets, they
proclaim, yields economic inefficiency, making society worse off.

But the economic principle underlying this fanfare is shaky indeed. Since the
late 19th century, mainstream economists have struggled to prove that Smith was
right—that the chaos of free markets leads to a blissful economic order. In the
1950s, U.S. economists Kenneth Arrow and Gerard Debreu finally came up with a
theoretical proof, which many orthodox economists view as the centerpiece of modern economic theory.

Although this proof is the product of the best minds of mainstream economics,
it ends up saying surprisingly little in defense of free markets. The modern theory
of the Invisible Hand shows that given certain assumptions, free markets reduce the
wasteful use of economic resources—but perpetuate unequal income distribution.

To prove free markets cut waste, economists must make a number of far-fetched
assumptions: there are no concentrations of economic power; buyers and sellers know
every detail about the present and future economy; and all costs of production are
borne by producers while all benefits from consumption are paid for by consumers (see
box for a complete list). Take away any one of these assumptions and markets can lead
to stagnation, recession, and other forms of waste—as in fact they do.

In short, the economic theory invoked by conservatives to justify free markets
instead starkly reveals their limitations.

The Fruits of Free Markets

The basic idea behind the Invisible Hand can be illustrated with a story. Suppose
that I grow apples and you grow oranges. We both grow tired of eating the same
fruit all the time and decide to trade. Perhaps we start by trading one apple for one

orange. This exchange satisfies both of us, because in fact I would gladly give up more than one apple to get an orange, and you would readily pay more than one orange for an apple. And as long as swapping one more apple for one more orange makes us both better off, we will continue to trade.

Eventually, the trading will come to a stop. I begin to notice that the novelty of oranges wears old as I accumulate a larger pile of them and the apples I once had a surplus of become more precious to me as they grow scarcer. At some point, I draw the line: in order to obtain one more apple from me, you must give me more than one orange. But your remaining oranges have also become more valuable to you. Up to now, each successive trade has made both of us better off. Now there is no further exchange that benefits us both, so we agree to stop trading until the next crop comes in.

Note several features of this parable. Both you and I end up happier by trading freely. If the government stepped in and limited fruit trading, neither of us would be as well off. In fact, the government cannot do anything in the apple/orange market that will make both of us better off than does the free market.

Adding more economic actors, products, money, and costly production pro-cesses complicates the picture, but we reach the same conclusions. Most of us sell our labor time in the market rather than fruit; we sell it for money that we then use to buy apples, oranges, and whatever else we need. The theory of the Invisible Hand tells us a trip to the fruit stand improves the lot of both consumer and seller; likewise, the sale of labor time benefits both employer and employee. What's more, according to the theory, competition between apple farmers insures that consumers will get apples produced at the lowest possible cost. Government intervention still can only make things worse.

This fable provides a ready-made policy guide. Substitute "Japanese autos" and "U.S. agricultural products" for apples and oranges, and the fable tells you that import quotas or tariffs only make the people of both countries worse off. Change the industries to airlines or telephone services, and the fable calls for deregulation. Or re-tell the tale in the labor market: minimum wages and unions (which prevent workers from individually bargaining over their wages) hurt employers and workers.

Fruit Salad

Unfortunately for free-market boosters, two major short-comings make a fruit salad out of this story. First, even if free markets perform as advertised, they deliver only one benefit—the prevention of certain economically wasteful practices—while preserving inequality. According to the theory, competitive markets wipe out two kinds of waste: unrealized trades and inefficient production. Given the right assumptions, markets ensure that when two parties both stand to gain from a trade, they make that trade, as in the apples-and-oranges story. Competition compels producers to search for the most efficient, lowest-cost production methods—again, given the right preconditions.

Though eliminating waste is a worthy goal, it leaves economic inequality untouched. Returning once more to the orchard, if I start out with all of the apples and oranges and you start out with none, that situation is free of waste: no swap can make us both better off since you have nothing to trade! Orthodox economists acknowledge that even in the ideal competitive market, those who start out rich stay rich, while the poor remain poor. Many of them argue that attempts at redistributing income will most certainly create economic inefficiencies, justifying the preservation of current inequities.

But in real-life economics, competition does lead to waste. Companies wastefully duplicate each other's research and build excess productive capacity. Cost-cutting often leads to shoddy products, worker speedup, and unsafe working conditions. People and factories stand idle while houses go unbuilt and people go unfed. That's because of the second major problem: real economies don't match the assumptions of the Invisible Hand theory.

Of course, all economic theories build their arguments on a set of simplifying assumptions about the world. These assumptions often sacrifice some less important aspects of reality in order to focus on the economic mechanisms of interest.

Assumptions and Reality

The claim that free markets lead to efficiency and reduced waste rests on eight main assumptions. However, these assumptions differ sharply from economic reality. (Assumptions 1, 3, 4, and 5 are discussed in more detail in the article.)

ASSUMPTION ONE: *No market power.* No individual buyer or seller, nor any group of buyers or sellers, has the power to affect the market-wide level of prices, wages, or profits.
REALITY ONE: Our economy is dotted with centers of market power, from large corporations to unions. Furthermore, employers have an edge in bargaining with workers because of the threat of unemployment.

ASSUMPTION TWO: *No economies of scale.* Small plants can produce as cheaply as large ones.
REALITY TWO: In fields such as mass-production industry, transportation, communications, and agriculture, large producers enjoy a cost advantage, limiting competition.

ASSUMPTION THREE: *Perfect information about the present.* Buyers and sellers know everything there is to know about the goods being exchanged. Also, each is aware of the wishes of every other potential buyer and seller in the market.
REALITY THREE: The world is full of lemons—goods about which the buyer is inadequately informed. Also, people are not mind-readers, so sellers get stuck with surpluses and willing buyers are unable to find the products they want.

ASSUMPTION FOUR: *Perfect information about the future.* Contracts between buyers and sellers cover every possible future eventuality.
REALITY FOUR: Uncertainty clouds the future of any economy. Futures markets are limited.

But in the case of the Invisible Hand, the theoretical preconditions contradict several central features of the economy.

For one thing, markets are only guaranteed to prevent waste if the economy runs on "perfect competition": individual sellers compete by cutting prices, individual buyers compete by raising price offers, and nobody holds concentrated economic power. But today's giant corporations hardly match this description. Coke and Pepsi compete with advertising rather than price cuts. The oil companies keep prices high enough to register massive profits every year. Employers coordinate the pay and benefits they offer to avoid bidding up compensation. Workers, in turn, marshal their own forces via unionization—another departure from perfect competition.

Indeed, the jargon of "perfect competition" overlooks the fact that property ownership itself confers disproportionate economic power. "In the competitive model," orthodox economist Paul Samuelson commented, "it makes no difference whether capital hires labor or the other way around." He argued that given perfect

---

ASSUMPTION FIVE: *You only get what you pay for.* Nobody can impose a cost on somebody else, nor obtain a benefit from them, without paying.
REALITY FIVE: Externalities, both positive and negative, are pervasive. In a free market, polluters can impose costs on the rest of us without paying. And when a public good like a park is built or roads are maintained, everyone benefits whether or not they helped to pay for it.

ASSUMPTION SIX: *Price is a proxy for pleasure.* The price of a given commodity will represent the quality and desirability and or utility derived from the consumption of the commodity.
REALITY SIX: "Conspicuous Consumption" (Veblen) and or "snob effects" will often distort prices from underlying utility and marketers will try to position commodities accordingly.

ASSUMPTION SEVEN: Self-interest only. In economic matters, each person cares only about his or her own level of well-being.
REALITY SEVEN: Solidarity, jealousy, and even love for one's family violate this assumption.

ASSUMPTION EIGHT: No joint production. Each production process has only one product.
REALITY EIGHT: Even in an age of specialization, there are plenty of exceptions to this rule. For example, large service firms such as hospitals or universities produce a variety of different services using the same resources.

—Chris Tilly and Bryan Snyder

competition among workers and among capitalists, wages and profits would remain the same regardless of who does the hiring. But unemployment—a persistent feature of market-driven economies—makes job loss very costly to workers. The sting my boss feels when I "fire" him by quitting my job hardly equals the setback I experience when he fires me.

Perfect Information?

In addition, the grip of the Invisible Hand is only sure if all buyers and sellers have "perfect information" about the present and future state of markets. In the present, this implies consumers know exactly what they are buying—an assumption hard to swallow in these days of leaky breast implants and chicken à la salmonella. Employers must know exactly what skills workers have and how hard they will work—suppositions any real-life manager would laugh at.

Perfect information also means sellers can always sniff out unsatisfied demands, and buyers can detect any excess supplies of goods. Orthodox economists rely on the metaphor of an omnipresent "auctioneer" who is always calling out prices so all buyers and sellers can find mutually agreeable prices and consummate every possible sale. But in the actual economy, the auctioneer is nowhere to be found, and markets are plagued by surpluses and shortages.

Perfect information about the future is even harder to come by. For example, a company decides whether or not to build a new plant based on whether it expects sales to rise. But predicting future demand is a tricky matter. One reason is that people may save money today in order to buy (demand) goods and services in the future. The problem comes in predicting when. As economist John Maynard Keynes observed in 1934, "An act of individual saving means—so to speak—a decision not to have dinner today. But it does not necessitate a decision to have dinner or to buy a pair of boots a week hence...or to consume any specified thing at any specified date. Thus it depresses the business of preparing today's dinner without stimulating the business of making ready for some future act of consumption." Keynes concluded that far from curtailing waste, free markets gave rise to the colossal waste of human and economic resources that was the Great Depression—in part because of this type of uncertainty about the future.

Free Lunch

The dexterity of the Invisible Hand also depends on the principle that "You only get what you pay for." This "no free lunch" principle seems at first glance a reasonable description of the economy. But major exceptions arise. One is what economists call "externalities"—economic transactions that take place outside the market. Consider a hospital that dumps syringes at sea. In effect, the hospital gets a free lunch by passing the costs of waste disposal on to the rest of us. Because no market exists where the right to dump is bought and sold, free markets do nothing to compel the hospital to bear the costs of dumping—which is why the government must step in.

Public goods such as sewer systems also violate the "no free lunch" rule. Once the sewer system is in place, everyone shares in the benefits of the waste disposal, regardless of whether or not they helped pay for it. Suppose sewer systems were sold in a free market, in which each person had the opportunity to buy an individual share. Then any sensible, self-interested consumer would hold back from buying his or her fair share—and wait for others to provide the service. This irrational situation would persist unless consumers could somehow collectively agree on how extensive a sewer system to produce—once more bringing government into the picture.

Most orthodox economists claim that the list of externalities and public goods in the economy is short and easily addressed. Liberals and radicals, on the other hand, offer a long list: for example, public goods include education, healthcare, and decent public transportation—all in short supply in our society.

Because real markets deviate from the ideal markets envisioned in the theory of the Invisible Hand, they give us both inequality and waste. But if the theory is so far off the mark, why do mainstream economists and policymakers place so much stock in it? They fundamentally believe the profit motive is the best guide for the economy. If you believe that "What's good for General Motors is good for the country," the Invisible Hand theory can seem quite reasonable. Business interests, government, and the media constantly reinforce this belief, and reward those who can dress it up in theoretical terms. As long as capital remains the dominant force in society, the Invisible Hand will maintain its grip on the hearts and minds of us all. ❑

Article 1.3

PURSUING PROFITS—OR POWER?

BY JAMES K. BOYCE
July/August 2013

Do corporations seek to maximize profits? Or do they seek to maximize power? The two may be complementary—wealth begets power, power begets wealth—but they're not the same. One important difference is that profits can come from an expanding economic "pie," whereas the size of the power pie is fixed. Power is a zero-sum game: more for me means less for you. And for corporations, the pursuit of power sometimes trumps the pursuit of profits.

Take public education, for example. Greater investment in education from pre-school through college could increase the overall pie of well-being. But it would narrow the educational advantage of the corporate oligarchs and their privately schooled children—and diminish the power that comes with it. Although corporations could benefit from the bigger pie produced by a better-educated labor force, there's a tension between what's good for business and what's good for the business elite.

Similarly, the business elite today supports economic austerity instead of full-employment policies that would increase growth and profits. This may have something to do with the fact that austerity widens inequality, while full employment would narrow it (by empowering workers). If we peel away the layers of the onion, at the core again we find that those at the top of the corporate pyramid put power before profits.

As one more example, consider the politics of government regulation. Corporations routinely pass along to consumers whatever costs they incur as a result of regulation. In the auto industry, for instance, the regulations that mandated seat belts, catalytic converters, and better fuel efficiency added a few hundred dollars to car prices. They didn't cut automaker profit margins. If the costs of regulation are ultimately borne by the consumer, why do they face such stiff resistance from the corporations? The answer may have less to do with profits than with power. Corporate chieftains are touchy about their "management prerogatives." They simply don't like other folks telling them what to do.

In a famous 1971 memorandum to the U.S. Chamber of Commerce, future Supreme Court Justice Lewis Powell wrote, "The day is long past when the chief executive office of a major corporation discharges his responsibility by maintaining a satisfactory growth of profits." To counter what he described as an attack on the American free-enterprise system by labor unions, students, and consumer advocates, Powell urged CEOs to act on "the lesson that political power is necessary; that power must be assiduously cultivated; and that when necessary, it must be used aggressively and with determination." He was preaching to a receptive choir.

The idea that firms single-mindedly maximize profits is an axiom of faith of neoclassical Econ 101, but alternative theories have a long history in the broader profession. Thorstein Veblen, John Maynard Keynes, and Fred Hirsch all saw an individual's position relative to others as a key motivation in economic behavior.

Today a sound-bite version of this idea is encountered on bumper stickers: "He Who Dies with the Most Toys Wins."

In his 1972 presidential address to the American Economics Association, titled "Power and the Useful Economist," John Kenneth Galbraith juxtaposed the role of power in the real-world economy to its neglect in orthodox economics: "In eliding power—in making economics a nonpolitical subject—neoclassical theory ... destroys its relation with the real world."

On the free-marketeer side of the ideological spectrum, the pursuit of power is depicted as a pathology distinctive to the State. "Chicago school" economist William Niskanen theorized that public-sector bureaucrats seek to maximize the size of their budgets, taking this as a proxy for "salary, perquisites of the office, public reputation, power, patronage, ease of managing the bureau, and ease of making changes." He called this "the peculiar economics of bureaucracy."

But the pursuit of power isn't unique to government bureaucracies. It's commonplace in corporate bureaucracies, too. In his presidential address, Galbraith made the connection: "Between public and private bureaucracies—between GM and the Department of Transportation, between General Dynamics and the Pentagon—there is a deeply symbiotic relationship."

Recognizing the real-world pursuit of power not only helps us understand behavior that otherwise may seem peculiar. It also redirects our attention from the dichotomy between the market and the state toward a more fundamental one: the divide between oligarchy and democracy. ❑

Sources: Sarah O'Connor, "OECD warns of rising inequality as austerity intensifies," *Financial Times*, May 15, 2013 (ft.com); Lewis F. Powell, Jr., "Confidential Memorandum: Attack on American Free Enterprise System," Aug. 23, 1971 (law.wlu.edu); John Kenneth Galbraith, "Power and the Useful Economist," *American Economic Review*, March 1973; William A. Niskanen, "The Peculiar Economics of Bureaucracy," *American Economic Review*, May 1968.

Article 1.4

FREEDOM, EQUITY, AND EFFICIENCY
Contrasting Views of Labor Market Competition

BY ALEJANDRO REUSS
April 2012

The basic world-view of neoclassical economists is that, in markets, people engage voluntarily in exchanges with each other, and that this means market exchanges leave both parties better off. If someone cannot be forced to make a trade, they will only do so if it leaves them at least a little better off than they would have been otherwise. Left to their own devices, people will find and exhaust all the possibilities for trades that boost the overall social well-being. Policies that interfere with people's ability to make voluntary trades, then, can only subtract from the well-being of society as a whole.

The neoclassical narrative depends on many (often unspoken) *assumptions*. Individuals must be rational and self-interested. The assumption of "rationality" means they must act in ways that further their objectives, whatever these objectives may be. The assumption of "self-interest" means that, in making decisions, they must only take into account benefits and costs to themselves. They must have perfect information about all factors (past, present, and future) that could affect their decisions. Their actions must not affect any "third parties" (anyone other than those directly involved in the exchange and agreeing to its terms). There must be many buyers and sellers, so that no single buyer or seller (and no group of buyers or sellers colluding together) can impose the prices they want. Several other assumptions may also be important.

The Neoclassical View

Implicitly, the neoclassical story appeals to ideas about freedom, equity (fairness), and efficiency. Very few people would say they are against any of these virtues, but different people embrace different definitions. Different people, for example, have different ideas about what people should have the freedom to do, and what "freedoms" would impinge on the freedoms, rights, or well-being of others. So really the issue is, when neoclassical economists say that unregulated market competition is desirable, for example, as a matter, of "freedom," what view of freedom are they basing this on?

Freedom

By "freedom," neoclassical economists mean freedom from force or threat of force. They would recognize that someone making an exchange when threatened with violence—when confronted with "an offer they can't refuse," in the *Godfather* sense of that phrase—is not really engaging in a voluntary transaction. That person could very well make an exchange leaving them worse off than they would have been otherwise (except that they may have saved their own neck). On the other hand, suppose a person is faced only with very undesirable alternatives to engaging in a trade. Suppose they have "no choice" but to accept a job, because the alternative is to starve. Neoclassical economists would point out that these circumstances are not of the potential employer's making. It is quite unlike, in their view, conditions that are directly imposed by the other party (like having a gun held to one's head). If the impoverished worker accepts a job offer, even at a very low wage or under very bad working conditions, the neoclassical economist would argue that this is evidence that he or she really is made better off by the exchange. Restricting his or her freedom to engage in this exchange, in the neoclassical view, only makes him or her worse off.

Equity

Neoclassical economists argue that restrictions on market competition can unfairly benefit some market participants (buyers or sellers) or potential market participants at the expense of others. This kind of equity concern enters into neoclassical theory in several ways:

First, restrictions on competition may affect the ability of different people (or firms) to participate in a market—to offer what they have for sale or to bid on what others offer for sale. Suppose that the government issues special licenses to some people or firms that permit them to engage in a certain trade, like driving a taxi, while denying such licenses to others. (Such policies create "barriers to entry," in the language of neoclassical economics.) Such restrictions are, in the neoclassical view, unfair to the unlucky (or less-influential) individuals or firms who do not receive licenses and so are locked out of the market.

Second, restrictions may affect the ability of different people to use whatever advantage they may have, to compete in a market. A price floor, for example, prevents lower-cost sellers from using their cost advantage (their willingness to accept a lower price) to compete in the market. In the neoclassical view, this favors higher-cost sellers at the expense of their lower-cost competitors.

Third, restrictions may affect the ability of sellers to fetch the highest price they can, constrained only by competition from other sellers, and of buyers to pay the lowest price they can, constrained only by bidding from other buyers. A price floor, by restricting producers from competing on price (preventing any from offering prices below the floor), may favor producers in general at the expense of consumers. By the same token, a price ceiling (a maximum legal price) may favor consumers at the expense of producers.

Efficiency

In the neoclassical view, a resource is used "efficiently" as long as the benefit from using that resource is greater than the cost. Let's think about a company—say, an auto company—that has to decide how many machines to rent or how many workers to hire for its operations. It will consider how many extra cars it can produce if it rents one additional machine, or hires one additional worker. The company will figure out how much income it will get from the sale of those additional cars. That is, it will multiply the number of additional cars by the price it will get per car. Ultimately, it will compare this extra income against the rental cost paid for the machine, or the wage paid to the worker. The company will rent a machine, or hire a worker, as long as the extra income it gets is more than the additional cost it has to pay.

In the neoclassical view, this is "efficient" not only from the standpoint of the company, but from the standpoint of society as a whole. If the cost of using an extra machine or hiring an extra worker is less than value of the extra cars produced, the use of the machine or worker is also "efficient" from the standpoint of society as a whole.

There's just one more problem. In the neoclassical view, for private actors to make decisions that are also "efficient" form the standpoint of society as a whole, the prices they base their decisions on have to be the *right* prices. That is, each price has to reflect the true cost of a good to society as a whole. So how do we know, in this view, what is the "right price"?

The "Right" Wage

Let's look at an example using, in the language of neoclassical economics, the "price of labor" (or wage). Suppose that the going wage in a certain place is $20 per hour. According to neoclassical economists, a company will hire a worker as long as the extra benefit it gets from each extra hour of labor (the extra units produced times the price the company gets per unit) is at least as much as the additional cost it pays for that extra hour of labor ($20). Suppose, however, that the wage was only this high because there were barriers to competition in the labor market. If the wage without barriers would have only been, say, $10, then a company would hire an extra worker as long as the extra benefit it got from each extra hour of labor was at least $10 per hour.

How do we know whether the "right" wage is $20 or $10? In the view of neo-classical economists, the right wage—like any other right price—reflects the true cost to society of the good involved (here, an hour of labor). The cost of labor is whatever pains the worker endures as a result of that hour of work. This includes having to show up for work, when one might prefer to be someone else, having to follow the employer's orders, when one would rather be "doing one's own thing," putting up with the conditions at work, which could be dangerous, unhealthy, or unpleasant, and so on. It is competition in the labor market that makes workers reveal what they really require to compensate them for the burdens of labor.

If the price of labor, due to barriers to labor-market competition, is "too high," then employers will use "too little" labor. If the wage is $20, due to barriers, then employers will not hire an extra hour of labor unless it results in the production of at least $20 of additional goods. As a result of the inflated price of labor, society will have turned its back on who-knows-how-many opportunities to get between $10 and $20 of goods at a true cost of $10 worth of labor. In other words, wages that are inflated by barriers to competition result in an "inefficient" use of resources.

Critiques of the Neoclassical View

Economists associated with different schools of thought may use normative concepts like "freedom," "equity," or "efficiency," but mean something very different by these ideas than what neoclassical economists mean. (Some may choose not to use these terms, and instead invoke other normative concepts, like "justice," "equality," "the good life," and so on.) Here, however, we will focus on contrasts with the neo-classical views of freedom, equity, and efficiency described above.

Freedom

Neoclassical economists emphasize workers' freedom of choice to accept low wages, long hours, bad working conditions, and so on. Workers would not accept those conditions, they argue, unless doing so would leave them better off than they would be otherwise. In this view, institutions like unions or policies like minimum-wage laws interfere with workers' freedom to make a deal that would leave them better off.

Many liberal and almost all radical economists, on the other hand, emphasize how the conditions that an individual will "freely" accept depend on the alternatives available to them. If the only alternative is to starve in the street, most people would work even very long hours, under very bad conditions, for very low pay. Instead of seeing these workers as having "freely" accepted such agreements, however, one could view them as lacking any real freedom to *refuse* these conditions.

Union contracts, minimum-wage laws, and other restraints on competition between workers do, indeed, restrict each individual worker's "freedom" to accept lower wages, worse conditions, and so on, just as neoclassical economists argue. However, this view ignores the benefit to each worker—that these institutions also *protect* each worker from other workers undercutting him or her. Instead of seeing restraints on labor competition as robbing workers of the freedom to accept lower wages or worse conditions, one can instead see them as giving workers the freedom to demand higher wages or better conditions.

Equity

Barriers to labor-market competition, neoclassical economists argue, favor some workers at the expense of others and workers at the expense of consumers. An alternative view is that restraints on labor-market competition allow workers to get a better deal (higher pay, better conditions, etc.) from employers. The absence of these restraints, on the other hand, may result in higher profits for employers while relegating workers to lower pay and worse conditions. Which outcome one prefers depends on how one values benefits to one group of people (workers) compared to benefits to another (employers).

There are several reasons that someone might favor the interests of workers over those of employers, and therefore approve of changes that benefit workers even if these benefits come at the expense of employers:

1. **Ideas of "fairness" based on social "custom" or "convention."** In most societies where people work for wages, there are evolving ideas about what is a "fair" wage or "decent" living. Partly, such ideas may be based on what people have become accustomed to in the past. Partly, they may reflect expectations that conditions of life will improve over time, and especially from one generation to the next.

2. **Commitment to greater economic and social equality.** People who get most of their income from property (ownership of businesses, land or buildings, or financial wealth) are likely to be at the top of the income ladder. Most of the people at the bottom or in the middle, on the other hand, get most of their income from work. Therefore, changes that benefit workers as a group (at the expense of employers) tend to bring about a more equal distribution of income in society.

3. **Ideas about who creates and deserves to keep society's wealth.** Some "radical" economists argue that labor is the source of all new wealth produced in society.

Owners of property take a piece of this wealth by controlling things (like farms, mines, factories, etc.) that everyone else needs in order to work and live. In this view, there is no such thing as a "fair" distribution of income between workers and employers, since the employing class exists only by virtue of taking part of what workers produce.

Much of the history of labor movements around the world centers on attempts to *restrain* competition between workers, to keep workers from undercutting each other on the wages or conditions they will accept, and therefore to benefit workers as a group. Unions, for example, are compacts by which each member agrees *not* to accept a lower wage or worse conditions than the other members. Unions also set conditions on hours, benefits, and conditions of work. No individual can bargain a lower wage or worse conditions, in order to get a job, and thereby force other workers to do the same. Labor legislation like the minimum-wage laws, maximum hours (or overtime) laws, and laws regulating labor conditions, likewise, all restrain competition between workers.

Efficiency

We have already described one concept of efficiency used by neoclassical econo-mists: The key idea is that resources are used if (and only if) the benefit to society is greater than the cost. Neoclassical economists also use another concept of effi-ciency: An efficient condition is one in which nobody can be made better off with-out making someone worse off. This definition, pioneered by the Italian neoclassical economist Vilfredo Pareto, is known as "Pareto efficiency." The two definitions are connected: If resources were being wasted (used inefficiently), they could be used to make someone better off without making anyone worse off.

Neoclassical economists call a *change* that makes some people better off with-out making anyone worse off a "Pareto improvement." There are very few changes in public policies, however, that make some people better off while literally mak-ing nobody worse off. Most policy changes, potentially affecting millions of people, make some people better off and others worse off. In these cases, neoclassical econo-mists apply what they call the "compensation test." They compare the benefits to the "winners" from some change in public policy to the losses to the "losers." If the total gains are greater than the total losses, neoclassical economists argue, the winners could compensate the losers—and leave everyone at least a little better off.

In most cases where there are both winners and losers due to a change in public policy, however, the winners do not actually compensate the losers. These are not, then, actual efficiency improvements in the sense that some people are made bet-ter off while nobody is made worse off. Restraints on labor-market competition, for example, may benefit workers at the expense of their employers. (Eliminating such policies, meanwhile, may have the opposite effect.)

Judging whether these changes are for the better, then, involves weighing the benefits to some people against the losses to others. How one resolves such an issue depends on one's normative ideas, or values, about whose interests should take pre-cedence. In other words—which side are you on? ❏

Article 1.5

WHATEVER HAPPENED TO THE WORKING CLASS?
Overcoming the idea that nearly everyone is "middle class."

BY MARTIN OPPENHEIMER
September/October 2017

The dominant view of social class in American society is that most of us, aside from a very few at the top and the poor at the bottom, are "middle class." This is a story that has been a basic motif of American culture for more than a century. Even many labor leaders refer to their members as "middle class." Social scientists have devoted numerous volumes to the topic of "class," which most of them define by income level, collar color (white collar workers are defined as "middle class" due to their somewhat higher levels of formal education), and lifestyle (housing type, neighborhood, consumer and leisure time activities, religion, or some combination of these).

The idea that most Americans are "middle class" is based on a confusion, whether intentional or not, between middle *income* and middle *class*. In a 2012 Pew Research Center report, 49% of survey respondents chose "middle class" among available choices (no "working class" choice was available, so that the result reinforces the "fact" that a large plurality of Americans are "middle class"). They ranged in income from $30,000 to over $100,000. The Pew report, titled *The Lost Decade of the Middle Class*, defines the middle-income "tier" as household income from two-thirds of the median ($39,500) to twice the median ($118,000). This large middle bloc is decreasing as a percentage of all income earners, which leads politicians to bemoan the decline of the great American "middle class" and pose as saviors of it.

Workers at the lower end of this "middle" have little in common with people earning close to $120,000, not only in their lifestyles but more important in their sources of income. At the upper end those sums are often earned in part or in whole from the profits of business while the rest earn their wages from their labor. Thus, within the "middle class" category it is not only the working class—but even some of the capitalist class—that has disappeared.

As these categories disappear, so does the idea of class conflict, for if people belong to a "class" defined only on the basis of their income level (or perhaps also some other lifestyle indicators) then the distinction between classes is a matter of an arbitrary number (dollars plus maybe some numerical rating of consumption patterns like housing values). The middle class-ization of America consequently obscures the possibility that there might be a conflict between one part of this "middle class" which is working class and another part which is capitalist—since the income of the latter depends in large part on the exploitation of the former.

What, then, is the actual middle class? The "old" or traditional middle class includes some 22.2 million business owners with no employees (who are oddly classified in government data as "employed persons" because the employ themselves). They may not hire workers, but many exploit the labor of family members "off the books." Then there are about 2.7 million owners of establishments with 1-19 employees (this includes franchisees). Within these two groups are between three and four million self-employed professionals, some of whom employ workers. Add to this about 1.9 million small-scale farmers who are also called "self-employed."

Above this middle class are medium to large capitalists—the owners of enterprises, whether industrial, agricultural, extractive or financial, and regardless of the number of employees—whose profits put them into income brackets far above twice the median U.S. family income, which today is about $60,000.

"Old middle class" employers objectively stand in a conflictual, exploitative relationship to their employees. Surveys sponsored by business organizations show that the politics of the middle class, with the possible exception of many professionals, trend conservative, anti-tax, anti-regulatory, Republican, Trumpish. However, these results do reflect a bias towards the better-off segment because it is highly likely they miss many small "mom-and-pop" (especially immigrant) enterprises. The annual profit for a small business owner ranges, depending on number of years in business, type of business, region, and gender (with women owners typically making less than men, and running smaller businesses) from around $30,000 to $100,000, with franchisees clustering around $66,000. These incomes depend in part on keeping wages down, hence their general antagonism to unionization, the "Fight for $15" movement, measures providing paid sick leave, and so on. Although the bankruptcy rate for small business start-ups is considerable, Bureau of Labor Statistics data indicate that sector is quite stable after a dip following the Great Recession. A major factor is the outsourcing and subcontracting of work by larger corporations and the public sector in order to lower their labor costs.

People of color play a major role in small business. The smaller the firm, the more likely the owners will be people of color (and/or women). Although the data do not break out immigrants as such, while about 72% of owners are white, some 13.5% of owners are Latino and 6.2% are Asians. Both groups are over-represented relative to their populations. And both groups have a business startup rate twice that of whites. However, the categories "Latino" and "Asian" don't give us the complete picture by any means, since percentage and type of business varies considerably by country background (especially among Asians). Chinese, Koreans, and Cubans particularly outstrip the national average of the self-employed. African-Americans, by contrast, are considerably underrepresented at only 6.2%. There are several reasons for this (difficulty in obtaining bank loans being one) but the whole answer is still unclear.

Some class analysts (including some Marxists) propose that there is also a "new middle class," a clustering of administrators, supervisors, and mid-level bureaucrats. This grouping, although dependent on wages like other workers, is somewhat different from the working class because its function is to support exploitative relations within capitalism even as they are themselves exploited. The key is the level of authority associated with the occupation. The BLS calls these "managerial occupations." Excluding top executives (both private-sector capitalists and top government officials), there are close to seven million of them. As managers, their job implies a certain expectation that they will administer and control the workers under their jurisdictions, so that in varying degrees they too stand in an antagonistic relationship to their underlings.

That leaves the working class, those whose primary source of income is their wages, at about 60% of all employed people. There are about 92 million workers, divided among service, sales, workers in extractive industries, repairs, and production, and transportation workers. Actual production workers, the former heart of the U.S. blue collar proletariat, were only about 9% of wage earners in 2016. No matter how one juggles the data, the working class, not the middle class, constitutes a clear majority of U.S. income earners.

Suddenly, the election of Donald Trump has thrown a spotlight on white workers, including the 43% of union members who voted for Trump and other Republicans. Books by and about the "angry" white working class and its travails are trawled for clues on what the white working class thinks and how to win it back to the Democratic Party. Sen. Chuck Schumer (D-N.Y.) recently unveiled a "Better Deal" focusing on economic issues (but ignoring "social" issues such as abortion rights and protection of immigrants, and without mentioning labor unions). The suffering and rage of the "forgotten working class" has suddenly become as concerning as the decline of the "middle class." But not all of the working class—only the whites who live in areas of economic depression, especially in the deindustrialized Rust Belt and former mining centers who seemingly voted Republican against their own interests. The fact that African-American and Latina/o workers also live in areas of economic depression, including many of the same ones as the whites, and typically have even higher unemployment rates, does not seem to provoke the same concern.

Class consciousness appears to be quite robust within the upper, or capitalist class, which is why this group generally resists regulations and the reforms that would make a more decent life available to workers. The working class has a weaker sense of itself as a class, and this may be in part because many workers continue to see themselves (and are labeled by others) as "middle class." Yet when surveys include the option of choosing "working class," "middle class" identification shrinks. Recent Gallup surveys, which provide a choice between "Upper Middle/Middle" class and "Working/Lower" class, have shown considerable fluctuation in recent years. During the Great Recession, respondents split almost evenly (50-47%) between the two choices, as they had earlier in the 20th century. With the "recovery," they diverged (62-36% in June 2017) as incomes improved. White collar workers historically tend see themselves as "middle class," although unionization does alter their perceptions.

Our society is practically unique in the "developed" world in not having a social-democratic political party with historical roots in the labor movement. We lack an active working-class political and cultural infrastructure. Working-class communities clustered around workplaces are mostly gone. The myth of our society as "middle class" fills the void. Correspondingly, manual work is devalued as accolades and tangible rewards go to those who live off the labor of others.

The inability of unions to hold their own against an increasingly hostile political environment, much less gain ground, is at least partially the result of weak working-class consciousness. This weakness is also an obstacle to progressive social change more generally. Although we cannot create class consciousness out of thin air, it is important for each of us to contribute to demythologizing social class in the United States. ❑

Article 1.6

SHARING THE WEALTH OF THE COMMONS

BY PETER BARNES
November/December 2004

We're all familiar with private wealth, even if we don't have much. Economists and the media celebrate it every day. But there's another trove of wealth we barely notice: our common wealth.

Each of us is the beneficiary of a vast inheritance. This common wealth includes our air and water, habitats and ecosystems, languages and cultures, science and technologies, political and monetary systems, and quite a bit more. To say we share this inheritance doesn't mean we can call a broker and sell our shares tomorrow. It does mean we're responsible for the commons and entitled to any income it generates. Both the responsibility and the entitlement are ours by birth. They're part of the obligation each generation owes to the next, and each living human owes to other beings.

At present, however, our economic system scarcely recognizes the commons. This omission causes two major tragedies: ceaseless destruction of nature and widening inequality among humans. Nature gets destroyed because no one's unequivocally responsible for protecting it. Inequality widens because private wealth concentrates while common wealth shrinks.

The great challenges for the 21st century are, first of all, to make the commons visible; second, to give it proper reverence; and third, to translate that reverence into property rights and legal institutions that are on a par with those supporting private property. If we do this, we can avert the twin tragedies currently built into our market-driven system.

Defining the Commons

What exactly is the commons? Here is a workable definition: The commons includes all the assets we inherit together and are morally obligated to pass on, undiminished, to future generations.

This definition is a practical one. It designates a set of assets that have three specific characteristics: they're (1) inherited, (2) shared, and (3) worthy of long-term preservation. Usually it's obvious whether an asset has these characteristics or not.

At the same time, the definition is broad. It encompasses assets that are natural as well as social, intangible as well as tangible, small as well as large. It also introduces a moral factor that is absent from other economic definitions: it requires us to consider whether an asset is worthy of long-term preservation. At present, capitalism has no interest in this question. If an asset is likely to yield a competitive return to capital, it's kept alive; if not, it's destroyed or allowed to run down. Assets in the commons, by contrast, are meant to be preserved regardless of their return.

This definition sorts all economic assets into two baskets, the market and the commons. In the market basket are those assets we want to own privately and manage for profit. In the commons basket are the assets we want to hold in common and manage for long-term preservation. These baskets then are, or ought to be, the yin and yang of economic activity; each should enhance and contain the other. The role of the state should be to maintain a healthy balance between them.

The Value of the Commons

For most of human existence, the commons supplied everyone's food, water, fuel, and medicines. People hunted, fished, gathered fruits and herbs, collected firewood and building materials, and grazed their animals in common lands and waters. In other words, the commons was the source of basic sustenance. This is still true today in many parts of the world, and even in San Francisco, where I live, cash-poor people fish in the bay not for sport, but for food.

Though sustenance in the industrialized world now flows mostly through markets, the commons remains hugely valuable. It's the source of all natural resources and nature's many replenishing services. Water, air, DNA, seeds, topsoil, minerals, the protective ozone layer, the atmosphere's climate regulation, and much more, are gifts of nature to us all.

Just as crucially, the commons is our ultimate waste sink. It recycles water, oxygen, carbon, and everything else we excrete, exhale, or throw away. It's the place we store, or try to store, the residues of our industrial system.

The commons also holds humanity's vast accumulation of knowledge, art, and thought. As Isaac Newton said, "If I have seen further it is by standing on the shoulders of giants." So, too, the legal, political, and economic institutions we inherit—even the market itself—were built by the efforts of millions. Without these gifts we'd be hugely poorer than we are today.

To be sure, thinking of these natural and social inheritances primarily as economic assets is a limited way of viewing them. I deeply believe they are much more than that. But if treating portions of the commons as economic assets can help us conserve them, it's surely worth doing so.

How much might the commons be worth in monetary terms? It's relatively easy to put a dollar value on private assets. Accountants and appraisers do it every day, aided by the fact that private assets are regularly traded for money.

This isn't the case with most shared assets. How much is clean air, an intact wetlands, or

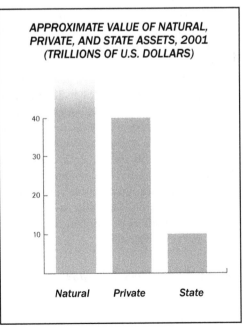

APPROXIMATE VALUE OF NATURAL, PRIVATE, AND STATE ASSETS, 2001 (TRILLIONS OF U.S. DOLLARS)

Natural   Private   State

Darwin's theory of evolution worth in dollar terms? Clearly, many shared inheritances are simply priceless. Others are potentially quantifiable, but there's no current market for them. Fortunately, economists have developed methods to quantify the value of things that aren't traded, so it's possible to estimate the value of the "priceable" part of the commons within an order of magnitude. The surprising conclusion that emerges from numerous studies is that the wealth we share is worth more than the wealth we own privately.

This fact bears repeating. Even though much of the commons can't be valued in monetary terms, the parts that can be valued are worth more than all private assets combined.

It's worth noting that these estimates understate the gap between common and private assets because a significant portion of the value attributed to private wealth is in fact an appropriation of common wealth. If this mislabeled portion was subtracted from private wealth and added to common wealth, the gap between the two would widen further.

Two examples will make this point clear. Suppose you buy a house for $200,000 and, without improving it, sell it a few years later for $300,000. You pay off the mortgage and walk away with a pile of cash. But what caused the house to rise in value? It wasn't anything you did. Rather, it was the fact that your neighborhood became more popular, likely a result of the efforts of community members, improvements in public services, and similar factors.

Or consider another fount of private wealth, the social invention and public expansion of the stock market. Suppose you start a business that goes "public" through an offering of stock. Within a few years, you're able to sell your stock for a spectacular capital gain.

Much of this gain is a social creation, the result of centuries of monetary-system evolution, laws and regulations, and whole industries devoted to accounting, sharing information, and trading stocks. What's more, there's a direct correlation between the scale and quality of the stock market as an institution and the size of the private gain. You'll fetch a higher price if you sell into a market of millions than into a market of two. Similarly, you'll gain more if transaction costs are low and trust in public information is high. Thus, stock that's traded on a regulated exchange sells for a higher multiple of earnings than unlisted stock. This socially created premium can account for 30% of the stock's value. If you're the lucky seller, you'll reap that extra cash—in no way thanks to anything you did as an individual.

Real estate gains and the stock market's social premium are just two instances of common assets contributing to private gain. Still, most rich people would like us to think it's their extraordinary talent, hard work, and risk-taking that create their well-deserved wealth. That's like saying a flower's beauty is due solely to its own efforts, owing nothing to nutrients in the soil, energy from the sun, water from the aquifer, or the activity of bees.

The Great Commons Giveaway

That we inherit a trove of common wealth is the good news. The bad news, alas, is that our inheritance is being grossly mismanaged. As a recent report by the advocacy group

Friends of the Commons concludes, "Maintenance of the commons is terrible, theft is rampant, and rents often aren't collected. To put it bluntly, our common wealth—and our children's—is being squandered. We are all poorer as a result."

Examples of commons mismanagement include the handout of broadcast spectrum to media conglomerates, the giveaway of pollution rights to polluters, the extension of copyrights to entertainment companies, the patenting of seeds and genes, the privatization of water, and the relentless destruction of habitat, wildlife, and ecosystems.

This mismanagement, though currently extreme, is not new. For over 200 years, the market has been devouring the commons in two ways. With one hand, the market takes valuable stuff from the commons and privatizes it. This is called "enclosure." With the other hand, the market dumps bad stuff into the commons and says, "It's your problem." This is called "externalizing." Much that is called economic growth today is actually a form of cannibalization in which the market diminishes the commons that ultimately sustains it.

Enclosure—the taking of good stuff from the commons—at first meant privatization of land by the gentry. Today it means privatization of many common assets by corporations. Either way, it means that what once belonged to everyone now belongs to a few.

Enclosure is usually justified in the name of efficiency. And sometimes, though not always, it does result in efficiency gains. But what also results from enclosure is the impoverishment of those who lose access to the commons, and the enrichment of those who take title to it. In other words, enclosure widens the gap between those with income-producing property and those without.

Externalizing—the dumping of bad stuff into the commons—is an automatic behavior pattern of profit-maximizing corporations: if they can avoid any out-of-pocket costs, they will. If workers, taxpayers, anyone downwind, future generations, or nature have to absorb added costs, so be it.

For decades, economists have agreed we'd be better served if businesses "internalized" their externalities—that is, paid in real time the costs they now shift to the commons. The reason this doesn't happen is that there's no one to set prices and collect them. Unlike private wealth, the commons lacks property rights and institutions to represent it in the marketplace.

The seeds of such institutions, however, are starting to emerge. Consider one of the environmental protection tools the United States currently uses, pollution trading. So-called cap-and-trade programs put a cap on total pollution, then grant portions of the total, via permits, to each polluting firm. Companies may buy other firms' permits if they want to pollute more than their allotment allows, or sell unused permits if they manage to pollute less. Such programs are generally supported by business because they allow polluters to find the cheapest ways to reduce pollution.

Public discussion of cap-and-trade programs has focused exclusively on their trading features. What's been overlooked is how they give away common wealth to polluters.

To date, all cap-and-trade programs have begun by giving pollution rights to existing polluters for free. This treats polluters as if they own our sky and rivers. It means that future polluters will have to pay old polluters for the scarce—hence valuable—right to dump wastes into nature. Imagine that: because a corporation polluted in the past, it gets free income forever! And, because ultimately we'll all pay for limited pollution via higher prices, this amounts to an enormous transfer of wealth—trillions of dollars—to shareholders of historically polluting corporations.

In theory, though, there is no reason that the initial pollution rights should not reside with the public. Clean air and the atmosphere's capacity to absorb pollutants are "wealth" that belongs to everyone. Hence, when polluters use up these parts of the commons, they should pay the public—not the other way around.

Taking the Commons Back

How can we correct the system omission that permits, and indeed promotes, destruction of nature and ever-widening inequality among humans? The answer lies in building a new sector of the economy whose clear legal mission is to preserve shared inheritances for everyone. Just as the market is populated by profit-maximizing corporations, so this new sector would be populated by asset-preserving trusts.

Here a brief description of trusts may be helpful. The trust is a private institution that's even older than the corporation. The essence of a trust is a fiduciary relationship. A trust holds and manages property for another person or for many other people. A simple example is a trust set up by a grandparent to pay for a grandchild's education. Other trusts include pension funds, charitable foundations, and university endowments. There are also hundreds of trusts in America, like the Nature Conservancy and the Trust for Public Land, that own land or conservation easements in perpetuity.

If we were to design an institution to protect pieces of the commons, we couldn't do much better than a trust. The goal of commons management, after all, is to preserve assets and deliver benefits to broad classes of beneficiaries. That's what trusts do, and it's not rocket science.

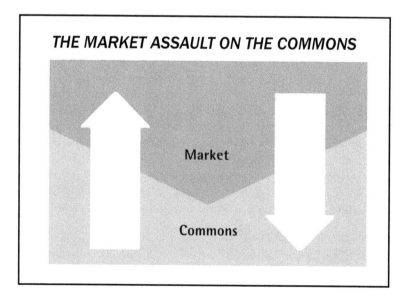

THE MARKET ASSAULT ON THE COMMONS

Market

Commons

Over centuries, several principles of trust management have evolved. These include:

- Trustees have a fiduciary responsibility to beneficiaries. If a trustee fails in this obligation, he or she can be removed and penalized.
- Trustees must preserve the original asset. It's okay to spend income, but don't invade the principal.
- Trustees must assure transparency. Information about money flows should be readily available to beneficiaries.

Trusts in the new commons sector would be endowed with rights comparable to those of corporations. Their trustees would take binding oaths of office and, like judges, serve long terms. Though protecting common assets would be their primary job, they would also distribute income from those assets to beneficiaries. These beneficiaries would include all citizens within a jurisdiction, large classes of citizens (children, the elderly), and/or agencies serving common purposes such as public transit or ecological restoration. When distributing income to individuals, the allocation formula would be one person, one share. The right to receive commons income would be a nontransferable birthright, not a property right that could be traded.

Fortuitously, a working model of such a trust already exists: the Alaska Permanent Fund. When oil drilling on the North Slope began in the 1970s, Gov. Jay Hammond, a Republican, proposed that 25% of the state's royalties be placed in a mutual fund to be invested on behalf of Alaska's citizens. Voters approved in a referendum. Since then, the Alaska Permanent Fund has grown to over $28 billion, and Alaskans have received roughly $22,000 apiece in dividends. In 2003 the per capita dividend was $1,107; a family of four received $4,428.

What Alaska did with its oil can be replicated for other gifts of nature. For example, we could create a nationwide Sky Trust to stabilize the climate for future generations. The trust would restrict emissions of heat-trapping gases and sell a declining number of emission permits to polluters. The income would be returned to U.S. residents in equal yearly dividends, thus reversing the wealth transfer built into current cap-and-trade programs. Instead of everyone paying historic polluters, polluters would pay all of us.

Just as a Sky Trust could represent our equity in the natural commons, a Public Stock Trust could embody our equity in the social commons. Such a trust would capture some of the socially created stock-market premium that currently flows only to shareholders and their investment bankers. As noted earlier, this premium is sizeable—roughly 30% of the value of publicly traded stock. A simple way to share it would be to create a giant mutual fund—call it the American Permanent Fund—that would hold, say, 10% of the shares of publicly traded companies. This mutual fund, in turn, would be owned by all Americans on a one share per person basis (perhaps linked to their Social Security accounts).

To build up the fund without precipitating a fall in share prices, companies would contribute shares at the rate of, say, 1% per year. The contributions would be the price companies pay for the benefits they derive from a commons asset, the large, trusted market for stock—a small price, indeed, for the hefty benefits. Over time, the mutual fund would assure that when the economy grows, everyone benefits. The top 5% would still own more than the bottom 90%, but at least every American would have some property income, and a slightly larger slice of our economic pie.

Sharing the Wealth

The perpetuation of inequality is built into the current design of capitalism. Because of the skewed distribution of private wealth, a small self-perpetuating minority receives a disproportionate share of America's nonlabor income.

Tom Paine had something to say about this. In his essay "Agrarian Justice," written in 1790, he argued that, because enclosure of the commons had separated so many people from their primary source of sustenance, it was necessary to create a functional equivalent of the commons in the form of a National Fund. Here is how he put it:

> There are two kinds of property. Firstly, natural property, or that which comes to us from the Creator of the universe—such as the earth, air, water. Secondly, artificial or acquired property—the invention of men. In the latter, equality is impossible; for to distribute it equally, it would be necessary that all should have contributed in the same proportion, which can never be the case .... Equality of natural property is different. Every individual in the world is born with legitimate claims on this property, or its equivalent.

Enclosure of the commons, he went on, was necessary to improve the efficiency of cultivation. But:

> The landed monopoly that began with [enclosure] has produced the greatest evil. It has dispossessed more than half the inhabitants of every nation of their natural inheritance, without providing for them, as ought to have been done, an indemnification for that loss, and has thereby created a species of poverty and wretchedness that did not exist before.

The appropriate compensation for loss of the commons, Paine said, was a national fund financed by rents paid by land owners. Out of this fund, every person reaching age 21 would get 15 pounds a year, and every person over 50 would receive an additional 10 pounds. (Think of Social Security, financed by commons rents instead of payroll taxes.)

A Progressive Offensive

Paine's vision, allowing for inflation and new forms of enclosure, could not be more timely today. Surely from our vast common inheritance—not just the land, but the atmosphere, the broadcast spectrum, our mineral resources, our threatened habitats and water supplies—enough rent can be collected to pay every American over age 21 a modest annual dividend, and every person reaching 21 a small start-up inheritance.

Such a proposal may seem utopian. In today's political climate, perhaps it is. But consider this. About 20 years ago, right-wing think tanks laid out a bold agenda. They called for lowering taxes on private wealth, privatizing much of government, and deregulating industry. Amazingly, this radical agenda has largely been achieved.

It's time for progressives to mount an equally bold offensive. The old shibboleths—let's gin up the economy, create jobs, and expand government programs—no longer excite. We need to talk about fixing the economy, not just growing it; about income for everyone, not just jobs; about nurturing ecosystems, cultures, and communities, not just our individual selves. More broadly, we need to celebrate the commons as an essential counterpoise to the market.

Unfortunately, many progressives have viewed the state as the only possible counterpoise to the market. The trouble is, the state has been captured by corporations. This capture isn't accidental or temporary; it's structural and long-term.

This doesn't mean progressives can't occasionally recapture the state. We've done so before and will do so again. It does mean that progressive control of the state is the exception, not the norm; in due course, corporate capture will resume. It follows that if we want lasting fixes to capitalism's tragic flaws, we must use our brief moments of political ascendancy to build institutions that endure.

Programs that rely on taxes, appropriations, or regulations are inherently transitory; they get weakened or repealed when political power shifts. By contrast, institutions that are self-perpetuating and have broad constituencies are likely to last. (It also helps if they mail out checks periodically.) This was the genius of Social Security, which has survived—indeed grown—through numerous Republican administrations.

If progressives are smart, we'll use our next New Deal to create common property trusts that include all Americans as beneficiaries. These trusts will then be to the 21st century what social insurance was to the 20th: sturdy pillars of shared responsibility and entitlement. Through them, the commons will be a source of sustenance for all, as it was before enclosure. Life-long income will be linked to generations-long ecological health. Isn't that a future most Americans would welcome? ❑

Chapter 2

SUPPLY AND DEMAND

INTRODUCTION

Textbooks tell us that supply and demand work like a well-oiled machine. The Law of Supply tells us that as the price of an item goes up, businesses will supply more of that good or service. The Law of Demand adds that as the price rises, consumers will choose to buy less of the item and seek available substitutes. Only one equilibrium price can bring businesses' and consumers' intentions into balance. Away from this equilibrium point, surpluses or shortages tend to drive the price back toward the equilibrium. Of course, government actions such as taxation or setting a price ceiling or floor can move the economy away from its market equilibrium, and create what economists call "deadweight losses" and chronic surpluses (gluts) and shortages.

Marc Breslow argues that supply and demand do not always produce the best outcomes for society. He notes that the "price gouging" that we suffer during shortages or feared shortages—especially for hard-to-substitute goods like gasoline—is simply supply and demand at work (Article 2.1).

The next two articles take on the mainstream textbook criticisms of price ceilings and price floors. Economist Ellen Frank questions the textbook models' conclusion that rent controls (and other price ceilings) lead to permanent shortages. She maintains that rent control helps to equalize power between landlords and tenants, and also to assure a supply of affordable housing (Article 2.2).

What would the effects be of raising the federal minimum wage to $15 per hour? In "What Are the Effects of a $15/hour Minimum Wage?"(Article 2.3), Arthur MacEwan finds that there will be very little disruption in urban and regional economies with a move towards a $15 minimum wage. In "low-wage" states, the move to a $15 per hour minimum wage can be gradually introduced to minimize any sticker shock with local labor markets.

Dean Baker, in "Bubbles: Are They Back?"(Article 2.4), reminds us that markets can often deviate from the textbook dogma of efficient equilibrium-seeking mechanisms for allocating scarce goods. "Bubbles" can and do occur when a rapid rise in prices create a self-reinforcing further rise of prices. Stock-market prices and real-estate prices were the two major culprits that blew up both the U.S. and world economies in 2008. Dean acknowledges that both bubbles are back, but finds them a bit less perilous than the bubbles we faced in 2008.

In "The Airfare Mystery" (Article 2.5), Arthur MacEwan argues that "supply and demand" is just a starting point for understanding what causes variation in air fares. We need to delve deeper, according to MacEwan, into issues of market power (does a particular airline monopolize a particular route?), price discrimination (are some buyers, like business travelers, charged more than others?), and government intervention (what roles do taxes and subsidies play?).

In "Want Free Trade? Open the Medical and Drug Industry to Competition" (Article 2.6), Dean Baker describes how companies in this sector are protected from market competition. Doctors are protected from international competition, even as "free trade" agreements have put blue-collar workers squarely in competition with workers all over the world. Meanwhile, pharmaceutical companies enjoy monopoly protections lasting decades, thanks to patents, without a significant counterweight from government price regulation. Baker calls the bluff of those pushing trade deals to truly open up domestic markets that have long been protected by significant market power and allow for the domestic prices of pharmaceuticals and doctors to fall to the "world price" of those goods and services. It appears that "global competition" is only for working people not those enjoying these administered prices and profits.

Taken together, these articles call into question the claims that markets always operate efficiently and lead to the best social allocation of resources. The articles also imply a constructive role for the "visible hand" of government.

Discussion Questions

1. (General) Several of these articles call for a larger government role in regulating supply and demand. What are some possible results of expanded government involvement, positive and negative? On balance, do you agree that government should play a larger role?

2. (Article 2.1) Breslow says that shortages have different effects on prices in the short run and the long run. Explain the difference. How is this difference related to the concepts of elasticity of demand and elasticity of supply?

3. (Article 2.2) Frank states that because modern rent-control laws are "soft," they do not lead to housing shortages. Explain. Do you agree with her reasoning?

4. (Article 2.3) Which approach do you believe would be more effective in reducing poverty: raising the minimum wage to $15 per hour nationally, or an across-the-board increase in government assistance (social welfare programs)?

5. (Article 2.3) Would an employee be more productive at $15 per hour or $9 per hour? Explain in detail and include in your answer as many factors that you can think of that might influence your conclusion.

6. (Article 2.4) What is a "bubble?" Describe a bubble's characteristics using the housing market, stock market, or car-loan market as an example. Should we be concerned about bubbles in the U.S. economy today?

7. (Article 2.5) MacEwan sees "supply and demand" as a shorthand for the various kinds of forces operating in real-world markets. What kinds of influences does he describe that may affect air fares? Which have an impact mainly on the supply side? Which on the demand side?

8. (Article 2.6) Baker argues that trade agreements have protected U.S. doctors and pharmaceutical companies from international competition. Why do you think this has been the case, when other kinds of workers and industries have borne the full brunt of global competition? Would policies to reduce the prices charged by the medical sector be desirable? What policies?

9. (Article 2.6) Baker argues that trade policy will often reflect domestic political and economic power and thus sees very little chance that the U.S. government would enact trade policy to allow for greater domestic competition in pharmaceuticals and medical services. Since world suppliers are prohibited from coming to the United States to provide drugs and medical services, can American consumers "vote with their feet" and follow the logic of the market to other countries? Explain the phenomenon of "medical tourism" and the relationship of our NAFTA partners Canada and Mexico to this market phenomenon.

Article 2.1

PRICE GOUGING: IT'S JUST SUPPLY AND DEMAND

BY MARC BRESLOW
October 2000, updated May 2015

Critics of the oil industry charge that the companies conspire to raise prices during shortages, ripping off consumers and gaining huge profits through illegal behavior. The industries respond that there is no conspiracy, prices rise due to the simple functioning of supply and demand in the market. The media debate the question: can evidence be found of a conspiracy? Or are rising prices simply due to increased costs as supplies are short? Politicians ask whether companies are guilty of illegal activity, and demand that investigations be opened.

What's going on? In reality, critics of the industries are missing the point of how a capitalist "free market" operates during times of shortages. The industry spokespersons are more on target in their explanations—but that doesn't mean what the companies are doing is okay. In fact, they *are* profiting at the expense of everyone who is forced to pay outrageous prices.

Both the media and public officials want to know whether rising costs of operation are causing the high prices, and therefore the companies are justified. Why? Because simple textbook economics says that in a competitive market we should get charged according to costs, with companies only making a "normal" profit. But a careful reading of the texts shows that this is only in the "long run" when new supplies can come into the market. In the short run, when a shortage develops, "supply and demand" can force prices up to unbelievable levels, especially for any product or service that is really a necessity. It doesn't have any relationship to the cost of supplying the item, nor does it take a conspiracy. The industry spokespeople are right that market pressures are the cause.

What confuses consumers is why a relatively small shortage can cause such a huge price jump, as it did for gasoline and electricity. Why, if OPEC reduces world oil supplies by only 1% or 2%, can the price of gasoline rise by perhaps 50%? Why shouldn't prices rise by the 1% or 2%? The answer lies in a common-sense understanding of what happens during a shortage. Everyone who owns a car, and still needs to get to work, drop the kids off at child care, and buy groceries, still needs to drive. In the short run, you can't sell your car for a more energy-efficient one, nor move someplace where public transit is more available, nor find a new day care center closer to home. Even if there are subways or buses available where you live, tight work and family time schedules probably make it difficult for you to leave the car at home.

So, as prices rise, everyone continues trying to buy as much gasoline as they did before (in technical terms, the "short-run price elasticity of demand" is very low). But there is 2% less gas available, so not everyone can get as much as they want. Prices will continue rising until some people drop out of the market, cutting back on their purchases because they simply can't afford to pay the higher prices. For something as essential to modern life as gasoline, this can take quite a price jump. If the price goes from $3.00 to $3.50 will you buy less? How about $4.00? Or $4.50? You can see the problem. Prices can easily rise by 50% before demand falls by the 2% needed for supply and demand to equalize.

Note that this situation has nothing to do with the costs of supplying gasoline, nor do oil companies in the United States have to conspire together to raise prices. All they have to do is let consumers bid for the available gasoline. Nothing illegal has taken place—OPEC is acting as a cartel, "conspiring," but the United States has no legal power over other countries. Profits can go up enormously, and they may be shared between OPEC, oil companies such as Exxon/Mobil and Royal Dutch Shell, and firms lower on the supply chain such as wholesalers and retail gas stations.

Housing is perhaps the worst of these situations, as no one should be forced to leave their home. But the "invisible hand" of the market will raise prices, and allocate housing, according to who has the greatest purchasing power, not who needs the housing. A highly-skilled computer programmer, moving into San Francisco from elsewhere, will get an apartment that some lesser-paid worker, maybe a public school teacher or a bus driver, has been living in, perhaps for many years.

In all these cases, the market has done what it does well—allocate sales to those who can afford to buy, without regard to need; and allocate profits to those who have a product in short supply, without regard to costs of production. The human costs to people of moderate- and low-incomes, who are priced out of the market, can be severe. But they can be prevented—by price controls that prevent price-gouging due to shortages. Such controls have been used many times in the United States—for rent in high-demand cities, for oil and gas during the "crises" of the 1970's, and for most products during World War II. Maybe it's time we made them a staple of sensible economic policy. ❑

Sources: "In Gas Prices, Misery and Mystery," Pam Belluck, *New York Times*, 6/14/2000; "Federal action sought to cut power prices from May," Peter J. Howe, *Boston Globe*, Aug. 24, 2000; "Industry Blames Chemical Additives for High Gas Prices," Matthew L. Wald, *New York Times*, June 26, 2000.

Article 2.2

DOES RENT CONTROL HURT TENANTS?

BY ELLEN FRANK
March/April 2003

> Dear Dr. Dollar:
> *What are the merits of the argument that rent control hurts tenants by limiting the incentives to create and maintain rental housing?*
> —Sarah Marxer, San Francisco, Calif.

The standard story of rent control, laid out in dozens of introductory economics textbooks, goes like this. In the housing market, landlords are willing to supply more rental units when prices are high, and tenants are willing to rent more units when prices are low. In an unregulated market, competition should result in a market-clearing price at which the number of apartments landlords are willing and able to provide just equals the number tenants are willing and able to rent. Thus, when prices are allowed to rise to their correct level, shortages disappear. Rent controls, in this story, disrupt the market mechanism by capping rents at too low a level. Artificially low rents discourage construction and maintenance, resulting in fewer available apartments than would exist without the controls. At the same time, low rents keep tenants in the area, searching for apartments that don't exist. The result: permanent housing shortages in rent-controlled markets.

What's wrong with this story? Just about everything.

First, the story ignores the unequal power that landlords and tenants exercise in an unregulated market. Boston College professor Richard Arnott notes that tenants are, for a number of reasons, averse to moving. This gives landlords inordinate pricing power even in a market where housing is not in short supply—and in areas where vacancy rates are low, land is scarce, and "snob zoning" commonplace, landlords can charge truly exorbitant prices. In Boston, rent controls were eliminated in 1997, and average apartment rents have since climbed nearly 100%. The city's spiraling rents show that without controls, landlords can—and do—gouge tenants.

Second, rent control opponents misrepresent the structure of controls. As practiced in the real world, rent control does not place fixed caps on rent. New York City enacted an actual rent freeze after World War II, and a small number of apartments still fall under this "old-law" rent control. But most rent-controlled apartments in New York and all controlled apartments in other U.S. cities fall under what Arnott calls "second generation" or "soft" controls, which simply restrict annual rent increases. Soft rent controls guarantee landlords a "fair return" on their properties and require that owners maintain their buildings. They allow landlords to pass along maintenance costs, and many allow improvement costs to be recouped on an accelerated schedule, making building upkeep quite lucrative.

Consequently, controlled apartments are not unprofitable. And as Occidental College professor and housing specialist Peter Dreier points out, landlords won't walk away as long as they are making a decent return. Residential landlords are not very mobile: they have a long-term interest in their properties, and only abandon them when *market* rents fall below even controlled levels as a result of poverty, crime, or economic depression. Rent controls themselves do not foster abandonment or poor maintenance.

Third, all second-generation rent control laws—enacted chiefly in the 1970s—exempted newly constructed buildings from controls. Thus, the argument that controls discourage new construction simply makes no sense. As for the oft-heard complaint that developers fear that rent controls, once enacted, will be extended to new buildings, the 1980s and 1990s construction booms in New York, Boston, San Francisco, and Los Angeles—all cities with controls—indicate that developers aren't all that worried. There is plenty of housing and construction in cities with and without rent controls.

Nevertheless, even in many cities with rent controls, there is a shortage of *affordable* apartments. Market housing costs have been rising faster than wages for at least two decades. That some apartments in New York and San Francisco are still affordable to low- and middle-income families is due primarily to rent control.

Indeed, limited as they might be, rent controls deliver real benefits. They prevent price-gouging and ration scarce apartments to existing tenants. The money tenants save in rent can be spent in the neighborhood economy, benefiting local businesses. Meanwhile, more secure tenants create neighborhoods that are stable, safe, and economically diverse. And rent controls are essential if tenants are to have credible legal protection against slumlords: the legal right to complain about lack of heat or faulty plumbing is meaningless if landlords can retaliate by raising rents.

There are many problems with the U.S. housing market. High prices, low incomes, and lack of public housing or subsidies for affordable housing all contribute to homelessness and housing insecurity in major American cities. Rent control is not the cause of these problems, nor is it the whole solution. But along with higher wages and expanded public housing, it is part of the solution. As Dreier puts it, "Until the federal government renews its responsibility to help poor and working-class people fill the gap between what they can afford and what housing costs to build and operate, rent control can at least help to keep a roof over their heads." ❑

Sources: Richard Arnott, "Time for Revisionism on Rent Control?" *Journal of Economic Perspectives,* Winter 1995. Dreier and Pitcoff, "I'm a Tenant and I Vote," *Shelterforce,* July/August 1997 (nhi.org).

Article 2.3

WHAT ARE THE EFFECTS OF A $15/HOUR MINIMUM WAGE?

BY ARTHUR MacEWAN
May/June 2018

> Dear Dr. Dollar:
> *While I am all for raising the wages of low-income workers, it seems that there are some problems with setting the minimum wage at $15 per hour. Wouldn't pushing up the minimum wage lead to less employment for low-wage workers, as employers find it more profitable to use more machinery in place of workers and some employers actually shut down their operations, maybe moving offshore? And does it make sense to have the same minimum throughout the country, when income levels are so different in different states—West Virginia and Massachusetts, for example?*
> —Rebecca G., Hagerstown, W.V.

Although Bernie Sanders and others have called for raising the national minimum wage to $15 per hour, this is not going to happen as long as Republicans control Congress and Donald Trump is in the White House. The national minimum wage remains at $7.25 per hour, where it has been since 2010. Real action, however, is taking place at the state and local level.

Seattle paved the way with 2014 legislation that is slated to raise the city's minimum wage to $15 an hour by 2021. Since then, there have been efforts in many cities and states to follow Seattle's lead. Under the "Fight for $15" banner, a national movement has emerged. In California, San Francisco will have a $15 minimum this year, Los Angeles by 2020, and the whole state by 2022.

New York's minimum wage will reach $15 at different times in different regions, with New York City's hitting the mark at the end of this year for large employers and at the end of 2019 for small employers (less than 10 employees); the phase-in will be slower in other regions of the state. In Washington, DC, the minimum wage will rise to $15 per hour in 2020.

In 2017, either by legislatures' actions or by the ballot box, 19 states raised their minimum wage. While none moved immediately to $15, and in some states the increases were very small, these changes illustrate the extent to which minimum wage action has moved out of Washington.

Not a Lot of Money, But....

Fifteen dollars an hour is not a lot of money. Forty hours a week for 52 weeks a year at this rate yields an annual income of $31,200, roughly half the median household income in the country. By 2021, when the $15 rate will be reality in some states and cities, inflation will have reduced the figure to less than $14 in current dollars (perhaps lower).

Still, the increase of the minimum wage to $15 could make a real difference for low-income workers and their families. In Massachusetts, for example, an increase of the minimum to $15 is under consideration by the legislature, and, if the legislature does not act favorably, the increase will be on the ballot in November. The Massachusetts law would raise the minimum wage from its current $11 per hour in $1 increments over the next four years. This increase would improve the economic well-being of over a million workers, close to 30% of the state's workforce. Fully 91% of affected workers are age 20 or older. Over half are women. Fifty-eight percent work full-time. Some 400,000 children (28% of all Massachusetts children) have at least one working parent who would get a raise.

At the current $11 per hour minimum in Massachusetts, even with more than one person working, a family with kids can make it only with several public supports, such as housing and daycare vouchers, food stamps, and MassHealth (a program that combines Medicaid and the Children's Health Insurance Program). Fifteen dollars an hour won't solve all this family's economic problems, but it will help.

Opposition and Response

Nonetheless, there are opponents of the new minimum wage laws. They argue that if the minimum wage is raised, the level of employment will fall—especially for low-wage workers. So instead of being helped, they claim, many low-wage workers would lose their jobs. It is a simple—and, unfortunately, a simplistic—argument. It is true that if the prices of tomatoes, cars, or many other items rise, people will buy less of those items. So, the argument goes, the same is true for low-wage workers. Employers, for example, will find ways, perhaps by using more equipment or cutting back services, to hire fewer employees.

But labor is different than tomatoes or cars. If a higher price is paid for the same tomato, that doesn't mean the tomato will become tastier. The same with the car; paying more for the same car won't make it run any better. But pay the same worker more and things change.

Workers who are paid better tend to be more productive, either because they feel better about their jobs or they now have a greater desire to keep that job, or both. Greater productivity lowers costs per unit of output. Also, better pay means less turnover, which can also lower employers' costs. While these cost reductions may not outweigh the higher wage, they certainly reduce the negative impact of the higher wage on employers' bottom lines.

Also, insofar as the higher costs are a burden on employers, much of that burden can be passed on to customers with relatively little impact on purchases. In Massachusetts, for example, even ignoring cost savings from higher productivity and lower turnover, McDonald's could fully cover the costs of raising the minimum wage from $11 to $15 by raising prices by 1.3% per year for four years.

Furthermore, when a city or state raises its minimum wage, low-wage firms are unlikely to move away. A large share of the low-wage labor force is employed in fast food sites and retail stores. Their very nature ties them to the location of their clientele. Very few low-wage workers are in manufacturing firms that might flee abroad.

It should be no surprise, then, that many economic studies have shown that in various states negative employment impacts of increases in the minimum wage have been either non-existent or trivial. To again use the Massachusetts example: As the state's minimum wage was raised over three years from $8 per hour to its current $11 per hour in recent years, there was no apparent negative impact on employment. To be sure, some studies of minimum wage increases show negative employment impacts. But, on balance, the increasing number of studies that show no negative impacts are more convincing. (See box.)

Variations

There are major differences among the states in the minimum wage, income levels, and the cost of living. States like Maryland, New Jersey, and Massachusetts have median household incomes about 70% higher than states like Mississippi, West Virginia, and Louisiana. In the lowest-income states, the cost of living is also quite low, so people in those states are not worse off to the degree that the income difference would imply. However, in the lowest-income states, in which the minimum wage is only the federal minimum of $7.25, a jump to $15 could be very disruptive to local firms and damaging to employment.

Yet there are also major differences within states in the minimum wage, income levels, and the cost of living. New York, as noted above, has taken at least some of this intra-state difference into account by setting different schedules for the establishment of the $15 minimum wage in different regions. If a $15 minimum were established nationally, means could be developed to ease the adjustment in areas where this would be an especially large increase. The New York procedure is one option, but others could be developed.

Seattle: A Tale of Two Studies

In June 2017, two papers were released evaluating the impact on employment of the increase of the minimum wage in Seattle. At that time, the minimum had increased to $13 an hour.

The first study, "Seattle's Minimum Wage Experience 2015–6," written by a group at the University of California Berkeley, found that there was no significant impact on employment of the move toward the $15 minimum wage.

The second study, "Minimum Wage Increases, Wages, and Low-Wage Employment: Evidence from Seattle," by a group at the University of Washington yielded, a very different result—that the impact on employment of low-wage workers was large and negative. This second study has been widely touted by opponents of increasing the minimum wage.

But in spite of the attention it received, the second study was unconvincing, in part because the large negative impact it found was very much larger than had been found in similar studies of minimum wage increase elsewhere by researchers critical of minimum wage increases. Also, this study excluded data from multi-site firms, which included most fast food and many retails sales operations. Further, it failed to effectively take account of the rapid growth of the Seattle economy, which appears to have moved many low-wage workers into higher-higher wage categories.

The Berkeley study focused on the Seattle food service industry, which is an intense user of minimum wage workers. If employment impacts resulted from the increase of the minimum wage, they should show up in this industry. As a control group, this study used cities elsewhere in the country which had economic experiences similar to Seattle over the years leading into the Seattle wage increase. Its methodology makes its result—no negative impact on employment—more convincing.

In whatever manner the introduction would be handled, there would be considerable value in moving toward economic equality among the states. Until the late 1970s, there was a general convergence among income levels across different states. In the 1930s, Mississippi had had a per capita income level about 30% as high as in Massachusetts, and by the late 1970s, that figure was almost 70%. But today, Mississippi is down to 55% of Massachusetts. (See Gerald Friedman, "Growing Together, Flying Apart," *D&S*, March/April 2018.)

This shift from convergence to divergence has been associated with the general rise of economic inequality in the country and surely has been driven by some of the same factors. Regional inequality is a problem in itself, but it is not unreasonable to see it as associated with the political and cultural polarization in the United States. Establishing a much higher national minimum wage, which would have its greatest impact in low-income regions, would be one step in reducing this undesirable—indeed, poisonous—inequality and polarization. ❏

Sources: Multistate Insider, "Minimum Wages Rise in 19 States" (multistate.us); National Employment Law Project, "City Minimum Wage Laws: Recent Trends and Economic Evidence" (nelp.org); GovDocs, "New York State $15 Minimum Wage and Paid Family Leave" (govdocs.com); Aaron C. Davis, "D.C. gives final approval to $15 minimum wage," *Washington Post*, June 21, 2016 (washingtonpost.com); Federal Reserve Bank of St. Louis, Personal Income Per Capita and Median Household Income (fred.stlouisfed.org); Nicole Rodriguez, "Frequently Asked Questions Related to the $15 Minimum Wage," Massachusetts Budget and Policy Center, May 31, 2017, updated January 2018 (massbudget.org); David Cooper, "Raising the minimum wage to $15 an hour would lift wages for 41 million American workers," Economic Policy Institute, April 26, 2017 (epi.org); by Robert Pollin and Jeannette Wicks-Lim, "A $15 U.S. Minimum Wage: How the Fast-Food Industry Could Adjust Without Shedding Jobs," *Journal of Economic Issues*, 2016; Arindrajit Dube, T. William Lester and Michael Reich, "Minimum Wage Effects Across State Borders: Estimates Using Contiguous Counties," Review of Economics and Statistics, 2010; Michael Reich, Sylvia Allegretto, and Anna Godoey, "Seattle's Minimum Wage Experience 2015-16," Center for Wage and Employment Dynamics, Institute for Research on Labor and Employment, University of California Berkeley, June 2017 (irle.berkeley.edu); Eeaterina Jardim et al, "Minimum Wage Increases, Wages, and Low-Wage Employment: Evidence from Seattle," NBER Working Paper No. 23532, June 2017, revised in October 2017 (nber.org); Ben Zipperer and John Schmitt, "The 'high road' Seattle labor market and the effects of the minimum wage increase: Data limitations and methodological problems bias new analysis of Seattle's minimum wage increase," Economic Policy Institute, June 26, 2017 (epi.org).

Article 2.4

BUBBLES: ARE THEY BACK?

BY DEAN BAKER

December 2017; Center for Economic and Policy Research

There has been much greater concern about the danger of asset bubbles ever since the collapse of the housing bubble sank the economy. While it is good that people in policy positions now recognize that bubbles can pose a real danger, it is unfortunate that there still seems very little understanding of the nature of the problem.

First, an economy-threatening bubble does not just sneak up on us. Often the discussion of bubbles implies that we need some complex measuring tools to uncover an economy-threatening bubble that's lurking in some far corner of the data.

This is absurd on its face. If a bubble is large enough to threaten the economy, it is hard to miss. This was true of both the stock bubble in the 1990s and the housing bubble in the last decade.

At the peak of the stock bubble in 2000, the ratio of stock prices-to-trend corporate profits was more than twice its long-term average. This may have been justified if there was an expectation that profit growth was going to be much faster in the future, but almost no economic analysts projected this speed up.

Higher price-to-earnings ratios could also be justified if stockholders were prepared to accept lower returns on their stock than they had in the past. But there was no evidence this was the case. In fact, most stockholders seemed to expect that the double-digit returns of the recent past would continue.

In the case of the housing bubble, inflation-adjusted house prices had risen by more than 70% above their long-term trend. This unprecedented run-up in house prices occurred at a time when rents were essentially moving in step with the overall rate of inflation, suggesting that there was no major shift in the fundamentals of the housing market. Furthermore, vacancy rates were already at record highs even before the bubble burst, providing clear evidence that house prices were not being driven by a shortage of housing.

And, both bubbles were clearly moving the economy. In the case of the stock bubble, investment hit its highest share of GDP since the late early 1980s, as start-ups were taking advantage of sky-high share prices to finance crazy schemes. Also, the wealth generated by the stock bubble led to a surge in consumption that pushed the savings rate to a then-record low.

In the case of the housing bubble, high prices led to a flood of new construction, raising the residential investment share of GDP to almost 6.5%, compared to a long period average of less than 4%. The wealth created by the housing bubble led to an even larger consumption boom than the stock bubble.

All of this was easy to see from widely available government data sets. It required no more than an Excel spreadsheet to analyze these data. So this was not rocket science, it was basic economic logic and arithmetic.

Should we be concerned about a bubble now? Stock prices and housing prices are both high by historical standards. The ratio of stock prices-to-trend corporate earnings is more than 27-to-one; this compares to a long-term average of 15-to-one.

House prices are also high by historic standards. Inflation-adjusted house prices are still well below their bubble peaks, but are about 40% above their long-term average.

In both cases, these markets are high, although in ways that are at least partly explained by the fundamentals of the market. In the case of stock prices, the profit share of GDP is almost 30% above its trend level. If this persists, then the ratio of prices-to-earnings is much closer to the long-term average. Of course, a big cut in the corporate tax rate increases the likelihood that a high-profit share in GDP will continue.

Extraordinarily low-interest rates (both real and nominal) also mean that stocks provide a relatively better return compared with alternatives like bonds and short-term deposits. This also would change if interest rates rise substantially, but for now, that doesn't seem likely.

The run-up in house prices also seems less disconcerting when we consider there has been a parallel run up in rents. While rents have not increased as much as house prices, they have been substantially outpacing the overall rate of inflation for the last five years. Low-interest rates would also help to explain house prices being above long-term trends, as they justify a higher ratio of sales prices-to-rents.

Here also, there is a risk that higher rates could send prices tumbling. This could be an especially bad story for moderate-income homeowners, since the bottom tier of the housing market has seen the largest price increases over the last five years.

But even in a bad story, where for example higher interest rates send both stock and house prices back towards their trend levels, we don't have to fear an economic collapse and probably not even a recession. The high stock market is not driving investment, which remains very modest despite near record-high after-tax profits. Housing construction has come back from its post-crash lows, but is roughly in line with its long-term average share of GDP.

The loss of trillions of dollars of wealth would be a hit to consumption. Consumption has been unusually high in recent years with the savings rate averaging just 3.6% of disposable income in the last year. A more normal savings rate would be closer to 6%. But even if the savings rate were to rise to 6% over a span of a year or two, it would likely dampen growth rather than cause a recession.

In short, there is little reason to think that the economy is threatened by the risk of collapsing bubbles at the moment. This doesn't mean that holders of large amounts of Bitcoin or Amazon stock may not have something to worry about, but most of us don't. ❑

Article 2.5

THE AIRFARE MYSTERY

BY ARTHUR MacEWAN
January/February 2014

Dear Dr. Dollar:
Boston is 3,280 air miles from London, only 27% further than the 2,580 air miles from Boston to San Diego. So why does a flight from Boston to London cost more than twice as much as a flight from Boston to San Diego, 100% more, for the same dates? Is it just supply and demand?   —Kathleen M. Gillespie, Lexington, Mass.

Airfares do seem to pose a mystery. Supply and demand may help explain things, but these are really little more than categories into which explanations can be placed. If someone says that the flights to London are so expensive because supply is limited relative to demand, we have no real explanation until we explain why supply is limited.

On the surface, the high price of flights on the Boston-London route suggests that this is a very profitable route. So why don't more airlines fly this route more often, expanding supply, to get a share of the profits?

Beneath the surface (on travel web sites), it turns out that a large part of the price difference between these two routes is not the actual payment to the airline, but taxes and fees. I found one Boston-London-Boston trip for $1,082, where taxes and fees accounted for $656 of that total. On the Boston-San Diego-Boston flight, however, taxes and fees accounted for only $33 out of the $436 cost.

In general, European governments charge much higher taxes and fees than is the case in the United States. From an environmental perspective, the Europeans are probably on the right track, as air travel is an especially polluting (greenhouse gas-creating) form of travel. The European governments, however, may simply be motivated by the opportunity to capture revenue.

There are seemingly strange airline fare differences within the United States that are not explained by tax and fee differences. For example, a non-stop round-trip Boston-Detroit flight (630 miles each way) costs about twice as much as a non-stop Boston-Chicago flight (860 miles each way)—$458 compared to $230 for the same times and dates.

This difference is explained by the fact that Delta has a lock on the Boston-Detroit route, while United, American, US Airways, and Jet Blue all fly the Boston-Chicago route. That is, Delta is a monopoly on the Boston-Detroit route and can charge high fares without facing competition. (Northwest used to control this route until it merged with Delta a couple of years ago.)

Why have no other airlines entered this apparently lucrative Boston-Detroit route? That's not clear. Perhaps Delta has long-term leases on Detroit airport gates. Or perhaps other airlines, recognizing the economic and population decline of Detroit, believe this market has limited potential. Whatever the reason, it is clear that monopoly control of this route is the issue.

Also, the Boston-Detroit fare portends an ominous future as airline mergers reduce competition further. Following the Delta-Northwest merger, Continental and United came together. American Airlines and US Airways have also been moving toward a merger. In August, however, the federal government acted to block the move. "According to the Justice Department," reported the *New York Times*, the proposed merger "would substantially reduce competition in over 1,000 city pairs served by the two airlines."

While monopolistic situations and taxes and fees explain some of the "mystery" of airline fares, there is more. Flights and times that are heavily used by business travelers tend to have high fares because business travelers are less concerned about the price. This is partly because they often have limited flexibility, but also because airfares are deductible as a cost of business—i.e., the taxpayers pick up part of the tab.

Also, on a flight with the same airline, prices can change dramatically within a day or even within hours. Trying to book a flight one evening, the cheapest ticket I could find was about $600, but by the next morning I got the ticket for about $300. I suspect that in this case the airline (using computer-based forecasting) recognized that the flight was not filling up and therefore reduced the price to attract more customers.

And things can work in the other direction. Making a reservation at the last minute, the potential passenger is often faced with a very high fare because the airline views the traveler as having little flexibility. For example, if I make a reservation to fly Boston-Chicago-Boston, leaving tomorrow and returning two days later, the fare would be over $900, as compared to the $230 I would pay if I made the reservation a few weeks in advance.

So, yes, supply and demand can help explain the variation in airfares. But to really understand what is going on we need to know a good deal more. ❏

Sources: "Airline Merger Mania," *New York Times*, June 22, 2013; James B. Stewart, "For Airlines, It May Be One Merger Too Many," *New York Times*, Aug. 16, 2013.

Article 2.6

WANT FREE TRADE? OPEN THE MEDICAL AND DRUG INDUSTRY TO COMPEITITON

BY DEAN BAKER
November 2013; Center for Economic and Policy Research

Free trade is like apple pie, everyone is supposed to like it. Economists have written thousands of books and articles showing how everyone can gain from reducing trade barriers. While there is much merit to this argument, little of it applies to the trade pacts that are sold as "free-trade" agreements.

These deals are about structuring trade to redistribute income upward. In addition, these agreements also provide a mechanism for over-riding the democratic process in the countries that are parties to the deals. They are a tool whereby corporate interests can block health, safety, and environmental regulations that might otherwise be implemented by democratically elected officials. This is the story with both the Trans-Pacific Partnership (TPP) now being negotiated by General Electric, Merck, and other major corporations who have been invited to the table, as well as the European Union-United States (EU-U.S.) trade agreement.

But trade agreements don't have to be designed to make the rich richer. It is possible to envision trade deals that actually would liberalize trade. NAFTA and it successors were designed to push down the wages of manufacturing workers by making it as easy as possible to set up operations overseas. This put U.S. steelworkers and autoworkers in direct competition with the low-wage workers in the developing world, pushing down wages of manufacturing workers in the United States, and by reducing the number of manufacturing jobs, the wages of less educated workers more generally.

This is all very simple and straightforward. But suppose that instead of designing trade deals to give us cheaper manufacturing workers we designed trade deals to give us cheaper doctors. In the United States, we pay our doctors almost twice as much as the average in other wealthy countries, and almost three times as much as in countries like Sweden or Norway. Suppose we structured a trade deal to get our doctors' pay in line with pay in other wealthy countries.

If we could save an average of $100,000 per doctor, this would translate to savings of roughly $85 billion a year, which would come to more than $1 trillion over the next decade. Throw in dentists and a few other highly paid professions and we would be talking real money. Just the savings on doctors' pay would come to more than $12,000 for an average family of four over ten years. This dwarfs the potential gains that are projected even by supporters of the trade agreements now being negotiated.

But we can be sure that freer trade in physicians' services will not be on the agenda in these trade deals. While the United States brings in Stem workers, nurses, and even teachers from other countries in order to keep their wages down in the United States, no one in a policy position will talk about doing the same with doctors.

The reason is very simple: doctors have lots of money and power. Roughly a third of them can be found in the top 1%, and nearly all would be in the top 3% of the income distribution.

Of course, trade can be used to bring down prices in other areas as well. The United States pays close to twice as much for its prescription drugs as people in other wealthy countries. This is the deliberate result of a patent policy that gives unchecked monopolies to drug companies for decades. In contrast, every other wealthy country couples patent monopolies with price controls, negotiated prices or some other policy that limits the extent to which drug companies can exploit their monopoly.

The United States could simply change its patent policy, but with that route being politically blocked, it could in principle use free trade to bring about the same result. With the country spending over $300 billion a year on drugs at present, the potential gains here also could be well over $1 trillion over the course of a decade.

The industry will claim that lower drug prices will hurt the incentive to develop new drugs, but we can switch to more modern and efficient methods for financing research. By raising prices by tens or even hundreds of times above their free market price, drug patents create the same sort of distortions and waste that we would expect from tariffs of several thousand percent. It's not hard to envision a system that leads to less waste and corruption.

There are many other areas where trade could, in principle, be used to bring about gains for large segments of the U.S. population as well as its trading partners. Unfortunately, we are not likely to see trade agreements that will produce such broad gains. This has nothing to do with trade per se, it has due to with the fact that these trade deals are developed and negotiated by corporate interests for corporate interests.

With the drug companies sitting at the negotiating table at the TPP, does anyone think the deal will actually lower drug prices? Do we expect good rules regulating fracking when the oil and gas industries are writing them? And will the big banks working on the financial section produce good rules for regulating finance?

Yes, free trade can benefit the country as a whole. But the trade deals we will see in the next year have nothing to do with free trade, they are just one more item on the agenda for redistributing wealth upward. ❑

Chapter 3

CONSUMERS

INTRODUCTION

The "two economies" described in the introduction to this book—the textbook economy and the economy portrayed by critics of the status quo—come into sharp contrast when we consider the theory of consumer choice. In the textbook model of consumer choice, rational individuals seek to maximize their well-being by choosing the right mix of goods to consume and allocating their "scarce" resources accordingly. They decide for themselves how much they would enjoy various things, and make their choices based on full information about their options. More of any good is always better, but diminishing marginal utility says that each additional unit of a good consumed brings less additional enjoyment than the one before. The theory attempts to assess the utility of each individual uniquely. Yet, we soon discover that it is difficult if not impossible to "measure pleasure" for a single individual and impossible to compare utility between individuals.

The first article in this chapter contends that the idea of consumer sovereignty—that consumer wishes determine what gets produced—does not fit the facts. Helen Scharber notes, in "The 800-Pound Ronald McDonald in the Room" (Article 3.1), how the advertising that saturates our daily lives constantly creates new wants. In recent years, advertisers have been increasingly targeting children in order to convince them to nag their parents into buying products they suddenly "need."

Deborah M. Figart's "Underbanked and Overcharged" (Article 3.2) argues that low-income communities are ill-served by both conventional banks and "alternative financial service providers" (AFSPs), such as check-cashing outlets. Low-income areas may lack convenient nearby outlets for conducting financial transactions, and community members typically face high fees and interest rates from both banks and AFSPs. Figart points to a possible solution: recent proposals for the revival of "postal banks" operated by the U.S. Postal Service.

The next article, "Neutralized," turns to a service that most students consume daily—internet communications (Article 3.3). Rob Larson reviews the shifting fortunes of the battle for net neutrality. The major activist victory of 2015 in which neutrality provisions became law lasted until the late-2017 decisions by the Trump Administration's FCC to reverse the regulations, allowing telecommunication companies to control how data flows through cable and cell signals.

Next, in "Campus Struggles Against Sweatshops Continue" (Article 3.4), Sarah Blaskey and Phil Gasper turn our attention to activism around global labor conditions. They show how people on the consumption side, in this case students and faculty at U.S. colleges and universities, have banded together with workers on the other side of the world to fight "sweatshop" conditions in apparel production.

In "A Flying Public Finally Erupts" (Article 3.5), Sam Pizzigati discusses the notorious consumer dissatisfaction in the airline industry and argues that it stems from the consolidation that resulted from deregulation of the industry in the late 1970s. The "magic" of the free market led to cost-cutting, declining service for the consumer, and stark differences between first-class travel and coach.

The chapter's final article, an interview with economist Juliet Schor (Article 3.6), explores the causes behind U.S. consumerism. Schor looks beyond some of the "usual suspects"—like advertising—by linking the rise of consumerism to labor-market forces that have prevented the reduction of work time. She argues that future changes in U.S. consumption behavior, and therefore long-term environmental sustainability, depend on reducing hours of work.

Discussion Questions

1. (Article 3.1) Standard consumer theory still applies if advertising is simply a way to inform consumers. But critics suggest that advertising shapes our tastes and desires. Think of some of your recent purchases. For which purchases was advertising primarily a source of information, and for which was it more of a taste-shaper?

2. (Article 3.1) According to Scharber, what are the negative impacts of advertising directed at children? Would you support a law banning advertising to young children? Why or why not?

3. (Article 3.2) Why might private for-profit enterprises not supply desired services at affordable prices, as in the case of financial services in low-income communities? Is the establishment of public service providers a good solution?

4. (Article 3.3) Larson suggests that the reversal of net neutrality requirements in the United States was partially because of the shifting positions of the big online companies, like Google and Amazon. Why does he suggest their loyalties on this issue may have changed?

5. (Articles 3.4) How can consumers overcome the problem of "asymmetric information" in making purchases? Consider cases when consumers are interested in something (like labor conditions) that they cannot directly observe from the product itself.

6. (Articles 3.4) Why might people on the consumption side of a market (like apparel buyers) consider factors other than product price and quality in their purchasing decisions? Do you think changes in consumer purchasing behavior are enough to bring about social change, in terms of things like labor conditions and environmental impacts of production methods?

7. (Article 3.5) Dramatic video of the forced removal of a doctor from a boarded United flight went viral in 2017 and caused a sensation, especially among regular airline travelers. According to Pizzigati, what less-conspicuous economic changes, in government regulation and airline policy, led to this dramatic event?

8. (Article 3.6) Schor argues that, far from being the consequence of human beings' inherently insatiable wants, consumerism is the result of various social and institutional factors. What does she see as the key factors pushing people to consume more and more? What are the main reasons, in her view, that consumer behavior in the United States has differed from that in other countries?

Article 3.1

THE 800-POUND RONALD McDONALD IN THE ROOM

BY HELEN SCHARBER

January 2007

When your child's doctor gives you advice, you're probably inclined to take it. And if 60,000 doctors gave you advice, ignoring it would be even more difficult to justify. Last month, the American Academy of Pediatrics (AAP) issued a policy statement advising us to limit advertising to children, citing its adverse effects on health. Yes, banning toy commercials might result in fewer headaches for parents ("Please, please, pleeeeeeease, can I have this new video game I just saw 10 commercials for????"), but the AAP is more concerned with other health issues, such as childhood obesity. Advertising in general—and to children specifically—has reached astonishingly high levels, and as a country, we'd be wise to take the doctors' orders.

Advertising to kids is not a new phenomenon, but the intensity of it is. According to Juliet Schor, author of *Born to Buy*, companies spent around $100 million in 1983 on television advertising to kids. A little more than 20 years later, the amount earmarked for child-targeted ads in a variety of media has jumped to at least $12 billion annually. That's over $150 per boy and girl in the United States. And it's not as though kids only see ads for action figures and sugary cereal; the other $240 billion spent on advertising each year ensures that they see ads for all kinds of products, everywhere they go. According to the AAP report, "the average young person views more than 3,000 ads per day on television, on the Internet, on billboards, and in magazines." Ads are also creeping into schools, where marketers have cleverly placed them in "educational" posters, textbook covers, bathroom stalls, scoreboards, daily news programs, and bus radio programming.

If advertising to children is becoming increasingly ubiquitous, it's probably because it's becoming increasingly profitable. Once upon a time, kids didn't have as much market power as they do today. The AAP report estimates that kids under 12 now spend $25 billion of their own money annually, teenagers spend another $155 billion, and both groups probably influence around $200 billion in parental spending. Not too surprising, considering that 62% of parents say their children "actively participate" in car-buying decisions, according to a study by J.D. Power & Associates. Marketers are also becoming more aware of the long-term potential of advertising to children. While they may not be the primary market now, they will be someday. And since researchers have found that kids as young as two can express preferences for specific brands, it's practically never too early to begin instilling brand loyalty.

But while small children have an incredible memory for commercial messages, they may not have developed the cognitive skills necessary to be critical of them. In 2004, the American Psychological Association (APA) also called for setting limits on advertising to kids, citing research that "children under the age of eight are unable to critically comprehend televised advertising messages and are prone to accept advertiser messages as truthful, accurate and unbiased." Many people take offense at the idea that we might be manipulated by marketing. Aren't we, after all, intelligent enough to make up our own minds about what to buy? The research cited by the APA, however, shows that children are uniquely vulnerable to manipulation by advertising. Marketers therefore should not be allowed to prey on them in the name of free speech.

Such invasive advertising to children is not only an ethical problem. The American Academy of Pediatrics cited advertising's effects on health through the promotion of unhealthy eating, drinking and smoking as the main motivation for setting limits. Children's health issues certainly merit attention. The Center for Disease Control, for example, has found that the prevalence of overweight children (ages 6 to 11) increased from 7% in 1980 to about 19% in 2004, while the rate among adolescents (ages 12 to 19) jumped from 5% to 17%. In addition to physical health problems, Schor argues that extensive marketing has negative effects on children's emotional well being. In her research for Born to Buy, Schor found links between immersion in consumer culture and depression, anxiety, low self esteem and conflicts with parents. The big push to consume can also lead to financial health problems, as many Americans know all too well, with credit card debt among 18 to 24-year-olds doubling over the past decade.

Not even the staunchest critics of marketing to children would argue that advertisements are completely at fault for these trends. Yet, the commercialization of nearly everything is negatively affecting children's well being in rather profound ways. Why, then, is hardly anyone paying attention to the 800-pound Ronald McDonald in the room? Perhaps it's because advertising appears to be a necessary evil or a fair tradeoff—maybe little Emma's school couldn't afford a soccer team without Coke on the scoreboard, for example. Or perhaps some would argue that parents who don't approve of the commercial culture should limit their kids' exposure to it. Increasingly invasive marketing techniques make it practically impossible to simply opt out of commercial culture, though. Thus, decisions to limit marketing to children must be made by the country as a whole. Sweden, Norway, Greece, Denmark, and Belgium have already passed laws curbing kid-targeted advertising, and according to 60,000 pediatricians, if we care about the health of our kids, we should too. ❏

Sources: American Association of Pediatrics, Policy Statement on Children, Adolescents, and Advertising, December 2006 (pediatrics.aappublications.org/cgi/content/full/118/6/2563); American Psychological Association, "Television Advertising Leads to Unhealthy Habits in Childen" February 2004 (releasees/childrenads.html); Jennifer Saranow, "Car makers direct more ads at kids," *Wall Street Journal*, November 9th, 2006 (www.commercialexploitation.org/news/carmakers.html); David Burke, "Two-year olds branded by TV advertising" (www.whitedot.org/issue/isssory.aps?slug=Valkenburg); Center for a New American Dream, *Kids and Commercialism* (www.newdream.org/kids/);; Juliet Schor, Born to Buy: The Commercialized Child and the New Consumer Culture (New York: Scribner, 2004); "Facts about Childhood Overweight," Center for Disease Control (www.cdc.gov/Healthy Youth/overweight/index.html).

Article 3.2

UNDERBANKED AND OVERCHARGED
Creating alternatives to the "alternative financial service providers."

BY DEBORAH M. FIGART
July/August 2014

Driving down Atlantic Avenue, the main commercial thoroughfare in Atlantic City, N.J., one can easily count at least three times as many check-cashing outlets as banks. At these stores, you can cash your paycheck or government check (for a fee), send a wire transfer to a relative or friend overseas, or pay some bills.

Many traditionally African-American neighborhoods and poor census tracts, like this one, do not have a single bank nearby. The U.S. banking system is working for well-heeled customers. It isn't working for poor people.

Over 30 million households—more than one in four–are unbanked or underbanked. That means they have no access to traditional banking services or that they have a bank account but also rely on Alternative Financial Service Providers (AFSPs). According to the Federal Deposit Insurance Corporation's 2011 FDIC National Survey of Unbanked and Underbanked Households, the number of financially excluded households has increased since the publication of its first survey in 2009, with the number of unbanked alone increasing by over 800,000. The incidence of financial exclusion is highest among households that are African-American, Hispanic, lower-income, younger, or less-educated (see Figure 1).

The FDIC asked people why they had never had a bank account or why they had closed any prior account. Some reasons are listed in Figure 2. (Respondents were able to select more than one option.) Since the exact language of the FDIC's survey choices changed between 2009 and 2011, four reasons from the 2009 survey are included for further information.

FIGURE 1: PERCENTAGES OF HOUSEHOLDS, BY CHARACTERISTIC OF HOUSEHOLDER, UNBANKED OR UNDERBANKED, 2011

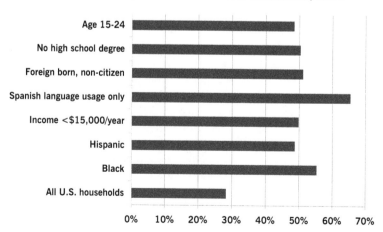

The responses suggest how difficult it is to survive at the lower end of the income distribution. Living paycheck to paycheck, the unbanked feel they do not have enough money to open and maintain a bank account, especially if there is a minimum balance requirement or the bank charges low-balance fees. The survey also reveals social barriers to being a bank customer. If your primary language is not spoken at the bank, for example, then you may feel banks are unwelcoming. This is one reason that over half of immigrant/non-citizen households, and that nearly two-thirds of households where only Spanish is spoken, are unbanked or underbanked

Logistical problems can be a major barrier. "Do I have the proper documents to open an account?" "Is there a bank near me that is convenient?" Banks and savings-and-loans ("thrifts") are under-represented in minority and low-income areas, and AFSPs cluster in those communities. (Scholars who study the issue call this the "spatial void hypothesis.") These spatial voids have only intensified since the 2008 financial crisis, as mainstream banks have ostensibly become more risk-averse—at least regarding low- and moderate-income households and communities.

Alternative financial services are big business in the United States, with an FDIC estimate of $320 billion in annual revenues. The sheer number of check-cashing outlets, payday lenders, auto-title lenders, and issuers of loans on anticipated tax refunds—over 13,000 according to the trade association Financial Service Centers of America—places them nearly on par numerically with banks and credit unions. (Combined, banks and credit unions number almost 15,000, according to the FDIC and National Credit Union Association.) AFSPs are not a "fringe" phenomenon in another sense—many are owned by large mainstream banks that have sought to profit in the market niches left unexploited by regular banking.

In states where check-cashing stores are regulated, fees are clearly posted in business locations, so it is fairly easy to determine the costs to customers. For example, cashing a

FIGURE 2: SOME REASONS HOUSEHOLDS DO NOT HAVE AN ACCOUNT OR CLOSED THEIR ACCOUNT, 2011 AND 2009

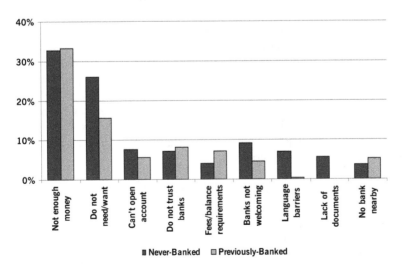

Note: The last four categories appeared only in the 2009 survey.

government check (or direct deposit services for these checks) costs 1-3% of the face value of the check. Paychecks from businesses typically carry a 1-5% fee. Determining the typical fees for transaction services in mainstream banks is more difficult because of complicated fee structures that are dependent upon minimum balances. For people with limited needs for transaction services, and who would risk low balance penalties if they used a mainstream bank, AFSPs may in fact be a reasonable alternative.

Fees for transaction services, however, pale in comparison to the cost of credit. To make ends meet, 12 million Americans rely on short-term payday loans each year, at interest rates of about 300-750% (annual percentage rate, or APR). (Thirty-five states allow payday lending.) For the average borrower, a two-week payday loan stretches into five months of debt, with total interest payments greater than the amount of the loan. Wanting in on the action, big banks have issued payday loans to their own customers, terming them "deposit-advance loans," presumably to make them sound more legitimate.

With increased pressure from the new Consumer Financial Protection Bureau (CFPB) and the FDIC, the greedy practices of payday lenders, especially those operating on the internet, are gradually being investigated and curtailed. Now, banks are pulling back from deposit-advance loans. They are also beginning to cut off accounts for payday lenders and are allowing bank customers to halt automatic withdrawals to payday lending companies. What a difference the Dodd-Frank financial regulation law and the CFPB are beginning to make.

U.S. Senator Elizabeth Warren (D-MA) wants to take the solutions to financial exclusion one step further, beyond regulatory protections against harmful lending and transaction practices. In a recent Huffington Post opinion piece, she urges a serious consideration of postal banks, backing a new report from the U.S. Postal Service (USPS) Office of the Inspector General. The Postal Service, she argues, could partner with banks to offer basic services, including bill paying, check cashing, and small loans.

The idea has precedents. The United States had a postal savings system for accepting and insuring small deposits from 1911 to 1967. The government was thought to be a safe place to stash savings. Savers were paid interest on money that the postal service accepted and redeposited in local banks. After World War II, banks offered higher interest rates to compete for deposits and postal deposits fell. The convenience of the local post office faded in importance as Americans increasingly enjoyed access to cars.

But the idea of postal banks is once again garnering widespread support (44% in favor vs. 37% opposed in a recent YouGov/Huffington Post poll). For millions of Americans, the local post office is one of the geographically closest retail outlets. Unlike private financial-service providers subject to patchy state-by-state regulations, federal postal banks would be regulated in all U.S. states. They would help ease the spatial void in poorer communities and guard against exploitative practices by unregulated banking "alternatives." ❏

Sources: 2011 FDIC National Survey of Unbanked and Underbanked Households, September 2012; FDIC National Survey of Unbanked and Underbanked Households, December 2009; Sen. Elizabeth Warren, "Coming to a Post Office Near You: Loans You Can Trust?" Huffington Post Blog, Feb. 1, 2014 (huffingtonpost.com); Office of the Inspector General, U.S. Postal Service, "Providing Non-Bank Financial Services for the Underserved," Report Number RARC-WP-14-2007, Jan. 27, 2014; Pew Charitable Trusts reports on Payday Lending in America (pewstates.org).

Article 3.3

NEUTRALIZED
The net neutrality victory turns to defeat

BY ROB LARSON
July/August 2018

When the Federal Communications Commission (FCC) decided to regulate Internet providers through "net neutrality" principles, the conservative *Wall Street Journal* predicted a "Telecom Backlash." The great regional cable monopolies like Comcast and AT&T, as well as the wireless carriers like Verizon and Sprint, opposed the net neutrality orders because they would prevent them from further monetizing their control over the "pipes" that online data takes to reach end users. Under the Trump administration, they ultimately got their way: The FCC reversed itself and undid the crucial "Title II" classification on December 14, 2017.

Meanwhile, giant tech companies like Facebook and Google subsidiary YouTube are usually viewed as supportive of Title II, and they had meaningfully opposed the telecoms earlier this decade in support of neutrality. However Silicon Valley's growing dominance is drawing it into the telecommunication industry itself, diminishing its support for the popular neutrality principles. This change has the potential to reshape Internet access, a pivotal change with ramifications for the entire U.S. economy.

Neutering Net Neutrality

The basic argument of net neutrality is relatively easy to understand: information traveling over a network shouldn't be subject to discrimination or favor, like speeding up the data flow for companies that can afford to pay the network operator, or slowing down (or even blocking) info from entities the operator doesn't care for. This basic principle has long applied to many familiar networks, like the traditional phone system. When you make a phone call for pizza delivery, for example, the mobile carriers can't steer your call to another pizzeria that paid for the privilege. They have to connect you to the one you dialed, and maintain a common standard of call quality.

Given the rapid growth of the Internet over the last 20 years, the stakes for abandoning these principles online are great. Leaving the cable monopolists and the cell carrier oligopolists a free hand allows them to consider collecting unearned "rent" income by charging popular, cash-flush sites higher rates for faster or more consistent content delivery, while slowing down (or "throttling") content from poorer or unfavored sites. It gives the telecom industry enormous discretionary power.

The issue came to real national attention in 2014, when rising media giant Netflix refused to pay telecom colossus Comcast for the rising proportion of its traffic coming from users streaming its library of TV shows and movies. In retaliation, Comcast "throttled" Netflix data, causing users of its service to experience prolonged wait and downgraded quality. This became popularly associated with the "spinning wheel of death" displayed as Netflix's content streamed through relatively tiny network connections. This was risky move for Comcast, as it represented coming between America and its TV shows—about as smart as stepping between a bear and her cubs.

Historically, the FCC had been unable to impose neutrality standards on the industry since Internet access was technically classified as an information service, rather than a telecommunication service. If it were reclassified as a telecom service, the cable and wireless firms' data plans could be designated "common carriers" like the traditional phone lines, considered to be too important to the economy to be unregulated. This would subject Internet service to Title II of the Telecommunications Act, which would effectively impose net neutrality norms on the industry. This is what the FCC did in 2015, and undid in 2017.

A Net Neutrality Glossary

Artificial scarcity: Most goods and services are necessarily "scarce," meaning that the labor and resources required to make them are limited in supply relative to demand. Others could be abundant, meaning there could be enough to meet demand, but producers limit supply, making them "artificially scarce." Many artificially scarce goods or services have negligible costs of production after development, for example drugs or software, but may be limited deliberately by an entity with market power, like the holder of a patent right.

Broadband: High-speed Internet access, via wired cable or fiber connection, a cell phone tower network, satellite service, or a local wireless hotspot.

Captured regulator: A government body created to regulate certain market practices in an industry, but which has become largely taken over by the industry itself, through lobbying or political action.

Common carrier: A provider of network services that obeys net neutrality rules, like the phone system under Title II classification.

Interconnection: The connections between networks, like those operated by ISPs and those operated by large content-providing firms, such as streaming video companies.

ISP: Internet service provider. Usually a private company (although a few embattled municipal networks exist) that runs a broadband network to consumers' computers and phones, transmitting data from content providers like websites.

Market power: The ability of a market actor (or combination of them) to influence prices or market conditions.

Net neutrality: The principle that all data traveling through information networks to consumers should be treated equally. Practices that violate the principle include throttling of data to collect payment, discrimination among users or types of data, or paid promotion to ensure faster delivery.

Network effect: A service used in a network gains value as more users join. (If everyone you need to contact regularly has a telephone, telephone service is worth more to you than if they did not.) This feature tends to create market concentration and monopoly.

The first of three rounds of battle over neutrality in the United States began before the Netflix debacle, in December 2010, and was indicative of the FCC's long-standing reputation as a "captured" regulator. The FCC's then-chairman, Tom Wheeler, was a former cable industry lobbyist, and unsurprisingly the FCC's first attempt at a neutrality policy was literally written by people from the industry.

This FCC order was prepared by lobbyists and attorneys for AT&T, Verizon, and Google, and actually did ban the net neutrality violations of blocking and discrimination among data transmission. But a gigantic omission pointed toward the reason for the phone corporations' participation: The rule confined itself to the "wired" Internet, completely exempting service via a wireless signal. Liberal legal scholar Tim Wu, coiner of the term "net neutrality," observed the significance of this exemption in his fine book *The Master Switch*: "That enormous exception— AT&T and Verizon's condition for support of the rule—is no mere technicality, but arguably the masterstroke on the part of [the cell carriers]. It puts the cable industry at a disadvantage, while leaving the markets on which both AT&T and Verizon have bet their future without federal oversight."

Wireless was correctly understood at the time to be the growth center of the industry, so this exemption gave the cell service oligopoly a free hand to charge for prioritization and block content they didn't care for. Still, the telecom companies found even this infringement on their corporate liberty to be too much to tolerate, and their major trade associations, the United States Telecom Association and the National Cable & Telecommunications Association, filed lawsuits immediately after the decision. The regulation, the Open Internet Order 2010, was ultimately struck down in court in 2014, leading to the next round of the struggle.

Title II: The Quickening

To understand the second round of net neutrality confrontation, we need to look at the lineup of corporate forces on either side of the issue. On one side were the great telecom giants AT&T, Comcast, and Verizon, which opposed to net neutrality so they could charge more for choice access to their "bandwidth," or data flow capacity. Household-name tech platforms like Google, Facebook, and Amazon were on the opposing side, eager to continue their rapid online growth without increased costs for access to the telecom networks.

Title II

Title II of the 1934 Communications Act requires network-operating companies to treat communications equally and not discriminate among users or with respect to content. The classic example is telephone service, where Title II requires that if you call your doctor, for example, your call can't be routed instead to another practice that paid the network operator. This means phone service is a "common carrier" of information, and the FCC's reclassification of the ISPs as common carriers means net neutrality principles will be instated for cable and wireless broadband markets.

In November 2014, President Obama recorded a video statement calling for Title II reclassification, largely in response to a groundswell of public comments on the FCC's online facility, reaching over four million and largely supporting net neutrality. This was the result of a major activist campaign, combining online and offline action.

Despite claims of "regulatory overreach," the FCC's 2015 neutrality order specifically elected to "forbear" using several of the regulatory tools of Title II, including price limits, and left several important issues unresolved. But it confirmed the main net neutrality provisions. The FCC explicitly drew attention to the tsunami of public comments in justifying its decision: "Because the record overwhelmingly supports adopting rules and demonstrates that three specific practices invariably harm the open Internet—blocking, throttling, and paid prioritization—this order bans each of them, applying the same rules to both fixed and mobile broadband Internet access service."

A predictable chorus of conservative and neoliberal opposition quickly arose, led by Republican FCC Commissioner Ajit Pai. Among the usual cant about overreach, Pai claimed no action was needed since "The Internet is not broken." Netflix subscribers watching the spinning wheel while Comcast and other cable firms were throttling its data capacity might disagree. For their part, the cable and cellular service providers claimed that the threat of FCC interference would limit their infrastructure investments—meaning the networks would have to lay less cable and upgrade fewer cell towers because of rising expenses. This oft-repeated claim was countered by reporting from the *MIT Technology Review*, which found that the telecom networks have a hilarious 97% profit margin on bandwidth investments. They're unlikely to walk away in the face of mild regulation; indeed, they haven't deserted European markets, where some network neutral provisions are in effect.

The Empires Strike Back

The advent of the Trump administration amounted to a major setback for net neutrality, as it did for so many other important economic, social, and environmental policies. Trump appointed the leading Republican on the FCC, Pai, to head the agency, and shortly thereafter announced that the agency was reevaluating the Title II classification. Pai's main justification for doing so was his repeated claim that net neutrality was depressing investment in the telecommunications network, despite the industry's absurd profit rates. In fact, Comcast and other large broadband providers had continued to increase their yearly capital investments in the years after the FCC's neutrality rules were issued. On December 14, 2017, the Commission voted to formally overturn the Title II ruling, despite continued telecom investment, and despite the lack of major competition among the cable companies that supply the wired broadband for Wi-Fi service.

Activism to save neutrality this time around was somewhat less dramatic than in the previous round, owing in part to the diminishing support of the influential tech titans. However, public comments poured in at the FCC once again, forcing them to "rate limit" submissions, ensuring tranches of comments were gradually submitted so as not to overwhelm their docket facility yet again. Twenty-three million comments were submitted by the time of the repeal vote, but many were generated by software programmed to churn them out. Many were alleged to have been submitted by public figures; others were posted under the names of deceased or fictional people. Some of the fake comments supported net neutrality, but the *Wall Street Journal* reported that one anti-neutrality email was posted at "a near-constant rate—1,000 every 10 minutes—punctuated by periods of zero comments, as if web robots were turning on and off. ...The Comment has been posted on the FCC website more than 818,000 times." A report by telecom firms found many of the comments were attributable to "FakeMailGenerator.com." It's a pity that the public comment process at the FCC and other regulatory agency websites has been so heavily gamed.

Exactly what this major reversal for freedom means as far as market conditions will take time to materialize. There are clues at coffee shops and with in-flight airline-sponsored Internet access, which are exempt from neutrality rules since the companies are not telecom firms and provide web access as a perk. There, tech giants like Amazon prominently sponsor the service, and users are steered toward those sites, although differences in bandwidth access aren't yet common. On mobile, the telecoms have been experimenting for some time with "zero rating," a practice of not counting use of certain partner websites or services against a data plan. These modest neutrality violations can be expected to expand over time, likely leading to poorer service and restricted access for those less able to pay.

From Platforms to Pipes

The dramatically waxing and waning fortunes of net neutrality owe a lot to the shifting stances of the giant tech platforms over neutrality. In the proposed 2010 rule written by industry, Google had agreed with Verizon that neutrality rules weren't necessary on wireless systems. When Obama made his famous November 2014 video calling for Title II reclassification, Google founder Eric Schmidt told an administration official that the position was a mistake. As the *Wall Street Journal* put it, "Google and Net Neutrality: It's Complicated."

While in 2010, the tech giants directly signed on to the effort to support net neutrality, in 2014 they mostly left neutrality policy to the lower-profile Internet Association, their trade group. The *National Journal* found "big Web companies like Facebook and Google mostly stayed on the sidelines of the debate." Several prominent online companies did stage an "Internet Slowdown," replacing their normal home pages with a graphic of the spinning "loading" wheel, dramatizing the risks posed by fast- and slow-lanes. Participating firms included Web mid-weights like Mozilla, Kickstarter, WordPress, and of course Netflix. Notably absent were the heavyweights like Google, Facebook, or Apple.

In 2017 their support was thinner still, and some tech figures argued that the reclassification wasn't necessary for effective neutrality. The business coverage ran headlines like "Web Firms Protest Efforts to Roll Back Net Neutrality," but the fine print reveals the companies involved are led by second-tier firms like Netflix, Reddit, and GoDaddy. And Netflix itself, the very poster child for net neutrality, was "less vocal" on the subject after it worked out satisfactory commercial deals with the telecom giants to route its data. The *Wall Street Journal* bluntly reported that the company "says it is less at risk now that it is big enough to strike favorable deals with telecom companies. The company did just that, reaching several deals in recent years to pay broadband providers for ample bandwidth into their networks." And "some big players," including Google and Amazon, "were content with relatively low-key efforts."

While the smaller firms were purposely displaying the annoying pinwheel, Google couldn't be bothered to include the image on the front of its incredibly prominent search engine page. Instead, the firm ran a post on its relatively obscure policy blog, while Amazon deployed a noncommittal button linking to the FCC comment facility, and Facebook CEO Zuckerberg posted that he supported Title II but was "open to working with members of Congress." Hardly an aggressive stance. In 2017, Netflix, Reddit, and others did reprise the display of the slow-loading pinwheel, but they were increasingly lonely among the towering tech colossi in doing so.

Why the hesitance to stick up for net neutrality? After all, these firms do rely on open access to the telecom industry's "pipes" of the Internet to deliver their oceans of free user content to their platforms globally.

The answer is clear economics: the companies are themselves becoming Internet service providers like the telecom companies, investing heavily in new cables and other infrastructure to bring content and their platforms' services to users. They are losing their previously stark opposing interest to the telecom giants.

Big tech has been moving further in this direction since the 2014–5 neutrality struggle. The business media frequently report on these changes. In early 2016 the *Wall Street Journal* reported that Microsoft and Facebook were jointly investing in a transatlantic data cable to add redundancy to the networks their platforms rely on. Because the project costed hundreds of millions of dollars, "only the very largest Internet companies have made the plunge" into digital infrastructure on this scale. The deal indicated, according to the *Journal*, that "the biggest U.S. tech companies are seeking more control over the Internet's plumbing."

Amazon has also invested in an undersea bundle of fiberoptic cables, and in late 2016 Facebook and Google announced major investments in a high-speed line between Los Angeles and Hong Kong. Google is also laying an incredible 6,200-mile-long fully private cable from LA to its data center in Chile, part of an effort to catch up to Amazon and Microsoft in cloud computing. Fascinatingly, a Google cloud computing exec is reported to claim the company's telecommunications infrastructure "adds up the world's biggest private network, handling roughly 25% of the world's internet traffic...without relying on telecom companies." Except that now, Google *is* a telecom company.

Indeed, all the tech giants have invested in high-speed data lines between major world cities for years. These investments are intended to ensure enough capacity to route information among the giants' enormous data centers. The business press suggests, amazingly, that "the investments have pushed aside the telephone companies that dominated the capital-intensive market for more than a century." The process is strikingly reminiscent of Rockefeller's money-gushing Standard Oil empire, which first conquered energy, and then began taking over the rail lines carrying that energy.

These market developments make it easy to understand why the big tech firms are less and less interested in confronting the telecom industry: They are increasingly members of that industry, and they are gaining an economic interest in the possibility of prioritizing or restricting different data. They are gaining control. This is a major long-term trend that will see the future blurring of the lines between tech and telecom. Let this be a lesson to social and political movements: Capitalists are bad social-change allies.

Despite the blow to leftist morale from the Trump FCC's reversal and the spreading desertion of the mega-cap tech giants from the neutrality struggle, positive signs persist. Notably, in May 2018 U.S. Senate Democrats successful voted with a handful of Republicans to restore the Title II classification, a surprising victory, but one doomed to die in the GOP-run House of Representatives. But the vote speaks to the enduring popularity of the idea. Net neutrality has a future with legislatures and administrations that are less devoted to the unfettered freedom of enormous cable monopolists to steer public attention toward pleasant corporate propaganda and pop songs. ❏

Sources: Tim Wu, *The Master Switch* (Vintage, 2011); David Talbot, "When Will the Rest of Us Get Google Fiber?" *MIT Technology Review*, February 4 2013; Mark Scott, "Dutch Offer Preview of Net Neutrality," *New York Times*, Feb. 26 2015; Miriam Gottfried, "Don't Get Too Excited About the FCC's New Rules," *Wall Street Journal*, April 16 2017; Cecilia Kang, "F.C.C. Repeals Net Neutrality Rules," *New York Times*, Dec. 14, 2017; "Net Neutrality breaks records," Fight for the Future, July 13, 2007; James Grimaldi and Paul Overberg, "Lawmakers Seek Checks on Phony comments before 'Net Neutrality' Vote, *Wall Street Journal*, Dec. 13 2017; James Grimaldi and Paul Overberg, "Millions of People Post Comments on Federal Regulations. Many Are Fake." *Wall Street Journal*, December 12 2017; John McKinnon and Ryan Knutson, "Want to See a World Without Net Neutrality? Look at These Old Cellphone Plans," *Wall Street Journal*, December 11 2017; Alistair Barr, "Google and Net Neutrality: It's Complicated," *Wall Street Journal*, February 4 2015; Brendan Sasso, "Despite fierce opposition from the major Internet providers, the FCC is poised to seize expansive new regulatory powers," *National Journal*, February 5 2015; John McKinnon, "Web Firms Defend Net Neutrality As GOP Takes Aim," *Wall Street Journal*, April 13 2017; Drew FitzGerald, "Netflix backs away From Fight Over Internet Rules Now That Traffic is Flowing," *Wall Street Journal*, Dec. 13 2017; John McKinnon and Douglas MacMillan, "Web Firms Protest Efforts to Roll Back Net Neutrality," *Wall Street Journal*, July 12, 2017; Drew FitzGerald, "Facebook and Microsoft to Build Fiber Optic Cable Across Atlantic," *Wall Street Journal*, May 27, 2016; Drew FitzGerald, "Google, Facebook to Invest in U.S.-China Data Link," *Wall Street Journal*, Oct. 12, 2016; Drew FitzGerald, "Google Plans to Expand Huge Undersea Cables to Boost Cloud Business," *Wall Street Journal*, Jan. 16 2018.

Article 3.4

CAMPUS STRUGGLES AGAINST SWEATSHOPS CONTINUE
Indonesian workers and U.S. students fight back against Adidas.

BY SARAH BLASKEY AND PHIL GASPER
September/October 2012

Abandoning his financially ailing factory in the Tangerang region of Indonesia, owner Jin Woo Kim fled the country for his home, South Korea, in January 2011 without leaving money to pay his workers. The factory, PT Kizone, stayed open for several months and then closed in financial ruin in April, leaving 2,700 workers with no jobs and owed $3.4 million of legally mandated severance pay.

In countries like Indonesia, with no unemployment insurance, severance pay is what keeps workers and their families from literal starvation. "The important thing is to be able to have rice. Maybe we add some chili pepper, some salt, if we can," explained an ex-Kizone worker, Marlina, in a report released by the Worker Rights Consortium (WRC), a U.S.-based labor-rights monitoring group, in May 2012.

Marlina, widowed mother of two, worked at PT Kizone for eleven years before the factory closed. She needs the severance payment in order to pay her son's high school registration fee and monthly tuition, and to make important repairs to her house.

When the owner fled, the responsibility for severance payments to PT Kizone workers fell on the companies that sourced from the factory—Adidas, Nike, and the Dallas Cowboys. Within a year, both Nike and the Dallas Cowboys made severance payments that they claim are proportional to the size of their orders from the factory, around $1.5 million total. But Adidas has refused to pay any of the $1.8 million still owed to workers.

Workers in PT Kizone factory mainly produced athletic clothing sold to hundreds of universities throughout the United States. All collegiate licensees like Adidas and Nike sign contracts with the universities that buy their apparel. At least 180 universities around the nation are affiliated with the WRC and have licensing contracts mandating that brands pay "all applicable back wages found due to workers who manufactured the licensed articles." If wages or severance pay are not paid to workers that produce university goods, then the school has the right to terminate the contract.

Using the language in these contracts, activists on these campuses coordinate nationwide divestment campaigns to pressure brands like Adidas to uphold previously unenforceable labor codes of conduct.

Unpaid back wages and benefits are a major problem in the garment industry. Apparel brands rarely own factories. Rather, they contract with independent manufacturers all over the world to produce their wares. When a factory closes for any reason, a brand can simply take its business somewhere else and wash its hands of any responsibilities to the fired workers.

Brands like Nike and Russell have lost millions of dollars when, pressed by United Students Against Sweatshops (USAS), universities haver terminated their contracts. According to the USAS website, campus activism has forced Nike to pay severance and Russell to rehire over 1,000 workers it had laid off, in order to avoid losing more collegiate contracts. Now many college activists have their sights set on Adidas.

At the University of Wisconsin (UW) in Madison, the USAS-affiliated Student Labor Action Coalition (SLAC) and sympathetic faculty are in the middle of a more than year-long campaign to pressure the school to terminate its contract with Adidas in solidarity with the PT Kizone workers.

The chair of UW's Labor Licensing Policy Committee (LLPC) says that Adidas is in violation of the code of conduct for the school's licensees. Even the university's senior counsel, Brian Vaughn, stated publicly at a June LLPC meeting that Adidas is "in breach of the contract based on its failure to adhere to the standards of the labor code." But despite the fact that Vaughn claimed at the time that the University's "two overriding goals are to get money back in the hands of the workers and to maintain the integrity of the labor code," the administration has dragged its feet in responding to Adidas.

Instead of putting the company on notice for potential contract termination and giving it a deadline to meet its obligations as recommended by the LLPC, UW entered into months of fruitless negotiations with Adidas in spring of 2012. In July, when these negotiations had led nowhere, UW's interim chancellor David Ward asked a state court to decide whether or not Adidas had violated the contract (despite the senior counsel's earlier public admission that it had). This process will delay a decision for many more months—perhaps years if there are appeals.

Since the Adidas campaign's inception in the fall of 2011, SLAC members have actively opposed the school's cautious approach, calling both the mediation process and the current court action a "stalling tactic" by the UW administration and Adidas to avoid responsibility to the PT Kizone workers. In response, student organizers planned everything from frequent letter deliveries to campus administrators, to petition drives, teach-ins, and even a banner drop from the administration building that over 300 people attended, all in hopes of pressuring the chancellor (who ultimately has the final say in the matter) to cut the contract with Adidas.

While the administration claims that it is moving slowly to avoid being sued by Adidas, it is also getting considerable pressure from its powerful athletics director, Barry Alvarez, to continue its contract with Adidas. As part of the deal, UW's sports programs receive royalties and sports gear worth about $2.5 million every year.

"Just look at the money—what we lose and what it would cost us," Alvarez told the *Wisconsin State Journal*, even though other major brands would certainly jump at the opportunity to replace Adidas. "We have four building projects going on. It could hurt recruiting. There's a trickle-down effect that would be devastating to our whole athletic program."

But Tina Treviño-Murphy, a student activist with SLAC, rejects this logic. "A strong athletics department shouldn't have to be built on a foundation of stolen labor," she told *Dollars & Sense*. "Our department and our students deserve better."

Adidas is now facing pressure from both campus activists in the United States and the workers in Indonesia—including sit-ins by the latter at the German and British embassies in Jakarta. (Adidas' world headquarters are in Germany, and the company sponsored the recent London Olympics.) This led to a meeting between their union and an Adidas representative, who refused to admit responsibility but instead offered food vouchers to some of the workers. The offer amounted to a tiny fraction of the owed severance and was rejected as insulting by former Kizone workers.

In the face of intransigence from university administrations and multinational companies prepared to shift production quickly from one location to another to stay one step ahead of labor-rights monitors, campus activism to fight sweatshops can seem like a labor of Sisyphus. After more than a decade of organizing, a recent fundraising appeal from USAS noted that "today sweatshop conditions are worse than ever."

Brands threaten to pull out of particular factories if labor costs rise, encouraging a work environment characterized by "forced overtime, physical and sexual harassment, and extreme anti-union intimidation, even death threats," says Natalie Yoon, a USAS member who recently participated in a delegation to factories in Honduras and El Salvador.

According to Snehal Shingavi, a professor at the University of Texas, Austin who was a USAS activist at Berkeley for many years, finding ways to build links with the struggles of the affected workers is key. "What I think would help the campaign the most is if there were actually more sustained and engaged connections between students here and workers who are in factories who are facing these conditions," Shingavi told *Dollars & Sense*. Ultimately, he said, only workers' self-activity can "make the kind of changes that I think we all want, which is an end to exploitative working conditions."

But in the meantime, even small victories are important. Anti-sweatshop activists around the country received a boost in September, when Cornell University President David Skorton announced that his school was ending its licensing contract with Adidas effective October 1, because of the company's failure to pay severance to PT Kizone workers. The announcement followed a sustained campaign by the Sweatfree Cornell Coalition, leading up to a "study in" at the president's office. While the contract itself was small, USAS described the decision as the "first domino," which may lead other campuses to follow suit. Shortly afterwards, Oberlin College in Ohio told Adidas that it would not renew its current four-year contract with the company if the workers in Indonesia are not paid severance.

Perhaps just as significant are the lessons that some activists are drawing from these campaigns. "The people who have a lot of power are going to want to keep that power and the only way to make people give some of that up is if we make them," Treviño-Murphy said. "So it's really pressure from below, grassroots organizing, that makes the difference. We see that every day in SLAC and I think it teaches us to be not just better students but better citizens who will stand up to fight injustice every time." ❑

Sources: Worker Rights Consortium, "Status Update Re: PT Kizone (Indonesia)," May 15, 2012 (workersrights.org); Andy Baggot, "Alvarez Anxiously Awaits Adidas Decision," *Wisconsin State Journal*, July 13, 2012 (host.madison.com); United Students Against Sweatshops (usas.org), PT Kizone update, June 15, 2012 (cleanclothes.org/urgent-actions/kizoneupdate).

Article 3.5

A FLYING PUBLIC FINALLY ERUPTS

BY SAM PIZZIGATI

April 2017; Inequality.org

America's top airline execs have every incentive to treat average passengers as cattle and chattel. Could United's now infamous aisle drag upset their gravy train?

Those of us on the shady side of 60 can remember a time when ordinary people could actually enjoy traveling on an airplane. Meals on all but short-hop flights. Comfortable seats with ample legroom. Plenty of space to stow your bags, since flights seldom took off much more than three-quarters full. On cross-country trips, flight attendants on United used to hand out menus that proudly proclaimed the meal choices that even coach passengers could make.

We lucky travelers owed that golden age to regulation. Before 1978, airlines operated like electrical utilities. The government determined fares, routes, and schedules and essentially guaranteed the private airlines a reasonable rate of profit in return.

But America's movers and shakers considered this entire system unreasonable. If we only deregulated the airline industry and let the free market work its magic, they promised, the resulting competition would lower fares and give passengers a much wider array of choices. Lawmakers—from both parties—would enthusiastically swallow this free-market-magic line, with America's liberal lion, Senator Edward Kennedy (D-Mass.), leading the way. In 1978, Congress deregulated the airline industry.

Deregulation at first seemed to bring nothing but good news. Jazzy new "low-fare" airlines jumped into the airline market, and prices sank. But then reality set in. The new airlines came and went; none lasted. A regulated industry essentially became an unregulated monopoly, with corporate executives—instead of public officials—calling the shots. The shots these execs called would feather their nests at the expense of average travelers. Passengers soon found themselves bouncing at hubs instead of flying direct to their destinations. These hubs cut airline costs but added long hours to travel days.

The cost-cutting continued inside the planes. Airlines eliminated meals for average travelers and the comfy legroom between coach seats. Then they did their best to pack most every seat on every flight, creating ever longer delays in boarding and exiting.

But coach didn't become truly cruel until earlier this week when United had a 69-year-old doctor dragged off his seat and down the airline aisle. Videos of the incident went viral and generated headlines worldwide.

First-class passengers at United never, of course, have to worry about getting dragged off a flight. America's airline giants bend over backwards to move deep-pocketed passengers only in the greatest of comfort. United even drives top customers with tight connections from gate to gate in Porsches and Mercedes. Once aboard United planes, these lucky few can relax in fold-out beds, notes one press report, "complete with mood lighting, adjustable lumbar supports, and bedding from Saks Fifth Avenue."

The modern airplane, the University of Toronto's Katherine DeCelles and Harvard's Michael Norton observed last year, has become "a social microcosm of class-based society." And all that anger airline travelers have been feeling this week as they view the doctor-dragging videos? That anger, the DeCelles-Norton research suggests, can best be understood "through the lens of inequality."

The contemporary airline business model rests on what some analysts like to call the "velvet rope economy." Airlines make much more on premium seats than on seats in coach. Their goal: make coach seating unpleasant enough to keep the enormously lucrative premium seats filled.

For this scheme to work, the inequality involved has to be clearly visible. Coach passengers need to know that passengers upfront are luxuriating while they, cramped and hungry, sit and stew. This stark, in-your-face inequality, DeCelles and Norton found in their research, seems to be contributing more to the misery of air travel than no-stretch seats and interminable delays.

Air rage incidents among economy-class passengers, the data show, turn out to be "nearly four times" more likely on planes that sport a first-class section. If coach-class passengers have to walk through first-class to reach their own seats, air rage incidents become, one analysis of the DeCelles-Norton research notes, "twice as likely again."An even more startling stat: Having coach passengers walk through first class appears to be "roughly as likely to produce an air rage incident as a six-hour travel delay." Corporate America, conclude researchers DeCelles and Norton, has built physical and situational inequality "into people's everyday environments."

How to end that inequality? Maybe we could get a little head start by discouraging lavish rewards for corporate execs who see average passengers as little more than sardines to be squeezed. How lavish? United's immediate past CEO, Jeff Smisek, had to step down in 2015 after a federal corruption probe implicated him in a favor-trading scheme. He walked away with $37 million in compensation, "including a car, free flights, and lifetime parking privileges at two major airports."

Airline execs like Smisek all regularly rely on various subsidies that our tax dollars make possible. We could, if we so chose, start leveraging those tax dollars. We could, for instance, deny tax-funded airport subsidies to airlines that pay their top execs over 25 times what they pay their typical workers.

And if that doesn't work? We can make the execs fly coach. ❑

Sources: Chico Harlan, "Airlines have never been better at making certain your flight is full," *Washington Post*, September 8, 2014; Daniel Victor and Matt Stevens, "United Airlines Passenger Is Dragged From an Overbooked Flight," *New York Times*, April 10, 2017; Harold Meyerson, "Et Tu, Jet Blue? The Airlines' War on the 99%," *American Prospect*, May 14, 2014; Helaine Olen, "United Is Not Alone," *New York Times*, April 11, 2017; Katherine A. DeCellesa and Michael I. Norton, "Physical and situational inequality on airplanes predicts air rage," *Proceedings of the National Academy of Sciences*, March 30, 2016; Nelson D. Schwartz, In an Age of Privilege, Not Everyone Is in the Same Boat," *New York Times*, April 23, 2016; Henry Farrell, "If You Want to Know Why Americans Are Angry About Inequality, Try Flying Coach," *Washington Post*, May 3, 2016; Hugo Martin, "United Airlines pays $37 million to ex-CEO who quit amid a corruption investigation," *Los Angeles Times*, May 3, 2016; Gregory Karp, "America's airline CEOs cry foul about foreign competition," *Chicago Tribune*, April 21, 2015.

Article 3.6

THE FUTURE OF WORK, LEISURE, AND CONSUMPTION

AN INTERVIEW WITH JULIET SCHOR
May/June 2014

Economist Juliet Schor is known worldwide for her research on the interrelated issues of work, leisure, and consumption. Her books on these themes include The Overworked American: The Unexpected Decline of Leisure, The Overspent American: Upscaling, Downshifting, and the New Consumer, and Plenitude: The New Economics of True Wealth (retitled True Wealth for its paperback edition). She is also a professor of sociology at Boston College. —Eds.

DOLLARS & SENSE: We wouldn't expect patterns of work, leisure, and consumption to change overnight, but we're now more than half a decade into a profound crisis. Obviously it's had a big impact on employment, incomes, and so forth, but do you see any lasting changes emerging?

JULIET SCHOR: Some of the trends that were pretty significant before the crash have abated. I'm thinking most particularly about what I've called the "fast fashion model" of consumption—cheap imports of manufactured goods that people were acquiring at accelerating rates, the acceleration of the fashion cycle, and the cycle of acquisition and discard. The trend was people buying things, holding them for shorter and shorter periods of time and then discarding them either into some kind of household storage, into a waste stream, or into secondary markets. You had an amazing period of acquisition of consumer goods. I first started looking at this in the realm of apparel, but it was also in consumer electronics, ordinary household appliances, and pretty much across the board in consumer goods.

Of course, a lot of it was financed by debt or longer working hours, but manufactured goods just became so cheap. The idea that you could buy a DVD player for $19—and yes, people were trampling each other in the stores on Black Friday to get them—but that's just an extraordinary period. So that has changed, because the economics of that have changed. Going forward, I don't think we're going to see that level of availability of cheap goods that we saw before. So I think that cycle has slowed down.

The other big thing has been the bifurcation of the consumer market. That's something that's been going on for a long time—the falling out of the middle as a result of the decline of the middle class, the growth of a really low-end in the consumer market with dollar stores and a retail sector where even Walmart is considered expensive. The other side was the expansion of the hyper-luxury market.

Trends in income and wealth are reflected in the consumer sphere. There's more reluctance to take on debt, so debt-fueled consumer buying is lessened. There's also less availability of consumer credit for households now. The other big thing that I've been looking at is the rise of "alternative cultures" of consumption; that is, people moving out of the branded, advertised goods and the mass-produced lifestyles that dominated in the last couple of decades into more ecologically aware lifestyles with more artisanal and self-production.

D&S: Stepping back and looking more broadly at the emergence of this mass consumer culture in the United States after the Second World War, what do you see that are the key factors that are at the root of consumer capitalism in the United States? It seems a little facile to focus too narrowly on just advertising. Some scholars point to mass media images and what kinds of lifestyles people aspire to. Galbraith pointed more generally to the relentless stream of new products fueling new desires—the so-called "dependence effect." How do you see those influences, as well as others, sorting out?

JS: I don't want to completely dismiss factors like the old monopoly capital idea or the advertising and marketing story, which is that shortfalls of demand led to a big effort to get people to buy things, but I don't buy that story, for the most part. If you think about the postwar period, you had a labor market in which firms were unwilling to use productivity growth to reduce hours of work, and I wrote a book about that, *The Overworked American*. Part of that was about firms and why they don't want to do that. So in the post-war period, you have, from the labor market side, a situation where all productivity growth is getting channeled into income—into expansion of output—so it goes to wages and profits.

Now, of course, workers aren't getting the benefits of productivity growth, but in the post-war era, they did. There were contracts that were explicitly tied—3% productivity, 3% real wage growth. So that creates consumer demand, because that income is getting into people's pockets. Now you can ask the question: Why don't they save it? I don't think it's advertising, primarily, that determines why people didn't save more. There, I think, you have to look at social competition, and the fact that you have an unequal society in which how you live, what you buy, and what you have are important determinants of social position. Rising income gives you a constantly rising norm, and people consume to keep up with that norm. I think it would have played out more or less similarly if there weren't any advertising. The products might have been different but this sort of "consumer escalator," the fact that you have growing levels of consumption, is really coming much more from the production side. So in that way, I'm much more Marxian than Keynesian, I would say.

D&S: Turning to the contrast between the United States and other high-income capitalist countries, especially in terms of the shape of the labor movement and the role of the state: How did working hours get reduced in other countries? In France or Germany, for example, the average employed person works about 300 hours less per year than in the United States. So that strikes me as quite central, in your analysis, in terms of understanding consumption patterns in different countries.

JS: In the United States in the post-war period, the state devoted a lot of energy to the promotion of consumption, whether it was the highway system or suburbanization. That was in part out of a fear of the "Keynesian problem" of inadequate demand after the Second World War. In Europe, I guess I would point to two things. First, after the war, they had a supply-side problem, which was that they had to rebuild productive capacity rather than what we had, which was the demand-side problem. So our state was much more oriented to promoting consumption than European states, which were more oriented towards rebuilding their societies. In Europe, working hours continued to fall and they didn't in the United States.

That's the way you need to think about it—everybody was on a common trajectory of work-hours decline from about 1870. Of course, the United States was the leader in all of that. We had the shortest working hours and we were the first ones to put in reforms of working hours: The United States was the leader on no Sunday work, no Saturday work, etc. I think the factors are the role of trade unions—both that trade unions were much stronger in Europe and also that in the United States, trade unions turned against the reduction of working hours after the Second World War. That has to do mostly with the Cold War, and with the conservative nature of U.S. trade unions. So in the 1950s, the AFL-CIO became—"hostile" may be too strong a word—became extremely disinterested in the idea of shorter hours of work. That's something that did not happen in Europe.

The other thing is that the incentives facing firms in the United States were really different, in terms of U.S. employers having much higher per worker fixed costs, because of health insurance. There are some European countries where health insurance is provided at the firm level, but mostly not. In the United States that turns out to be a powerful disincentive to reduce working hours, and it becomes a powerful incentive for raising working hours. The growth in inequality, which is more pronounced in the United States, also raised working hours. I think those are the key factors which lead the United States and Europe to diverge quite rapidly on the issue of work time. That divergence turns out to have all sorts of very important consequences.

One of the things you have seen in the patterns of leisure time activities in the United States is you've got time-stressed households doing really money-intensive things like going to the Caribbean for three days, or spending a lot of money to "de-stress," or spending money to reward themselves for working so hard. So we definitely have quite a bit of that in the United States because work is so demanding and stressful and that shapes the leisure patterns. You get what economists call goods- or income-intensive leisure.

D&S: If we think of consumption behavior as social—as aiming to enhance a person's social status—can we think of any important social constraints on the amounts or patterns of consumption? If many people disapprove of polluting or wasteful forms of consumption, like the Hummer, can we observe a social constraint on that? Or, in what are very difficult economic times for a lot of people, is there any effect on people reining in unseemly levels of luxury consumption?

JS: Well, I'll start with the latter. I was reading about and experiencing people's reluctance to engage in ostentatious displays at the time of the crash, and in its early aftermath. I think, by now, that didn't last very long. One of the things about the most ostentatious stuff is that we're increasingly a gated society, so the wealthy are consuming lavishly outside of the view of the ordinary and the poor. There is certainly less celebration of it, and you see it less in the culture now than before the crash, for sure. The Hummers are a very interesting case. I have a friend who did research on the war between Hummer drivers and the Prius drivers, the Prius drivers being referred to as "pious" drivers by the Hummer folks. Now the Hummer vehicle has collapsed as a consumer product. Hummer drivers were subjected to a lot of social disapproval. It also became economically less-desirable when the price of gas went up.

There is definitely a rising ecological consciousness that is attempting to moralize consumption in ways that yield social approval or disapproval of low-carbon versus high-carbon lifestyles. It isn't mainstream yet. It's much more prevalent in highly educated groups, it tends to be more bicoastal, it's a kind of "forward trend" in the consumer culture. You do see more and more, as you move into the mainstream, people attempting to do more ecologically. I think there's widespread sentiment about that. Then, of course, you also have so many people who are just trying to make ends meet that they feel it is not possible for them to think about ecological impact. Of course, the irony is that the people who are just trying to make ends meet are the ones with the low carbon footprints, but the discourse of environmental impact is permeating through consumer culture.

D&S: Going back to something about advertising: It seems to have become more pervasive, both in terms of physical spaces that are filled with advertising and products advertised to users. In the last couple of decades, we've seen the advent of direct marketing of prescription pharmaceuticals, for example, directly to the people who will end up using them. There's a pushback, such as criticism of advertising to children, but it seems largely that there's widespread tolerance of this pervasiveness of advertising in daily life.

JS: This is a little counterintuitive, but part of why advertising has become so pervasive is that the core of advertising, which is television spots, have become so unimportant. People don't have to watch them anymore, and that's huge for advertisers. I think the 30- or 60-second TV spots are much more powerful than the kinds of things that advertisers have moved towards in terms of the spatial expansion of advertising. I think that advertising on the web is much less powerful. So, that's one of the paradoxes of advertising in the contemporary moment: the moment when advertising is much more pervasive in terms of space and place, is a moment when it's much less powerful. Advertisers have been able to move in a few directions that have been productive for them, like word of mouth advertising, and so forth, but those forms are also being delegitimized. People know the person sitting next to them in a bar telling them to drink this vodka might be paid by the company.

Prescription drugs are a big exception, because that came about as a regulatory change. Drug companies weren't allowed to advertise directly to consumers before. If it weren't for pharmaceuticals and ads directed at kids, the advertising industry would be in big trouble. Now the kid story is, I think, a little bit different than the adult story, in the sense that you have a much more powerful approach to children now than you did in the past. The approach to children, I think, is a lot more effective than the approach to adults, which I think is declining in effectiveness. So, you can see a theme in what I'm saying about advertising. Today, I would say I feel less worried about advertising than I did before I started studying it. I think people tune it out. I don't want to go too far on this, but to me it's not where the main action is in terms of what's driving consumer patterns.

D&S: We see some examples of people, in their purchasing decisions, transcending a kind of narrow consumer mentality: They're thinking about environmental impacts, say, in buying a hybrid or electric car. In terms of other products they may be thinking about labor conditions, such as buying fair trade goods or no sweatshop apparel or footwear. On the other hand, one might look at this as reinforcing a core aspect of consumerist capitalism: That whatever it is that you may want, it's for sale and you can buy it.

JS: There's a debate in sociology and the social sciences more generally—because there are other disciplines that have weighed in on this question—about the critique of ethical consumption, political consumption, green consumption. Some argue that it's actually detrimental because it leads people to think that this purchasing behavior can solve problems, and it leads them to be less likely to join in collective solutions to environmental problems, labor problems, poverty, and development in the global South.

I did a study of that, and I used two different data sets: One was a random sample survey of all Americans. The other was an intentional survey of people who are political or ethical consumers, or what we called "conscious consumers," with about 2,000 participants. What we found is that there are actually very high levels of correlation between people engaging in this kind of purchasing and being socially and politically involved in trying to solve these problems in collective ways. And we also looked at the time sequencing and found a group of people who are politically involved already and then you add on this "walk the talk" aspect—if you're going to be fighting sweatshops, then don't buy sweatshop clothing, and if you're concerned about environmental impacts then you don't want to be buying things that are at odds with your values.

So you have people who were political first, then extended to their purchasing behavior, and you have people who got into both at around the same time, and you have people who moved in the other direction—who first did the conscious consuming and then became politically active. Certainly the idea that becoming a "green consumer" undermines your likelihood of engaging in collective action around this is not at all supported by the data in the United States, and there have also been some studies in Europe that show the same thing.

I think the fact of the matter is that changing marketplace behavior in the kind of society we have today is an important component in a broad-based campaign, whether it's on the environment or labor conditions or whatever. We see a lot of the NGOs involved in campaigns that have a market-based dimension—and those have been some of the most successful campaigns in recent years—because it's so hard to get the state to act to do these things, because it is captured by business. People have turned to the market in part because it's an arena where it looks like you can have some results, at least in the short term.

Ultimately, can you stop climate change through consumer behavior and through just market behavior? Definitely not. Can you ensure good working conditions merely by market-oriented activity? Definitely not. To think that it's sufficient is the real mistake, but I don't think that most people who work in this field, who try to work on transforming consumer behavior, have such a naïve view.

D&S: We've already talked about ways in which consumption is connected to people's lives at work, and the availability of leisure time, as well as some changes in patterns of consumption related to broader social objectives. What kinds of changes in consumption—and in the forces shaping consumption—do you envision?

JS: Well, I have a hard time thinking about the future without orienting all of my thinking about climate, because I just don't see much of a positive future unless we can address climate change very significantly. And that means, for wealthy countries, pretty radical emissions cuts in a pretty short period of time. It actually means that for most countries. So, as I think about the future, I think about what we could do both to address climate change through radical emissions reductions and also increase social justice, reduce inequality, and start solving the enormous problems that we have in this country. My most recent book, *True Wealth*, is about how to do that. Obviously, we need to get onto a renewable energy system, there's no question about that. We need a carbon tax or carbon regulation, and that's stuff that is very well known. What is not understood, I don't think, is that we can't successfully address climate change with a model in which we continue to try to expand the size of the economy.

We're going to have to deal with working hours, because that's the only way to stop expanding the size of the economy in any sensible way. So the core of what we need to do is to get back on the trajectory of using productivity growth to reduce hours of work. And that then opens up incredible possibilities in terms of rebalancing the labor market, integrating the unemployed, and having a fairer distribution of hours. We're talking about the distribution of income, but not about the distribution of hours, which is one of the things that drives the distribution of income. So, fair access to the work that exists, giving people more time off from work, and doing much more as a society—and probably a lot on the local and community level—to ensure basic needs for people.

With declining work hours, people's incomes are pretty much stabilized, so you need to bring the incomes of the bottom up, and you need to bring the incomes of the top down. Part of that has to be a redistribution of work opportunity and creating community provisioning of basic needs, like publicly owned utilities which provide power and heat for people at reasonable prices, enhanced public transportation, more public provisioning of food. There are really interesting things going on in global-South countries bringing farmers and consumers together in local food economies that are not just about high-priced organic food, which is what we have here, but low-priced food that ensures food security for people. So, shorter hours, basic needs being met—including housing, education, healthcare—that's the direction I would like to see us go, and I think that really it all flows out from a kind of commitment to climate protection. It could all flow out from a commitment to basic needs, too. They really integrate.

Time use is central, and I think you get a totally different culture of consumption if people's incomes are on a basically stabilized trajectory and what they're getting is more and more free time. So, you have a new culture of consumption that is not about the acquisition of the new, it's not the "work and spend" pattern as I've called it, it's not "throw away" or media driven, it's more "true materialist," where you really pay attention to the things you have, and it's a kind of earthier consumption. ❑

Chapter 4

FIRMS, PRODUCTION, AND PROFIT MAXIMIZATION

INTRODUCTION

How do producers make decisions? Textbooks describe a process that is rational, benign, and downright sensible. There is one best—least costly and most profitable—way to produce any given amount of goods or services. Given a particular scale of operations, there is one most-profitable amount to produce. Businesses adjust their total output and the mix of inputs at the margin until they achieve these most profitable outcomes. They pay the going wage for labor, just as they pay the going price for any input. And when businesses have achieved the lowest possible costs, market competition ensures that they pass on savings to consumers.

This chapter describes a reality that is a bit more complicated, and in some ways uglier, than the textbook model. Very large companies are not the passive price-takers of neoclassical lore but do in fact affect the market-wide levels of prices, profits, and wages, and manufacture their own demand. Thus, large corporations are the very embodiment of market power (violating Tilly Assumption #1, Article 1.2).

Alejandro Reuss starts things off with a primer on corporations (Article 4.1). He describes the ways that corporations are "special"—that is, different from other capitalist enterprises—and why they have become the dominant form of business organization in many countries. He concludes by discussing how corporations' economic power—their control over investment and employment—can translate into political power.

In "If Corporations Are People, What Kind of People Are They?" (Article 4.2), Geoff Schneider holds corporate America up to the World Health Organization's guidelines for psychopathic behavior. The recent record of multinational corporate behavior checks off every box the WHO uses to diagnose psychopathy.

Arthur MacEwan discusses the recent trend of stock buybacks, what has given rise to it, and whether it has any benefit for the larger economy (Article 4.3, "Stock Buybacks: Any Positive Outcome?"). This topic is particularly timely with the recent Trump Administration tax cuts allowing corporations to engage in stock buybacks at much more rapid rates. Apple has announced it will use $100 billion of its tax cut on a stock buyback to reward its executives and shareholders. Next to none of this tax cut "trickles down" to Apple's workers or to Apple's loyal consumers.

In Article 4.4, "What's Good for Wal-Mart ...," Miller provides a salient example of firms' market power. He suggests that there may not be just "one best way" for retail businesses, but rather two: a "high road" based on high levels of service, skilled and decently paid employees, and higher prices, as exemplified by the business model at Costco; and a "low road" that offers low prices, no frills, and a low-paid, high-turnover workforce, which is Walmart's business model. Despite Walmart's growth and its position as the world's largest retailer, the author questions whether the business model has in fact proven beneficial for the U.S. economy as a whole.

Today's private equity firms engage in what used to be called "leveraged buy-outs." Economists Eileen Appelbaum and Rosemary Batt offer a forceful critique, describing how private equity firms buy out target companies with borrowed money, load them up with debt, strip them of valuable assets, and pay themselves extraordinary dividends and fees. Meanwhile, they raise important questions about the boundaries of the firm. Private equity firms, Batt and Appelbaum note, "act as managers and employers of the companies they take over, even though the law treats them as passive investors in the companies they own" (Article 4.5).

Next, in "High CEO Pay: It's What Friends Are For" (Article 4.6), Dean Baker argues that in spite of the "Chicago School" platitudes about corporate executives acting in the interests of the company as a whole, CEO pay is simply an extension of the "Old Boy's Network" and the ability to game the system.

Finally, economist Nancy Folbre looks at "Co-op Economics" (Article 4.7). Folbre considers not only the strengths of workers' cooperatives, in which the workers are also the owners of the firm, but also the problems that they face in growing and becoming more widespread.

Discussion Questions

1. (General) The authors of the articles in this chapter present various firm strategies as a choice, rather than an imperative. How does this compare with the standard microeconomic analysis of business decision-making?

2. (General) Miller suggests that we should change the rules of the competitive game to steer businesses toward better treatment of workers. Present-day capitalism already has some such rules (such as those forbidding slavery). What rule changes do articles in this chapter propose? What do you think of these proposals?

3. (Article 4.1) How do corporations differ from other capitalist firms? How should the fact that corporations are chartered by the government, and shareholders given special protections by law (such as limited liability), affect our attitudes about government regulation of corporate operations?

4. (Article 4.2) Schneider describes an episode in which General Motors (GM)

decided not to recall dangerously defective ignition switches in its vehicles due to the significant cost of doing so. Instead, the firm instructed dealerships to urge buyers to use lighter keychains. What sanction could a normal human expect if found guilty of this behavior? What sanction did GM receive?

5. (Article 4.3) Why does MacEwan call stock buybacks "a reversal of the conventional view of how firms operate"? What benefits for the economy might someone think there are from stock buybacks? Why does MacEwan think this is implausible?

5. (Article 4.4) John Miller implies that there is more than one "best" way to organize production. Do you agree? If other ways of organizing production are equally good, why are certain ways dominant, at least in particular industries?

6. (Article 4.5) Mainstream textbooks suggest that firms profit by offering something of positive value to the rest of society (like goods that consumers want). If private equity firms act in a way that is generally harmful, how do they profit?

7. (Article 4.6) Mainstream neoclassical theory explains prices and incomes as outcomes of market forces—supply and demand. What other forces, according to Baker, explain high CEO compensation? What is "crony capitalism?"

8. (Article 4.7) Folbre proposes a dramatically different power structure at the level of the individual firm, with workers democratically controlling the enterprises where they work. Why does she think that this alternative structure could be desirable for workers and for society? If it is so desirable, why is it not more common?

Article 4.1

WHAT ARE CORPORATIONS?

BY ALEJANDRO REUSS
April 2012

When people use the word "corporation," they are usually referring to certain private, for-profit businesses, especially the largest businesses in the United States or other capitalist economies. When we think of corporations, we usually think of "big business." Besides size, people often picture other features of corporations when they hear the word. A corporation can have many shareholders—all part-owners of the company—instead of being owned by a single owner or a couple of partners. A corporation has a board of directors, elected by some or all of the shareholders, which may direct the overall way the corporation is managed. The board usually hires a few top executives, who then make decisions about how the corporation in managed on a day-to-day basis.

Corporations do not have to be large. There are corporations of all different sizes. Even a small company with a few employees could be a corporation. There are some large companies that are not corporations, but the very largest companies, which may have hundreds of thousands of employees and may sell billions of dollars of goods each year, are almost always corporations. Various different kinds of businesses can be corporations, including manufacturing companies (such as General Motors), retail companies (like Wal-Mart), or financial companies (like Bank of America or Liberty Mutual).

Even though some not for-profit entities are also—legally speaking—corporations, people usually use the word "corporation" as shorthand for for-profit companies like General Motors or Wal-Mart. A corporation, in this sense, is a particular type of capitalist enterprise—a "capitalist corporation."

What Is a Capitalist Enterprise?

By "capitalist enterprise," we just mean a private, for-profit business whose owners employ other people in exchange for wages. By this definition, a private business where a "self-employed" owner works, but which does not hire other people for wages, is not a capitalist enterprise.

In the United States and other similar economies, relatively few people are business owners. Farm workers do not usually own the farms where the work. Miners do not usually own the mines. Factory workers usually do not own the factories. People who work in shops or offices usually do not own those businesses. Most workers do not own the buildings where they go to work, the materials or tools they use, or the products they produce. Instead, they work for pay at capitalist enterprises that are owned by others.

Workers get paid a wage or salary by the owner of the business, who in turn owns whatever the worker produces using the materials and tools provided. The owners of a business, of course, do not usually want the goods that employees produce, but want to sell these goods. If a capitalist enterprise cannot sell these goods for more than what it cost to produce them, it cannot make a profit.

Even a business that makes a profit may not stay in business for very long if the profit is less than "normal" (whatever that may be). The owners may decide that it is not worth investing in that business, if it is possible for them to make a larger profit in another business. In addition, businesses that make higher profits can reinvest these profits to expand and modernize, and may put the less profitable business at a competitive disadvantage in the future. Therefore, owners of capitalist enterprises are under competitive pressure to make the most profit they can.

How Are Corporations Special?

In many ways, capitalist corporations are like other capitalist enterprises. However, corporations are also defined by their special legal status, which makes them different from other capitalist enterprises. Corporations are granted a "charter" by the government, which means that the corporation exists as a legal entity. (In the United States, state governments grant corporate charters.)

All the things that make corporations different from other capitalist enterprises are determined by government policy. Corporate law creates certain special privileges for corporations that other businesses do not have. It also imposes special obligations on corporations (especially those whose shares are bought and sold on the stock market). The most important of these special characteristics are "limited liability," the "fiduciary responsibility" of management to the corporation's shareholders, "public disclosure" requirements, and the corporate "governance" structure.

Limited Liability

If a corporation cannot pay its debts, it can declare bankruptcy, and the people it owes can get paid off from the sale of its assets, like the buildings or machinery it owns. If the proceeds are not enough to pay off all the debts, however, the shareholders are not responsible (not "liable") to pay the rest. This is what we mean by the term "limited liability." Someone who buys stock in a corporation is risking whatever they paid for the stock, but cannot lose more than this amount. If the corporation goes bankrupt, the shareholders' stock becomes worthless, but the shareholders cannot be forced, legally, to pay whatever debts the corporation has left unpaid.

The justification usually given for the legal principle of limited liability is that it promotes economic growth and development. The idea is that, if companies were limited to what an individual or family, or perhaps a couple of partners, could scrape together to start a business, they would not be able to operate at the scale that modern corporations do. They would not have enough money to buy expensive machinery, let alone buy large factories or put together huge assembly lines.

Even if the reason given for limited liability is to fuel economic growth, however, we should remember that this is also a big favor from the government for the people who own shares in corporations. First, limited liability means that the government gives the shareholders of a corporation a certain kind a protection from other people's claims against it. Second, it means that corporations may take bigger risks in hopes of bigger profits, since the shareholders are not on the hook for all the corporation's liabilities if these risks do not pay off.

Fiduciary Responsibility

A single person who fully owns an entire company (known as a "privately held" company) can use the company's funds for whatever he or she likes, whether that is expanding the company's operations or buying luxury cars. In contrast, corporate executives receive a salary and other compensation (often lavish, in the case of large companies) decided by the board of directors or a committee of the board. They are legally free to spend this income as they wish.

Corporate executives also control how company funds are spent, but are not free to treat corporate funds as their own. This means that the chief executive of a company is not legally entitled to use company funds to remodel his or her house, buy fancy cars, take expensive vacations, and so on. Of course, executives still fly on private jets, take "business trips" to exotic locales, enjoy fancy "business dinners," and so on, but they have to justify these as necessary costs of doing business. If shareholders think that executives have failed in their fiduciary responsibility, they can actually sue the company.

Some legal scholars and economists have extended this idea to the logical extreme that corporate managers are legally obligated to the shareholders and only the shareholders. In this view, management decisions must be guided by the sole objective of enhancing "shareholder value" (in effect, the profitability of the corporation, and therefore the value of an ownership stake in it). This means that they cannot put other people's interests ahead of those of the shareholders. According to the "shareholder value" doctrine, if managers decide to pay workers more than they really have to, they are giving away the company's (that is, the shareholders') money. Likewise, they have no legal duty to the broader community, beyond abiding by the law. They do not have to "give back," say, by funding schools, libraries, or parks in the communities where they operate.

The shareholder value doctrine is not new, and it is not just something that pro-business comentators have made up. The doctrine was clearly articulated no later than 1919, in a Supreme Court opinion (*Dodge v. Ford Motor Company*) no less. However, in practice, the courts have been reluctant to intervene in disputes between shareholders and management (in effect, declining to open up the can of worms of deciding what the right business decisions would be).

Public Disclosure

Corporations that sell shares of stock on the stock market are called "publicly traded corporations." Each time a corporation sells a share of its stock to an individual or another company, it raises some money. This is one way the company can finance its operations. In actual fact, most stock sales do not involve a corporation selling stock to a member of the public, but one member of the public selling shares to another (that is, resale of shares that a corporation had previously issued). Therefore, most stock sales do not result in any money going to the corporation that originally issued it.

By law, publicly traded companies have to disclose certain business information. They have to file forms with the government listing their officers (board members and top executives), the officers' compensation (salaries and other benefits), the company's profits or losses, and other information. The idea behind disclosure requirements is to protect shareholders or people who might consider purchasing shares in a company, often referred to as the "investing public."

In practice, corporate "insiders" (board members, top executives, etc.) have much more information about the financial condition of a corporation than members of the public. This has led to well-publicized scandals in recent years, such as the Enron case. Corporate executives sold the stock they owned when the price was high, knowing that in reality the company was not as profitable as the public thought, and that the stock price would soon plummet.

Corporate Governance

When an individual buys a share (or many shares) of a corporation, he or she gets certain property rights. Shareholders are not legally entitled to receive a share of the company's profits each year. The company management decides how much of this money to pay out to shareholders (as "dividends") and how much to keep. A corporation might keep cash reserves, use profits to buy existing businesses, use them to expand its existing operations (for example, by buying or renting additional factory or office buildings, buying new machinery, hiring additional workers, etc.). It is not necessarily preferable for shareholders to receive all or most of the company's profit for a year in the form of dividends. By using "retained earnings" to expand, a corporation may increase in overall value. This increases the value of an ownership share in the company (the value of the stock that shareholders own).

Shareholders have the right to sell their shares if and when they wish. This gives them a stake in the profitability of the corporation, since the price of a share (on the stock exchange) is likely to go higher the more profitable the company is. A shareholder who does not want to be a part owner of the company anymore is not entitled to sell back the shares to the company, nor to take "their" piece of the company with them. The corporation is not required to give the shareholder any tangible asset—the shareholder cannot claim any particular thing owned by the corporation—nor is the corporation forced to sell off tangible assets in order to pay a shareholder who does not want his or her shares anymore. This way, shareholders come and go, but the corporation itself stays intact.

Shareholders also have a say in the governance structure of the corporation. You can think of a corporation as a political entity, like a small (or, in some cases, not so small) country. Shareholders are like the citizens. They are entitled to attend annual shareholder meetings, where they can address questions or comments to the corporation's directors (board members) and executives. Shareholders are entitled to vote in elections to the board of directors (except for those holding certain classes of "nonvoting" or "preferred" stock). They can even run for election to the board of directors, if they so wish.

Corporate elections are different from government elections. First, in corporate elections, only shareholders are allowed to vote. The decisions made by a corporation's management may affect many other people—workers, people in communities where the corporation has operations, etc.. However, if they are not shareholders in the corporation, they are not entitled to vote. In addition, in corporate elections, different shareholders do not get the same number of votes. Rather, each shareholder gets a number of votes equal to the number of shares he or she owns (excluding nonvoting stock). Someone who owns one share gets one vote; 10 shares, 10 votes; 100 shares, 100 votes.

In practice, a large shareholder does not need to own anywhere near a majority of the shares to effectively control a company. People who own very few shares in a company, if disgruntled with the management, are more likely to just sell their shares than to devote a lot of time and energy to getting the management replaced. Relatively small shareholders, in fact, usually just sign away their voting rights to other, larger shareholders. This way, a very wealthy individual may have effective control of a company even though he or she "only" owns, say, 5% of the total shares. Keep in mind that 5% of the stock in the largest corporate giants could be worth billions of dollars.

Corporations, Economic Power, and Political Power

Large corporations are certainly among the most powerful entities in the U.S. economy and politics. We can start by classifying the power of large corporations into economic power, on the one hand, and political power, on the other. Economic power has to do with the ability of large corporations to dictate to others (other businesses, workers, etc.) the conditions under which they will do business. Political power has to do with their ability to get what they want from the government, including both favors they can get from the government and influence over the overall direction of government policy.

Mainstream or "neoclassical" economists do not talk about economic power very much. Mostly, they talk about "market" economies as if nobody exercised any power over anyone else—buyers and sellers engaging in voluntary exchanges, each free from any kind of coercion from other buyers or sellers. The main form of economic power neoclassical economists do talk about is "market power"—basically, the ability of a seller (or buyer) to dictate higher (or lower) prices to others, because of a lack of competition.

In the view of radical political economists, employers as a group have economic power in a different sense. Most of the economic activity in capitalist economies depends on the economic decisions made by capitalist enterprises, such as how much output to produce, how many people to hire, whether to buy new machines or new buildings (this is what economists mean by "investment"), and so on. If capitalist employers decide not to hire people to produce goods and services, many people will be unemployed. Tax collections will be low, and governments are likely to experience budget deficits, unless they dramatically cut spending. Moreover, if capitalist enterprises are not hiring, unemployment is high, and many people are afraid of losing their jobs, the party in power probably will not survive the next election.

If the owners and managers of capitalist enterprises do not like the kinds of economic policies the government is putting in place, they may decide not to hire or invest. In some cases, where capitalists feel very threatened by government policies, they may actually do this with the conscious political aim of bringing down the government. More often, a decline in employment and investment can arise from a simple decline in "business confidence." The owners and managers of capitalist enterprises become pessimistic about being able to sell their goods at a profit, and make a business decision to cut back on production, employment, and investment. The effect, however, can still be to force the government to bend over backwards to maintain profitable conditions for business, in order to avoid an economic downturn. This way, the economic power of capitalist enterprises over the whole economy can result in their getting the kinds of government policies that favor them. ❑

Article 4.2

IF CORPORATIONS ARE PEOPLE, WHAT KIND OF PEOPLE ARE THEY?

BY GEOFF SCHNEIDER
June 2016

In 1886, the U.S. Supreme Court ruled, in *Santa Clara County v. Southern Pacific Railroad*, that corporations have the same legal status as persons. The legal rights of corporations gradually have been expanded in the United States since that time to include the right to free speech and to contribute unlimited amounts to political campaigns (a product of the Supreme Court's 2010 *Citizens United* ruling). A key question that emerges from U.S. corporate personhood is: If corporations are people, what kind of people are they?

One of the key characteristics of a corporation is that, by its very legal structure, it is an amoral entity. It exists for the sole purpose of making profits, and it will do whatever is necessary to increase profits, without considering ethical issues except insofar as they impinge on the bottom line. A crucial reason for this behavior is that chief executive officers (CEOs) and other executives have a legal "fiduciary duty" to act in the best financial interests of stockholders. As conservative economist Milton Friedman stated in his book *Capitalism and Freedom*, "there is one and only one social responsibility of business—to use its resources and engage in activities designed to increase its profits so long as it stays within the rules of the game, which is to say, engages in open and free competition without deception or fraud." Thus, those who control corporations are obligated to do whatever they can within the law to make as much money as possible.

This can lead to behavior that some have called psychopathic. In the provocative 2003 film, "The Corporation," the filmmakers argue that corporations meet the diagnostic criteria used by psychiatrists to determine if a person is psychopathic. Those criteria are:

- Callous disregard for the feelings of others;
- Reckless disregard for the safety of others;
- Incapacity to maintain enduring relationships;
- Deceitfulness: repeated lying and conniving others for profit;
- Incapacity to experience guilt; and
- Failure to conform to social norms with respect to lawful behaviors.

Although at first blush the claim that corporations are psychopaths seems incredible, if we consider the worst behaviors of corporations over the last few decades, and the disturbing frequency with which such behaviors seem to recur, it is possible to see why so many people hold corporations in such low esteem. Below, we describe briefly some of the most horrific behaviors of large corporations in recent years.

Rana Plaza Building Collapse, 2013:

An Example of Corporate Abuses of Subcontracting and Sweatshops

For decades, U.S. and European clothing manufacturers have been moving their operations overseas to countries with extremely low wages and with few safety or environmental regulations. One of their favorite destinations in recent years has been Bangladesh, where wages for clothing workers are the lowest in the world (only $0.24 per hour until the minimum wage was raised to $0.40 per hour in 2014), and where few safety standards are enforced. Bangladesh now has more than 5,000 garment factories handling orders for most of the world's top brands and retailers, and is second in garment manufacturing output behind China.

In 2013, the Rana Plaza building that housed several clothing factories collapsed, killing 1,134 people in the worst disaster in garment-industry history. It was later discovered that the building was constructed with substandard materials in violation of building codes. Even more disturbing was the fact that the owners of the factories insisted that employees return to work even after an engineer inspected the building the day before the collapse and deemed it unsafe due to cracks in the walls and clear structural deficiencies. The factories were making clothes for Walmart, Benetton, and many other large, multinational companies.

Disasters like this one, along with the torture and killing of a Bangladeshi labor activist in 2012, are a product of the subcontracting system used by large clothing manufacturers. The corporations issue specifications for the garments that they want to have manufactured, and contractors around the world bid for the right to make the garments. The lowest bidder wins. But what kind of factory is likely to have the lowest bid? Given the regular occurrence of disasters and labor abuses in garment factories, it appears that the contractors who win bids are those who are the most likely to pay workers the least under the most unsafe conditions. Huge multinational clothing companies are only too eager to participate, while at the same time claiming that they are not responsible for the deaths and abuses because they themselves were not the factory owners. The factory owners in Bangladesh were charged with murder, but there were no major consequences for the clothing companies. The callous disregard for the feelings and safety of others and incapacity to experience guilt that many clothing manufacturers display is certainly consistent with the definition of a psychopath.

BP Oil Spill in the Gulf of Mexico, 2010:

Taking Chances with People's Lives and the Environment

The 2010 BP oil spill in the Gulf of Mexico was the worst in U.S. history. The Deepwater Horizon oil rig exploded on April 20, 2010, killing 11 people and spilling 210 million gallons of oil into the Gulf. Investigations into the causes of the spill indicated significant negligence.

- Deepwater drilling procedures were adapted from shallow-water techniques, without adequate consideration of the differences of the deep-water environment.
- Federal regulators relaxed requirements for environmental reviews, tests,

and safety plans at the request of BP, and encouraged but did not require key backup systems.
- BP used well casings, cement, and other equipment that violated company safety guidelines and industry best practices, despite concerns raised by BP engineers.
- Warning signs were ignored, and safety tests delayed despite the warning signs.

The human and environmental costs of the spill were devastating. In addition to the human deaths, millions of birds, turtles, dolphins, and fish were killed. The Gulf tourism industry was devastated for several years, costing businesses $23 billion in lost revenue. And the Gulf still has not recovered, with ongoing problems cropping up related to the environment and wildlife.

The primary culprit here was BP's relentless pursuit of lower costs. Poor quality materials plus skimping on safety measures created conditions for the explosion and meant that BP was unable to deal with the disaster once it happened. Although BP was found guilty of negligence and fined a record $18.7 billion, that amount was only about 8% of their annual revenue, and no BP official went to prison.

ExxonMobil and Climate Change Denial, 1981-2008:

Lying to People for Profit
In 1981, a team of researchers at Exxon conclusively established the connection between thew burning of fossil fuels, the spewing of greenhouse gases into the air (especially carbon), and climate change. Their research was supported by dozens of other studies by climate scientists. These studies have been so convincing that over 97% of climate scientists agree that climate change is occurring and that human activity is a significant cause. As anyone who studies scientific research will know, it is rare to have near-universal agreement on something as complex as climate change, which helps us to understand that the evidence for climate change is overwhelming.

Despite this evidence, Exxon, which merged with Mobil in 1999, spent millions of dollars on a public-relations effort to deny the existence of climate change so that they could continue to sell as much of their oil as possible. As documented in the book *Merchants of Doubt* (later adapted as a film of the same name), Exxon funded foundations who paid a small group of scientists and public-relations professionals to cast doubt on the idea of climate change in order to prevent action from being taken. And their impact in the United States was dramatic. While much of the world was taking climate change seriously and enacting policies to begin reducing greenhouse gas emissions, the United States was increasing its use of fossil fuels and its emissions.

ExxonMobil now states publicly that it accepts the idea that climate change is occurring, and the company has stopped formally funding climate change denialism. However, ExxonMobil's reduction in public funding of denialism has coincided with a dramatic increase in untraceable "dark money" being used to fund climate change denialism. One cannot help but wonder who is funding such efforts.

Thanks to ExxonMobil and others who have prevented progress on climate change, we are now faced with the prospect of dramatic climate events that will cost many people their lives. We are likely to see increasing droughts, food shortages, heat waves, sea-level rise, floods, and other disasters that threaten our very existence. All so that ExxonMobil and other giant companies could sell more barrels of oil. As is so often the case, there have been no criminal prosecutions related to these incidents.

Enron's Fraudulent Use of Derivatives and Shell Companies, 1990-2002:

Financial Deregulation Plus Executive Stock Options are a Toxic Mix
One of the arguments in favor of corporations is that, thanks to the profit motive, they tend to innovate in order to make money. But, what kind of innovations might result from the profit motive? Enron executives Kenneth Lay and Jeffrey Skilling used the deregulated environment in financial markets in the 1990s and early 2000s (the same environment that also produced the financial crisis) to create an innovative financial model build on fraud and subterfuge.

Enron was the world's largest energy trading company, with a market value of $68 billion. But its real innovation was in shady accounting practices. Enron would start by undertaking a legitimate investment, such as building a power plant. They would then immediately claim all of the expected profit from the power plant on their books, even though they had yet to make any money on the investment, making them appear to be an incredibly profitable company. If the power-plant profits ever came in below expectations, Enron would transfer the unprofitable assets to a shell company—a company that did not really exist formally, other than as a vehicle for Enron to dispose of losses—thereby hiding Enron's losses from its investors. Shell-company investors were given shares of Enron common stock to compensate them for the shell-company losses. Thus, Enron appeared to be incredibly profitable even while it was incurring losses, which caused its stock price to soar.

Much of the reason for this behavior was the incentive system created by financial markets. At the time, most CEOs and highly placed executives were paid most of their salaries in stock options. This meant that they could make more money if they could get the company's stock price to increase, which would allow them to cash in their stock options at a higher value. In theory, paying CEOs in stock options gave them an incentive to run the company in the most profitable way possible, which would then cause the stock price to go up. But stock options also gave executives an incentive to artificially prop up stock prices in order to cash in, which is what the Enron executives did. Meanwhile, the accounting auditors who were supposed to flag questionable and illegal financial transactions looked the other way in order to keep Enron's business.

As Enron's losses mounted, the executives cashed in all of their stock options and left the company bankrupt. More than 5,000 employees lost their jobs and millions of investors lost their savings. Lay, Skilling and 15 other Enron executives were found guilty of fraud. But these sordid events didn't stop an even bigger financial market manipulation from dragging down the entire global economy less than a decade later.

Goldman Sachs, CMOs, and the Financial Crisis of 2007-2008:

Betting Against Your Own Clients
The global financial crisis of 2007–2008 was a product of a number of corporate misdeeds, fueled by greed and the deregulation of financial markets. To increase their profits in the early 2000s, banks started loaning money to extremely risky, subprime borrowers with very poor credit scores to purchase houses. The banks then bundled large groups of these subprime mortgage loans into securities called collateralized mortgage obligations (CMOs). The banks did not care about the creditworthiness of borrowers because they immediately sold these securities to investors.

As more and more subprime borrowers took out mortgage loans, the real-estate market boomed, forming a huge bubble. At the peak of the bubble in 2006-2007, default rates on mortgages started to increase rapidly. Realizing that subprime loans were likely to fail, Goldman Sachs and several other big investment banks began to do something highly unethical: they sold bundles of subprime mortgages (as CMOs) to investors, and they used financial instruments called credit default swaps to bet that the mortgages in the CMOs they sold were going to default and that the CMOs would become worthless. In other words, they sold investors CMO securities that they believed were going to fail, and they even made bets in financial markets that the CMOs they sold would fail. Goldman Sachs was not the only investment bank to do this. Deutsche Bank and Morgan Stanley also engaged in similar transactions to profit at the expense of their own investors.

As in so many other cases of corporate malfeasance, the consequences amounted to little more than a slap on the wrist. Goldman Sachs paid a $550 million fine in 2010 to settle the fraud case brought by the Securities and Exchange Commission (SEC), an amount that was just 4% of the $13.4 billion in profits Goldman Sachs made in the previous year. In 2016, Goldman Sachs agreed to an additional $5.1 billion fine for misleading investors about the quality of the CMOs they sold them. However, not a single Goldman Sachs official went to jail.

VW Programs Cars to Cheat on Emissions Tests, 2009-2015:

The Things a Company Will Do to Become #1
Martin Winterkorn, Volkswagen's chief executive officer from 2007 to 2015, established the goal of making VW the largest car company in the world, and he embarked on an ambitious plan to achieve that goal. Much of his plan hinged on developing fuel-efficient, clean diesel cars as an alternative to hybrids. But, when VW discovered that it could not develop an inexpensive technology to remove pollution without compromising the car's gas mileage and overall performance, they turned to a fraudulent approach. VW programmed 10.5 million cars so that the cars would detect when they were being tested for emissions, and during testing the cars' engines would run in a way that they would meet

emissions standards. But when the cars were driven normally, they would spew pollutants at a rate much higher than allowed by law.

A nonprofit group, the International Council on Clean Transportation, discovered the problem when they tested numerous diesel cars in 2013. They alerted the Environmental Protection Agency (EPA), which launched an investigation in 2014. As is so often the case, VW responded to the investigation aggressively, accusing regulators and testers of being incompetent. But additional testing established conclusively that VW cars had been programmed to reduce emissions when tested, and to spew large amounts of pollutants when driven normally. The EPA told VW that it would no longer allow the company to sell diesel cars in the United States in 2015, and accused them of violating the Clean Air Act. Particularly problematic was the fact that VW diesels spewed large amounts of nitrogen oxide, in amounts up to 40 times the legal limit. Nitrogen oxide is a pollutant that causes emphysema, bronchitis, and contributes to many other respiratory diseases. The EPA estimates that the additional pollution from VW diesel cars will cause as many as 34 deaths and sicken thousands of people in the United States. Other studies predicted up to 200 premature deaths.

VW did briefly become the largest car company in the world in July of 2015 when they surpassed Toyota, but since the scandal became public the company has fallen back. On June 27, 2016, VW agreed to pay $14.7 billion in fines to the government and compensation for VW diesel car owners. A criminal inquiry is also underway.

General Motors' Faulty Ignition Switches, 2005-2007:

Why Would Anyone Sell a Product That They Knew Could Kill People?

Imagine yourself as a CEO or vice president of a major corporation. An engineering report comes across your desk, noting that a part in one of your products is faulty, and that the consequences of that part failing could be the injury or even deaths of some of your customers. Would you still sell the faulty product, even knowing that it might kill people? This is what General Motors (GM) did with its faulty ignition switch.

This particular sordid story starts in 2010, when a 29-year-old nurse named Brooke Melton died in a car crash after losing control of her car. Her parents, who knew that she was a safe driver and that her car had been behaving oddly, sued GM and hired engineering experts to try to determine the cause of the crash. They discovered that the problem was the ignition switch that had been installed on over 22 million GM cars manufactured from 2001 to 2007. The ignition switch could turn from "On" to "Acc" just by being bumped lightly or if the key was on a particularly heavy keychain. The shift from "On" to "Acc" could disable the power steering, anti-lock braking, and airbags and cause the car to stall.

As the investigation progressed, the full scale of GM's deceit became apparent. In 2001, GM engineers initially detected the defective part, labelling it the "switch from hell." Problems with the switch cropped up repeatedly over the next several years. In 2005, internal documents show that GM acknowledged the problem but chose not to fix it because it would be too costly. Instead, they sent a note to GM dealerships telling them to urge customers to use lighter key chains. Each year, people died as ignition switches failed and air bags failed to deploy, but GM continued to hide the problem and refused to recall cars and repair the problem.

Finally, thanks to the Melton lawsuit and government investigations that followed, GM recalled the vehicles and repaired the faulty switch. But not before at least 124 people died in crashes related to the faulty part. GM paid a $900 million fine in 2015, and other settlements with victims brought the total cost of the debacle to $2 billion. While this put a dent in the company's 2015 profits of $9.7 billion, no individuals faced criminal charges for their actions.

Are Corporations Psychopaths?

Above, we highlighted seven examples of horrific corporate behavior. In each case, corporations exhibited many of the behaviors characteristic of psychopaths, especially a callous disregard for the feelings and safety of others, deceitfulness, avoidance of admitting guilt and taking responsibility for their actions, and failure to respect social and ethical norms and the law. But, are these behaviors typical of powerful, profit-hungry corporations, or are they exceptions?

As we all know, many corporations behave ethically, and many invent useful and innovative products that improve our lives. Yet, every year a certain number of corporations cast ethics and morality to the side and engage in unscrupulous behavior, resulting in economic harm, injury, and even deaths. There appear to be aspects of the corporate structure that encourage such behavior, including the relentless quest for maximum profits, the lack of personal responsibility for any illegal actions taken by the corporation, and the power corporations have to manipulate the legal system and government regulators.

Regarding the last point, one of the elements to every story above was the inadequate efforts of government regulators. The push for deregulation by various politicians directly facilitated many of the above corporate misdeeds. And government regulators are often overmatched by corporate legal teams with almost unlimited resources, which allows many corporations to avoid serious consequences even in cases where they have done something horrible. Even when corporations have been caught red handed in clear violation of the law, the penalties are usually little more than a slap on the wrist and are often far less than the profits from the offense in question. Corporate wealth and power appear to allow them to avoid significant checks on their behavior. Thus, instead of engaging in "open and free competition without deception or fraud," as Milton Friedman hoped that they would, some corporations use deception and fraud with near impunity in order to outdo the competition.

Such problems could be fixed. We need a regulatory system with teeth, where corporate lobbyists don't have undue influence over how they are regulated. And we need real consequences for corporate crime. When corporations find out that their actions or products may harm people, if they refuse to take action and to inform the public and regulators of the problem, the people who make those decisions should go to prison.

Finally, like real people, corporations should face real consequences when they break the law. A corporation that engages in particularly egregious behavior, especially a corporation that does so repeatedly, should face sanctions that have a real impact on executives and stockholders. For cases in which a corporation causes deaths, the corporation should face the "death penalty": having its charter revoked and its assets seized by the public. If stockholders could potentially lose all of their investment in a company that behaved illegally, they would begin checking up on companies and we would see much less illegal and unethical behavior.

Of course, all of these solutions require us to get corporate money out of politics. As long as corporations can buy off politicians, they can continue to act as psychopaths and face very little in the way of consequences. ❏

Selected Sources: Julfikar Ali Manik and Nida Najar, "Bangladesh Police Charge 41 With Murder Over Rana Plaza Collapse," *New York Times*, June 1, 2015 (nytimes.com); Julfikar Ali Manik and Jim Yardley, "Building Collapse in Bangladesh Leaves Scores Dead," *New York Times*, April 24, 2013; "One Year After Rana Plaza" (editorial), *New York Times*, April 27, 2014; Lauren McCauley, "Workers Decry Multinationals' Greed Following Disaster in Bangladesh," Common Dreams, April 25, 2013 (commondreams.org); Ian Urbina, "In Gulf, It Was Unclear Who Was in Charge of Rig," *New York Times*, June 5, 2010; Ben Bryant, "Deepwater Horizon and the Gulf Oil Spill—the Key Questions Answered," *The Guardian*, April 20, 2011 (theguardian.com); Douglas Fischer, "'Dark Money' Funds Climate Change Denial Effort," *Scientific American*, Dec. 23, 2013 (scientificamerican.com); Oliver Milman, "Oil Industry Knew of 'Serious' Climate Concerns More Than 45 Years Ago," *The Guardian*, April 13, 2016; Suzanne Goldenberg, "Exxon Knew of Climate Change in 1981, Email Says—but it Funded Deniers for 27 More Years," *The Guardian*, July 8, 2015; Bill Keller, "Enron for Dummies," *New York Times*, Jan. 26, 2002; Gretchen Morgenson and Louise Story, "Banks Bundled Bad Debt, Bet Against It and Won," *New York Times*, Dec. 23, 2009; "Senate Panel Says Goldman Misled Clients, Lawmakers on CDOs," Bloomberg News, April 13, 2011 (bloomberg.com); Guilbert Gates, Jack Ewing, Karl Russell, and Derek Watkins, "How Volkswagen's 'Defeat Devices' Worked," *New York Times*, March 16, 2017.

Article 4.3

STOCK BUYBACKS: ANY POSITIVE OUTCOME?

BY ARTHUR MacEWAN

January/February 2017; updated June 2018

Dear Dr. Dollar:
When a corporation buys back some of its own stock, is there any positive outcome (for the economy) other than making upper management richer?
—Julia Willebrand, New York, N.Y.

In early 2018, shortly after Congress and the President enacted sweeping new tax legislation, the Apple corporation said it would use $100 billion of its gains from the new tax laws to buy back shares of its own stock. Apple is not new to the buy-back game, but this 2018 action takes it to a new high. Exxon, which before Apple held the top buyback position, was spending only $20 billion per year on buybacks before 2015.

According to research by the Morgan Stanley bank, corporations expect to spend 43% of their tax cut gains on buybacks. They expect that another 26% will go to paying down debt and to mergers and acquisitions, whereas capital spending would account for 17%. Only 13% would go to wage increases. (The extent to which wages will be increased by investment is an open question; but new investment is a relatively small share of firms' tax change gains.) Yet although buybacks are a major part of the tax change story in 2018, they are not a new phenomenon.

Usually we think of firms issuing—i.e., selling—shares of stock to raise money for their investments. However, firms can also buy back those shares, which are shares of ownership in the firms. In recent years, buy-backs have become a big deal. In the decade 2006 to 2015, U.S. nonfinancial corporations' total net equity issues—new share issues minus shares taken off the market through buybacks and merger-and-acquisition deals—averaged negative $416 billion per year.

These buybacks, this reversal of the conventional view of how firms operate, do not generate a positive outcome for the economy. That is, these buybacks do not lead to economic growth or other changes that would benefit those of us who neither manage a company nor hold large amounts of its stock—just about everybody. Certainly, a firm's executives can gain through buybacks. As can some shareholders, both the ones who sell their shares in the buyback and the ones who, continuing to hold the company's stock, may see its value rise.

A driving force in the buyback game is that it generally serves to raise the incomes of companies' top executives. They are gaming the system to raise their own incomes. Yet, top executives have always wanted more income, and buybacks were relatively insignificant until the mid-1980s. So why have stock buybacks become so substantial in more recent years?

In a 2014 article in the Harvard Business Review, William Lazonick, a professor at the University of Massachusetts Lowell emphasizes two new developments. The first is Wall Street's increasing focus on earnings per share (EPS) as a principal means to evaluate the well-being of a firm. EPS is the amount of net earnings (i.e., profits after taxes) divided by the total number of shares of stock outstanding, usually calculated for a three-month period. A firm's spending on buybacks is not counted as an operating expense and therefore does not affect net earnings, but the buybacks do reduce the number of shares outstanding. So the buybacks increase EPS.

Focusing on EPS means focusing on the immediate or short-run performance of a firm, and it tells little about the firm's long-run prospects. Furthermore, the firm's long-run prospects can be harmed by the buybacks, since, though not counted as an operating expense, the buyback expenditure reduces the firm's retained earnings that are the financial foundation for investing in productive capabilities.

Associated with this EPS emphasis is that the salaries of top executives are often tied to their firms' EPS. Moreover, executives are often paid in company stock. By buying back a firm's stock (i.e., raising demand for the stock), executives are able to lift the stock price, even if only temporarily. So buybacks and the consequent increase in a firm's EPS are a way that top executives can game the system all the way to the bank.

The second factor that Lazonick points to in explaining the change is that in 1982, the Securities and Exchange Commission (SEC) instituted Rule 10b-18 of the Securities Exchange Act, which greatly facilitated stock buybacks without meaningful regulation. Lazonick points out: "In essence, Rule 10b-18 legalized stock market manipulation [by a firm] through open market purchases." (An "open market" purchase is the purchase of a company's stock in the securities market or, if the purchase is directly between the buyer and seller, at the securities market price.)

There is also a third factor, which helps explain the surge of buybacks in the most recent years—namely the poor performance of the U.S. economy. In a slow-growth economy, the opportunities to profit from productive investment are limited, which raises the relative appeal of gaming the system through buybacks and other means. Yet, devoting funds to buybacks and abandoning productive investment contributes to the economy's poor performance.

During the decade ending in 2015, large firms with familiar names dominated in terms of the amount spent on buybacks (as shown in the table). ExxonMobil led, spending $206.3 billion on buybacks during this period, amounting to nearly 60% of its net income (profits after taxes). Then came Microsoft and IBM, with the latter's spending on buybacks amounting to 89% of its net income. For the top fifty firms in terms of amount spent on buybacks, the total spending was $3.7 trillion in the years 2006-2015, an amount equal to 60% of their total net income over that period. In more recent years, as noted above, Apple has become the leader of the pack.

In a 2016 paper, which supplies additional data and analysis of buybacks, Lazonick sums up the phenomenon: "Given the importance of these corporations to the operations and performance of the economy, it is fair to say that the 21st century U.S. industrial economy has become a 'buyback economy.'"

Of course, there are those who claim that buybacks are good for the economy. In a rather trite attack on Lazonick's Harvard Business Review article, Greg Satell in a Forbes article claims that buybacks can put more of their "excess cash" in the hands of investors who will be able "to create new value." One wonders: If so many major firms themselves cannot find, or choose not to find, productive investments "to create new value," why will those who sell stock back to the firms make productive investments? Most likely, they too will use the funds to game the system, entering into the grand casino we call "Wall Street." ❏

Sources: William Lazonick, "How Stock Buybacks Make Americans Vulnerable to Globalization," AIR Working Paper #16-0301, March 2016 (theairnet.org); William Lazonick, "Profits without Prosperity," *Harvard Business Review*, September 2014 (hbr.org); Greg Satell, "Why Stock Buybacks Are Good For The Economy And The Country," *Forbes*, May 9, 2015 (forbes.com); Steven Rattner, "Testimony Before the House Ways and Means Committee," May 16, 2018 (waysandmeans.house.gov); Jack Nicas, "Apple Says It Will Buy Back $100 Billion in Stock," The *New York Times*, May 1, 2018 (nytimes.com).

Article 4.4

WHAT'S GOOD FOR WAL-MART . . .

BY JOHN MILLER

January/February 2006

> "Is Wal-Mart Good for America?"
>
> It is a testament to the public relations of the anti-Wal-Mart campaign that the question above is even being asked.
>
> By any normal measure, Wal-Mart's business ought to be noncontroversial. It sells at low costs, albeit in mind-boggling quantities. ...
>
> The company's success and size ... do not rest on monopoly profits or price-gouging behavior. It simply sells things people will buy at small markups and, as in the old saw, makes it up on volume. ... You may believe, as do service-workers unions and a clutch of coastal elites—many of whom, we'd wager, have never set foot in Wal-Mart—that Wal-Mart "exploits" workers who can't say no to low wages and poor benefits. You might accept the canard that it drives good local businesses into the ground, although both of these allegations are more myth than reality.
>
> But even if you buy into the myths, there's no getting around the fact that somewhere out there, millions of people are spending billions of dollars on what Wal-Mart puts on its shelves. No one is making them do it. ... Wal-Mart can't make mom and pop shut down the shop anymore than it can make customers walk through the doors or pull out their wallets.
>
> What about the workers? ... Wal-Mart's average starting wage is already nearly double the national minimum of $5.15 an hour. The company has also recently increased its health-care for employees on the bottom rungs of the corporate ladder.
>
> —*Wall Street Journal* editorial, December 3, 2005

"Who's Number One? The Customer! Always!" The last line of Wal-Mart's company cheer just about sums up the *Wall Street Journal* editors' benign view of the behemoth corporation. But a more honest answer would be Wal-Mart itself: not the customer, and surely not the worker.

The first retail corporation to top the Fortune 500, Wal-Mart trailed only Exxon-Mobil in total revenues last year. With 1.6 million workers, 1.3 million in the United States and 300,000 offshore, Wal-Mart is the largest private employer in the nation and the world's largest retailer.

Being number one has paid off handsomely for the family of Wal-Mart founder Sam Walton. The family's combined fortune is now an estimated $90 billion, equal to the net worth of Bill Gates and Warren Buffett combined.

But is what's good for the Walton family good for America? Should we believe the editors that Wal-Mart's unprecedented size and market power have redounded not only to the Walton family's benefit but to ours as well?

Low Wages and Meager Benefits

Working for the world's largest employer sure hasn't paid off for Wal-Mart's employees. True, they have a job, and others without jobs line up to apply for theirs. But that says more about the sad state of today's labor market than the quality of Wal-Mart jobs. After all, less than half of Wal-Mart workers last a year, and turnover at the company is twice that at comparable retailers.

Why? Wal-Mart's oppressive working conditions surely have something to do with it. Wal-Mart has admitted to using minors to operate hazardous machinery, has been sued in six states for forcing employees to work off the books (i.e., unpaid) and without breaks, and is currently facing a suit brought by 1.6 million current and former female employees accusing Wal-Mart of gender discrimination. At the same time, Wal-Mart workers are paid less and receive fewer benefits than other retail workers.

Wal-Mart, according to its own reports, pays an average of $9.68 an hour. That is 12.4% below the average wage for retail workers even after adjusting for geography, according to a recent study by Arindrajit Dube and Steve Wertheim, economists at the University of California's Institute of Industrial Relations and long-time Wal-Mart researchers. Wal-Mart's wages are nearly 15% below the average wage of workers at large retailers and about 30% below the average wage of unionized grocery workers. The average U.S. wage is $17.80 an hour; Costco, a direct competitor of Wal-Mart's Sam's Club warehouse stores, pays an average wage of $16 an hour.

Wal-Mart may be improving its benefits, as the *Journal*'s editors report, but it needs to. Other retailers provide healthcare coverage to over 53% of their workers, while Wal-Mart covers just 48% of its workers. Costco, once again, does far better, covering 82% of its employees. Moreover, Wal-Mart's coverage is far less comprehensive than the plans offered by other large retailers. Dube reports that according to 2003 IRS data, Wal-Mart paid 59% of the healthcare costs of its workers and dependents, compared to the 77% of healthcare costs for individuals and 68% for families the average retailer picks up.

A recent internal Wal-Mart memo leaked to the *New York Times* confirmed the large gaps in Wal-Mart's healthcare coverage and exposed the high costs those gaps impose on government programs. According to the memo, "Five percent of our Associates are on Medicaid compared to an average for national employees of 4 percent. Twenty-seven percent of Associates' children are on such programs, compared to a national average of 22 percent. In total, 46 percent of Associates' children are either on Medicaid or are uninsured."

A considerably lower 29% of children of all large-retail workers are on Medicaid or are uninsured. Some 7% of the children of employees of large retailers go uninsured, compared to the 19% reported by Wal-Mart.

Wal-Mart's low wages drag down the wages of other retail workers and shutter downtown retail businesses. A 2005 study by David Neumark, Junfu Zhang, and Stephen Ciccarella, economists at the University of California at Irvine, found that Wal-Mart adversely affects employment and wages. Retail workers in a community with a Wal-Mart earned 3.5% less because Wal-Mart's low prices force other businesses to lower prices, and hence their wages, according to the Neumark study. The same study also found that Wal-Mart's presence reduces retail employment by 2% to 4%. While other studies have not found this negative employment effect, Dube's research also reports fewer retail jobs and lower wages for retail workers in metropolitan counties with a Wal-Mart. (Fully 85% of Wal-Mart stores are in metropolitan counties.) Dube figures that Wal-Mart's presence costs retail workers, at Wal-Mart and elsewhere, $4.7 billion a year in lost earnings.

In short, Wal-Mart's "everyday low prices" come at the expense of the compensation of Wal-Mart's own employees and lower wages and fewer jobs for retail workers in the surrounding area. That much remains true no matter what weight we assign to each of the measures that Wal-Mart uses to keep its costs down: a just-in-time inventory strategy, its ability to use its size to pressure suppliers for large discounts, a routinized work environment that requires minimal training, and meager wages and benefits.

How Low Are Wal-Mart's Everyday Low Prices?

Even if one doesn't subscribe to the editors' position that it is consumers, not Wal-Mart, who cause job losses at downtown retailers, it is possible to argue that the benefit of Wal-Mart's low prices to consumers, especially low-income consumers, outweighs the cost endured by workers at Wal-Mart and other retailers. Jason Furman, New York University economist and director of economic policy for the 2004 Kerry-Edwards campaign, makes just such an argument. Wal-Mart's "staggering" low prices are 8% to 40% lower than people would pay elsewhere, according to Furman. He calculates that those low prices on average boost low-income families' buying power by 3% and more than offset the loss of earnings to retail workers. For Furman, that makes Wal-Mart "a progressive success story."

But exactly how much savings Wal-Mart affords consumers is far from clear. Estimates vary widely. At one extreme is a study Wal-Mart itself commissioned by Global Insight, an economic forecasting firm. Global Insight estimates Wal-Mart created a stunning savings of $263 billion, or $2,329 per household, in 2004 alone.

At the other extreme, statisticians at the U.S. Bureau of Labor Statistics found no price savings at Wal-Mart. Relying on Consumer Price Index data, the BLS found that Wal-Mart's prices largely matched those of its rivals, and that instances of lower prices at Wal-Mart could be attributed to lower quality products.

Both studies, which rely on the Consumer Price Index and aggregate data, have their critics. Furman himself allows that the Global Insight study is "overly simplistic" and says he "doesn't place as much weight on that one." Jerry Hausman, the M.I.T. economist who has looked closely at Wal-Mart's grocery stores, maintains that the CPI data that the Bureau of Labor Statistics relies on systematically miss the savings offered by "supercenters" such as Wal-Mart. To show the difference between prices at Wal-Mart and at other grocers, Hausman, along with Ephraim Leibtag, USDA Economic Research Service economist, used supermarket scanner data to examine the purchasing patterns of a national sample of 61,500 consumers from 1988 to 2001. Hausman and Leibtag found that Wal-Mart offers many identical food items at an average price about 15%-25% lower than traditional supermarkets.

While Hausman and Leibtag report substantial savings from shopping at Wal-Mart, they fall far short of the savings alleged in the Global Insight study. The Hausman and Leibtag study suggests a savings of around $550 per household per year, or about $56 billion in 2004, not $263 billion. Still, that is considerably more than the $4.7 billion a year in lost earnings to retail workers that Dube attributes to Wal-Mart.

But if "Wal-Mart hurts wages, not so much in retail, but across the whole country," as economist Neumark told *BusinessWeek*, then the savings to consumers from Wal-Mart's everyday low prices might not outweigh the lost wages to all workers. (Retail workers make up just 11.6% of U.S. employment.)

Nor do these findings say anything about the sweatshop conditions and wages in Wal-Mart's overseas subcontractors. One example: A recent Canadian Broadcasting Corporation investigative report found that workers in Bangladesh were being paid less than $50 a month (below even the United Nation's $2 a day measure of poverty) to make clothes for the Wal-Mart private label, Simply Basic. Those workers included ten- to thirteen-year-old children forced to work long hours in dimly lit and dirty conditions sewing "I Love My Wal-Mart" T-shirts.

Making Wal-Mart Do Better

Nonetheless, as Arindrajit Dube points out, the relevant question is not whether Wal-Mart creates more savings for consumers than losses for workers, but whether the corporation can afford to pay better wages and benefits.

Dube reasons that if the true price gap between Wal-Mart and its retail competitors is small, then Wal-Mart might not be in a position to do better—to make

---

The Costco Alternative? Wall Street Prefers Wal-Mart

In an April 2004 online commentary, *BusinessWeek* praised Costco's business model but pointed out that Costco's wages cause Wall Street to worry that the company's "operating expenses could get out of hand." How does Costco compare to low-wage Wal-Mart on overhead expenses? At Costco, overhead is 9.8% of revenue; at Wal-Mart, it is 17%. Part of Costco's secret is that its better paid workers are also more efficient: Costco's operating profit per hourly employee is $13,647; each Wal-Mart employee only nets the company $11,039. Wal-Mart also spends more than Costco on hiring and training new employees: each one, according to Rutgers economist Eileen Appelbaum, costs the company $2,500 to $3,500. Appelbaum estimates that Wal-Mart's relatively high turnover costs the company $1.5 to $2 million per year.

Despite Costco's higher efficiency, Wall Street analysts like Deutsche Bank's Bill Dreher complain that "Costco's corporate philosophy is to put its customers first, then its employees, then its vendors, and finally its shareholders. Shareholders get the short end of the stick." Wall Street prefers Wal-Mart's philosopy: executives first, then shareholders, then customers, then vendors, and finally employees.

In 2004, Wal-Mart paid CEO Lee Scott $5.3 million, while a full-time employee making the average wage would have received $20,134. Costco's CEO Jim Senegal received $350,000, while a full-time average employee got $33,280. And *BusinessWeek* intimates

up its wage and benefit gap and still maintain its price advantage. But if Wal-Mart offers consumers only minor price savings, then its lower wages and benefits hardly constitute a progressive success story that's good for the nation.

If Wal-Mart's true price gap is large (say, the 25% price advantage estimated by Hausman), then Wal-Mart surely is in a position to do better. For instance, Dube calculates that closing Wal-Mart's 16% overall compensation gap with other large retailers would cost the company less than 2% of sales. Raising prices by two cents on the dollar to cover those increased compensation costs would be "eminently absorbable," according to Dube, without eating away much of the company's mind-boggling $10 billion profit (2004).

Measures that set standards to force Wal-Mart and all big-box retailers to pay decent wages and provide benefits are beginning to catch on. Chicago, New York City, and the state of Maryland have considered or passed laws that would require big-box retailers to pay a "living wage" or to spend a minimum amount per worker-hour for health benefits. The Republican board of Nassau County on Long Island passed an ordinance requiring that all big-box retailers pay $3 per hour toward healthcare. Wal-Mart's stake in making sure that such proposals don't become law or spread nationwide goes a long way toward explaining why 80% of Wal-Mart's $2 million in political contributions in 2004 went to Republicans.

Henry Ford sought to pay his workers enough so they could buy the cars they produced. Sam Walton sought to pay his workers so little that they could afford to shop nowhere else. And while what was good for the big automakers was probably never good for the nation, what is good for Wal-Mart, today's largest employer, is undoubtedly bad for economic justice. ❑

---

that the top job at Costco may be tougher than at Wal-Mart. "Management has to hustle to make the high-wage strategy work. It's constantly looking for ways to repackage goods into bulk items, which reduces labor, speeds up Costco's just-in-time inventory, and boosts sales per square foot. Costco is also savvier ... about catering to small shop owners and more affluent customers, who are more likely to buy in bulk and purchase higher-margin goods."

Costco's allegedly more affluent clientele may be another reason that its profit per employee is higher than Wal-Mart's and its overhead costs a lower percentage of revenue. However, Costco pays its employees enough that they could afford to shop there. As the *BusinessWeek* commentary noted, "the low-wage approach cuts into consumer spending and, potentially, economic growth." —*Esther Cervantes*

Average Hourly Wage		Percentage of U.S. Workforce in Unions		Employees Covered by Company Health Insurance		Employees Who Leave After One Year	
Wal-Mart	Costco	Wal-Mart	Costco	Wal-Mart	Costco	Sam's Club*	Costco
$9.68	$16.00	0.0%	17.9%	48%	82%	21%	6%

* Sam's Club is the Wal-Mart unit that competes directly with Costco.

Sources: "Is Wal-Mart Good for America?" *Wall Street Journal*, 12/3/05; "Gauging the Wal-Mart Effect," *WSJ*, 12/03/05; Arindrajit Dube & Steve Wertheim, "Wal-Mart and Job Quality—What Do We Know, and Should We Care?" 10/05; Jason Furman, "Wal-Mart: A Progressive Success Story," 10/05; Leo Hindery Jr., "Wal-Mart's Giant Sucking Sound," 10/05; A. Bernstein, "Some Uncomfortable Findings for Wal-Mart," *BusinessWeek* online, 10/26/05, and "Wal-Mart: A Case for the Defense, Sort of," *BusinessWeek* online, 11/7/05; Dube, Jacobs, and Wertheim, "The Impact of Wal-Mart Growth on Earnings Throughout the Retail Sector in Urban and Rural Counties," *Institute of Industrial Relations Working Paper*, UC Berkeley, 10/05; Dube, Jacobs, and Wertheim, "Internal Wal-Mart Memo Validates Findings of UC Berkeley Study," 11/26/05; Jerry Hausman and Ephraim Leibtag, "Consumer Benefits from Increased Competition in Shopping Outlets: Measuring the Effect of Wal-Mart," 10/05; Hausman and Leibtag, "CPI Bias from Supercenters: Does the BLS Know that Wal-Mart Exists?" *NBER Working Paper No. 10712*, 8/04; David Neumark, Junfu Zhang, and Stephen Ciccarella, "The Effects of Wal-Mart on Local Labor Markets," *NBER Working Paper No. 11782*, 11/05; Erin Johansson, "Wal-Mart: Rolling Back Workers' Wages, Rights, and the American Dream," American Rights at Work, 11/05; Wal-Mart Watch, "Spin Cycle"; CBC News, "Wal-Mart to cut ties with Bangladesh factories using child labour," 11/30/05; National Labor Committee, "10 to 13-year-olds Sewing 'I Love My Wal-Mart' Shirts," 12/05; Global Insight, "The Economic Impact of Wal-Mart," 2005.

Article 4.5

HOW PRIVATE EQUITY WORKS—AND WHY IT MATTERS

BY EILEEN APPLEBAUM AND ROSEMARY BATT

January/February 2016

Private equity (PE) firms are financial actors that raise billions of dollars in investment funds each year. They use these funds to buy out well-performing companies using high amounts of debt, take them private, and promise their investors outsized returns in the process. They advertise that they improve the operations of companies they buy. Sometimes they do. But more often PE firms engage in financial engineering techniques that extract wealth from companies and leave them more financially at risk than before—and sometimes bankrupt. While discredited as "leveraged buyouts" in the 1980s, these tactics have returned with a vengeance in the last fifteen years. And they are perfectly legal.

PE firms typically charge pension funds and other investors an annual management fee of 2% of capital committed to the private equity fund. Not satisfied with these payments for managing their private equity funds, PE firms also charge investors in their funds numerous other fees and expenses. This part isn't always legal: In May 2014, the Securities and Exchange Commission (SEC) revealed that its examinations of PE funds had uncovered numerous examples, some bordering on outright fraud, where PE firms had inappropriately charged fees and expenses to pension funds and other investors. In 2015, Fenway Partners, Blackstone, and KKR were the first PE firms to pay fines to the SEC to settle charges—a meager $80 million among the three.

Management fees are specified in contracts between private equity funds and the investors in these funds. But these are not the only fees that PE firms charge. They typically claim 20% of any profit the PE fund realizes on its investments as a bonus or performance fee. This performance fee—so-called "carried interest" taxed at half the rate of ordinary income—is generally not reported to investors. Private equity funds simply report returns net of these performance fees. But these fees cut deeply into the returns earned by pension funds and other private equity investors—and workers, retirees, and taxpayers have a right to know how large these payments are.

Private Equity: The Impact

Between 2000 and 2014, U.S. private equity firms invested $5.2 trillion in 32,200 leveraged buyouts that affected some 11.3 million workers in U.S. companies—considerably more than the number of workers who are currently union members. Over that period, the number of active PE firms globally grew from under 1,500 to over 3,500—a 143% rise. And, while PE investments fell sharply during the Great Recession, they have since largely recovered their pre-crisis levels. Currently, there are 3,883 U.S. private equity firms and 12,992 PE-owned companies headquartered in the United States.

In our book, *Private Equity at Work: How Wall Street Manages Main Street*, we explain how private equity firms have become such an important force in the economy and why regulators need to rein in their activities. That is because they are investors that actively manage the companies they buy, but are treated as passive investors and not held accountable for their actions. Before a company is ever purchased, the general partners of the PE fund (who make all decisions for the fund) develop a plan for how much debt can be leveraged on the company, how the company's cash flow will be used to service the debt, and how the PE firm will exit the company at a profit within a five-year window. They oversee company operations; make decisions that affect workers jobs, pay, and pensions—and then walk away. While law treats PE funds as investors, they behave as managers and employers in the companies they own.

Sometimes private equity does perform as advertised—providing access to management expertise and financial resources that help small companies grow and improve their competitiveness. Small companies have relatively few assets that can be mortgaged, but many opportunities for operational improvements in information technology, accounting, management, and distribution systems. Most PE investments, however, are in larger companies that already have modern management systems in place and also have substantial assets that can be mortgaged. Here, private equity firms use debt and financial engineering strategies to extract wealth from healthy companies, and workers, managers, and suppliers often pay the price. Job destruction outweighs job creation.

Private equity affects the lives of Americans in many ways—as workers, retirees, consumers, renters, and community members. Despite the fact that private equity ownership often leads to job and wage loss for workers, pension funds ("workers' capital") account for fully 35% of all investments in PE funds. Most workers do not know that their retirement savings are invested in these funds and may be putting other companies and their workers at risk. And despite the hype, these investments often don't yield the high returns for retirement funds that private equity firms promise. Moreover, since the Great Recession, private equity and hedge funds have bought up more than 100,000 troubled mortgages and are renting them back to people who lost their homes. In October 2015 alone, Blackstone

Case Study: Michael's Stores

Private Equity firms Bain and Blackstone used most of the tactics described here when they bought arts-and-crafts supplies retailer Michael's Stores in 2006 and took it private.

At the time, the company had 1,108 stores employing about 43,100 workers and $3.9 billion in sales. Its high sales revenue, healthy profits, and low debt made it an attractive takeover target. But the leveraged buyout saddled the chain with a $4 billion dollar debt. Bain and Blackstone also had Michael's sign a management services agreement through 2016 for an annual fee of $12 million—including a stipulation that if the company went public or was sold, the PE sponsors would continue to collect the fees for the remaining years of the contract even though the services would never be provided. In 2013, the PE funds did a dividend recapitalization, which yielded them $714 million, or about 70% of what the PE funds had invested. When Michael's went public in June 2014, it still carried long-term debt of $3.7 billion, and it had to pay the PE firms $30 million to cover the years remaining on the management services contract.

bought up 1000 rental units in New York City as well as the City's iconic rent-controlled Stuyvesant Town-Peter Cooper Village—making the PE firm one of the city's largest landlords.

How Do Private Equity Firms Make Money?

Debt, or "leverage," is at the core of the private equity business model. (Hence the term "leveraged buyout.") Debt multiplies returns on investment and the interest on the debt can be deducted from taxes owed by the acquired (or "portfolio") company. Private equity partners typically finance the buyout of a Main Street company with 30% equity coming from the PE fund and 70% debt borrowed from creditors— the opposite of the 30% debt and 70% equity typical of publicly traded companies. Private equity funds use the assets of the portfolio company as collateral, and put the burden of repaying the debt on the company itself.

The private equity firm also has very little of its own money at risk. The general partners of a PE fund typically put up $1 to $2 for every $100 that pension funds and other investors contribute. PE partners invest less than 1% of the purchase price of acquired companies (2% of the 30% equity is $0.02 \times 0.30 = .006$, or 0.6%). Yet they claim 20% of any gains from the subsequent sale of these companies.

In other words, PE firms play with other people's money—money contributed by pension funds and other investors in its funds and borrowed from creditors. Leverage magnifies investment returns in good times—and the general partners of the PE fund collect a disproportionate share of these gains. But if the debt cannot be repaid, the company, its workers, and its creditors bear the costs. The private equity business model is a low-risk, high-reward strategy for the PE firms and their partners.

Post buyout, PE firms often engage in financial engineering that further compromises their portfolio companies.

- They may have portfolio companies take out loans at "junk bond" rates and use the proceeds to pay themselves and their investors a dividend—a so-called "dividend recapitalization."

- They may sell company assets and claim the proceeds for themselves. They may split an asset-rich company into an operating company (OpCo) and a property company (PropCo) and sell off the real estate. Proceeds of the sale are used to repay the investors, while the operating company must lease back the property, often at inflated rates. Companies in cyclical industries are especially at risk of failure as owning their property provides a buffer against market downturns. For example, the Darden Restaurants sold its struggling Red Lobster restaurant chain to the PE firm Golden Gate, which immediately sold off most of Red Lobster's property and used the proceeds to repay most of the equity investment of the PE firm and its investors. The restaurants, however, now have to pay rent, and their annual earnings are cut substantially.

- They may "waive" the management fees they charge their limited partners in exchange for a higher share in the profits, which are then taxed at the

---

CalPERS (Finally) Releases Data on Performance Fees Paid to Private Equity

On November 24, 2015, CalPERS, the large California public employee pension fund, re-leased long-awaited figures on the amounts it has paid private equity firms in performance fees—so-called "carried interest" that is taxed at the lower capital gains rate rather than as ordinary income. For years, the pension fund failed to ask the PE firms for this informa-tion or to report on these fees. Recently this changed under pressure from unions, media, and the tax-paying public. As widely anticipated, the number is ginormous. Over the 25 years since 1990, CalPERS acknowledges it has paid $3.4 billion in performance fees—a number it admits understates the full amount paid.

Private equity has persuaded public pension funds that its high management and performance fees are warranted by exceptionally high returns on private equity invest-ments, but the evidence is weak. Moreover, because private equity investments are risky and require a 10-year commitment by pension fund investors, returns need to be high enough to be worth the risk and long-term investment—about three percentage points higher than stock market returns according to CalPERS benchmark. Unfortunately, half of the PE funds launched after 2005 have failed to beat this benchmark, and this is true of the PE funds in which CalPERS is invested. CalPERS's PE investments failed to beat its own benchmark in three-year, five-year and ten-year time frames.

More recently, having failed to meet their strategic objective to "maximize risk-adjusted rates of return," CalPERS staff proposed removing the requirement from the pension fund's PE policy. However, we and others concerned about the fund's risky invest-ments urged CalPERS board members to vote it down, which they did at their December 14 meeting.

---

much lower capital gains tax rate, rather than as ordinary income. The IRS recently released guidance making it crystal clear that this violates tax law.

- They may require portfolio companies to pay monitoring or "consulting" fees to the PE firm for unspecified services. Payment of the fees reduces the companies' cash cushion and puts them at risk in an economic downturn. The Securities and Exchange Commission (SEC) has found that many PE firms fail to share this fee income with their investors, as legally required. Moreover, in some cases where the monitoring fee contract fails to spec-ify the services to be provided, these payments may actually be dividends (which are not tax deductible) disguised as monitoring fees (which are)—and this tactic allows the portfolio company to reduce its tax liabilities.

- Monitoring-fee contracts typically have a term of ten years, even though the PE firms expect to re-sell portfolio companies in three to five years. As a result, at the time of the re-sale, the remaining years in the contract must be paid off, even though the PE firm will never provide any services once the company is sold.

What Happens to Companies and Workers?

The results of financial engineering are predictable. The high debt levels of highly leveraged companies make them much more likely to default on their loans or declare bankruptcy. And in cyclical industries, companies that have to pay rent rather than own their own property are more likely to go under in a recession. As we report in our book, a 2008 study by the World Economic Forum found that for the period 1980-2005, PE-owned companies were twice as likely to go bankrupt as comparable publicly owned companies. Another study of more than 2,000 highly leveraged companies found that, during the last recession (from 2007 to the first quarter of 2010), roughly a quarter of them defaulted on their debts. The financial crisis officially ended in 2009, but bankruptcies among private equity owned companies continued through 2015. Energy Future Holdings (EFH), for example, was acquired in 2007 by a PE consortium led by KKR and TPG and defaulted in 2014 with the largest debt for any leveraged buyout on record—$35.8 billion. By mid-2014, nine other private-equity owned companies defaulted on $6.5 billion in bonds and institutional loans. By 2014, defaults on the high-yield and leveraged loans that financed the 2004-2007 boom in leveraged buyouts affected a total of $120 billion (out of nearly $500 billion) in bonds and institutional loans.

In 2015, Harrah's (now known as Caesar's Entertainment) also declared bankruptcy. The company, with 30,440 unionized employees, was acquired in 2006 by Apollo Global Management and Texas Pacific Group (TPG Capital). By June of 2007, the casino chain's long-term debt had more than doubled. The gambling industry slumped in the recession and Harrah's struggled under its debt burden. The company cut staff, reduced hours, outsourced jobs, and scaled back operations, but in the end was not able to meet its debt obligations.

These examples of job loss following private equity takeovers are backed by rigorous economy-wide statistical studies by economists at Chicago, Harvard, and Maryland universities. One study, covering the period 1980-2005, found that post-buyout, private-equity-owned establishments and companies had significantly lower levels of employment and wages than their publicly traded counterparts. In the year of the PE buyouts, the target companies had higher levels of wages and employment growth than comparable public companies. Post-buyout, however, both wages and employment levels were lower in the PE-owned companies. Depending on the data and estimation techniques, PE-owned establishments registered employment levels that were, in the first two years after the buyout, 3.0 to 6.7% lower than similar establishments; after five years, 6% lower.

Bankruptcies of PE-owned companies threaten not only workers' jobs, but also their defined-benefit pensions. In typical bankruptcy proceedings, the pension plan can make its case for better treatment of workers under a court-approved Plan of Reorganization. If the bankrupt company is unable to fulfill its pension obligations, then an insurance program run by the Pension Benefit Guarantee Corporation (PBGC) provides employees with basic benefits, although not at the level they would have received had the pension remained solvent. In light of the higher rates of bankruptcy in PE-owned companies, the PGBC has disproportionately absorbed the pension liabilities of these companies.

Private equity firms have figured out a number of ways to take advantage of the bankruptcy code and more easily shift pension liabilities to the PBGC. One strategy is to use a special provision in the code—Section 363—that allows for the stream-lined sale of company assets, including auctioning off the entire assets of a company

---

Dumping Pension Plans

A Sun Capital private equity fund bought Friendly's Ice Cream Restaurant chain in a leveraged buyout in 2007. Sun Capital immediately sold much of the company's real estate and leased the property back to Friendly's outlets. After a series of cutbacks and layoffs, it filed for bankruptcy in November 2011. Soon after, Friendly's was acquired by another Sun Capital-sponsored PE fund in a Section 363 bankruptcy sale, with its pension obligations offloaded onto the PBGC. Sun Capital was able to retain ownership of Friendly's, but neither the PE firm nor any of its funds had any responsibility for the pensions of Friendly's 6,000 employees and retirees. Oxford Automotive and Relizon, among other companies, also went bankrupt while in private equity hands and were also sold from one affiliate of a PE firm to another affiliate.

Private equity funds' strategies to avoid pension liabilities are particularly offensive given that pension funds represent over one-third of the investors in PE. These pension funds are in the contradictory position of hoping to benefit from activities that sometimes undermine the retirement security of beneficiaries in funds like their own. This raises troubling questions: are the actions of pension funds that invest in private equity consistent with the interests and values of their own members?

Finally, private equity firms have sought to avoid liability under the Workers Adjustment and Retraining Notification (WARN) Act, which requires companies that close down plants to give workers 60 days' notice and pay, whether or not they continue to work. In the recent case of PE-owned Golden Guernsey dairy, OpenGate Capital has argued that it is not liable under the WARN Act. In a surprising verdict in October 2015, the court ruled that OpenGate Capital was indeed responsible for back pay under the law.

---

without first putting in place a Plan for Reorganization for the distribution of proceeds. While the secured creditors get paid, there is no requirement to renegotiate pension obligations—typically the largest unsecured creditor in a bankruptcy case. As a result, pension liabilities typically get shifted to the PBGC, and employees receive only the basic guaranteed retirement benefits.

Section 363 sales were extremely rare in the 1990s (only 4% of large publicly traded companies), but they represent 21% of bankruptcies in the 2000s. According to the PBGC, employees and retirees lost more than $650 million in 363 sales of bankrupt companies owned or controlled by private equity firms from 2003 to 2012. Exploitation of the 363 loophole, in addition, has severely strained the financial stability of the PBGC in recent years.

How Should Private Equity Be Regulated?

Private equity partners act as managers and employers of the companies they take over, even though the law treats them as passive investors in the companies they own. Several legal and regulatory changes would curb the negative effects of private equity on companies and working people, while preserving the benefits of private pools of capital to stimulate growth and development in small and mid-sized companies.

A simple first step is greater transparency. With the exception of a few large publicly traded firms (including Blackstone, Apollo, and Carlyle), PE firms face far less stringent Securities and Exchange Commission (SEC) reporting requirements than public corporations, and very little of what they report can legally be made public. And privately owned PE portfolio companies have no reporting requirements at all.

Even the limited partners who invest in private equity have little information about, for example, how decisions are made or how fund performance is measured.

Limiting the amount of debt that can be loaded onto portfolio companies is critical to reduce the risk of bankruptcy by PE-owned companies. Federal bank regulators took a first step in 2013 by issuing guidelines effectively reducing the willingness of banks to make loans that raise a company's debt level above six times its earnings. This has had some effect on PE firms' ability to overleverage the companies they acquire. But KKR and other large PE firms have responded by making loans available to other PE funds for leveraged buyouts. More direct steps to limit excessive use of debt include limiting the tax deductibility of interest payments or simply capping the use of debt over a certain percentage of the purchase price.

Eliminating the "carried interest" loophole in the capital gains tax would make the tax code fairer. This loophole lets private equity general partners pay the capital gains tax rate on their share of PE fund profits. Profit-sharing income of other managers, meanwhile, is taxed at the higher rate applied to ordinary income. More broadly, the carried-interest tax loophole comes at the expense of other taxpayers, who must either pay higher taxes or receive fewer or lower-quality public services. Changing the tax code to eliminate the loophole would also have the positive effect of reducing the incentive to load acquired companies with excessive levels of debt.

Reforms are also needed to hold private equity partners accountable for their actions as managers and employers in the same way as public corporations are. Private equity general partners make decisions that affect a portfolio company's debt structure, operations, human resources management, staffing levels, and plant closures. The PE firm and its funds are not passive investors and should be viewed, along with the portfolio company, as the joint employer of the portfolio company's workers. Employment laws such as the WARN Act and Employee Retirement Income Security Act (ERISA) need to be updated to explicitly reflect this new reality. Loopholes in the bankruptcy code must be closed to prevent PE firms from offloading pension liabilities onto the PBGC.

In sum, a set of legal and regulatory changes are needed to ensure that PE firms are transparent and accountable for their actions, that they pay their fair share of taxes, and that they assume the same liability as publicly traded companies for any negative effects of their actions on the jobs, incomes, and pensions of the workers in the companies they own. ❏

Sources: Eileen Appelbaum and Rosemary Batt, *Private Equity at Work: When Wall Street Manages Main Street* (Russell Sage Foundation, 2014); Steven J. Davis, John C. Haltiwanger, Ron S. Jarmin, Josh Lerner, and Javier Miranda, "Private Equity and Employment," National Bureau of Economic Research, NBER Working Paper 17399, 2011 (nber.org); Matthew Goldstein, "As Banks Retreat, Private Equity Rushes to Buy Troubled Home Mortgages," *New York Times*, Sept. 28, 2015 (nytimes.com); Andrew McIntyre, "5 Firms Steer $690M Deal for Manhattan Rental Portfolio," Law360, Sept. 11, 2015 (law360.com); Private Equity Growth Capital Council, "Private Equity by the Numbers" (pegcc.org); Eileen Appelbaum, "CalPERS Releases Data on Performance Fees Paid to Private Equity," Center for Economic and Policy Research blog, November 25, 2015 (cepr.net/blogs/cepr-blog).

Article 4.6

HIGH CEO PAY: IT'S WHAT FRIENDS ARE FOR

BY DEAN BAKER
March 2018; Center for Economic and Policy Research

The explosion in the pay of corporate CEOs is well documented. While the heads of major corporations were always well paid, we saw their pay go from 20- to 30-times the pay of ordinary workers in the 1960s and 1970s to 200- or 300-times the pay of ordinary workers in recent years. Paychecks of more than $20 million a year are now standard, and it's not uncommon to see a top executive haul in more than $40 or $50 million in a single year.

Soaring CEO pay is an important part of the story of the rise in inequality over the last four decades. These people are all in the top 0.01% or even 0.001% of the income distribution.

The high pay of CEOs lifts the pay for other top executives. If the CEO is getting $25 million a year, it is likely that people directly under her are making salaries of $3 to $5 million, and quite possibly considerably more. If CEOs were earning $2 million, most likely the next tier of workers would be earning in the neighborhood of $1 million. And, it's just straight logic that higher pay at the top means less for everyone else.

In addition, the high pay at the top of the corporate ladder gets transmitted to other sectors. It is now common to see university presidents and heads of charities and other nonprofits get pay in excess of $1 million or even $2 million a year. They can truthfully say that they would get far higher pay if they ran comparably sized organizations in the corporate sector.

There is an ongoing debate in the economics profession over the reason for the jump in CEO pay. Many economists argue that higher pay reflects the growing importance of CEO performance to the company. Their argument is that a good CEO, who can skillfully steer a company through a rapidly changing market environment, can add billions of dollars to shareholder value. In this context, the shareholders can still come out way ahead even if they are paying out $40 or $50 million a year to their CEOs.

The contrasting position is that CEOs often walk away with massive paychecks even when they have done little or nothing to add value for shareholders. (It is assumed that CEOs are being rewarded for helping shareholders, not for benefitting employees or society as a whole.) The CEOs of major oil companies got huge pay raises as a result of the rise in world oil prices in the last decade, a factor that was pretty much out of their control. This implies that high pay is a result of the failure of corporate governance, where shareholders lack the ability to effectively control CEO pay.

In a new paper, Jessica Schieder of the Economic Policy Institute and I examined the impact of a cap in the deductibility of CEO pay. A provision in the Affordable Care Act (ACA) prevented health insurers from deducting more than $500,000 of CEO pay from their taxes. This meant that a dollar of CEO pay went from costing companies 65 cents in after-tax dollars to costing them a full dollar, an increase of more than 50%.

If CEO pay was closely related to the returns the CEOs provided to shareholders, this provision should have led to a fall in the pay of CEOs at health insurers, relative to other companies. We tested the impact of this ACA provision, controlling for profits, revenues, stock prices and other factors expected to affect CEO pay. We could find zero evidence that the provision had any effect whatsoever in lowering the pay of CEOs in the insurance industry.

The fact that making CEO pay more costly to the company had no effect on their compensation supports the broken corporate governance view. CEOs don't get paid the big bucks because they are so valuable to their companies. They get paid the big bucks because the boards of directors, who most immediately determine their pay, are their friends.

The directors are appointed through a process that is dominated by top management. Being a director is a very cushy job, typically paying in the hundreds of thousands of dollars for perhaps a 150 hours of work annually. As long as directors have the support of management, it is almost impossible for them to be removed. Over 99% are reelected. In this context, directors have no incentive to ask questions like "can we pay our CEO less?"

It is possible to change the incentive structure. A provision in the Dodd-Frank financial reform bill requires a triannual "say on pay" vote by shareholders. This is a nonbinding vote in which shareholders vote yes or no on a CEO pay package. Less than 3% of packages are voted down. Interest is generally low because there is little consequence from a no vote.

But the law could be changed to have more consequence. Suppose directors sacrificed their pay if the shareholders voted no. This would give them a real incentive to ask whether they could pay their CEO less. ❑

Sources: Jessica Schieder and Dean Baker, "Does Tax Deductibility Affect CEO Pay? The Case of the Health Insurance Industry," Economic Policy Institute, March 22, 2018 (epi.org).

Article 4.7

CO-OP ECONOMICS
What can economics teach us about the challenges and potential of cooperation?

BY NANCY FOLBRE
September/October 2013

I teach economics, a discipline largely inhabited by people skeptical of human potential for cooperation. But I live in a small New England town and work in a university environment that are, for the most part, cooperative. If I eat lunch on campus, I buy it from a student-managed, democratically run business that offers the tastiest, healthiest, cheapest provisions available. If I need to buy bread or milk on the way home, I pull into the Leverett Village Co-op. If my car needs attention, it goes to a worker-owned business, Pelham Auto, where I know both service managers by name. My money sits at the Five College Federal Credit Union, where it earns more interest and gains me better service than I've ever gotten at any other bank.

About four years ago, I began to weave economic theory more closely into my everyday life. The threads began coming together when Adam Trott and Michael Johnson, two members of the local Valley Alliance of Worker Cooperatives, reached out to tell me about their efforts to promote locally owned and democratically managed firms.

Although we lived in the same community, they found me as a result of a short post I wrote for the *New York Times'* "Economix" blog, describing a collaborative agreement between the United Steel Workers and the largest worker-owned business in the world, Mondragón Corporation. It seemed ironic, but also encouraging, that we first connected online, and that it might be possible to go from the global to the local and then back again.

Even in our cooperative-rich area of Western Massachusetts, Adam and Michael explained, most potential worker/owners knew virtually nothing about the principles involved (beyond liking the general idea). Why couldn't a public university provide better education and training for students potentially interested in starting up or joining a worker-owned business? Of course it could, and should. We decided to try to make that happen.

In a collaborative process that involved interested faculty and graduate students, as well as representatives from the Valley Alliance, we developed a new upper-division economics course and designed a Certificate Program for Applied Economic Research on Cooperative Enterprises centered on a summer research internship with a local cooperative.

Here, I want to share some of the ideas and opinions I've formed in the process of developing this program, which we believe could be a good model for other colleges and universities.

History Matters

Most people, including most college students, seem to think that cooperatives are a counter-cultural leftover from the 1960s, a niche phenomenon confined to hip neighborhoods and college towns. The economic history of the United States is typically portrayed as the steady march of corporate capitalism, trampling all other institutional forms. Many on the right see it as a march of progress; many on the left, as a march of doom.

Ironically, the traditional left preoccupation with corporate capitalism may simply feed the beast—overstating its hegemonic role, as though it can't be contained until the revolution comes. J.K. Gibson-Graham makes this point persuasively in *The End of Capitalism (As We Knew It)*: What we call "capitalism" involves many different creatures. Families, communities, non-profit organizations, and the state actually account for a larger share of economic activity—broadly defined—than capitalist firms.

Though standard economics texts hardly mention them, consumer cooperatives and worker-owned businesses have shaped our history. Their influence, however, has been uneven, greater in some industries and regions than others.

Marxist scholars have often associated cooperatives with the so-called "utopian socialists"—whom they have traditionally considered well-meaning but misguided. Efforts to establish alternative businesses have often been labeled a form of co-optation less politically virtuous than trade-union organizing or socialist political parties. Yet cooperative efforts have typically been closely linked to and complementary with larger anti-corporate organizing efforts. In a fascinating article entitled "Toward an Organizationally Diverse American Capitalism? Cooperative, Mutual, and Local, State-Owned Enterprise," sociologist Mark Schnaiberg traces the history of cooperative marketing efforts in the grain and dairy industries, originally dominated by large monopsonies that used their market power to pay farmers as little as possible. (A monopsony is a single buyer that dominates a market, just as a monopoly is a single seller.) When farmers successfully started up cooperatives, other members of the community also became more likely to organize on their own behalf.

Even when cooperative enterprises represent only a small proportion of market transactions in a local community, they often exercise a disproportionate influence, disciplining capitalist enterprises or pioneering innovations that are later adopted by them. Local food cooperatives were the first to begin marketing organic and local produce, and large supermarket chains gradually followed suit. Local credit unions have made it harder for large banking institutions to charge excessive fees. Worker-owned businesses have pulled the small-business community in a more progressive direction, serving as a counterweight to large, footloose firms.

By demonstrating the viability of businesses aimed to serve larger social goals, cooperatives have altered our economic ecology.

Culture Matters

As an economist, I was trained to emphasize the difference between for-profit and non-profit firms. But that difference may be less significant than the moral and cultural values central to the definition of cooperative enterprises.

Consumer cooperatives seek to provide high-quality products at minimal cost. Worker-owned businesses need to generate profits both to pay themselves and to finance investment. Both, however, are committed to seven "cooperative principles" (see box, next page) that include democracy and concern for community.

In this respect, cooperative enterprises can be seen as a subset of efforts to develop a solidarity economy, which also includes non-profit businesses and community organizations. They are also closely aligned with "buy local" efforts that urge consumers to shop in locally owned stores and build a local supply chain (for instance, by patronizing restaurants utilizing locally grown products).

Not that it's always clear how "concern for community" should be defined. Almost by their very nature as small, decentralized businesses, co-ops prioritize those with whom they are most likely to come into contact. But local solidarity is not automatically consistent with broader forms of solidarity. In fact, it risks a kind of parochialism that could lead to happy little enclaves embedded in a larger economy built on hierarchy and exploitation.

On the other hand, co-op culture can promote values that may lead people toward other forms of positive engagement, with the goal of steadily expanding the cooperative reach and linking many kinds of progressive efforts together. Co-op ventures also offer people the opportunity to build something new, rather than merely trying to tear down something old.

The Seven Cooperative Principles

Cooperatives around the world generally operate according to the same core principles and values, adopted by the International Co-operative Alliance (www.ica.coop) in 1995. Cooperatives trace the roots of these principles to the first modern cooperative, founded in Rochdale, England, in 1844.

1. **Voluntary and Open Membership**: Cooperatives are voluntary organizations, open to all people able to use its services and willing to accept the responsibilities of membership, without gender, social, racial, political or religious discrimination.
2. **Democratic Member Control**: Cooperatives are democratic organizations controlled by their members—those who buy the goods or use the services of the cooperative— who actively participate in setting policies and making decisions.
3. **Members' Economic Participation**: Members contribute equally to, and democratically control, the capital of the cooperative. This benefits members in proportion to the business they conduct with the cooperative rather than on the capital invested.
4. **Autonomy and Independence**: Cooperatives are autonomous, self-help organizations controlled by their members. If the co-op enters into agreements with other organizations or raises capital from external sources, it is done so based on terms that ensure democratic control by the members and maintains the cooperative's autonomy.
5. **Education, Training and Information**: Cooperatives provide education and training for members, elected representatives, managers and employees so they can contribute effectively to the development of their cooperative. Members also inform the general public about the nature and benefits of cooperatives.
6. **Cooperation among Cooperatives**: Cooperatives serve their members most effectively and strengthen the cooperative movement by working together through local, national, regional and international structures.
7. **Concern for Community**: While focusing on member needs, cooperatives work for the sustainable development of communities through policies and programs accepted by the members.

From the National Cooperative Business Association, International Year of Cooperatives (usa2012.coop).

The commitment to democratic decision-making distinguishes worker-owned businesses from other institutional forms that aim to enlarge economic goals (such as the new "social benefit" corporate charters) or to help incentivize workers (such as profit-sharing or employee-stock-ownership plans). This commitment reflects a cultural value—as well as a political principle. Other shared values encouraging respect and concern for others may help lubricate the democratic process by making collective decision-making less contentious.

Democratic values and skills may grow stronger in communities where they are consistently exercised, explaining why some regions of the world seem to foster more cooperative enterprises than others. The famous Mondragón cooperatives grew up in the Basque area of northern Spain, among people who felt embattled and impoverished by their minority status and strengthened by their progressive Catholic traditions. Many small cooperatives have prospered in northern Italy, an area with a long history of labor radicalism and a strong Communist Party. In Canada, the province of Quebec has successfully encouraged the cooperative provision of social services under the banner of the "social economy."

In the United States, cooperatives have often helped improve living standards in African-American communities, from a cooperative shipyard in 1860s Baltimore, to a co-op buying club in Depression-era Gary, Ind., to the Common Ground Collective in post-Katrina New Orleans. As Jessica Gordon-Nembhard and Ajowa Nzinga point out (see *Dollars & Sense*, July/August 2006), a common history of economic exclusion and hardship can foster cooperation.

Public policies have also played a role in developing these epicenters of cooperative development. But culture is surely one of the factors shaping the political alignments that generate such policies.

Efficiency Matters

Economists often overstate the value of efficiency, or define it in excessively narrow terms. But that doesn't mean it's not important. Efficiency is an important arbiter of success in competition and, in the world we live in, co-operators need to compete. Since competition between firms is, to some extent a "team sport," successful cooperation among team members can prove advantageous.

Democratically managed firms may be more efficient than others, even from the relatively narrow perspective of costs and benefits. The British economist John Stuart Mill made this argument in the mid-19th century, pointing out that workers who were also owners would be likely to work harder and smarter than those merely paid an hourly wage.

This issue never received much attention from early-20th-century Marxists convinced of the virtues of central planning. However, it came to the fore with Yugoslavian experiments in worker self-management in the mid-20th century and has since had a big impact on progressive economic thinking—in part because it helps frame a critique of both the traditional family firm and the modern corporation.

A long-standing favorite of neoclassical economists is an argument, developed by economists Armen Alchian and Harold Demsetz, that workers will have a tendency to shirk on the job unless they are overseen by an owner who can capture any profits (or "residual") left over after the workers are paid. This gives the "residual claimant" an incentive to crack the whip and make them work as hard as possible. Ownership in most modern corporations is highly fragmented, but owners presumably hire managers—from the chief executive officer or CEO down to supervisors and foremen—to fulfill this disciplinary role.

Radical economist Samuel Bowles effectively rebuts this argument, pointing out that it is difficult and costly to monitor effort. Workers seeking to resist capitalist exploitation may be especially likely to shirk unless managers can find a way to either secure their loyalty or threaten them with costly job loss.

Unfortunately, worker ownership alone doesn't necessarily solve this incentive problem. Workers either have to be really good at monitoring one another's efforts (so that no one can free ride without being sanctioned), or they have to feel such strong solidarity toward one another that no one even tries to free ride. (The latter is preferable, since it's often hard for a collective to fire someone who is slacking off.)

Other tensions among owner-workers can arise. For instance, young owner-workers have a stronger incentive to reinvest firm profits to increase their future earnings than older owner-workers, who would prefer to retain more earnings and/or fund their pensions. The success of a worker-owned enterprise depends on the ability of worker-owners to anticipate and creatively respond to such conflicts of interest. But the process of doing so—negotiating and resolving differences of opinion—can itself be quite costly, in two ways.

First, democratic decision-making can be quite time-consuming, especially if based on rules of consensus. Worker-owned firms generally treat time in meetings as part of their paid work, and the time they devote to it can cut down on directly productive activities.

Second, democratic decision-making can prove emotionally costly, as when good friends disagree about important matters and find it difficult to accommodate one another. On the other hand, conflict avoidance—such as a desire not to discipline a fellow worker who is also a friend—can also lower efficiency. This problem can be described as a "second order" free-rider problem—that is, a reluctance to openly point to or discourage free riding.

Representative democracy and delegation to a manager can help minimize these problems, but also at some cost. Majority rule can alienate the minority, and unstable factions can lead to lack of continuity in decision-making.

Worker-owned firms will be more likely to prosper if they cultivate an awareness of decision-making problems and develop the institutional structures and skills necessary to over-come them.

Here comes the Catch-22. Neither our educational system nor most employers do much to help people develop democratic management skills, so there's a big start-up problem. If we could just create more opportunities for people to develop and practice such skills, worker-owned businesses could enjoy more success.

Efficiency gains can also come at the macro level. Worker-owned businesses that get off the ground tend to be more stable than other small businesses, in part because workers have an incentive to hang in over the long haul, even if revenue slumps. This can buffer the effects of recession on the economy as a whole.

Most importantly, worker-owned businesses depend more on positive incentives than on the threat of job loss. Unlike employer-owned businesses, they don't rely on the labor discipline imposed by a high unemployment rate. And consistently high unemployment rates are among the most inefficient features of our current economic system.

Collaboration Matters

For all the reasons given above, the cooperative movement may need to reach a certain critical mass before it can really take off. More collaboration among cooperatives—and between cooperatives and other institutions such as public universities—could make a big difference.

Relatively few worker-owned businesses are started up in a given year, leading some to speculate that they are inherently less expansionary than capitalist firms (for the simple reason that worker-owners care about more than the rate of return on their capital investment). They also care about the quality of their work life and their place in the community. Some of the decision-making problems described above, moreover, may be more easily solved in small firms where everyone knows everyone else. Expansion can lead to complications.

However, collaboration and expansion could help worker-owned businesses in several ways. First, it could help them gain access to more and better financing. By definition, worker-owned firms can't sell equity shares in their business (because all owners must be workers). They can develop other forms of self-financing, including bonds that can be especially attractive to socially responsible investors. But they can also develop ways of pooling resources and helping to finance one another. Each firm belonging to the Valley Alliance of Worker Coops sets aside a percentage of its profits to promote local cooperative development. One can even imagine a kind of franchise model in which one firm could spin off smaller firms, which could become financially independent, but remain closely allied.

Second, vertical networking along the supply chain could increase efficiency and the ability to compete with large conglomerate capitalist enterprises. International networking among cooperatives holds particular promise, because it advances a larger fair-trade agenda, and also helps escape parochialism. Many examples of this kind of networking exist, such as the People's Market at UMass-Amherst buying only cooperatively produced coffee and actively seeking other cooperatively produced goods and services.

Third, more networking could help develop the distinctive managerial and decision-making skills described above. Indeed, the more worker-owners gain experience in different types of firms, the richer the skills they bring to the task of democratic management. And the more visible worker-owners become, the more young people are likely to become attracted to new prospects for more socially meaningful and economically rewarding work.

Finally, the more worker-owned businesses and other cooperative enterprises expand, the easier it becomes to build political coalitions and implement policies that promote their efforts. These synergies help explain how regional economies in the Basque area of Spain, northern Italy, and the Canadian province of Quebec have evolved.

A worker-owned business is what economists call a "microeconomic structure." But its ultimate success may depend on its ability to change the macroeconomic structure, which can, in turn, improve its microeconomic efficiency. Even a small cooperative firm can help a community enhance its standard of living and quality of life. More importantly, however, it can provide a catalyst for social and political changes that not only bring more and more worker-owned businesses into being, but also enable them to compete more effectively with capital-owned firms.

That's why worker-owned businesses fit the description of what the 20th-century Italian theorist and revolutionary Antonio Gramsci called a "non-reformist reform" and what sociologist Erik Olin Wright terms a "real utopia." Take another look at those seven cooperative principles. They offer a pretty good guide to running not just a business, but a whole society. ❏

Sources: J.K. Gibson-Graham, *The End of Capitalism (As We Knew It)* (University of Minnesota Press, 2006); Mark Schnaiberg, "Toward an Organizationally Diverse American Capitalism? Cooperative, Mutual, and Local, State-Owned Enterprise," *Seattle University Law Review*, Vol. 34, No. 4 (2011); Jessica Gordon-Nembhard and Ajowa Nzinga, "African-American Economic Solidarity," *Dollars & Sense*, July/August 2006; Erik Olin Wright, *Envisioning Real Utopias* (Verso, 2010).

Chapter 5

MARKET FAILURE I: MARKET POWER

INTRODUCTION

With monopoly, we finally encounter a situation in which most economists, orthodox and otherwise, agree that unfettered markets lead to an undesirable outcome. If a firm is able to create a monopoly, it faces a downward-sloping demand curve—that is to say, if it reduces output, it can charge a higher price. Economists argue that competitive forces tend to undermine any monopoly, but failing this, they support antitrust policy as a backstop. The concept of monopoly not only points to an important failing of markets, but it opens the door to thinking about many possible market structures other than perfect competition, including oligopoly, in which a small group of producers dominates the market. Monopoly and oligopoly are examples of market structures in which firms wield "market power" (violating Tilly Assumption #1—see Article 1.2). That is, individual firms can affect the market-wide level of prices, profits, and wages. Market power alters how markets function from the ideal of perfect competition and delivers significantly less optimal results.

We begin this chapter with another seminal article by Chris Tilly, "Is Small Beautiful? Is Bigger Better? Small and Big Businesses Both Have Their Drawbacks" (Article 5.1). This article walks through the pluses and minuses of large and small businesses, and finds both wanting.

The recent financial crisis has provided particularly egregious examples of what happens when we institute laissez-faire (hands-off) regulatory regimes, especially in the area of finance. In "A Brief History of Mergers and Antitrust Policy" (Article 5.2), Edward Herman provides a long-term context for the discussion, reviewing the history of U.S. antitrust law over the last century. He also criticizes economists for justifying a hands-off policy toward big business mergers over the last few decades.

Article 5.3 takes a much-needed break for drinks with "Hopsopoly," a review of the beer industry. Years of corporate consolidation at the top of the industry have led to a few gigantic firms dominating global beer brewing. These enormous brewers are also buying the distribution networks through which beer reaches consumers, giving them a powerful new lever of control over the market to fight the popularity of craft labels.

Next, Arthur MacEwan discusses the relevance of the concept of "monopoly capital" in an age of globalized competition (Article 5.4). MacEwan finds that firm size and market concentration have continued to grow throughout the era of globalization and that large firms still exhibit extraordinary market power.

The last two articles look at two examples of the exercise of market power today. Sasha Breger Bush focuses on the unequal relationship between farmers and the companies that dominate the food industry (Article 5.5). Breger Bush describes how, in the United States, poultry farmers find themselves under the thumb of giant "integrators" like Perdue, Tyson, and Pilgrim's Pride. In developing countries where coffee is widely grown, farmers face a similar relationship with coffee processors. In both cases, there is a fundamental relationship of "unequal exchange."

Finally, Dean Baker focuses, in his article "Facebook: The Sorry Company" (Article 5.6), on the important issues the company has been compelled to apologize for, and some decisive measures that could prevent the company from having to go back before Congress for a fresh round of apologies.

Discussion Questions

1. (Article 5.1) List the pros and cons of large and small businesses that Tilly discusses. How does this compare with the problems associated with market structure that your textbook mentions? Be sure to compare Tilly's list of small-business flaws with what your textbook has to say about small business.

2. (Articles 5.1 and 5.2) In what ways do these articles show that corporations control "the marketplace of ideas"? What are the possible consequences? What, if anything, should be done about it?

3. (Article 5.3) Describe the multiple layers of the beer industry, from production to wholesaling to retail. What limits has the Justice Department placed on AB InBev's ability to buy and control distributors? Do you feel this will be enough to preserve consumer access to smaller craft labels?

4. (Article 5.4) Mainstream economists view competition among many small firms as a prerequisite for "efficient" market outcomes. Some touted globalization as a way to increase competition and benefit consumers. What problems, if any, result from the large size and market dominance of a few global firms? Should this change our view of globalization in any way?

5. (Articles 5.5) Breger Bush notes that food producers (like chicken farmers or coffee farmers) occupy a highly competitive market segment, while food industry "integrators" occupy an much less competitive segment. What are the consequences of this set-up? Are they undesirable and, if so, what remedy would you propose?

6. (Article 5.6) Baker outlines three measures that would address Facebook's past data scandals, and significantly relieve users' anxieties. Describe these policy proposals. What could they be expected to do to Facebook's business model?

Article 5.1

IS SMALL BEAUTIFUL? IS BIG BETTER?
Small and big businesses both have their drawbacks.

BY CHRIS TILLY
July/August 1989, revised April 2002

Beginning in the late 1980s, the United States has experienced a small, but significant boom in small business. While big businesses have downsized, small enterprises have proliferated. Should we be glad? Absolutely, declare the advocates of small business. Competition makes small businesses entrepreneurial, innovative, and responsive to customers.

Not so fast, reply big business's boosters. Big corporations grew big because they were efficient, and tend to stay efficient because they are big—and thus able to invest in research and upgrading of technology and workforce skills.

But each side in this debate omits crucial drawbacks. Small may be beautiful for consumers, but it's often oppressive for workers. And while big businesses wield the power to advance technology, they also often wield the market power to bash competitors and soak consumers. In the end, the choices are quite limited.

Big and Small

Is the United States a nation of big businesses, or of small ones? There are two conventional ways to measure business size. One is simply to count the number of employees per firm. By this measure, small businesses (say, business establishments with less than 20 employees) make up the vast majority of businesses (Table 1). But they provide only a small fraction of the total number of jobs.

The other approach gauges market share—each firm's share of total sales in a given industry. Industries range between two extremes: what economists call "perfect competition" (many firms selling a standardized product, each too tiny to affect the market price) and monopoly (one business controls all sales in an industry). Economy-wide, as with employment, small businesses are most numerous, but control only a small slice of total sales. Sole proprietorships account for 73% of established businesses, far outnumbering corporations, which are 20% of the total (the remainder are partnerships). But corporations ring up a hefty 90% of all sales, leaving sole proprietors with only 6%. It takes a lot of mom and pop stores to equal General Motors' 1999 total of $177 billion in sales.

Industry by industry, the degree of competition varies widely. Economists consider an industry concentrated when its top four companies account for more than 40% of total sales in the industry (Table 2). At the high end of the spectrum are the cigarette, beer, and aircraft industries, where four firms account for the bulk of U.S. production.

No market comes close to meeting the textbook specifications for perfect competition, but one can still find industries in which a large number of producers compete for sales. The clothing and restaurant industries, for example, remain relatively competitive. Overall, about one-third of U.S. goods are manufactured in concentrated industries, about one fifth are made in competitive industries, and the rest fall somewhere in between.

Beating the Competition

Those who tout the benefits of small, competitive business make a broad range of claims on its behalf. In addition to keeping prices low, they say the quality of the product is constantly improving, as companies seek a competitive edge. The same desire, they claim, drives firms toward technological innovations, leading to productivity increases.

The real story is not so simple. Competition does indeed keep prices low. Believe it or not, clothing costs us less—in real terms—than it cost our parents. Between 1960 and 1999, while the overall price level and hourly wages both increased nearly sixfold, apparel prices didn't even triple. And small businesses excel at offering variety, whether it is the ethnic restaurants that dot cities or the custom machine-tool work offered by small shops. Furthermore, however powerful small business lobbies may be in Washington, they do not influence the legislative process as blatantly as do corporate giants.

But those low prices often have an ugly underside. Our sportswear is cheap in part because the garment industry increasingly subcontracts work to sweatshops—whether they be export assembly plants in Haiti paying dollar-a-day wages, or the "underground" Los Angeles stitcheries that employ immigrant women in virtual slavery. Struggling to maintain razor-thin profit margins, small businesses cut costs any way they can—which usually translates into low wages and onerous working conditions.

"There is a rule of survival for small business," Bill Ryan, president of Ryan Transfer Corporation, commented some years ago. "There are certain things you want to have [in paying workers] and certain things you can afford. You had better go with what you can afford." Bottom line, workers in companies employing 500 or more people enjoy average wages 30% higher than their counterparts in small businesses.

Part of this wage gap results from differences other than size—unionization, the education of the workforce, the particular jobs and industries involved. But University of Michigan economist Charles Brown and his colleagues

TABLE 1:
SMALL BUSINESS NATION?

Most businesses are small, but most employees work for big businesses

Company size (number of employees)	Percent of all firms	Percent of all workers
1–4	54%	6%
5–9	20%	8%
10–19	13%	11%
20–49	8%	16%
50–99	3%	13%
100–249	2%	16%
250–499	0.4%	10%
500–999	0.2%	7%
1,000 or more	0.1%	13%

Note: "Businesses" refers to establishments, meaning business locations.

Source: County Business Patterns, 1998.

controlled for all these differences and more, and still found a 10% premium for big business's employees. A note of caution, however: Other recent research indicates that this wage bonus is linked to long-term employment and job ladders. To the extent that corporations dissolve these long-term ties—as they seem to be rapidly doing—the pay advantage may dissolve as well.

Small business gurus make extravagant claims about small businesses' job-generation capacity. An oft-quoted 1987 report by consultant David Birch claimed that businesses with fewer than 20 employees create 88% of new jobs. The reality is more mundane: over the long run, businesses with 19 or fewer workers account for about one quarter of net new jobs. One reason why Birch's statistics are misleading is that new small businesses are created in great numbers, but they also fail at a high rate. The result is that the *net* gain in jobs is much smaller than the number created in business start-ups.

For companies in very competitive markets, the same "whip of competition" that keeps prices down undermines many of competition's other supposed benefits. The flurry of competition in the airline industry following deregulation, for example, hardly resulted in a higher quality product. Flying became temporarily cheaper, but also less comfortable, reliable, and safe.

Technological innovation from competition is also more myth than reality. Small firms in competitive industries do very little research and development. They lack both the cash needed to make long-term investments and the market power to guarantee a return on that investment. In fact, many of them can't even count on surviving to reap the rewards: only one-third to one-half of small business startups survive for five years, and only about one in five makes it to ten years. A 1988 Census Bureau survey concluded that in manufacturing, "technology use is positively correlated with plant size." Agriculture may be the exception that proves the rule. That highly competitive industry has made marked productivity gains, but its research is supported by the taxpayer, and its risks are reduced by government price supports.

Of course, the biggest myth about competition is that it is in any way a "natural state" for capitalism. In fact, in most markets the very process of competing for high profits or a bigger market share tends to create a concentrated, rather than a competitive, market structure.

TABLE 2: WHO COMPETES, WHO DOESN'T	
Industry	*Percent of sales by top four firms*
Light truck and utility vehicle manufacturing	96%
Breweries	91%
Home center stores	91%
Breakfast cereal manufacturing	78%
General book stores	77%
Credit card issuing	77%
Lawn equipment manufacturing	62%
Cable providers	63%
Computer and software stores	51%
Sock manufacturing	30%
Hotels and motels (excl. casinos)	22%
Gas stations	9%
Real estate	4%
Bars	2%

Source: 2002 Economic Census.

This process occurs in several ways. Big firms sometimes drive their smaller competitors out of business by selectively cutting prices to the bone. The smaller firms may lack the financial resources to last out the low prices. In the 1960s, several of IBM's smaller competitors sued it for cutting prices in a pattern that was designed to drive the smaller firms out of the market. Large corporations can also gain a lock on scarce resources: for example, large airlines like United and American operate the comprehensive, computerized information and reservation systems that travel agents tap into—and you can bet that each airline's system lists their own flights first. Or businesses may exploit an advantage in one market to dominate another, as Microsoft used its control of the computer operating system market to seize market share for its Internet browser.

Other firms eliminate competitors by buying them out—either in a hostile takeover or a friendly merger. Either way, a former competitor is neutralized. This strategy used to be severely limited by strict antitrust guidelines that prohibited most horizontal mergers—those between two firms that formerly competed in the same market. The Reagan administration's team at the Justice Department, however, loosened the merger guidelines significantly in the early 1980s. Since that time, many large mergers between former competitors have been allowed to go through, most notably in the airline industry.

The Power of Concentration

Concentration, then, is as natural to market economies as competition. And bigness, like smallness, is a mixed bag for us as consumers and workers. For workers, bigness is on the whole a plus. Whereas competition forces small businesses to be stingy, big firms are on average more generous, offering employees higher wages, greater job security, and more extensive fringe benefits. In 1993, 97% of businesses with 500 or more workers provided health insurance; only 43% of businesses with 25 or fewer employees did so. Large firms also provide much more employee training. The strongest unions, as well, have historically been in industries where a few firms control large shares of their markets, and can pass along increased costs to consumers—auto, steel, and tires, for example. When profits are threatened, though, firms in concentrated markets also have more resources with which to fight labor. They are better able to weather a strike, oppose unionization, and make agreements with rivals not to take advantage of each other's labor troubles. In addition, large companies, not surprisingly, score low on workplace autonomy.

What about consumers? Corporations in industries where there are few competitors may compete, but the competitive clash is seldom channeled into prolonged price wars. The soft drink industry is a classic example. David McFarland, a University of North Carolina economist, likens soft drink competition to professional wrestling. "They make a lot of sounds and groans and bounce on the mat, but they know who is going to win," he remarked.

Coke and Pepsi introduce new drinks and mount massive ad campaigns to win market share, but the net result is not lower prices. In fact, because competition between industry giants relies more on product differentiation than price, companies pass on their inflated advertising expenses to consumers. In the highly concentrated breakfast cereal market, the package frequently costs more than the contents. And of every dollar you pay for a box, nearly 20 cents goes for advertising.

It takes resources to develop and market a new idea, which gives large corporations distinct advantages in innovation. The original idea for the photocopier may have come from a patent lawyer who worked nights in his basement, but Xerox spent $16 million before it had a product it could sell. RCA invested $65 million developing the color television. RCA could take this gamble because its dominance in the television market ensured that it would not be immediately undercut by some other firm.

But market dominance can also translate into complacency. The steel industry illustrates the point. A few major producers earned steady profits through the 1950s and 1960s but were caught off-guard when new technologies vaulted foreign steel-makers to the top of the industry in the 1970s. Similarly, when IBM dominated the computer industry in the 1960s and early 1970s, innovation proceeded quite slowly, particularly compared to the frantic scramble in that industry today. With no competitors to worry about, it was more profitable for IBM to sit tight, since innovation would only have made its own machines obsolete.

And large corporations can also put their deep pockets and technical expertise to work to short-circuit public policy. In the 1980s, when Congress changed corporate liability laws to make corporate executives criminally liable for some kinds of offenses, General Electric's lobbyists and legal staff volunteered to help draft the final regulations, in order to minimize the damage.

Big businesses sometimes hide their lobbying behind a "citizen" smokescreen. The largest-spending lobby in Washington in 1986 was Citizens for the Control of Acid Rain. These good citizens had been organized by coal and electric utility companies to oppose tighter pollution controls. Along the same lines, the Coalition for Vehicle Choice (now, who could be against that?) was set up by Ford and General Motors in 1990 to fight higher fuel efficiency standards.

Concentration or Conglomeration

Over the last couple of decades, the mix of big and small businesses has changed, but the changes are small and—at first glance—contradictory. Over time, employment has shifted toward smaller firms, though the shift has been subtle, not revolutionary. Meanwhile, the overall level of industry-by-industry sales concentration in the economy has increased, but only slightly. As older industries become more concentrated, newer, more competitive ones crop up, leaving overall concentration relatively steady. In his book *Lean and Mean*, economist Bennett Harrison points out that there is actually no contradiction between the small business employment boomlet and big firms' continued grip on markets. Big businesses, it turns out, are orchestrating much of the flowering of small business, through a variety of outsourcing and subcontracting arrangements.

But if industry-by-industry concentration has changed little over the decades, conglomeration is a different matter. Corporate ownership of assets has become much more concentrated over time, reflecting the rise in conglomerates—corporations doing business in a variety of industries. Five decades ago, the top 200 manufacturing firms accounted for 48% of all sales in the U.S. economy. By 1993, the 200 biggest industrial businesses controlled 65% of sales.

Most mainstream economists see these groupings as irrelevant for the competitive structure of the economy. Antitrust laws place no restrictions on firms from different industries banding together under one corporate roof. But sheer size can easily affect competition in the markets of the individual firms involved. A parent company can use one especially profitable subsidiary to subsidize start-up costs for a new venture, giving it a competitive edge. And if one board of directors controls major interests in related industries, it can obviously influence any of those markets more forcefully.

A case in point is the mega-merger of Time Inc. and Warner, which will soon be joining with America Online. The resulting conglomerate will control massive sections of the home entertainment business, bringing together Time's journalists, film and television producers, and authors, Warner's entertainment machine, which includes Home Box Office, the nation's largest pay television channel, and AOL's huge share of the Internet access market. The conglomerate can influence the entertainment business from the initial point—the actors, writers, and directors—up to the point where the finished products appear on people's televisions or computers. Conglomeration also multiplies the political clout of large corportions. No wonder Disney and other entertainment giants have also hopped on the conglomeration bandwagon.

Choose Your Poison

Competition, concentration, or conglomeration: The choice is an unsavory one indeed. Opting for lots of tiny, competing firms leaves labor squeezed and sacrifices the potential technological advantages that come with concentrated resources. Yet the big monopolies tend to dominate their markets, charge high prices, and waste countless resources on glitzy ad campaigns and trivial product differentiation. And the big conglomerate firms, while not necessarily dominant in any single market, wield a frightening amount of political and economic power, with budgets larger than those of most countries.

Of course, we don't have much to say about the choice, no matter how much "shopping for a better world" we engage in. Market competition rolls on—sometimes cutthroat, other times genteel. Industries often start out as monopolies (based on new inventions), go through a competitive phase, but end up concentrating as they mature. As long as bigness remains profitable and the government maintains a hands-off attitude, companies in both competitive and concentrated industries will tend to merge with firms in other industries. This will feed a continuing trend toward conglomeration. Since bigness and smallness both have their drawbacks, the best we can do is to use public policies to minimize the disadvantages of each. ❏

Sources: *Lean and Mean: The Changing Landscape of Corporate Power in the Age of Flexibility*, Bennett Harrison, 1994; *Employers Large and Small*, Charles Brown, James Hamilton, and James Medoff, 1990.

Article 5.2

A BRIEF HISTORY OF MERGERS AND ANTITRUST POLICY

BY EDWARD HERMAN
May/June 1998

Government efforts to prevent or break up monopolies are called antitrust policy. They assume that when a few companies dominate an industry, this weakens competition and hurts the public by reducing production, raising prices, and slowing technical advance. Antitrust has gone through cycles during this century. In some years, strongly pro-business presidencies (usually Republican) have allowed businesses to merge at will. These have often been followed by "reform" administrations, which tend to restrain, but not to reverse, concentrations of corporate power.

The federal government first took on a strong antitrust role with the Sherman Act of 1890, which outlawed monopoly and efforts to obtain it. In 1914 the Clayton Act also put restrictions on stock purchases and interlocking directorates that would reduce competition. This legislation responded to public anger and fears about "trusts," which brought separate firms under common control. Most notorious were Rockefeller's Standard Oil Trust and James Duke's American Tobacco Company, which employed ruthless tactics to drive their competitors out of business.

Early on the antitrust laws also treated organized labor as a "monopoly," and were used in breaking the Pullman strike in 1892. In 1908, the Supreme Court awarded damages to an employer against whom unions had organized a secondary boycott. This led to the Clayton Act exempting unions from its restrictions.

Otherwise, the federal government only minimally enforced the Sherman Act until Theodore Roosevelt was elected in 1900. Then in 1911 the Supreme Court decided that both the Standard Oil and American Tobacco trusts were "bad trusts," and ordered their dismantling. But in 1920 the Court refused to condemn the U.S. Steel consolidation, because it was a "good trust" that didn't attack its smaller rivals. This began a long period when the Antitrust Division and the courts approved mergers that produced industries with a few dominant firms, but which were "well-behaved." And in the 1920s, Republicans virtually ended antitrust enforcement.

The Golden Age

Franklin Roosevelt revived antitrust during 1938 to 1941, and antitrust law had its golden age from 1945 to 1974, fueled by a liberal Supreme Court, anti-merger legislation passed in 1950, and mildly progressive enforcement (though less so in the Republican years). During this period Alcoa's monopoly over aluminum production was broken (1945), and the Court found the tobacco industry guilty of "group monopoly" (1946), although the companies were only assessed a modest fine.

During the 1960s, when antitrust law blocked mergers among companies in the same industry, businesses adapted by acquiring firms in unrelated industries. Many such "conglomerate" mergers took place during 1964-68, when Lyndon Johnson was president. Companies like International Telephone and Telegraph, Ling-Temco-Vought, Gulf & Western, Tenneco, and Litton Industries grew rapidly.

The Reagan-Bush Collapse

Antitrust policy went into recession around 1974, then plunged during the presidencies of Ronald Reagan and George H. W. Bush. They aggressively dismantled antitrust, imposing drastic cuts in budgets and manpower, installing officials hostile to the antitrust mission, and failing to enforce the laws. During 1981-89, the Antitrust Division of the Justice Dept. challenged only 16 of over 16,000 pre-merger notices filed with them.

Despite his high-profile contest with Microsoft, Bill Clinton largely accepted the conservative view that most mergers are harmless. During his two terms, federal authorities approved or ignored many giant mergers. These included Westinghouse's buyout of CBS, the joining of "Baby Bells" Bell Atlantic and Nynex, and the combination of Chemical Bank and Manufacturers Hanover. During 1997 alone, 156 mergers of $1 billion or more, and merger transactions totalling more than *$1 trillion*, passed antitrust muster.

Clinton's failure to attack giant mergers rests nominally on the alleged efficiency of large firms and the belief that globalized markets make for competition. FTC head Robert Pitofsky said, "this is an astonishing merger wave," but not to worry because these deals "should be judged on a global market scale, not just on national and local markets."

But the efficiency of large size—as opposed to the profit-making advantages that corporations gain from market power and cross-selling (pushing products through other divisions of the same company)—is eminently debatable. And many markets are not global—hospitals, for example, operate in local markets, yet only some 20 of 3,000 hospital mergers have been subjected to antitrust challenge. Even in global markets a few firms are often dominant, and a vast array of linkages such as joint ventures and licensing agreements increasingly mute global competition.

The Clinton administration's failure to contest many giant mergers did not rest only on intellectual arguments. It also reflected political weakness and an unwillingness to oppose powerful people who fund elections and own or dominate the media. This was conspicuously true of the great media combinations—Disney and Cap-Cities/ABC, and TimeWarner and Turner—and the merger of Boeing and McDonnell-Douglas, which involved institutions of enormous power, whose mergers the stock market greeted enthusiastically.

The Economists Sell Out

Since the early 1970s, powerful people and corporations have funded not only elections but conservative economists, who are frequently housed in think-tanks such as the American Enterprise, Hoover, and Cato Institutes, and serve as corporate consultants in regulatory and anti-trust cases. Most notable in hiring economic consultants have been AT&T and IBM, which together spent hundreds of millions of dollars on their antitrust defenses. AT&T hired some 30 economists from five leading economics departments during the 1970s and early 1980s.

Out of these investments came models and theories downgrading the "populist" idea that numerous sellers and decentralization were important for effective competition (and essential to a democratic society). They claimed instead that the market can do it all, and that regulation and antitrust actions are misconceived. First, theorists showed that efficiency gains from mergers might reduce prices even more than monopoly power would cause them to rise. Economists also stressed "entry," claiming that if mergers did not improve efficiency any price increases would be wiped out eventually by new companies entering the industry. Entry is also the heart of the theory of "contestable markets," developed by economic consultants to AT&T, who argued that the ease of entry in cases where resources (trucks, aircraft) can be shifted quickly at low cost, makes for effective competition.

Then there is the theory of a "market for corporate control," in which mergers allow better managers to displace the less efficient. In this view, poorly-managed firms have low stock prices, making them easy to buy. Finally, many economists justified conglomerate mergers on three grounds: that they function as "mini capital markets," with top managers allocating capital between divisions of a single firm so as to maximize efficiency; that they reduce transaction costs; and that they are a means of diversifying risk.

These theories, many coming out of the "Chicago School" (the economics department at the University of Chicago), suffer from over-simplification, a strong infusion of ideology, and lack of empirical support. Mergers often are motivated by factors other than enhancing efficiency—such as the desire for monopoly power, empire building, cutting taxes, improving stock values, and even as a cover for poor management (such as when the badly-run U.S. Steel bought control of Marathon Oil).

Several researchers have questioned the supposed benefits of mergers. In theory, a merger that improves efficiency should increase profits. But one study by Dennis Mueller, and another by F. W. Scherer and David Ravenscraft, showed that mergers more often than not have reduced returns to stockholders. A study by Michael Porter of Harvard University demonstrated that a staggering 74% of the conglomerate acquisitions of the 1960s were eventually sold off (divested)—a good indication that they were never based on improving efficiency. William Shepherd of the University of Massachusetts investigated the "contestable markets" model, finding that it is a hypothetical case with minimal applicability to the real world.

Despite their inadequacies, the new apologetic theories have profoundly affected policy, because they provide an intellectual rationale for the agenda of the powerful. ❑

Sources: "Competition Policy in America: The Anti-Antitrust Paradox," James Brock, *Antitrust Bulletin*, Summer 1997; "The Promotional-Financial Dynamic of Merger Movements: A Historical Perspective," Richard DuBoff and Edward Herman, *Journal of Economic Issues*, March 1989; "Antimerger Policy in the United States: History and Lessons," Dennis C. Mueller, *Empirica*, 1996; "Dim Prospects: effective competition in telecommunications, railroads and electricity," William Shepherd, *Antitrust Bulletin*, 1997.

Article 5.3

HOPSOPOLY
Global beer mergers reach a new level.

BY ROB LARSON
January/February 2017

When major beer label Budweiser announced that they would rename their product "America" through the 2016 U.S. election, it raised droll hackles from a variety of observers. George Will suggested in the conservative *National Review* that the beer was less than fully American because it was produced by a foreign-owned firm, an irony also observed in the more liberal *Washington Post*. John Oliver's HBO staff did what most US media did in 2016, and took the opportunity to give more TV time to the Trump campaign, in this case to mock Trump's taking credit for the name change. Most commenters counted themselves clever for being aware the Bud label is foreign-owned, but all of them missed the real point: It's not that "America" is foreign-owned, but that it's owned by a brand-new global semi-monopoly that perfectly represents the power-mongering of neoliberal capitalism.

Macrobrew

There are indeed American men and women who will tell you it broke their hearts when in 2008 Anheuser-Busch was bought by the InBev transnational. InBev is itself a product of the merged Belgian InterBrew giant and the Brazilian conglomerate AmBev, as Barry Lynn reviews in his book on market concentration, *Cornered*. Lynn observes that this merger, along with 2007's union of Miller and Coors under South African Breweries' control, meant that beer-loving America was subject to corporate decisions made further and further away, and thus "basically reduced to reliance on a world-bestriding beer duopoly, run not out of Milwaukee or St. Louis but out of Leuven, Belgium, and Johannesburg, South Africa."

And now, just Belgium! Unmentioned in any of the recent rash of commentary was that "America's" owner AB InBev itself announced this year a $108 billion purchase of SAB Miller, which together would sell about 30% of the world's beer, including 45% of total beer sales in the United States. The merger would create a "New World of Beer" in which AB InBev will have "operations across multiple continents and a host of countries," as the business press described it. The *Financial Times* projected that the combined global giant is expected "to control almost half the industry's total profits." SAB Miller will also benefit from bringing its operations under AB InBev's umbrella, since the latter pays an incredibly low effective tax rate in its Belgian corporate home, paying well under 1% on its nearly $2 billion profit in 2015.

Of course, regulators have to approve large-scale mergers in each of the many, many countries in which the merged empires do business. The European Union's competition laws, and antitrust law in the United States, are meant to bring legal action against monopolists, or firms planning to merge into something close to one. But in the neoliberal era, a capital fact is the steep drop-off of anti-monopoly suits—the business press has reported that, from Reagan to Obama, the repeated promise to aggressively enforce limits to market concentration "hasn't worked out that way." And indeed, for the proposed hopsopoly the news is so far, so good. In addition to Australia and South Africa, the European Union is set to allow the consolidation, China's Ministry of Commerce okayed the plan and the U.S. Justice Department approved the $100 billion deal, with reservations (see below).

These approvals require certain divestments—sales of pieces of the corporate empires before, or just after, they merge. Such sales can keep market concentration numbers just low enough for regulators to sign off. Yet these deals are so big that the divestments are *themselves* concentrating the market—Molson Coors is buying AB InBev's share of their currently joint-owned MillerCoors for $12 billion. These spun-off assets mean Molson Coors will itself have a 25% share of the U.S. beer market, second only to the new SAB-AB InBev combination. In the same way, Constellation Brands became the third-largest American brewer by buying several beer labels from the Mexican firm Grupo Modelo back in 2013, when InBev was buying it and needed to divest a few brands to appease regulators.

Tapping the Craft Keg

Smaller-batch craft beers produced by independent microbrewers provides limited escape from monopolized beer. Constellation paid a full $1 billion for the California craft brewer Ballast Point, in a move the *Wall Street Journal* suggested "signals that the craft-beer industry, which has a roughly 10% market share in the U.S., has crossed a threshold and become a big business that large brewers expect to continue to grow in the years to come." The growth potential of microbrews is a valuable opportunity for the majors, especially considering that beer's share of total U.S. alcoholic-beverage spending fell in 2015 for the sixth straight year, and not just to its perennial foe—wine—but also to liquor as the craft cocktail trend flourishes. And this is in spite of the industry spending over a billion (yes, billion) dollars annually just on TV ads.

This all means that the future growth center of microbrews is increasingly essential to the industry majors, as are export markets. But the growth hopes for microbrews are dimming. The industry must look fearfully at the slowing growth of craft labels, with a mid-single digit growth rate in 2015–16, down from double digits in previous years. What growth there is, is concentrated in the labels held by the industry giants. Market observers notice that while niche labels are still taking market share from the majors, albeit more slowly, "AB InBev's own U.S. craft portfolio … increased sales 36% in the first half [of 2016]. After a spate of acquisitions, most notably that of Goose Island, AB InBev is the third-largest craft brewer in the country," although that reflects the fragmented, unconcentrated contours of that market segment. The *Journal* notes, "Craft beer accounts for just 1% of the company's total volume," still an important future growth center for what they call "big beer."

That slowing craft growth is having big effects on the markets for beer ingredients, especially hops, the flowering body of the *Humulus lupulus* plant used to give beers their bitter or sweet flavors. Hops suppliers haven't been able to keep up with spiking demand from craft brews for a wide array of obscure varieties, despite a growing proportion of U.S. hops growers producing for small labels since the global brands' hops are now mostly grown in Germany. The slow-growing plant, and the fast-changing demand for particular varieties have limited the ability of hops growers to keep pace, and with the market's own growth now slowing, the fear is rising of an oversupply in the industry if crops are only harvested as demand fades. The very small size of the many craft labels, and their uncertain prospects, means farmers are often resistant to committing their production to obscure microbrewers.

Growth-seeking is also driving the major brewers toward foreign markets, as the *New York Times*' DealBook feature observes that "in China, Anheuser-Busch InBev and SABMiller are betting on premium products," with "the two beer behemoths" buying up large stakes in China's top-selling brands. "Together, the international brewers account for about one-third of the overall beer market in China. As they pursue a merger, given their dominance, Anheuser-Busch InBev and SABMiller are expected to prune their portfolio in China to keep regulators happy," and indeed the popular Snow brand was ultimately sold off to a Chinese state-owned company.

These different growth prospects are all threatened by a gradual worldwide reconsideration of health benefits of modest alcohol consumption. While public health agencies had for years considered small amounts of alcohol to have some health upsides (mostly heart-related), the emerging view is that these benefits are outweighed by health risks, leading to a growing number of health agencies amending their guidance to recommend lower levels of consumption.

Economies of Ale

Scale economies occur when a firm's per-unit costs decrease as the scale of production increases. Typically observed in industries, like manufacturing, that have high up-front costs, economies of scale arise from "spreading" a large starting investment over a growing amount of output. A brewery that cost $10 million to build, and which produces one million cans or bottles in a year, would have a per-unit fixed cost of $10. Producing ten million cans, the per-unit fixed cost is just a dollar per can. The big costs of brewing tanks, sturdy equipment for mixing the ground grains and the flavorful hops, the cost of the actual brewery structure itself—all add to a brewery's starting investment and create the potential for scale economies.

Economies of scale are usually observed at the plant or factory level, but can also arise at higher levels of operation, including in administration. For example, two large companies may merge and then lay off one of their human resources departments, if one computerized HR office can handle all the employees at the new, merged firm. But these returns to scale, associated with a higher level of market concentration, are often counterbalanced by increasing layers of corporate bureaucracy and the challenges of managing large commercial empires.

So returns to scale constitute strong incentives for firms to grow, both in dollar terms and in market share, gaining scale and profitability. They do have limits, but once firms have reached large and cost-efficient sizes they are often happy to go on growing or merging, in order to gain more market power. The result is that in many industries, from the manufacturing sector to telecommunications to financial services, rich competitive markets give way over time to other market structures, including the few large companies of an oligopoly or the single colossal monopolist.

As with other industries, from tobacco to chemicals, the industry is pushing back in significant part by getting directly involved in the research process. A former cigarette-industry executive now working for booze giant Diageo claimed in the press that a study critical of alcohol advertising was "junk science" and said, "We push back when there are dumb studies." This raises again the prospect of "science capture," the growing phenomenon of private entities with a material interest attempting to influence the scientific process. Indeed, some are funding their own research, the findings of which unsurprisingly support the economic activity of the industry doing the funding.

High-Proof Political Economy

The corporate beer empires aren't shy about using their newly enlarged market power, either. *Cornered* author Barry Lynn recounts a classic episode in which Anheuser-Busch targeted Boston Beer, the owner of Sam Adams:

For reasons still not entirely clear, the giant firm unleashed a devastating, multifront assault by armies of lawyers, lobbyists, and marketers who accused Boston Beer (to the government and to the public through the media) of deceptive packaging. Anheuser-Busch then followed up with an even more devastating second assault, in which it locked Boston Beer products out of the immensely powerful distribution networks that it controls. Ultimately, an arbitrator rejected all of the megafirm's contentions, and Boston Beer survived to brew another day, but the company, less than 1% the size of Anheuser-Busch, was left on the verge of bankruptcy.

Boston Beer remains the second-largest U.S. craft brewer, but the industry has not forgotten this power play.

And today's even-bigger corporations are brewing up new retail-level strategies. The *Journal* reports that AB InBev had planned to "offer some independent distributors in the U.S. annual reimbursements of as much as $1.5 million if 98% of the beers they sell are AB InBev brands." The money would come in the form of the conglomerate footing the bill for distributors' share of marketing costs, like displays at the retail level. The move has craft brewers crying foul, and understandably, since it leaves independents with a pitifully small fraction of store display space and promotion dollars left for them to fight over. The incentive plan also requires that distributors only carry craft brewers that operate below certain low thresholds of annual production, which most do.

The importance of this corporate proposal lies in the middle-man layer of the industry, created by state laws at the end of Prohibition. Beer brewers must sell their output to distributors, who then sell it on to the retailers where you pick up a six-pack. While there are hundreds of distributors in the United States, most are under agreement to sell exclusively either product from AB InBev or MillerCoors. But in addition to deals like these, the beer manufacturers are also able to buy and operate their own distributors—the state of California is investigating AB InBev after it bought two distributors in the state, with concerns about the giant declining to carry independent micros. The company presently owns 21 distributors in the United States and has further used its gigantic revenues to continue buying up independent brewers like Goose Island—now part of the global company and thus available to AB InBev's distributors—on its terms.

Raise a Glass

Popular opposition to the megamerger has been scattered, in a year punctuated by billion-dollar mergers in agriculture, chemicals, insurance, and drugs. In South Africa, a market important enough to require merger clearance as a condition of the deal (and the "SA" in "SABMiller"), a labor union objected to the deal's terms. Among those terms are rules covering a 2010 issue of SAB shares to workers and retailers, which would have matured in 2020. The union membership prefers to "cash out" earlier, or be granted an up-front payment in addition to the existing shares. Labor opposition to market concentration is always notable, although this case revolves more around the treatment of the workforce on a quite specific compensation issue, rather than an objection to capital accumulation in general.

The ultimate approval of the merger by the South Africa's Competition Tribunal was significantly a foregone conclusion. As *Bloomberg* observes, South Africa's bond rating has been downgraded, reflecting world investor fear of policy changes not to their advantage. This meant that the country's leader, President Jacob Zuma of the African National Congress (ANC), was especially eager to approve the megadeal, all the more after recent poor showings for the ANC in local races. This led to unusually prompt action by Zuma—*Bloomberg* noted in March 2016 that "SABMiller itself is still waiting for approval to merge its African soft-drink bottling assets, 15 months after it filed the request."

A number of other unions represent organized brewery workers in the United States, including the Machinists, the Operating Engineers, the Auto Workers, and the International Brotherhood of Teamsters (IBT). The IBT lodged an objection to a particular feature of the deal, writing a letter to the Attorney General requesting antitrust scrutiny of the related closure of the "megabrewery" operated by MillerCoors in Eden, N.C. While MillerCoors is to be sold to Molson as part of the deal, the closure does affect the market significantly, particularly since the huge facility produces 4% of all U.S. beer output, making the reduction more than can be compensated for at other facilities. This significant tightening of supply raised the question of antitrust violation to the IBT, due both to the further concentration of the market but also to the fact that the facility was essential for rival brewer Pabst, which for years has not brewed its own hipster swill but has had it produced by Miller under contract at the Eden brewery. Miller had previously indicated it has no interest in maintaining the deal past its expiration. The U.S. legal settlement appears to make no mention of this issue, but Pabst is now suing Miller over the terms of their brewing agreement, and the IBT lawsuit against Miller continues. For their part, unions from the acquiring company have also been skeptical, noting that the giant corporation has cut its Belgian workforce in half, to just 2,700 over ten years. The *Times* reports, "They also predict that the company will load up on debt to buy SABMiller, leading to pressure for further cutbacks."

Beyond labor, the large and still-growing craft sector of the marketplace has looked with suspicion on industry consolidation for some time and had a clear eye of the stakes, if not typically engaging in action beyond contacting legislators or regulators. The press in brewery-heavy St. Louis describes how craft independents view the deal "warily," as "smaller breweries remain worried a larger A-B InBev will have more influence on what beers retailers stock on their shelves and hamper access to supplies such as hops." They also see influence-building intent behind legislation the corporations have supported, like a bill passed by the Missouri state legislature allowing brewers to lease large commercial coolers to retailers. Craft brewers oppose the governor signing the bill, "arguing only large brewers such as A-B InBev can afford to buy the coolers, which will likely be filled by retailers with A-B brands."

Likewise, industry rag *All About Beer Magazine* has expressed enormous skepticism of not just the new megadeal but the whole history of consolidation in the industry, in the United States and the UK. In a beautiful expression of widespread market-skepticism, Lisa Brown wrote, "This is about a company that has historically used the strategy of controlling and purchasing the wholesale tier of the industry now getting much more influence and potential control of that sector, while also gaining a lot more spending money for lawyers and lobbying."

Reflecting these popular sentiments, the Brewers Association—the industry group representing the many small craft brewers and independent labels—requested significant safeguards from the Department of Justice should the deal clear. It wanted an end to AB InBev's preferential distribution and limits to its "self-

Opiate of the Masses

Fittingly, the first great scholar of capital concentration, Karl Marx, was a product of the beer-loving German people. Marx pioneered the study of capitalism's near-universal gravitational tendency, and for today's economy we have an analytical vocabulary to help understand the growth of capital.

- Concentration of capital, the growth of market share by a few big firms within a market.
- Consolidation, the growth of corporate capital by buying firms in separate industries.
- Capital accumulation, the overall growth in the capital stock of an economy.

Marx wrote in his giant classic study, *Capital*, that "The laws of this centralization of capitals, or of the attraction of capital by capital," depended ultimately on "the scale of production. Therefore, the larger capitals beat the smaller. It will further be remembered that, with the development of the capitalist mode of production, there is an increase in the minimum amount of individual capital necessary to carry on a business under its normal conditions." In other words, fancier technology and more expensive investments make it harder for small brewers to operate at the low costs of established firms.

Many more conservative economists have resisted this conclusion, and insisted that free markets have an enduringly competitive character, even in older industries. Friedrich Hayek, the Austrian economist and one of the conservative world's most revered thinkers, derided the argument that "technological changes have made competition impossible in a constantly increasing number of fields ... This belief derives mainly from the Marxist doctrine of the 'concentration of industry.'"

Marx might reply by raising a glass in toast, filled with amber-hued global corporate beer.

distribution" plans, since influence over distributors gives big brewers an additional potential lever of power over retailers. Evidently the DoJ heard the complaints, because happily for today's craft drinkers the department's allowance of the merger came with numerous conditions on top of the planned divestments, with some directed at these kinds of maneuvers. The department limited AB InBev from enforcing distributor incentive deals (like the one above), and crucially imposed a cap of 10% on the proportion of AB InBev's sales that can be sold through wholly-owned distributors. This is intended to limit the giant's influence over distribution and hopefully reserve shelf space for independent labels.

The agency further put the Big Beer giant under a new requirement to submit for approval all acquisitions of craft beers for the next ten years, benefiting consumers desiring a wider range of brews, and preserving more successful independents from corporate concentration. These requirements, resulting from demands for redress from retailers and craft brewers, do sound satisfyingly stringent. However, the firm retains enormous market power, is strategically positioned to grow in developing markets (especially in Africa), and can be expected to work to undermine or evade these rules in the future. As always, antitrust rules keep oligopoly form maturing into full monopoly, and impose meaningful limits on anticompetitive practices, at least when enforced aggressively. That enforcement tends to ebb and flow however, and it's unclear how the Trump administration will prioritize breaking up giant mergers with its emerging neoliberal shape.

With the worldwide trend for tighter corporate ownership and global oligopoly, it's the investor class that's getting fat off our beer. A more aggressive labor movement of organized malters and brewers, reinforced by irate craft consumers, could resist further job cuts and demand bolder regulatory roadblocks to this consolidation. Or better yet, rather than choosing your poison between super-concentrated markets or moderately concentrated ones, an incensed and tipsy anticapitalist movement could take over these global giants' facilities and brew the beers themselves.

There are few consumers who enjoy shop-talk about their personal favorites more than beer drinkers, providing a natural opportunity for sharing this and other episodes of capitalist globalization. Raising consciousness about capitalism's predations, even in beer, could encourage a movement to socialize brewing. In a democratically managed economic system, the freewheeling ethos of the microbrew movement would be free to flourish without being blackballed out of the market by the majors, or bought out if they manage to succeed.

Now *that* would be a happy hour! ❑

Sources: Tripp Mickle, "Budweiser to Rebrand Beer to America Through Elections," *Wall Street Journal*, May 11, 2016 (wsj.com); George Will, "This Bud's for You, America," *National Review*, May 18, 2016; Travis M. Andrews, "Budweiser seeks approval to be called 'America' this summer," *Washington Post*, May 10, 2015 (washingtonpost.com); Tripp Mickle and Saabira Chaudhuriab, "InBev's SABMiller Deal Still Faces Hurdles," *Wall Street Journal*, Nov. 11, 2015; Barry Lynn, *Cornered: The New Monopoly Capitalism and the Economics of Destruction* (John Wiley & Sons, 2009); James Fontanella-Khan and Patti Waldmeir, "China brewer sale clears path to AB InBev's £71bn SABMiller deal," *Financial Times*, March 2, 2016 (ft.com); James Kanter, "Anheuser-Musch InBev Aims Its Tax-Trimming Skills at SABMiller," *New York Times*, Oct. 19, 2015 (nytimes.com);

Leonard Silk, "Economic Scene; Antitrust Issues Facing Reagan," *New York Times*, Feb. 13, 1981; Brent Kendall, "Justice Department Doesn't Deliver on Promise to Attack Monopolies," *Wall Street Journal*, Nov. 7, 2015; Foo Yun Chee and Martinne Geller, "EU regulators to conditionally clear AB Inbev, SABMiller deal," Reuters, May 20, 2016; Tripp Mickle and Saabira Chaudhuriab, "SABMiller Board Backs AB InBev's Higher Offer," *Wall Street Journal*, July 29, 2016; Tripp Mickle and Brent Kendall, "Justice Department Clears AB InBev's Takeover of SABMiller," *Wall Street Journal*, July 20, 2016; Gina Chon and Scheherazade Daneshkhu, "AB InBev-SABMiller merger critics in US seek concessions," *Financial Times*, Dec. 8, 2015; Tripp Mickle, "Constellation Brands to Buy Craft-Beer Maker for $1 Billion," *Wall Street Journal*, Nov. 16, 2015; Tripp Mickle, "Cocktails Sip Away at Beer's Market Share," *Wall Street Journal*, Feb. 15, 2016; Nathalie Tadena, "Bud Light is a Heavier TV Ad Spender than its Peers," *Wall Street Journal* CMO TOday blog, May 22, 2014; Trefis Team, "Does The Declining U.S. Beer Trend Spell Doom For Brewers?," *Forbes*, June 29, 2015 (forbes.com); Stephen Wilmot, "Why Craft Brewing Slowdown Won't Benefit Big Beer," *Wall Street Journal*, Aug. 26, 2016; Tripp Mickle, "Trouble Brewing in the Craft Beer Industry," *Wall Street Journal*, Sept. 27, 2016; Amie Tsang and Cao Li, "China embraces Craft Beers, and Brewing Giants Take Notice," Dealbook, *New York Times*, Jan. 15, 2016; Justin Scheck and Tripp Mickle, "With Moderate Drinking Under Fire, Alcohol Companies Go on Offensive," *Wall Street Journal*, Aug. 22, 2016; Tripp Mickle, "Craft Brewers Take Issue With AB InBev Distribution Plan," *Wall Street Journal*, Dec. 7, 2015; Tripp Mickle, "Anheuser Says Regulators Have Questioned Pending Distributor Buyouts," *Wall Street Journal*, Oct. 12, 2015; Tripp Mickle, "AB InBev Defends SABMiller Buy to Senate," *Wall Street Journal*, Dec. 8, 2015; Tripp Mickle, "AB InBev Facing Union Opposition to SABMiller Acquisition," *Wall Street Journal*, June 3, 2016; Janice Kew, "Zuma Appeal to Business Bodes Well for AB InBev-SAB Beer Merger," Bloomberg News, March 15, 2016; James P. Hoffa, president, International Brotherhood of Teamsters, letter to U.S. Attorney General Loretta Lynch, June 6, 2016 (teamster.org); Bruce Vielmetti, "Historic brewing names Pabst, MillerCoors locked in legal battle," (Milwaukee) *Journal Sentinel*, May 5, 2016 (jsonline.com); Lisa Brown, "Craft brewers eye merger of A-B InBev and SABMiller warily," *St. Louis Post-Dispatch*, June 26, 2016 (stltoday.com); Lew Bryson, "Mega-Merger? How About No?," *All About Beer Magazine*, May 17, 2016; Brewers Association press release, "Brewers Association Statement on AB InBev Acquisition of SABMiller," July 20, 2016; U.S. District Court for the District of Columbia, United States of America v. Anheuser-Busch InBev SA/NV, and SABMiller plc, July 20, 2016; Karl Marx, *Capital*, vol. 1, ch. 25 (1867); Friedrich Hayek, *The Road to Serfdom* (1944).

Article 5.4

MONOPOLY CAPITAL AND GLOBAL COMPETITION

BY ARTHUR MacEWAN
September/October 2011

Dear Dr. Dollar:
Is the concept of monopoly capital relevant today, considering such things as global competition?
—Paul Tracy, Oceanside, Calif.

In 1960, the largest 100 firms on *Fortune* magazine's "annual ranking of America's largest corporations" accounted for 15% of corporate profits and had revenues that were 24% as large as GDP. By the early 2000s, each of these figures had roughly doubled: the top 100 firms accounted for about 30% of corporate profits and their revenues were over 40% as large as GDP.*

The banking industry is a prime example of what has been going on: In 2007 the top ten banks were holding over 50% of industry assets, compared with about 25% in 1985.

If by "monopoly capital" we mean that a relatively small number of huge firms play a disproportionately large role in our economic lives, then monopoly capital is a relevant concept today, even more so than a few decades ago.

Global competition has certainly played a role in reshaping aspects of the economy, but it has not altered the importance of very large firms. Even while, for example, Toyota and Honda have gained a substantial share of the U.S. and world auto markets, this does not change the fact that a small number of firms dominate the U.S. and world markets. Moreover, much of the rise in imports, which looks like competition, is not competition for the large U.S. firms themselves. General Motors, for example, has established parts suppliers in Mexico, allowing the company to pay lower wages and hire fewer workers in the states. And Wal-Mart, Target, and other large retailers obtain low-cost goods from sub-contractors in China and elsewhere.

Economics textbooks tell us that in markets dominated by a few large firms, prices will be higher than would otherwise be the case. This has generally been true of the auto industry. Also, this appears to be the case in pharmaceuticals, telecommunications, and several other industries.

Wal-Mart and other "big box" stores, however, often do compete by offering very low prices. They are monopsonistic (few buyers) as well as monopolistic (few sellers). They use their power to force down both their payments to suppliers and the wages of their workers. In either case—high prices or low prices—large firms are exercising their market power to shift income to themselves from the rest of us.

Beyond their operation within markets, the very large firms shift income to themselves by shaping markets. Advertising is important in this regard, including, for example, the way pharmaceutical firms effectively create "needs" in pushing their products. Then there is the power of large firms in the political sphere. General

Electric, for example, maintains huge legal and lobbying departments that are able to affect and use tax laws to reduce the firm's tax liability to virtually nothing. Or consider the success of the large banks in shaping (or eliminating) financial regulation, or the accomplishments of the huge oil companies and the military contractors that establish government policies, sometimes as direct subsidies, and thus raise their profits. And the list goes on.

None of this is to say that everything was fine in earlier decades when large firms were less dominant. Yet, as monopoly capital has become more entrenched, it has generated increasingly negative outcomes for the rest of us. Most obvious are the stagnant wages and rising income inequality of recent years. The power of the large firms (e.g., Wal-Mart) to hold down wages is an important part of the story. Then there is the current crisis of the U.S. economy—directly a result of the way the very large financial firms were able to shape their industry (deregulation). Large firms in general have been prime movers over recent decades in generating deregulation and the free-market ideology that supports deregulation.

So, yes, monopoly capital is still quite relevant. Globalization does make differences in our lives, but globalization has in large part been constructed under the influence and in the interest of the very large firms. In many ways globalization makes the concept of monopoly capital even more relevant. ❏

* The profits of the top 100 firms (ranked by revenue) were quite low in 2010, back near the same 15% of total profits as in 1960, because of huge losses connected to the financial crisis incurred by some of the largest firms. Fannie Mae, Freddie Mac, and AIG accounted for combined losses of over $100 billion. Also, the revenues of all firms are not the same as GDP; much of the former is sales of intermediate products, but only sales of final products are included in GDP. Thus, the largest firms' revenues, while 40% as large as GDP, do not constitute 40% of GDP.

Article 5.5

NO FRIENDSHIP IN TRADE
Farmers face modern-day robber barons, in the United States and worldwide.

BY SASHA BREGER BUSH
Mach/April 2015

Presiding over monopolies in shipping and railroads, U.S. robber baron Cornelius Vanderbilt once said that "there is no friendship in trade." During the 19th century, railroad magnates like Vanderbilt used their concentrated power to increase the price of freight, creating financial hardships for farmers who needed to ship their produce. Likewise, bankers like J.P. Morgan squeezed farmers, who were reliant on credit to get through the growing season, with high interest rates. By the latter part of the century, farmers "found the prices for their produce going down, and the prices of transportation and loans going up," wrote historian Howard Zinn, "because the individual farmer could not control the price of his grain, while the monopolist railroad and the monopolist banker could charge what they liked." The market dynamics set in motion by the robber barons ushered in decades of conflict between farmers and the railroad magnates, motivating populist movements and calls for government regulation of monopolies.

Biographer T.J. Stiles notes that a "blood-chilling ruthlessness infused all [of Vanderbilt's] actions." He continues, "Although Vanderbilt habitually dressed in the simple black-and-white outfit of a Protestant clergyman, his only religion was economic power." This religion of economic power is alive and well in today's global food system and farmers trade with the new robber barons of the global food system at their peril.

The small farmers and laborers who grow and process most of the world's food—who provide one of the few things we cannot live without—are themselves often hungry and poor. That is the simple, central paradox of the global food system.

Much of the explanation for this state of affairs focuses on processes of "unequal exchange." Unequal exchange results from trading relationships between parties with unequal levels of power, between powerful monopolies on the one hand and people who struggle in more competitive markets on the other. Unequal exchange is a mechanism for *exploitation* in the food system; that is, it siphons wealth away from farmers and workers and enriches multinational food and finance corporations.

Power, Inequality, and Unequal Exchange

Beginning in the 16th century, colonization, industrialization, and globalization have worked to undermine locally self-sufficient systems of food production, gradually replacing them with a system of global food interdependence. In this new system, food production, processing, distribution, and consumption are divided up among lots of different people and communities performing different food-related tasks, often in different parts of the world. In other words, there is now a "global division of labor" in food, and the people within this division of labor (who, these days, represent most of the global population) are dependent upon one another for the food they need to survive.

This new system is hierarchically ordered, with large multinational food and agriculture corporations controlling many aspects of production, processing, distribution, and consumption. Multi-national corporations' (MNCs) dominance over the global food system owes in large part to their *market power*. "Market power" refers to a firm's ability to influence the terms of trade—such as prices, but also quality and production standards—in a given market.

Today's food monopolies have consolidated their power thanks both to changes in national and international laws and regulations and to the policies of international institutions like the World Trade Organization (WTO), World Bank, and International Monetary Fund (IMF), among others. Of course, the capital- and technology-intensive nature of food processing, distribution, and retail these days—a key part of the process of food industrialization—also results in high barriers to entry in these markets. These barriers reduce competition for companies in the food industry.

The global food system is riddled with monopolistic markets, markets in which, on one side, stand only one or a few multinational corporate juggernauts, while on the other side there are many people jockeying for position. Inequalities in market power are magnified by geographical inequalities (e.g., between the global North and the global South), gender inequalities, racial inequalities, and inequalities in standards of living.

The U.S. Poultry Economy

The U.S. poultry chain, depicted opposite, is a good example. In the United States, three companies—Tyson, Perdue, and Pilgrim's Pride—control more than 50% of the market in broiler chickens. These large, industrial poultry companies are called "integrators," a reference to the "vertically integrated" poultry chain where big companies own and control almost every stage of the poultry production process. One recent commentator notes: "In fundamental ways, the meat business has returned to the state where it was 100 years ago, a time when just four companies controlled the market with a shared monopoly."

Poultry producers working in Arkansas, Mississippi, Georgia, or Kentucky compete with one another like dogs for scraps from the integrator's table, and thus end up with low incomes, low standards of living, and large debts. Poultry producers are largely "contract growers," meaning that they produce at the behest of the integrators and must accept whatever price the integrators offer for their chickens. In fact, the chickens themselves are actually owned by the integrator, with the "integrated out growers" (poultry producers) owning only the expensive chicken houses that chicks are raised in. The chicken houses are often purchased from the integrators on credit, burdening producers with large debts. Poultry producers also risk injury on the job, income losses associated with dead birds, antibiotic resistance and allergy (stemming from their regular contact with the antibiotics used to treat sick birds), among other serious risks. While the most risky and costly stage of the process—growing out the birds—is left to poultry producers, the integrators enjoy absolute control, massive profits and minimal competition in virtually every other stage of production. The integrators even operate under a "gentlemen's agreement" of sorts, with each integrator agreeing not to employ the growers contracted by the others, limiting competition among integrators and constraining poultry producers even further.

This trading relationship—between monopolistic integrators on the one hand and poultry producers facing high competition, serious risk, and large production costs on the other—is a stark example of unequal exchange and has concrete implications for the well-being of producers.

In an interview with the *American Prospect* magazine, Mike Weaver, who heads up a West Virginia poultry producer association, describes the tenuous financial position of producers in the United States. Weaver notes that "chicken farmers in his area are settling for almost an entire cent less per pound of meat *than they did in 1975*—when the median household income [in the United States] was around

---

Held Up: The Life of a Poultry Farmer

By Craig Watts

In December 1991, I signed a contract to raise chickens for one to the country's largest integrators. I was three years out of business school, where I had been introduced to the term "economic holdup." Little did I know that when I signed that contract I would begin to live this concept each and every day.

The term refers to a situation where two parties (in my case a farmer and an integrator) may be able to work most efficiently by cooperating, but refrain from doing so due to concerns that they may give the other party increased bargaining power, and thereby reduce their own profits. In my contract with my integrator, I have no bargaining power.

To get started, I borrowed approximately $200,000 to construct two poultry houses, following the specifications required by the integrator. Initially, all went well and in 1994 I borrowed another $200,000 to build two more houses. At that time, I was also forced to borrow an additional $40,000 to bring my older houses up to the specs of the new houses. The industry term is "upgrades." Upgrades can be additional equipment and/or changes to the structures themselves, as required by the integrator.

In the initial recruitment pitch, the integrator presented a rosy picture: that the poultry houses would provide a steady and primary income. They said I'd have the chicken houses paid off in ten years. None of these claims have proven to be true. I see it time and again: farmers are constantly forced to upgrade their facilities, with no rhyme or reason or any cost-benefit documentation, just more and more debt.

The snag is that if you don't upgrade, the company will terminate your contract. The holdup problem rears its head. Debt eliminates any bargaining power for the farmer. When the first upgrades were pushed on my operation, I was $400,000 in debt with one choice: lose my contract or make the upgrades and take on more debt.

In the fall of 2004, I actually paid my farm off. I had no mortgage payment for two years. But relief was short-lived: in 2006, the company began a major push for upgrades. Rumor was they were giving their service techs bonuses based on how much a farmer spent for upgrades. I had to borrow another $100,000.

Twenty-two years after I began as a contract poultry producer, my income is less than it was 15 years ago. Adjust that for inflation and you quickly realize if your poultry operation is treading water, then you're one of the lucky ones. Meanwhile, consumers are paying more at the grocery store and the industry is enjoying windfall profits.

$11,800. ... The number of companies buying livestock from farmers has declined, and the surviving companies have grown bigger by acquiring the smaller firms. For growers, that often means doing business with only one firm. ..."

The inequalities and injustices apparent in the poultry chain are replicated within the corporate hierarchy of integrators like Tyson: there is a dangerous division of labor between those who must compete to survive and those who do not need to do so. Highly paid executives, who are engaged in management work and are secure in their positions, lord over low-paid, interchangeable employees who work with their hands capturing chickens one-by-one at night in the chicken houses or performing dangerous work in slaughterhouses. Most of these managers are white men, while many of the workers that actually capture and slaughter the chickens are people of color, often with insecure immigration status. The Food Empowerment Project notes that workers in meat processing are mostly people of color from low-income communities. Historically populated by African Americans, this workforce has recently witnessed an influx of Latin American workers, with some 38% of workers in meat processing today hailing from outside of the United States.

The Global Coffee Economy

The power dynamics, inequalities and unequal exchanges apparent in the U.S. poultry chain are replicated in a variety of global food production systems. Take, for example, the diagram below of the global coffee economy, a chain connecting different parts of the global division of coffee labor to one another, taking us downstream from the green coffees harvested in the field by farmers, through various traders and processors, to the cups of roasted coffee consumed by final consumers.

The diagram illustrates how the global coffee economy operates and the severe inequalities that characterize it. International traders and roasters operate in a very uncompetitive market setting—they are monopolists. The six largest coffee trading

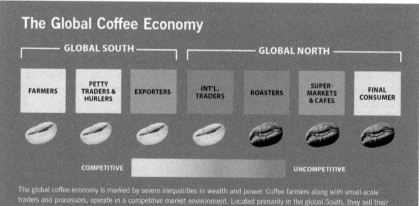

The Global Coffee Economy

GLOBAL SOUTH — GLOBAL NORTH

FARMERS | PETTY TRADERS & HURLERS | EXPORTERS | INT'L. TRADERS | ROASTERS | SUPER-MARKETS & CAFES | FINAL CONSUMER

COMPETITIVE _____ UNCOMPETITIVE

The global coffee economy is marked by severe inequalities in wealth and power. Coffee farmers along with small-scale traders and processors, operate in a competitive market environment. Located primarily in the global South, they sell their coffees onward, down the supply chain, to international traders and roasters. The traders and roasters operate in a relatively uncompetitive market environment and are located primarily in the global North. These inequalities in market power result in lower standards of living for coffee farmers and other marginalized actors in producing countries. Consumers (most of whom are from the global North) also have little negotiating power, when it comes to purchasing coffee from big retailers (supermarkets and corporate café chains like Starbucks). By contrast, the northern monopolies in trading, roasting, and retail earn high profits associated with their disproportionate market power. Monopolists thus push prices for growers down and prices for consumers up, capturing the super-profits generated in between.

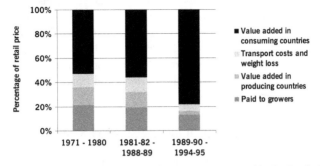

DISTRIBUTION OF INCOME IN THE GLOBAL COFFEE ECONOMY (% OF INCOME)

Source: John M. Talbot, "Where Does Your Coffee Dollar Go? The Division of Income and Surplus along the Coffee Commodity Chain," Studies in Comparative International Development, Vol. 32, No. 1 (1997), Tables 1 and 2.

Note: Data for 1971–1980 are for calendar years. Data for 1981–82 to 1988–89 and for 1989–90 to 1994–95 are for "coffee years" (Oct. 1–Sept. 30). Percentages of total retail price (reported by Talbot (1997)) for calendar years (1971–1980) or coffee years (1981–82 to 1988–89 and 1989–90 to 1994–95) were used to calculate means for intervals shown. Figures calculated did not add exactly to 100.0% due to rounding (in all cases between 99.9% and 100%). Bar graphs show each income category as percentage of sum of four income categories.

companies control over 50% of the marketplace at the trading step along the coffee chain (Neumann Kaffee Gruppe from Germany and ED&F Man based in London are the largest international traders). The roasting stage of coffee production is even more concentrated, with only two companies (Nestle and Phillip Morris) controlling almost 50% of the market. Market power gives these modern-day robber barons influence over prices and other terms of trade, allowing them to place downward pressure on prices they pay to farmers, and upward pressure on the prices they charge to consumers.

This inequality in market power introduces inequalities in incomes and standards of living between different actors in the coffee economy. Unsurprisingly, farmers operating in the shadow of the big traders and roasters have relatively low incomes and standards of living. By contrast, owners, managers, and some workers at the big coffee monopolies enjoy relatively high incomes and standards of living. There are also race and gender dimensions to consider: coffee farmers are disproportionately women of color, while owners and managers in the big coffee monopolies are generally white men. There is also a strong North-South dimension to this power inequality—coffee farmers from Latin America, Africa, and Asia compete fiercely with one another, their incomes undermined by the pricing power of monopolies headquartered in Europe and the United States.

Twenty-five million coffee farming families from Latin America, sub-Saharan Africa, South Asia, and Southeast Asia compete globally with one another to sell coffee to a handful of international coffee trading companies. Similar to the situation of poultry producers, there are in practice usually only one or two potential buyers for a farmer's coffee crop. Lacking the transport and information resources to effectively market their crops, many coffee farmers sell to whoever comes to the farm gate. Unsurprisingly, things do not usually go well for our coffee farmers.

The graph illustrates the distribution of income in the global coffee economy. Only a small percentage of total income is retained by those—growers, small-scale traders who transport coffee from the farm gate, and petty processors who transform dried coffee cherries into green beans in producing countries—who operate in competitive markets. Most of the income is appropriated in consuming countries, mainly by the coffee monopolists in trading and roasting, but also by large retailers (e.g., supermarkets and corporate café chains like Starbucks). The position of coffee growers deteriorated between the 1970s and 1990s. Expanded global trade in coffee since the late 1980s, with "free trade" increasing the market leverage of multinational traders and roasters over coffee farmers and final consumers, has led to decreasing relative income of growers.

Promoting Justice and Equity in the Global Food System

As the coffee and chicken examples suggest, unequal exchange is commonplace between farmers and producers on the one hand, and multinational, monopolistic middlemen (food traders, processors, and supermarkets) on the other. While larger corporate coffee farms may have some leverage in negotiating prices with these big middlemen, smaller and peasant farms have virtually no negotiating power. If a coffee farmer does not want to sell to the Neumann Kaffee Gruppe (NKG) at the price NKG offers, then NKG will simply move on until it finds a farmer who will. Similarly, if a poultry producer does not want to sell to Tyson at the company's offered price, the producer risks being cut out of the chain all together. Tyson will just move on to the next farm. In both cases, the market power of the monopolists also allows them to set conditions such as product quality and the specific technologies used in the production process. The same basic relationship holds for cattle ranchers and cocoa farmers selling to Cargill, pork producers selling to Smithfield (now owned by the China-headquartered WH Group), soy farmers selling to Archer Daniels Midland, vegetable producers selling to Walmart and Tesco, and orange producers selling to Coca-Cola Co. (to make Fanta Orange and Minute Maid juices), among many other global examples.

The Farmer and the Supplier

Unequal exchange is also common for farmers looking to purchase supplies for their businesses. In conventional farming systems, farmers and livestock growers regularly purchase seeds, young animals, feed, pesticides, or fertilizers from large multinational corporations like Tyson, Monsanto, and Cargill. In this unequal exchange, multinational giants charge farmers small fortunes for the supplies they need.

The farmers receive overpriced goods that often fail to work as advertised. In the case of expensive genetically modified seeds, farmers often end up with lower-than-promised yields and rising costs for fertilizers, pesticides, and water. Fertilizers and pesticides, for their part, erode the long-term health of the soil and increase irrigation requirements. Worse still, as farmers rack up these huge input costs, the prices that international traders offer them for their crop often fails to cover the rising costs of production. Farmers are thus "squeezed" between two monopolies, with unequal exchange ensuring that farmers pay too much for their inputs and receive too little for their crop. This trading mechanism thus works to rob especially small and peasant farmers of wealth and redistributes it to the monopolies.

The outcome for farmers is bleak and frequently results in rising debt. In India, the debts that result from this financial squeeze have led more than 200,000 peasant farmers to commit suicide, according to author Vandana Shiva. Agricultural laborers in rural areas also often suffer in this context, as temporary workers are laid off by small farmers experiencing hardship.

Unequal exchange helps to explain inequalities in wealth and power in the global food system, and how trade relationships work to facilitate exploitation—the unjust redistribution of wealth from people with less to people with more market power, from poor to rich, from black and brown to white, from women to men, from the global South to the global North. In answer to the question posed at the outset—how is it that the people who produce our food are themselves so often poor and hungry?—I answer simply: Because they engage in unequal exchange with powerful food monopolies, and there is no friendship in this trade.

A variety of policies, programs, and alternatives could help to make the global food system more equitable and fair. These include, but are certainly not limited to, anti-trust enforcement, public commodity price management, and producer unionization. In 1890, the U.S. Congress passed the Sherman Anti-Trust Act, a piece of legislation aimed at breaking up some of the large monopolies that dominated the U.S. economy at the time. Among the targets of the new anti-trust enforcers were the big meatpackers. The Supreme Court's 1905 decision in *Swift & Co. v. United States* found the Chicago "meat trust" to be engaging in price-fixing for meat and shipping rates. The case set the stage for more stringent government regulation of monopolies. Since the early 1980s, starting with the Reagan administration, anti-trust enforcement in the U.S. has waned. According to Barry Lynn, the author of *Cornered: The New Monopoly Capitalism and the Economics of Destruction*, this is partly due to increasingly pro-big business ideologies and political interests of public officials, like Reagan. Yet, the Sherman Act remains on the books and could be revived as a tool to break up the new meat trusts in the U.S. food system.

Historically, governments have also intervened in food markets to set and stabilize prices. While the system was not perfect, the International Coffee Agreement that regulated global coffee trading from 1962 to 1989 did indeed help many coffee farmers obtain better prices for their crops. A system of import and export quotas at the international level was complemented by public institutions at the national level that were responsible for purchasing coffee from producers at fixed prices and then exporting the coffee into the global market according to the quota arrangement. While the system was a mechanism for exploiting farmers in some cases (as in Uganda in the 1970s), in other cases (like in Mexico) public commodity price management helped farmers earn more money and stabilize their incomes. With the eruption of the global food crisis in 2006–7, global interest in such institutions has been revived, perhaps creating a political opening for new public price management programs.

As with most economic cases in which individuals are overpowered by large companies—be they integrators, coffee roasters, or employers—organization and unionization can help them increase their market leverage and bargaining power. In Colombia, some three quarters of the country's coffee farmers are organized under the umbrella of a single union. The union advocates for farmers in various political forums, and negotiates coffee prices with exporters and traders, often securing higher prices for farmers than they could obtain on their own. Support for such organizations, as well as related farmer cooperatives and producer associations, could help to empower and organize producers.

Such policies and programs are not mutually exclusive. Further, anti-trust enforcement, public price management, and producer unionization could be complemented by a wide variety of other mechanisms for promoting justice and equity in the global food system. For example, programs that support national and local food self-sufficiency, crop and income diversification, and organic farming techniques can potentially reduce producer reliance on global monopolists for income, financing and production inputs, among many other benefits. ❏

Sources: Oscar Farfan, "Understanding and Escaping Commodity Dependency: A Global Value Chain Perspective," World Bank, 2005; Food Empowerment Project, "Slaughterhouse Workers," Food Empowerment Project, 2015 (foodispower.org); Michael Kazin, "Ruthless in Manhattan," *New York Times*, May 7, 2009; Christopher Leonard, "How the Meat Industry Keeps Chicken Prices High," March 3, 2014 (slate.com); Barry Lynn, "Killing the Competition: How the New Monopolies are Destroying Open Markets," *Harper's Magazine,* February 2012; National Chicken Council, "Vertical Integration," 2015 (nationalchickencouncil.org); Stefano Ponte, "The Latte Revolution," *World Development*, 2002; Monica Potts, "The Serfs of Arkansas," *The American Prospect*, March 5, 2011; Vandana Shiva, "From Seeds of Suicide to Seeds of Hope," Huffington Post, May 29, 2009; Howard Zinn, *A People's History of the United States* (Harper, 2005).

Article 5.6

FACEBOOK: THE SORRY COMPANY

BY DEAN BAKER
April 2018; Center for Economic and Policy Research

Earlier this month, Facebook CEO Mark Zuckerberg apologized to Congress for allowing improper access to the data of tens of millions of Facebook users. This was just one of a long sequence of apologies that Zuckerberg has made for this and other failures of the social media giant.

Given this track record, it's probably will not be the last apology that Zuckerberg has to make for his company. It is long past time for Congress to take action so that Zuckerberg does not have to keep asking for our forgiveness. There are several simple steps the government can take to help him and his company in this area.

The first is to try to give Zuckerberg some competition. Facebook has an effective monopoly on the sort of social media platform it provides with no competitor having a reach that is even within an order of magnitude of Facebook's. In fact, when Zuckerberg was asked during his testimony who his competitors were he stumbled blindly and eventually suggested email.

The government can certainly force the company to end its practice of buying up potential competitors. In the last decade Facebook bought up both Instagram and WhatsApp, with the explicit purpose of eliminating potential competition. This is pretty much a textbook violation of anti-trust law in the United States, but the Obama administration chose to look the other way.

In addition to preventing Facebook from buying up potential competitors, the government can also prevent the company from using its near monopoly as a way to ply its way into new markets. This was the initial remedy proposed by the judge when Microsoft lost an antitrust case in the 1990s.

The judge ruled that Microsoft would be able to keep its near monopoly in the computer operating system market, but it would have to break off from its other divisions and would be prohibited from entering new markets. A new judge later reversed this ruling, but it would be a great precedent to apply to Facebook.

The second issue with Facebook is its tendency to pass on news items from phony sources. This turned out to be a big issue in the 2016 presidential campaign. Millions of people received fake news stories that were passed on from phony sources.

The best remedy for this problem would be to follow a practice now used for the enforcement of copyright law. The Digital Millennial Copyright Act (DMCA) requires websites to promptly remove material from their site after they have been notified of the alleged infringing material by the copyright holder. If they fail to do so, the website owner can face thousands of dollars of punitive damages for each act of infringement.

The comparable requirement for Facebook would be that it would have to promptly notify recipients of fake news after it has been called to their attention. If there were punitive penalties for failing to issue corrections that were comparable to those in the DMCA, it would give the company a strong incentive to limit the spread of fake news.

Finally, there is the problem that Zuckerberg was testifying to Congress over, the misuse of personal information that is collected through the system. The best remedy here is one that was suggested by the reporter and columnist David Dayen: simply ban individualized advertising.

As it stands, Facebook's great value is that it can narrowly target advertising based on its extensive knowledge of the interests and habits of its users. It knows what music you like, where you travel, what movies you see. It knows how much you use Facebook and at what times. It also likely knows what you are doing during your downtime from Facebook.

The best way to discourage Facebook and other companies from learning every detail about our lives is to take the money out of it. If they are prohibited from doing individualized marketing, they have no incentive to collect the data.

While Facebook will undoubtedly whine about its free speech rights being violated, it doesn't have much of a case. The courts have long accepted that commercial speech can be regulated; for example, we ban cigarette and alcohol ads from television. A ban on individualized advertising would be in the same vein.

This sort of ban would fundamentally change the Facebook model, but that is not the public's concern. Presumably, Zuckerberg and his team will be able to adapt to the new rules, but if not, that's capitalism.

An advantage of this sort of ban would be to increase the value of traditional advertising. Companies would again value placing ads in newspapers, magazines, or websites that they knew influenced a particular segment of the market. That might not be as cost effective for them as Facebook's individualized targeting, but if such targeting is prohibited, going the old-fashioned route will be the best they can do.

These three measures together will undoubtedly make Facebook a much smaller company. But it will also be a much better company. If such measures get implemented quickly, we might even have seen our last Mark Zuckerberg apology. ❑

Chapter 6

MARKET FAILURE II: EXTERNALITIES

INTRODUCTION

Markets sometimes fail. Mainstream economists typically focus on cases in which existing markets fail to facilitate exchanges that would make both parties better off. When a factory pollutes the air, people downwind suffer a cost. They might be willing to pay the polluter to curb emissions, but there is no market for clean air. In cases like this, one solution is for the government to step in with regulations that ban industries from imposing pollution costs on others. The same goes when private markets do not provide sufficient amounts of public goods, such as vaccines, from which everyone benefits whether they contribute to paying for them or not. Again, government may step in to correct the market failure. But what percentage of pollution should industries be required to eliminate? How much should be spent on public health? To decide how much government should step in, economists propose cost-benefit analysis, suggesting that the government weigh costs against benefits, in much the same way a firm decides how many cars to produce.

Orthodox economists typically see market failures as fairly limited in scope. In fact, they deny that many negative consequences of markets are market failures at all. When workers are paid wages too low to meet their basic needs, economists do not usually call their poverty and overwork market failures, but "incentives" to get a higher-paying job. When economists do recognize market failures, most argue that the problems are best solved by markets themselves. So pollution, for example, should be reduced by allowing firms to trade for the right to pollute. Finally, orthodox economists worry about government failure—the possibility that government responses to market failures may cause more problems than they solve. They conclude that the "invisible hand" of the market works pretty well, and that the alternatives, especially the "visible hand" of the state, will only make matters worse.

In "Pricing the Priceless: Inside the Strange World of Cost-Benefit Analysis" (Article 8.1), Lisa Heinzerling and Frank Ackerman point out key flaws in the use of cost-benefit analysis to guide government action. While weighing the costs of a course of action (like pollution limits) against the benefits has a superficial plausibility, cost-benefit analysis fails to clarify the nature of public choices. It fails, for example, to account for all relevant costs or benefits, it downgrades the importance of the future, and it does not deal with the problem of how costs and benefits are distributed.

In "How Growth Can Be Green" (Article 6.2), an interview with economist Robert Pollin, we discover that we can have both economic growth and a transformation to green-energy technologies. Pollin walks us through the arguments and the numbers behind "green growth."

Jeremy Brecher provides us with yet another antidote to the "either/or" scenario for pursuing a green energy path and meeting our climate commitments ("Jobs, Justice, and the Clean-Energy Future," Article 6.3). According to Brecher, not only is there no tradeoff between jobs and meeting our climate goals, but aggressively pursuing a green-energy path will in fact produce significantly more and better jobs than the jobs that they will be replacing.

In his article "Frackonomics: The Science and Economics of the Gas Boom" (Article 6.4), Rob Larson looks at the environmental impacts of hydraulic fracturing, a controversial new form of natural-gas extraction. He finds harms including everything from toxic pollution to increased seismic instability. Moreover, he argues, these problems are not well dealt with by neoclassical economics' usual prescription of strengthened private-property rights.

Arthur MacEwan's "Is Economic Growth Environmentally Sustainable?" (Article 6.5) asks the very important and timely question of whether we can have both an environmentally sustainable future and economic growth. MacEwan identifies two immediate problems with simply curtailing growth and then suggests solutions going forward.

When it comes to evaluating externalities in the energy sector, nuclear power presents us with some unique long- and short-term costs. Frank Ackerman answers a question about the costs of shutting down nuclear power plants ("Are Nuclear Plant Closures a Mistake?" Article 6.6). Ackerman evaluates Germany's experience with nuclear energy and their change of thinking in their transition to renewable forms of energy. It turns out that decommissioning nuclear power plants is worth it despite the costs.

Finally, in their article "Mapping Environmental Injustice" (Article 6.7), authors Klara Zwickl, Michael Ash, and James K. Boyce remind us that issues of race, class, and the distribution of power in society are never far off, including on environmental issues. They describe how the impacts of toxic air pollution fall along the contours of the American social hierarchy. Poor people tend to have higher exposure than rich people, and people of color tend to have higher exposure than whites.

Discussion Questions

1. (Article 6.1) Heinzerling and Ackerman point out a number of flaws in cost-benefit analysis. These weaknesses suggest that the cost-benefit approach will work better in some situations, worse in others. Describe when you would expect it to work better or worse, and explain.

2. (Article 6.1) Make a list of types of goods that are harder to put a price on (valuate) than others. Why is it so hard to price these types of goods?

3. (Article 6.2) What is "green growth?" Explain the advantages of green growth for developed countries and less developed countries.

4. (Article 6.3) Is there a tradeoff between jobs and achieving our climate goals of reducing greenhouse gasses? Explain Brecher's case for a labor-friendly "green energy policy."

5. (Article 6.4) What are the main harms, in Larson's view, from gas extraction by hydraulic fracturing ("fracking")? What are some possible solutions? Why does Larson doubt the viability of solutions based purely on private property and private legal action?

6. (Article 6.5) What are the two major problems associated with simply curtailing economic growth to reach environmental goals? MacEwan suggests that there are both "technical" and "political" solutions to these two problems. What are these solutions?

7. (Article 6.6) Why is Germany phasing out nuclear energy as part of the country's transition to renewable energy sources? What reasons does Ackerman give for thinking that that nuclear energy doesn't have much of a future?

8. (Article 6.7) Two possible explanations for disparities in environmental conditions along lines of income or race are "selection" and "move-in." "Selection" means that polluting industries make decisions to locate in predominantly low-income or non-white areas. "Move-in" means that people with fewer resources are more likely to move into areas where environmental quality is lower. What do you think of these two explanations? Would your views of "environmental injustice" differ depending on which factor is more important?

Article 6.1

PRICING THE PRICELESS
Inside the Strange World of Cost-Benefit Analysis

BY LISA HEINZERLING AND FRANK ACKERMAN
March/April 2003

How strictly should we regulate arsenic in drinking water? Or carbon dioxide in the atmosphere? Or pesticides in our food? Or oil drilling in scenic places? The list of environmental harms and potential regulatory remedies often appears to be endless. In evaluating a proposed new initiative, how do we know if it is worth doing or not? Is there an objective way to decide how to proceed? Cost-benefit analysis promises to provide the solution—to add up the benefits of a public policy and compare them to the costs.

The costs of protecting health and the environment through pollution control devices and other approaches are, by their very nature, measured in dollars. The other side of the balance—calculating the benefits of life, health, and nature in dollars and cents—is far more problematic. Since there are no natural prices for a healthy environment, cost-benefit analysis creates artificial ones. Researchers, for example, may ask a cross-section of the affected population how much they would pay to preserve or protect something that can't be bought in a store. The average American household is supposedly willing to pay $257 to prevent the extinction of bald eagles, $208 to protect humpback whales, and $80 to protect gray wolves.

Costs and benefits of a policy, however, frequently fall at different times. When the analysis spans a number of years, future costs and benefits are discounted, or treated as equivalent to smaller amounts of money in today's dollars. The case for discounting begins with the observation that money received today is worth a little more than money received in the future. (For example, if the interest rate is 3%, you only need to deposit about $97 today to get $100 next year. Economists would say that, at a 3% discount rate, $100 next year has a present value of $97.) For longer periods of time, or higher discount rates, the effect is magnified. The important issue for environmental policy is whether this logic also applies to outcomes far in the future, and to opportunities—like long life and good health—that are not naturally stated in dollar terms.

Why Cost-Benefit Analysis Doesn't Work

The case for cost-benefit analysis of environmental protection is, at best, wildly optimistic and, at worst, demonstrably wrong. The method simply does not offer the policy-making panacea its adherents promise. In practice, cost-benefit analysis frequently produces false and misleading results. Moreover, there is no quick fix, because these failures are intrinsic to the methodology, appearing whenever it is applied to any complex environmental problem.

It puts dollar figures on values that are not commodities, and have no price.

Artificial prices have been estimated for many benefits of environmental regulation. Preventing retardation due to childhood lead poisoning comes in at about $9,000 per lost IQ point. Saving a life is ostensibly worth $6.3 million. But what can it mean to say that one life is worth $6.3 million? You cannot buy the right to kill someone for $6.3 million, nor for any other price. If analysts calculated the value of life itself by asking people what it is worth to them (the most common method of valuation of other environmental benefits), the answer would be infinite. The standard response is that a value like $6.3 million is not actually a price on an individual's life or death. Rather, it is a way of expressing the value of small risks of death. If people are willing to pay $6.30 to avoid a one in a million increase in the risk of death, then the "value of a statistical life" is $6.3 million.

It ignores the collective choice presented to society by most public health and environmental problems.

Under the cost-benefit approach, valuation of environmental benefits is based on individuals' private decisions as consumers or workers, not on their public values as citizens. However, policies that protect the environment are often public goods, and are not available for purchase in individual portions. In a classic example of this distinction, the philosopher Mark Sagoff found that his students, in their role as citizens, opposed commercial ski development in a nearby wilderness area, but, in their role as consumers, would plan to go skiing there if the development was built. There is no contradiction between these two views: as individual consumers, the students would have no way to express their collective preference for wilderness preservation. Their individual willingness to pay for skiing would send a misleading signal about their views as citizens.

It is often impossible to arrive at a meaningful social valuation by adding up the willingness to pay expressed by individuals. What could it mean to ask how much you personally are willing to pay to clean up a major oil spill? If no one else contributes, the clean-up won't happen regardless of your decision. As the Nobel Prize-winning economist Amartya Sen has pointed out, if your willingness to pay for a large-scale public initiative is independent of what others are paying, then you probably have not understood the nature of the problem.

It systematically downgrades the importance of the future.

One of the great triumphs of environmental law is that it seeks to avert harms to people and to natural resources in the future, and not only within this generation, but in future generations as well. Indeed, one of the primary objectives of the National Environmental Policy Act, which has been called our basic charter of environmental protection, is to nudge the nation into "fulfill[ing] the responsibilities of each generation as trustee of the environment for succeeding generations."

The time periods involved in protecting the environment are often enormous—even many centuries, in such cases as climate change, radioactive waste, etc. With time spans this long, any discounting will make even global catastrophes seem trivial. At a discount rate of 5%, for example, the deaths of a billion people 500 years from now become less serious than the death of one person today. Seen in this way, discounting looks like a fancy justification for foisting our problems off onto the people who come after us.

It ignores considerations of distribution and fairness.

Cost-benefit analysis adds up all the costs of a policy, adds up all the benefits, and compares the totals. Implicit in this innocuous-sounding procedure is the assumption that it doesn't matter who gets the benefits and who pays the costs. Yet isn't there an important difference between spending state tax revenues, say, to improve the parks in rich communities, and spending the same revenues to clean up pollution in poor communities?

The problem of equity runs even deeper. Benefits are typically measured by willingness to pay for environmental improvement, and the rich are able and willing to pay for more than the poor. Imagine a cost-benefit analysis of locating an undesirable facility, such as a landfill or incinerator. Wealthy communities are willing to pay more for the benefit of not having the facility in their backyards; thus, under the logic of cost-benefit analysis, the net benefits to society will be maximized by putting the facility in a low-income area. In reality, pollution is typically dumped on the poor without waiting for formal analysis. Still, cost-benefit analysis rationalizes and reinforces the problem, allowing environmental burdens to flow downhill along the income slopes of an unequal society.

Conclusion

There is nothing objective about the basic premises of cost-benefit analysis. Treating individuals solely as consumers, rather than as citizens with a sense of moral responsibility, represents a distinct and highly questionable worldview. Likewise, discounting reflects judgments about the nature of environmental risks and citizens' responsibilities toward future generations.

These assumptions beg fundamental questions about ethics and equity, and one cannot decide whether to embrace them without thinking through the whole range of moral issues they raise. Yet once one has thought through these issues, there is no need then to collapse the complex moral inquiry into a series of numbers. Pricing the priceless just translates our inquiry into a different language, one with a painfully impoverished vocabulary. ❏

This article is a condensed version of the report Pricing the Priceless, *published by the Georgetown Environmental Law and Policy Institute at Georgetown University Law Center. The full report is available on-line at www. ase.tufts.edu/gdae. See also Ackerman and Heinzerling's book on these and related issues,* Priceless: Human Health, the Environment, and the Limits of the Market, *The New Press, January 2004.*

Article 6.2

HOW GROWTH CAN BE GREEN
Economic Growth, Clean Energy, and the Challenge of Climate Change

AN INTERVIEW WITH ROBERT POLLIN
November/December 2016

In a Gallup poll earlier this year, almost two-thirds of those polled said that global warming worried them "a great deal" or "a fair amount." Yet many are also worried that serious climate policy will require deep sacrifices—including big declines in production, incomes, and employment. In August, Robert Pollin, professor of economics and co-director of the Political Economy Research Institute (PERI) at UMass-Amherst, spoke with Dollars & Sense *co-editor Alejandro Reuss about these issues: Why "negative growth" is not a solution to climate change, why "green growth" is the best way to reduce greenhouse emissions, and how it can work in both high-income and low-income countries. —Eds.*

Dollars & Sense: You've argued in favor of "green growth" as a pathway for climate stabilization. That cuts against a conventional wisdom—both among advocates of serious action on climate policy and critics of such action—that greenhouse gas emissions reductions require a reduction in growth, no growth, or even negative growth. What's the basic case you make for green growth?

Robert Pollin: The argument for green growth is premised on the notion that, while an economy is growing, a given percentage of economic activity is devoted to the transformation of the energy sector—from fossil-fuel based energy to clean energy. According to my research, roughly speaking, if we look at about 1½% of GDP per year—and I've done it for different countries, so it could be the United States, it could be Spain, it could be Brazil, it could be South Africa, or it could be the world as a whole—1½% of GDP invested in clean energy—that is, clean renewable energy sources and energy efficiency—that I've costed this out and you could get to a global reduction in absolute CO_2 emissions on the order of 40% within twenty years, which is along the lines of the Intergovernmental Panel on Climate Change goals. That means that what you're doing is, as the economy is growing, you're taking part of economic activity and moving it from dirty activities to clean energy activity. So growth therefore becomes supportive of emissions and climate stabilization.

D&S: If the fruits of growth were heavily invested in projects to increase energy efficiency or develop sources of alternative "clean" energy (wind, water, solar), could a green growth approach actually achieve greater GHG emissions reductions than a hypothetical no-growth or de-growth alternative?

RP: If we're talking about a no-growth scenario, unless you're transforming the energy system you get no reduction in emissions. If you're at a flat level of economic activity, you get exactly the same level of emissions. If we cut GDP by 10%, and you keep the energy system the same, then emissions will go down by 10%, period. And a 10% emissions reduction is nowhere near what's required. On the other hand, reducing GDP by 10% would be the worst depression the world had ever experienced. GDP didn't go down by 10% during the 1930s. During the Great Recession of 2007-2008, global GDP went down by 2½%. So there's no way to get to a climate stabilization path just on the basis of cutting growth. If we want to go to zero growth, or we want to go to negative growth, we still have to transform the energy system, and the best way to transform the energy system is in a framework in which the economy is growing, because then you have a lot of opportunities and a lot of investment. You're creating more jobs. If you're trying to transform the energy system in a phase of no growth, you're imposing a depression, and who's going to be for that? Nobody, except the most fanatical environmentalists. But working people are going to see massive job loss, on a scale much greater than 2007–2009, greater than the 1930s. That has no political support and doesn't solve the problem anyway.

D&S: Is "green growth" a viable course of action for the developing world today? The high-income countries, including some that are now moving in the direction of greener energy, have mostly achieved high incomes through a carbon-intensive path. Can developing countries dramatically raise standards of living on the basis of a low-carbon-intensity path?

RP: Yeah, well the key is that the costs of delivering energy through clean renewable sources plus high efficiency are basically at parity now in developing countries, under average conditions. "Under average conditions" means that there is wide dispersion. It doesn't mean that in every single site if you put up a wind farm or install solar panels that the costs are going to be at parity with, say, the rich countries. But on average, if we believe the research that's out there, they are. And this also depends a lot on investments in high efficiency, because in developing countries the energy systems are very wasteful, so it's easy to get high returns from investing in raising efficiency standards. So actually the green growth path is even more effective in developing countries. I myself have written about it for India, for Brazil, for South Africa, for Indonesia. In a country like Indonesia or India—they expect to be high-growth countries, growing at 6, 7, or 8%—they can actually do that if they keep putting 1½% of GDP so that their growth dividend moves into clean energy, and you start to see their emissions going down as a feature of economic growth itself.

D&S: What about the means of promoting investment in energy efficiency and alternative energy that you're talking about? You've written about the importance of a leading government role in promoting investment in those sectors. Are you skeptical that governments can just re-set the incentives to private actors— through a carbon tax or emissions permits system—and have that bring about the necessary investments?

RP: Well, we have to be skeptical, because it hasn't happened. And we have to be skeptical because there are obviously extremely powerful interests that are quite pleased with the profits that they're receiving from burning fossil fuels. That's a political question. On the other hand, as I said, on average the costs of renewable energy are close to parity or on parity with fossil fuel energy. Energy efficiency pays for itself, by definition. In fact, in the United States in 2007, under President George W. Bush, a law was passed that required the federal government to raise efficiency standards in all federal buildings by 30% as of the year 2015. Now, we didn't do it, but in the buildings that were retrofitted—there's a website and it shows it was saving the taxpayers hundreds of millions of dollars. So why isn't it happening? One, there's inertia. You do have to do the up-front investment. Two, there's opposition from the fossil fuel industry. So we have to struggle around those things, at the same time recognizing that achieving these kinds of growth projections for clean energy are quite feasible economically and are good for jobs. That's the other big barrier, this notion that you're going to hurt jobs if you're going to protect the environment. Well, you know, the thing that I've been focusing on for several years is that it's actually beneficial for employment to pursue the green growth path as opposed to maintaining the fossil fuel infrastructure. ❏

Article 6.3

JOBS, JUSTICE, AND THE CLEAN-ENERGY FUTURE

BY JEREMY BRECHER

September/October 2016

Today, there are 400 parts per million (PPM) of carbon dioxide in the atmosphere, far above the 350 ppm climate scientists regard as the safe upper limit. Even in the unlikely event that all nations fulfill the greenhouse gas (GHG) reduction pledges they made at the Paris climate summit at the end of 2015, carbon in the atmosphere is predicted to increase to 670 ppm by the end of this century. The global temperature will rise an estimated 3.5 degrees Celsius (6.3 degrees Fahrenheit) above pre-industrial levels. For comparison, a one-degree increase was enough to cause all the effects of climate change we have seen so far, from Arctic melting to intensified hurricanes to desertification.

Limiting climate catastrophe will require drastic cuts in the burning of the fossil fuels that cause climate change. But many workers and their unions fear that such cuts will lead to drastic loss in jobs and economic well-being for working people—aggravating the shortage of good jobs and the burgeoning inequality we already face. Is there a way to escape the apparent lose-lose choice between saving the climate and saving jobs?

A Possible Clean Energy Future

A series of reports by the Labor Network for Sustainability (LNS), and partners provides good news: The U.S. can meet the targets for greenhouse gas (GHG) reduction that climate scientists say are necessary while also creating half-a-million jobs annually and reducing the cost of energy to consumers. The reports, gathered in the LNS Climate, Jobs, and Justice Project, also show that protecting the climate in a way that maximizes the benefit for working people and discriminated-against groups will take deliberate public policies and action by unions and their social movement allies.

In 2015, LNS asked Frank Ackerman of Synapse Energy Economics to assess the employment effects of meeting the Intergovernmental Panel on Climate Change (IPCC) target of reducing GHG emissions by 80% by 2050 (or "80x50"). Ackerman developed a Clean Energy Future model based on Synapse's many years of analysis of energy systems. [Disclosure: Ackerman is a longtime associate of *Dollars & Sense* and a former *D&S* collective member. —Eds.]

Ackerman and his coworkers set themselves the task of meeting three challenges simultaneously. The Clean Energy Future scenario should meet the IPCC target of reducing GHG emissions 80% by 2050. It should provide more good jobs than the business-as-usual scenario (what would happen if no changes are made to address climate change). And it should not place higher costs on American consumers.

The resulting report, "The Clean Energy Future: Protecting the Climate, Creating Jobs and Saving Money," shows that the United States can reduce GHG emissions 80% by 2050—while adding half-a-million jobs annually and saving Americans billions of dollars on their electrical, heating, and transportation costs.

The Clean Energy Future constructs a baseline "business as usual" reference case based primarily on projections from the federal Energy Information Administration's Annual Energy Outlook. It compares that reference case to a clean energy alternative based primarily on scenarios developed by the National Renewable Energy Laboratory (NREL) and original research by Synapse. It uses IMPLAN, a widely used model of employment impacts, to evaluate the jobs impacts of each of the two scenarios.

In the Clean Energy Future model, energy efficiency programs match the performance of today's most effective state programs. A national Renewable Portfolio Standard requires 70% renewable electricity by 2040. The cost of solar photovoltaic cells that convert sunlight into electricity drops 75% from 2010 to 2020. (The reference case already projects a 40% reduction.) Coal is entirely phased out. No new nuclear plants are built and existing plants are retired at the end of their 60-year life expectancy. By 2050, gas cars and light trucks are replaced by electric vehicles, and 80% of gas- and oil-fired space-heating and water-heating is replaced by electric heat. Wind and solar power grow enough to provide electricity for the new vehicles and heating. The Synapse team has prepared detailed analyses showing these projections are realistic, even conservative.

The Clean Energy Future plan covers electricity generation, cars and light trucks, space and water heating, fossil fuel supply, and waste management. It reduces GHG emissions across these sectors by 86% by 2050, compared to emissions in 1990.

If these reductions are made, meeting the "80x50" target (at least 80% reduction in emissions by 2050) for the entire economy will require far less stringent reductions in the remaining sectors. If non-electric industry, mass transit, freight transport, and agriculture reduce their emissions by 42%, the entire economy can meet the 80% reduction target. The report discusses a variety of studies indicating how those reductions could be achieved or indeed exceeded.

Creating New Jobs

The Clean Energy Future will create a substantial number of new jobs. The increase in jobs created, compared to the business-as-usual scenario, will start around 200,000 per year in 2016–2020 and rise to 800,000 a year in 2046–2050. The average job gain compared to business-as-usual scenario is 550,000 per year for the entire period. There are several reasons for this advantage. The Clean Energy scenario spends less on imported oil and less money ends up in the pockets of the owners of gas pipelines, coal mines, and oil wells and refineries, many of them overseas. Much of that money is spent instead paying workers to produce more labor-intensive forms of renewable energy and energy efficiency.

Nearly 80% of the new jobs provided by the Clean Energy Future will be concentrated in manufacturing and construction. The scenario will immediately start to create hundreds of thousands of new jobs in energy efficiency, ranging from insulation to high-efficiency heating and cooling, to fuel cells and combined heat and power (CHP) installations, to use of tree planting to cool urban areas. In the 2020s, a second

Jobs and Climate Policy In the States

The Climate, Jobs, and Justice Project includes three reports that take a closer look at what the Clean Energy Future will mean in three states, Illinois, Maryland, and Connecticut. These states were selected both because they present very different problems and potentials for climate policy and because they all have active organizing around climate and jobs that can test the relevance and usefulness of the Clean Energy Future.

If Illinois were an independent country, it would be the 20th largest economy in the world and the 34th largest emitter of GHGs. It is also a state with enormous potential for wind and solar energy. As a result, the state can phase out its coal and nuclear production while adding enough renewable energy capacity not only to replace it but also to run a new electric-vehicle fleet and export energy to other states.

The "Illinois Jobs and Clean Energy: Protecting the Climate and the State Economy" report lays out a climate protection strategy that will produce more than 28,000 net new jobs per year over business-as-usual projections through 2050. That represents almost 0.5% of total employment in the state, so it should reduce the unemployment rate by one-half percentage point. Three-quarters of the jobs created will be in the relatively high-wage construction and manufacturing sectors. The report indicates that even more jobs could be created if Illinois accelerated its climate timetable and made itself a center for export of renewable energy and renewable-energy-related manufactured goods such as wind-turbine components and solar-energy equipment.

"Maryland's Clean Energy Future: Climate Goals and Employment Benefits" presents a plan to reduce Maryland's net emissions of greenhouse gases (GHGs) to 80% less than the 2006 level by 2050—while adding more than ten thousand jobs per year. It identifies the state's major industrial emitters of GHGs and lays out strategies for reducing their emissions. The report also indicates that Maryland can use the burgeoning state and national demand for clean energy to create good, stable jobs in a growing climate-protection sector: manufacturing jobs, jobs for those who have been marginalized in the current labor market, and jobs for skilled union workers in the construction trades. It argues that Maryland needs a robust job-creation and clean-industry development strategy to realize that potential.

"The Connecticut Clean Energy Future: Climate Goals and Employment Benefits" shows how a largely non-industrial state with extreme economic inequality can create a rapidly growing climate-protection sector that creates stable jobs for unionized workers, effective job ladders for those previously excluded from good jobs, and expansion of energy efficiency, renewable energy, and other sectors. It presents a plan that meets the state's official goal of reducing GHG emissions 80% below the 2001 level by 2050 while adding more than 6000 jobs, most of them in construction and manufacturing.

Connecticut can achieve many of its other goals, such as reducing poverty and inequality, improving air quality, raising workforce skill levels, and reducing unemployment while implementing an aggressive climate-protection plan, but to realize these "co-benefits" it will need policies designed to do so. Public policy must assure that Clean Energy Future jobs are good, secure, permanent jobs with education, training, and advancement. New, high-quality jobs and/or dignified retirement must be provided for approximately 600 workers who may lose jobs in the Clean Energy Future—less than one-tenth of the jobs that will be gained. Existing inequality and racial, gender, and other injustices must be counteracted through job pathways, strong affirmative action provisions, and local hiring requirements. And a more local and less top-down energy system can be created through a rising Renewable Portfolio Standard requiring in-state electricity generation; shared solar generation; electric grid modernization; and encouragement for local clean-energy initiatives.

wave of jobs will develop producing, installing, and maintaining wind turbines, solar panels, and other forms of renewable energy. In the 2030s, new jobs will develop in the auto industry due to the increasing production of electric cars and trucks. Starting in the 2040s, the clean energy scenario will save so much money that a significant number of jobs will be created by the money saved on fossil fuels that will be spent instead on job-creating expenditures. Over the 35-year period, the average of 550,000 extra jobs per year will include 187,000 jobs in manufacturing and 240,000 in construction.

The Clean Energy Future will provide many new jobs for each that is lost. There will, however, be fewer jobs in coal, oil, and gas extraction and burning and in nuclear energy. For example, there will be about 100,000 fewer jobs each year in mining and extraction compared to the business-as-usual scenario. The report calls for a "just transition" for the workers who hold those jobs, including "assistance in training and placement in new jobs, or retirement with dignity."

Some studies have projected a far higher number of jobs created by climate protection policies, sometimes running in the millions. There are several reasons the numbers in the Clean Energy Future scenario are lower. It is based on the large and continuing reduction in the cost of renewable energy, which makes it possible to meet GHG reduction targets at far lower cost—but therefore also with considerably less labor. Unlike some studies, it is not based on extensive expansion of biofuel production, which creates large numbers of low-paid agricultural jobs. The program is designed to keep the cost of transition to a minimum, which also holds down the number of jobs created. Finally, the projections are based on conservative assumptions derived from a detailed knowledge of the electrical system. The report emphasizes that if society is prepared to spend more money, a far more rapid and job-intensive program could result.

The Costs Will Be Less

Over the 35-year period, the Clean Energy Future will actually cost slightly less than the business-as-usual case. It will actually save $7 per person annually in electricity, transportation, and heating costs—while meeting climate goals and creating jobs.

Why are the costs so modest? One reason is that the costs of solar, wind, and other forms of renewable energy have been getting dramatically lower and, according to Synapse's projections extrapolated from those of the federal Energy Information Administration and the National Renewable Energy Laboratory, they are likely to continue to do so.

"The Clean Energy Future" points out that there is another reason as well. Economists often assume that the status quo already represents the greatest possible efficiency; if it were possible to do things more efficiently, people would already be doing so in order to maximize their gains in the market. This is often put in the form of such adages as "there is no such thing as a free lunch" and "if there were pennies lying around on the ground someone would have already picked them up."

But in the case of energy in particular, the evidence indicates that there is so much waste in the current energy system that major cost savings can be realized by such available means as insulating buildings and co-generating heat and electricity.

Investment in such measures will be highly cost-effective and provide a high return. There are various reasons these "pennies" are not currently being picked up, including the market power of large energy corporations, the monopolies held by energy utilities, counterproductive government regulations, and incomplete knowledge. But those pennies can be picked up and utilized as part of the transition to the Clean Energy Future.

A Floor, Not a Ceiling

The Clean Energy Future plan provides a floor, not a ceiling, for what can be accomplished. It shows how we can meet climate goals with no net cost, and that doing so will create more jobs. But we can, and indeed should, do more. For example, mass transit can be expanded far faster. GHG reduction targets can be met earlier. GHG emissions can be reduced to near zero. We can achieve such goals just by accelerating the same basic plan.

We can also achieve other goals besides climate protection as part of the same process. To achieve maximum benefit from the Clean Energy Future, the project advocates four basic policies:

Pacific Northwest: Fossil Fuel vs. Clean Energy Jobs

Whenever there is opposition to a pipeline, fossil-fuel power plant, oil well, or other fossil-fuel project, it raises a legitimate question: Where are the people who would have built and operated the project going to find jobs? An LNS Climate, Jobs, and Justice project report, "The Economic Impact of Clean Energy Investments in the Pacific Northwest: Alternatives to Fossil Fuel Exports" by Noah Enelow of Ecotrust Knowledge Systems, examines job prospects for such an area, Grays Harbor County in western Washington State.

The report compares a recently defeated oil-export terminal to possible clean-energy projects. The Grays Harbor Westway and Imperium crude-oil storage-and-export terminal would have received oil brought by train from Utah and shipped it to Asia. The project would have created an estimated 231 construction jobs during its year of building and 148 operations jobs thereafter.

Enelow developed plans for two complementary clean-energy initiatives as an alternative. The first is a utility-scale solar photovoltaic array, with electrical components manufactured in-state. It would produce 478 construction jobs—more than twice as many jobs as the coal export terminal. But once built, the solar facility would produce only seven direct operations jobs compared with 148 direct operations jobs for the export terminal.

The report proposes a complementary investment in energy efficiency for commercial buildings, such as those financed by Property Assessed Clean Energy (PACE) programs. This would create 262 direct jobs in Grays Harbor County—exceeding the Westway/Imperium proposal by 114 jobs. In short, the combined utility-scale solar and energy-efficiency proposal would create far more jobs both in construction and in permanent operations than the oil-export terminal.

Source: Noah Enelow, Labor Network for Sustainability, "The Economic Impact of Clean Energy Investments in the Pacific Northwest: Alternatives to Fossil Fuel Exports," March 2016 (labor4sustainability.org).

Climate protection will require the creation of tens of thousands of new jobs. But there is no guarantee that they will be good jobs. Indeed, depending on other economic trends, spending on climate protection could increase inequality and provide increasingly insecure, contingent work. Climate protection strategy should be designed to provide the maximum number possible of good, secure, permanent jobs with opportunities for education, training, and advancement. The deterioration in the quality of jobs is directly related to the reduction in the size and bargaining power of labor unions; reinforcing the right of workers to organize and bargain collectively should be an explicit part of public policy for climate protection.

Because some jobs will be lost in fossil fuel-related industries, we need a vigorous program to provide new, high-quality jobs and/or dignified retirement for workers in those industries. A Superfund to protect workers and communities from negative side effects of climate policies should be a central part of any climate program. Anything less will be unjust to workers and will undermine political support for climate protection programs.

The Clean Energy Future plan opens up new opportunities to counter the growing inequality and rampant racial, gender, and other injustices of our society. But many of those opportunities will be lost unless we have deliberate policies to realize them. Climate protection programs should include job pathways and strong affirmative action provisions for those groups that have been most excluded from good jobs in the past.

The Clean Energy Future also opens up a wide range of opportunities for creating a more democratic economy and society. It allows for a less top-down and more distributed energy system, potentially reducing control by centralized utilities and increasing that of local and grassroots entities. It provides many opportunities for local economic initiatives, ranging from energy coops to local and community-based enterprises of many kinds. It will reduce the wealth and power of the fossil fuel corporations that have such a dominant role within our political system. These opportunities should not be squandered.

A Worker-Friendly Approach to Climate Protection

The Clean Energy Future laid out in the Climate, Jobs, and Justice Project represents a practical plan to reduce GHG emissions 80% by 2050. It shows that climate protection is not only affordable, but that it can actually save Americans money. The plan will create half a million more jobs than continuing on a fossil-fuel pathway, most of them in manufacturing and construction. It shows that—should we choose to do so—we can reduce carbon emissions enough to stabilize the climate, create growing numbers of good jobs, and at the same time avoid imposing new costs on consumers and taxpayers.

For unions, the Clean Energy Future presents a worker-friendly approach to climate protection. It overcomes the false assumption that workers must make a choice between climate protection on the one hand, and jobs and economic well-being on the other. It can form a key element in a workers' program for climate protection—one that can unify trade unionists, environmentalists, and the growing majority of Americans who are deeply concerned about climate change.

More and more unions are making climate protection a central part of their program. Unions and federations ranging from SEIU to the California Labor Federation have passed resolutions on climate change in the past few months. Climate caucuses have been formed in central labor councils up and down the West Coast. In January 2016, LNS organized the first Labor Convergence on Climate which brought together 75 labor leaders to forge a common strategy to change organized labor's approach to climate protection; the Convergence included invited representatives of state AFL-CIOs, city central labor councils, and individual unions, including building trades, manufacturing, public employee, and service unions, including elected officers. Such efforts open the way for organized labor to become a significant participant in the climate protection movement.

As the devastation caused by climate change grows the consciousness of the need to halt it is likely to grow as well—not only in the labor movement but throughout society. Whether it will grow strong enough fast enough to limit climate disaster is today an open question. (For discussion of the obstacles to climate protection and strategies for overcoming them, see my book, *Climate Insurgency: A Strategy for Survival* (2016) and my forthcoming books *Climate Solidarity: Workers vs. Warming* and *Against Doom: A Climate Insurgency Manual* (PM Press: 2017).)

The Clean Energy Future represents a pathway away from climate destruction that is also far better for workers and consumers than our current pathway based on fossil fuels. Should we let greed and inertia prevent us from taking it? ❏

Sources: "Clean Energy Future, 2016-2050," Climate, Jobs, and Justice Project, Labor Network for Sustainability, Sept. 21, 2015 (labor4sustainability.org); Brian Kahn, "A Global Milestone: CO2 Passes 400 PPM," Climate Central, May 6, 2015 (climatecentral.org); "Scoreboard Science and Data," Climate Interactive (climateinteractive.org); Andrew Jones, John Sterman, Ellie Johnston, and Lori Siegel, "With Improved Pledges Every Five Years, Paris Agreement Could Limit Warming Below 2C," Dec. 14, 2015 (climateinteractive.org).

Article 6.4

FRACKONOMICS
The Science and Economics of the Gas Boom

BY ROB LARSON
July/August 2013

Between 1868 and 1969, Cleveland's Cuyahoga River caught fire at least ten times, including one blaze that reached the Standard Oil refinery where storage tanks detonated. Ultimately, the seemingly impossible and unnatural phenomenon of burning water came to represent the dangers of unregulated industrial development and generated popular support for the environmental laws of the 1970s, including the Clean Water Act and the Safe Drinking Water Act.

Today the unsettling sight of burning water has returned, from a new industry that is exempt from both these laws. In homes near installations using the drilling technique known as hydraulic fracturing, or "fracking," the tap water has been known to ignite with the touch of a lighter. The industry is relatively new, so the scientific literature yields only tentative results and provisional research conclusions. But the early research suggests fracking has serious negative consequences for public health and local ecology, from flaming tap water to toxic chemicals to ground tremors. Industry spokesmen insist that the negative side-effects of fracking are insignificant. But there's one positive side-effect everyone should be able to agree upon: fracking is an ideal vehicle for explaining key economic concepts of market failure and market power, including *externalities, asymmetrical information,* and *regulatory capture,* along with brand-new ones, like *science capture.* Let's start with the firewater.

Liar Liar, Taps on Fire

In the fracking process, natural gas (methane) is released from shale rock strata up to a mile underground, by injecting millions of gallons of water, along with sand and a variety of synthetic chemicals. The huge pressure of the water makes new cracks in the rock, allowing the gas to dissolve and be extracted. Natural gas is now responsible for 30% of U.S. electricity production and for heating half of all U.S. homes. The national and business media have breathlessly reported huge growth in gas production, and the oil-and-gas industry projects that North America will return to exporting energy by 2025. Besides the sheer growth in production, the *Wall Street Journal* reported earlier this year, the fracking boom has brought other economic benefits, "improving employment in some regions and a rebound in U.S.-based manufacturing," and "greater defense against overseas turmoil that can disrupt energy supplies."

As made notorious by the documentary *Gasland*, water supplies are a major focus of concern about fracking, especially since the emergence of dramatic footage of a number of Pennsylvania homes, near fracking pads above the Marcellus Shale formation, producing fireballs from the kitchen tap. Duke University earth scientists conducted a more rigorous exploration of this phenomenon, published in the *Proceedings of the National Academy of the Sciences*. They surveyed rural Pennsylvanian water wells for residential use, measuring concentrations of methane, the main chemical component of natural gas. Concentrations rose far above natural levels closer to drill pads, spiking within one kilometer of active gas development sites to a level that "represents a potential explosion hazard." It was also found that the specific gas chemistry in the wells matched those produced through drilling, rather than through naturally occurring compounds. As the gas boom goes "boom," the cautious scientists conclude: "Greater stewardship, knowledge, and—possibly—regulation are needed to ensure the sustainable future of shale-gas extraction."

In parts of the country where water is scarcer, the issue is more ominous. The Environmental Protection Agency (EPA) and U.S. Geological Survey have found toxic alcohols, glycols, and carcinogenic benzene in underground aquifers in Wyoming, evidence that fracking has tainted precious underground water supplies. In press accounts, local residents who requested the study "expressed gratitude to the EPA, and perhaps a bit of veiled doubt about the zeal of local and state regulators." In parched Texas, the volume of water adequate for irrigating $200,000 worth of crops can be used to frack $2.5 billion-worth of gas or oil. The *Wall Street Journal* reports that "companies have been on a buying spree, snapping up rights to scarce river water—easily outbidding traditional users such as farmers and cities." A Texan rancher relates: "They're just so much bigger and more powerful than we are…We're just kind of the little ant that gets squashed."

Top-Secret Ingredients

The heavy use of often-secret synthetic chemicals has also cast a shadow over the fracking debate. Bloomberg News reported in 2012 that energy companies and well operators were refusing to disclose the chemical formulas of thousands of substances used in the fracking process, enough to "keep [the] U.S. clueless on wells." Many states have instituted a self-reporting law, modeled on one first developed in Texas, allowing drillers to withhold the ingredients used in their chemical mixes. Bloomberg reports that drillers "claimed similar exemptions about 19,000 times" in the first eight months of 2012 alone. The congressional exemption of the industry from federal water requirements (discussed below) makes this non-disclosure possible, so that "neighbors of fracked wells … can't use the disclosures to watch for frack fluids migrating into creeks, rivers and aquifers, because they don't know what to look for."

This development is a perfect example of what economists call *asymmetric information*, where one participant in a transaction knows relevant information that is unknown to the other party. The lack of information on one side can put the other party at an advantage, like the seller of a used car who knows more about the car's problems than the prospective buyer. For example, a team of Colorado endocrinologists set out to catalogue these synthetic compounds used in wells across the country, based on regulatory filings. The survey was limited due to the "void of environmental authority" to compel chemical disclosure, and thus the data sheets and reports are "fraught with gaps in information about the formulation of the products." Many of these reports only specify the general chemical class or use the label "proprietary," providing no additional information. Ultimately, the scientists found that over 75% of the chemicals were harmful for the sensory organs, nearly half could affect the nervous and immune systems, and 25% could cause "cancer and mutations."

Another report by Colorado scientists observed that fracking development is increasingly located "near where people live, work, and play." The study used air sampling to find strongly elevated health risks within a radius of about half a mile from fracking sites. The effects ranged from "headaches and eye irritation" up to "tremors, temporary limb paralysis, and unconsciousness at higher exposures." A larger review by Pennsylvania scientists reached similar conclusions, based on local resident reporting and finding a match of over two-thirds "between known health effects of chemicals detected and symptoms reported."

The scientists caution that their findings "do not constitute definitive proof of cause and effect," but they do "indicate the strong likelihood that the health of people living in proximity to gas facilities is being affected by exposure to pollutants from those facilities." They frequently advocate the *precautionary principle*—that careful study showing that a product or process is *not* harmful should precede its use—as when they recommend "health impact assessments before permitting begins," and note that "scientific knowledge about the health and environmental impacts of shale gas development … are proceeding at a far slower pace than the development itself." These conclusions contradict the industry's claim that fracking is both safe for public health and not in need of any further study. Especially considering the earthquakes.

Tectonic Economics

Perhaps more alarming than the burning water and secret chemicals is the association of fracking with earthquakes. An early report of this development came from the Oklahoma Geological Survey, which surveyed the timing of tremors and their proximity to fracking sites and found a "strong correlation in time and space" and thus "a possibility these earthquakes were induced by hydraulic fracturing." Earthquake epicenters were mostly within two miles of wells, and any earthquake disruption or damage caused by fracking-related activities represents an *externality*, a side effect of an economic transaction that affects parties outside the transaction.

These findings are backed up by a review in the prestigious research journal *Science*, in which cautious scientists note that fracking *itself* is not responsible for "the earthquakes that have been shaking previously calm regions." Yet they find that the induced earthquakes do arise from "all manner of other energy-related fluid injection—including deep disposal of fracking's wastewater, extraction of methane from coal beds, and creation of geothermal energy reservoirs." A surveyed area in Arkansas typically had about two quakes a year, before the beginning of fracking-water disposal. The year water disposal began, the number rose to ten. The next year, to 54. After water injection was halted, the quakes tapered off. The *Science* authors observe the "strongly suggestive" correlation between water disposal and seismic activity: "The quakes began only after injection began, surged when the rate of injection surged, were limited to the vicinity of the wells, and trailed off after injection was stopped." The scientists' main conclusion is the adoption of the precautionary principle: "look before you leap ... Stopping injection has stopped significant earthquakes within days to a year. ... The new regulations in Ohio and Arkansas at least move in the direction of such a learn-as-you-go approach."

Fracknapping

You might wonder why the EPA has not limited or regulated fracking operations, in light of the combustible water, cancer-causing chemicals, and earthquake clusters. The EPA might well have adopted significant national policies on fracking by now, had the practice not been made exempt from the main national environmental laws in the Energy Policy Act of 2005, an offspring of Dick Cheney's secretive energy committee. The exemptions from the Clean Water Act, the Safe Drinking Water Act, the Clean Air Act, and the Superfund law drastically limit the agency's authority to act on fracking.

The drive to limit even EPA *research* into fracking is decades old. An extensive *New York Times* report, based on interviews with scientists and reviews of confidential files, found that "more than a quarter-century of efforts by some lawmakers and regulators to force the federal government to police the industry better have been thwarted, as EPA studies have been repeatedly narrowed in scope and important findings have been removed." When Congress first directed the EPA to investigate fracking in the 1980s, the *Times* reported, EPA scientists found that some fracking waste was "hazardous and should be tightly controlled." But the final report sent to Congress eliminated these conclusions. An agency scientist relates, "It was like science didn't matter. ... The industry was going to get what it wanted, and we were not supposed to stand in the way."

Similarly, when an EPA public-advisory letter to the state of New York called for a moratorium on drilling, the advice was stripped from the released version. A staff scientist said the redaction was due to "politics," but could as well have said "business power." More importantly, the first major EPA review of fracking found "little or no threat to drinking water." This was an eyebrow-raising claim, given that five of seven members of the peer review panel had current or former energy industry affiliations, a detail noted by agency whistle-blower Weston Wilson. Other studies have been narrowed in scope or colored by similar conflicts of interest. More recently, the agency announced that its study finding contamination of Wyoming groundwater will not be subjected to outside peer review, and that further work instead will be funded directly by industry. As the EPA is presently drafting a brand-new report on the subject, these past embarrassments should be kept in mind.

This brings up the problem of *regulatory capture*, where an industry to be monitored gains major influence over regulators' policies. As mentioned above, fracking is very loosely regulated by the states, which is always a favorite outcome for corporate America since the regulatory resources of state governments are far smaller and the regulators are even more easily dominated than those of the federal government. The industry-sponsored FracFocus website is the state-sanctioned chemical-information clearing house, and a masterpiece of smooth PR design, suggesting clear water and full transparency. But Bloomberg News reports that "more than 40 percent of wells fracked in eight major drilling states last year had been omitted from the voluntary site."

Other state reactions have varied. In 2010, the New York State legislature voted to ban fracking, but then-Governor Paterson vetoed the bill and instead issued a temporary moratorium on the practice, though fracking remains illegal in the New York City watershed. Finally, while the EPA's main study is still pending, the agency has taken some steps, as in 2012 when it required well operators to reduce methane gas emissions from wells and storage pits to limit air pollution. But even here the regulation wears kid gloves: The new moves do not cut into industry profits. In fact, capturing the "fugitive" methane, the agency estimates, will *save* the industry $11 to $19 million annually. Also, the regulation won't take effect until 2015.

Neoclassical Gas

Mainstream, or "neoclassical," economic theory considers itself to have solutions to these problems—solutions centered as always on "free markets." The idea is that if firms create chronic health problems or combustible tap water, market forces should drive up their costs, as landowners learn of these firms' practices and demand higher payment for drilling. But as seen above, even households that have already leased their land for gas development remain unaware of the identities and effects of the obscure synthetic chemicals to which they are exposed. This *informational asymmetry*—the firms know things the landowners don't—significantly attenuates the ability of landowners to make informed choices.

On the other hand, households that are located near a drill pad but uninvolved in licensing the drilling will experience the ill effects as externalities. Neoclassicals suggest these can be fixed through a better property-rights system, where surrounding individuals can sue drillers for injuring their health. But this solution runs up against another problem: proving cause-and-effect from a drilling pad to a particular individual's health problems is extremely difficult. The tobacco industry notoriously made this point in court for many years, arguing that it was impossible to prove if a man's lung cancer was caused by a four-pack-a-day cigarette habit, as opposed to, say, local auto exhaust. If cause-and-effect is hard to prove in court for cigarettes, doing so for air-delivered volatile organic compounds will be almost impossible.

This problem is aggravated by the use of corporate resources to influence research. The showcase example is a study produced by the University of Texas, "Fact-Based Regulation for Environmental Protection in Shale Gas Development." The study gave fracking a guardedly positive bill of health, finding no evidence of negative health impacts. The commercial media gave the study a good deal of favorable attention, until the revelation that the lead researcher, Dr. Charles G. Groat, formerly of USGS, sits on the board of the Plains Exploration & Production Company, a Houston-based energy firm heavily invested in gas development. His compensation from the board was several times his academic salary, and he also held 40,000 shares of its stock. An in-house review by the university was outspoken, saying "the term 'fact-based' would not apply" to the paper, which was "inappropriately selective ... such that they seemed to suggest that public concerns were without scientific basis and largely resulted from media bias." Groat retired from the university the day the review was released, but this practice has become increasingly common from industries under fire for environmental or public-health impacts. Bloomberg News flatly stated that "producers are taking a page from the tobacco industry playbook: funding research at established universities that arrives at conclusions that counter concerns raised by critics." This raises the ugly possibility of *science capture*.

No Frackin' Way

Not that Americans are taking it lying down. A diverse popular coalition successfully fought to block a Gulf Coast gas terminal that stood to inflict major damage on local wildlife. The *Oil & Gas Journal* reports on the "firestorm" of activism: "In an unlikely but massive undertaking, environmental activists, sports fishermen, local politicians, media groups, and other citizens formed a coalition known as the 'Gumbo Alliance' that united opposition to the technology." The Louisiana governor vetoed the project "under considerable public pressure." Elsewhere, local residents have taken action to keep fracking and its negative externalities out of their communities. New York State "fractivists" have won an impressive 55 municipal bans and 105 local moratoriums against fracking, to date. The state's Court of Appeals—New York's highest court—recently upheld the bans against an industry lawsuit. These activist successes are an early challenge to what the *Wall Street Journal* called the new "shale barons."

American job markets remain highly depressed and state budgets are strained. What we need, instead of dogged extraction of every particle of fossil fuels from the ground, is a public employment program geared toward the construction of a new sustainable energy system. This would be a far superior alternative to fracking—on grounds of health, ecology, and employment. It could also serve as a springboard for a broader questioning of the suitability of capitalism for the challenges of the 21st century. That kind of radical approach would see the glass of water as half full, not half on fire. ❏

Sources: Russel Gold, "Gas Boom Projected to Grow for Decades," *Wall Street Journal*, February 28, 2013; Tom Fowler, "US Oil Sector Notches Historic Annual Gusher," *Wall Street Journal*, January 19, 2013; Stephen Osborn, Avner Vengosh, Nathaniel Warner, and Robert Jackson, "Methane contamination of drinking water accompanying gas-well drilling and hydraulic fracturing," *Proceedings of the National Academy of the Sciences*, Vol. 108, No. 20, May 17, 2011; Kirk Johnson, "EPA Links Tainted Water in Wyoming to Hydraulic Fracturing for Natural Gas," *New York Times*, December 8, 2011; Tennille Tracy, "New EPA Findings Test Fracking Site," *Wall Street Journal*, October 11, 2012; Felicity Barringer, "Spread of Hydrofracking Could Strain Water Resources in West, Study Finds," *New York Times*, May 2, 2013; Russel Gold and Ana Campoy, "Oil's Growing Thirst for Water," *Wall Street Journal*, December 6, 2011; Ben Elgin, Benjamin Haas and Phil Kuntz, "Fracking Secrets by Thousands Keep US Clueless on Wells," *Bloomberg News*, November 30, 2012; Theo Colborn, Carol Kwiatkowski, Kim Schultz and Mary Bachran, "Natural Gas Operations form a Public Health Perspective," *Human and Ecological Risk Assessment: An International Journal*, Vol. 17, No. 5, September 20, 2011; Lisa McKenzie,

Roxana Witter, Lee Newman, John Adgate, "Human health risk assessment of air emissions from development of unconventional natural gas resources," *Science of the Total Environment*, Vol. 424, May 1 2012; Nadia Steinzor, Wilma Subra, and Lisa Sumi, "Investigating Links between Shale Gas Development and Health Impacts Through a Community Survey Project in Pennsylvania," *New Solutions*, Vol. 23, No. 1, 2013; Austin Holland, Oklahoma Geological Survey, "Examination of Possibly Induced Seismicity from Hydraulic Fracturing in the Eolga Field, Garvin County, Oklahoma, August 2011; Richard Kerr, "Learning How NOT to Make Your Own Earthquakes," *Science*, Vol. 335, No. 6075, March 23 2012; Zoe Corbyn, "Method predicts size of fracking earthquakes," *Nature* News, December 9, 2011; Ian Urbina, "Pressure Limits Efforts to Police Drilling for Gas," *New York Times*, March 3, 2011; Devlin Barrett and Ryan Dezember, "Regulators Back 'Fracking' in New York," *Wall Street Journal*, July 1, 2011; John Broder, "US Caps Emissions in Drilling for Fuel," *New York Times*, February 4, 2012; Norman Augustine, Rita Colwell, and James Duderstadt, "A Review of the Processes of Preparation and Distribution of the report 'Fact-Based Regulation for Environmental Protection in Shale Gas Development,'" University of Texas at Austin, November 30, 2012; Jim Efsthathiou, "Frackers Fund University Research That Proves Their Case," Bloomberg News, July 23, 2012; Daron Threet, "US offshore LNG terminals face technical, legal maze," *Oil & Gas Journal*, December 24, 2007; Ellen Cantarow, "New York's Zoning Ban Movement Fracks Big Gas," Truthout, May 9, 2013 (Truthout.org); Alyssa Abkowitz, "The New Texas Land Rush," *Wall Street Journal*, April 25, 2013; Daron Threet, "US offshore LNG terminals face technical, legal maze," *Oil & Gas Journal*, December 24, 2007.

Article 6.5

IS ECONOMIC GROWTH ENVIRONMENTALLY SUSTAINABLE?

BY ARTHUR MacEWAN
January/February 2018

> Dear Dr. Dollar:
> *I keep hearing progressive economists talking about environmental sustainability, in particular in the context of the looming catastrophe of global climate change. But when it comes to macroeconomics, they seem to switch to talking "growth, growth, growth." Aren't the two contradictory?*
> —Anonymous, Washington, D.C.

> The first law of ecology is that everything is related to everything else.
> —*Barry Commoner*

As is the case with many questions, the answer is "yes and no."
Economic growth of the kind we have had for the last two hundred years—or longer—is in conflict with environmental sustainability. More growth has meant the use of more carbon-based fuels, so this growth has spewed more and more carbon dioxide into the atmosphere—and thus global warming. (Global warming is not the only environmental issue, but it is the danger that threatens the existence of human society as we know it. So let's focus on it here.)

Yet, the carbon intensity of economic growth is not something beyond social control. There are ways to grow—meeting human needs and desires—that greatly reduce, if not eliminate, the global warming impact. Most macroeconomic analyses, however, focus simply on growth without consideration of how this growth would affect the environment. There are two reasons for this error, one bad and one good.

The bad reason is that most economists take the basic arrangements of society for granted. They take the nature of technology as "given," and do not question either the technology itself or the social and political forces that maintain the existing path of technology.

The good reason is that we have more than one problem, and growth can provide positive social outcomes—reducing unemployment, general economic insecurity, and absolute poverty. None of this does any good if we are all soon washed away by rising tides, but it is a good reason that economic growth cannot be jettisoned out of hand.

Some Context

The environmental impact of human activity can be understood in terms of three factors:

- how many of us there are on the planet (population),

- the amount of output of goods and services produced per person (affluence), and
- the amount of environmental impact per unit of output (technology).

Over time, in terms of environmental impact, all three components of this relationship have gotten worse: population has grown and grown, the world as a whole has become more affluent, and technology has become more carbon intensive (more negative impact per unit of output). To halt global warming, it is necessary to pay attention to each of these factors.

What Can Change?

Population growth, at least in the long-run, can be reduced. Making contraception safe and widely available can help. Also, increased educational and employment opportunities for women tend to reduce fertility. But many people, especially in the agricultural sectors of low-income economies, choose to have several children. Children are their security, providing more hands to do a family's work and providing support for aging parents. Without greater affluence—hard to attain without economic growth—population will continue to grow. (That the most rapid population growth in the world is centered in African countries, which are among the least prosperous, illustrates the point.)

Curtailing economic growth as a means to contain environmental destruction has at least two main problems. First, unless it involves a massive, global redistribution of income and wealth, it condemns those at the bottom (countries and people) to their current economic level—both morally reprehensible and probably politically impossible. It is also probably politically impossible to overcome the obstacles to a massive redistribution. There are about 7.5 billion people in the world and total production is about $125 trillion, which means that average income is about $16,667. With no growth and redistribution getting everyone to this level, it would be necessary to reduce average income in the United States by over 70%, and in the Euro area and Japan by over 60%.

The second barrier to curtailing growth is that capitalism, which is pretty much the operating system of the whole world these days, is like a bicycle: If it stops, it (and the rider) falls over. The system depends on profits, and profits depend on either growth or redistributing income upward, and the latter has its limits. Getting rid of capitalism, running the world economy a different way, could have salutary results—though other social systems can do, and have done, substantial damage to the environment. Certainly, the political problems of getting rid of capitalism and insuring that its replacement would be environmentally friendly is a politically daunting tasks.

The Technology Option

Dealing with global warming needs to involve inhibiting population growth and curtailing economic growth—which means at least sharply constraining capitalism. But that's not enough. There need to be dramatic changes in the technology.

At the present time, the most promising energy production technologies are wind power and photovoltaics. Also, energy conservation has great potential for reducing the emissions of greenhouse gases.

The effectiveness of the technology option has been demonstrated in other countries. As Frank Ackerman points out in "Are Nuclear Plant Closures a Mistake?" (Article 6.6), renewable electricity generation expanded from 5% of total German power consumption in 1999 to over 30% in 2015. Over the same period, Ackerman concludes, "there has been no increase in [carbon] emissions from the electric sector ... [and] the reliability of the German electric system has continued to improve."

The problem, then, is not so much technical (i.e., developing ways to reduce emissions). The problem is political. Halting subsidies to the fossil fuel industries and providing support for environmentally friendly technological change would be good beginnings. Also, a great deal could be accomplished through encouragement of energy conservation programs. Further steps will require major limitations on firms' operations, limitations that prevent them from ignoring the health, safety, and, ultimately, the survival of the populations. A difficult task, of course, but we really have no choice. ❑

Article 6.6

IS NUCLEAR PLANT CLOSURE A MISTAKE?

BY FRANK ACKERMAN
May/June 2017

Dear Dr. Dollar:
Almost all the online search pieces regarding German decommissioning of nuclear power plants say it is too expensive, does not produce any benefits, and is generally a disaster in the making. Your thoughts would be greatly appreciated. —Julia Willebrand, New York, N.Y.

Nuclear decommissioning is always expensive. At the end of a nuclear power plant's lifetime, it must be disassembled, and safe storage must be found for a huge quantity of nuclear waste. Some of it will be hazardous for tens of thousands of years, and must be buried in a storage facility that will remain secure for much longer than the entire history of human civilization to date. The German government has allowed the country's electric utility companies to buy their way out of responsibility for nuclear waste storage at a price of 23.6 billion euros, but that may not be enough.

Germany has committed to closing all its nuclear plants by 2022. This deadline was first adopted in 2002 by a Social Democratic-Green coalition government, responding to Germany's strong anti-nuclear movement. In 2010, Chancellor Angela Merkel's conservative government extended the deadline by up to 14 years. Soon after Japan's Fukushima nuclear disaster in 2011, however, Merkel reinstated the 2022 deadline. Perhaps the only world leader who is also a physicist, she was newly impressed at the risk of nuclear accidents—and the risk of losing elections to the then-resurgent Green Party, riding the wave of post-Fukushima opposition to nuclear power. Of the 17 German reactors that were operating at the beginning of 2011, only eight are still on line. All will be permanently unplugged by the end of 2022.

Earlier retirement of nuclear plants affects the timing of decommissioning costs, but barely changes the magnitude. The main economic impact of early retirement for nukes is the loss of the low-cost electricity they could have produced in their remaining years. Most of the enormous costs of nuclear power are for initial construction and final decommissioning. With construction costs already paid via electric rates, and decommissioning costs already inescapable, the additional costs of operating a reactor for another year are relatively modest.

Does that mean that Germany's early retirement of nuclear plants is an expensive mistake, potentially destabilizing the grid, increasing carbon emissions from coal and gas plants, and pushing up electricity imports? In a word, no.

Germany has committed to the *Energiewende*—energy transition—aimed at rapid replacement of conventional power sources with renewable energy and improved efficiency. In the years of rapid nuclear retirement, since 2011, renewable energy has continued to expand, while coal and gas-fired power generation has remained roughly constant. As a share of power consumption in Germany, renewables represented only 5% as recently as 1999, rising to more than 30% in 2015—while nuclear power declined to 14% in 2015.

Generation of electricity from fossil fuels has not expanded, so there has been no increase in emissions from the electric sector. And in any case, emissions from power plants are subject to a cap under the EU's Emissions Trading System.

At the same time, the reliability of the German electric system has continued to improve. The duration of unplanned outages experienced by an average customer was 22 minutes per year in 2006, declining to 15 minutes by 2011, and to less than 13 minutes in 2015. France, with much greater dependence on nuclear power, averaged 65 minutes in 2013. The United States average was 115 minutes in 2015. Both nuclear and coal plants require large flows of cooling water, and can be forced to shut down during heat waves or droughts when river water is too warm, or too scarce, to provide effective cooling.

Is this rapid transition to renewable power propped up by electricity imports from France or other neighboring countries? No again. Before 2002, Germany's international trade in electricity was roughly in balance. Since then, during the era of renewable buildup and nuclear retirements, Germany has become a major exporter of electricity, selling more than 8% of its generation to other countries in 2016.

Stepping back from the details of Germany's impressive energy transition, is there a role for nuclear power in a sustainable future? For example, is nuclear power the only affordable low-carbon source of electrical power? The answer is still no. The only nuclear power that could be described as affordable comes from existing plants, where the construction costs have already been paid. As the costs of new reactors continue to mount, utilities throughout the U.S. and Europe have rejected the idea of building any more of them.

Most technologies have declining costs over time, as industry acquires more experience with them and learns how to apply them more efficiently. With nuclear power, more experience has led to discovery of more and more hazards, requiring an ever-longer list of expensive safeguards—and hence to increasing costs. Talk of new, safer designs for reactors, popular among nuclear researchers for decades, has remained nothing but talk. A few years ago, Westinghouse announced a new, standardized, "low-cost" reactor design. The attempt to build a few of them led directly to the recent bankruptcy of the company. It may yet bring down Toshiba, the owner of Westinghouse in its last, disastrous years.

Still, carbon emissions are undeniably lower for nuclear power than for fossil fuels. Some climate advocates, such as former NASA scientist Jim Hansen, insist that nuclear power is essential for carbon-emission reduction. Addressing this question requires a look at "lifecycle emissions"—from construction of facilities, through operation, to dismantlement and waste disposal. While there are no greenhouse-gas emissions from reactor operation, the reactor lifecycle includes significant emissions from construction. The same is true for wind and solar power, and for fossil fuel plants as well.

According to a recent literature review, coal plants have lifecycle emissions of about 1000 grams CO_2-eq/kWh (see table). Emissions for gas plants are about half as much. In contrast, nuclear plants have lifecycle emissions only about 1/15 as high as coal plants. But solar photovoltaics are even lower—about 1/20 as high as coal plants, while wind turbines are lower still.

To sum up, lifecycle emissions from nuclear-power plants are much lower than from fossil-fuel plants, and closer to renewables (only twice as much as from wind power!). But unlike renewables, nuclear power comes with horrendous construction costs and delays, uncertain nuclear accident risks, and unsolved very-long-term waste disposal problems.

Other than that, it's a bargain. ❏

LIFECYCLE EMISSIONS FOR SOURCES OF ELECTRICITY

Technology	g CO_2eq/kWh
Hydroelectric	10-13
Solar thermal	13
Wind	34
Solar photovoltaic	50
Nuclear	66
Natural gas	443-611
Coal	960-1,050

Source: Daniel Nugent and Benjamin K. Sovacool, "Assessing the lifecycle greenhouse gas emissions from solar PV and wind energy: A critical meta-survey," Energy Policy 65 (2014), 229-244.

Sources: The German Energiewende Book (book.energytransition.org); numerous entries on cleanenergywire.org; Wikipedia, "Energiewende in Germany" and sources cited there; Fraunhofer Institute, "Energy Charts," www.energy-charts.de/index.htm; German government energy data (bmwi.de/Navigation/EN/Topic/energiedaten.html).

Article 6.7

MAPPING ENVIRONMENTAL INJUSTICE
Race, Class, and Industrial Air Pollution

BY KLARA ZWICKL, MICHAEL ASH, AND JAMES K. BOYCE
November/December 2015

E ast St. Louis, Ill., just across the Mississippi River from St. Louis, Mo., is not your typical American town. It has a hazardous waste incinerator, numerous chemical plants, and multiple "national priority" toxic waste sites. It's also home to 26,000 residents, 98% of them African-American. The median household income is about $21,000—meaning that half the households in the city have annual incomes even lower. The rate of childhood asthma is among the highest in the nation.

America's polluters are not color-blind. Nor are they oblivious to distinctions of class. Studies of environmental inequality have found that minorities and low-income communities often bear disproportionate pollution burdens. One of the reasons was revealed in a consultant report to the California Waste Management Board that surfaced in the 1980s: "A great deal of time, resources, and planning could be saved and political problems avoided if people who are resentful and people who are amenable to Waste-to-Energy projects [a.k.a. incinerators] could be identified before selecting a site," the report observed. It recommended that "middle and higher-socioeconomic strata neighborhoods should not fall at least within the one-mile and five-mile radii of the proposed site."

Rather than being distributed randomly across the U.S. population, pollution mirrors the distribution of power and wealth. Pollution disparities reflect conscious

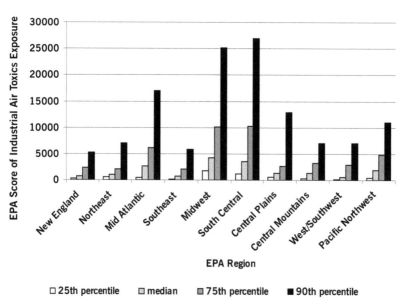

FIGURE 1: INDUSTRIAL AIR TOXICS EXPOSURE BY EPA REGION

□ 25th percentile   □ median   ▨ 75th percentile   ■ 90th percentile decisions—decisions by companies to locate hazardous facilities in vulnerable communities, and decisions by government regulators to give less priority to environmental enforcement in these communities. They can also reflect neighborhood changes driven by environmental degradation: pollution pushes out the affluent and lowers property values, while poorer people seeking low-cost housing move in, either unaware of the health risks or unable to afford alternatives. Even after accounting for differences related to income, however, studies find that racial and ethnic minorities often face higher pollution burdens—implying that disparities are the result of differences in political power as well as purchasing power.

The United States is a big, heterogeneous country. Electoral politics, social movements, industrial structure, residential segregation, and environmental policies differ across regions. So patterns of pollution may vary, too. Our recent study "Regional variation in environmental inequality: Industrial air toxics exposure in U.S. cities" examines these patterns to ask two key questions. First, is minority status or income more important in explaining environmental disparities? Second, does income protect minorities from pollution as much as it protects whites?

To tackle these questions, we used data on industrial air pollution from the U.S. Environmental Protection Agency (EPA). In the 1980s, in the wake of the deadly toxic gas release at a plant owned by the U.S.-based company Union Carbide in Bhopal, India, in which thousands of nearby residents were killed, environmental advocates in the U.S. demanded disclosure of information on hazards faced by communities near industrial facilities. In response, Congress passed the Emergency Planning and Community Right-to-Know Act of 1986, requiring corporations to disclose their releases of dangerous chemicals into our air, water, and lands. These are reported annually in the EPA's Toxics Release Inventory. The EPA has combined

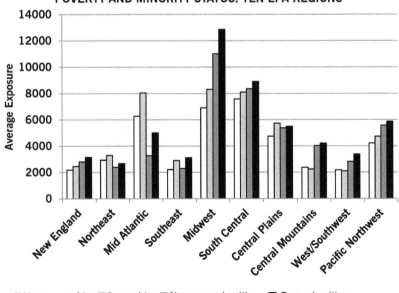

FIGURE 2: AVERAGE INDUSTRIAL AIR TOXICS EXPOSURE (EPA SCORE) BY POVERTY AND MINORITY STATUS, TEN EPA REGIONS

□ Non-poor white □ Poor white ▨ Non-poor minorities ■ Poor minorities these data with information on the toxicity and dispersion of hazardous chemical releases to create the Risk-Screening Environmental Indicators (RSEI), the database we use, that estimates the total human health risks in neighborhoods across the country from multiple industrial pollution sources and chemicals.

Industrial air pollution varies greatly across regions of the country. Figure 1 shows the level of health risk faced by the median resident (in the middle of the region's exposure distribution) as well as by more highly impacted residents (in the 75th and 90th percentiles of exposure). The Midwest and South Central regions have the highest levels, reflecting historical patterns of both industrial and residential development.

Figure 2 shows average pollution exposure by region for four groups: non-poor whites, poor whites, non-poor minorities and poor minorities. Poor minorities consistently face higher average exposure than non-poor minorities, and in most regions poor whites face higher average exposure than non-poor whites. In general, poor minorities also face higher exposure than poor whites, and non-poor minorities face higher exposure than non-poor whites. But in mapping environmental injustice we do find some noteworthy inter-regional differences—for example, in the contrast between racial disparities in the Midwest and Mid-Atlantic regions—that point to the need for location-specific analyses.

Finally, Figure 3 depicts the average pollution exposure for four racial/ethnic groups across income strata at the national level. The most striking finding here is that racial disparities in exposure are much wider among people who live in lower-income neighborhoods. At the lower-income end of the scale, the average exposures of African Americans are substantially greater than those of whites. The lower average exposures for Hispanics in low-income neighborhoods are largely explained by their concentration in western and southwestern cities with

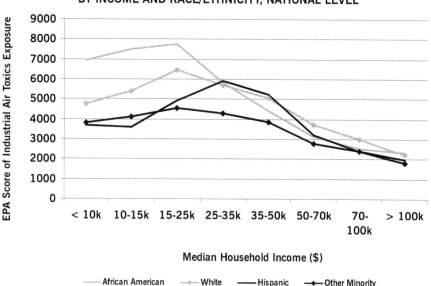

FIGURE 3: AVERAGE INDUSTRIAL AIR TOXICS EXPOSURE BY INCOME AND RACE/ETHNICITY, NATIONAL LEVEL

below-average pollution. Statistical analysis shows, however, that within these cities Hispanics also tend to live in the more polluted neighborhoods.

Pollution risk increases with average neighborhood income for all groups up to a turning point at around $25,000 per year. This can be explained by the positive association between industrialization and economic development. After that point, however, income becomes protective, and rising neighborhood income is associated with lower pollution exposure. Among these higher-income neighborhoods, racial and ethnic disparities in exposure are almost non-existent. But because of the correlation between minority status and income, minorities are more concentrated in lower-income communities whereas whites are more concentrated in upper-income communities. Based on where they live, whites may be more likely to see income as the main factor explaining disparities in pollution exposure, whereas African Americans are more likely to see the racial composition of neighborhoods as what matters most.

Environmental protection is not just about protecting nature from people: it's also about protecting people from other people. Those who benefit from industrial air pollution are the corporations that reap higher profits and their consumers, insofar as avoided pollution-control costs are passed on in the form of lower prices. Those who bear the greatest harm are the residents of nearby communities. Safeguarding the environment requires remedying this injustice and the imbalances of power that lie behind it. ❏

Sources: Michael Ash and T. Robert Fetter, "Who Lives on the Wrong Side of the Environmental Tracks?" *Social Science Quarterly*, 85(2), 2004; H. Spencer Banzhaf and Randall B. Walsh, "Do People Vote with Their Feet?" *American Economic Review*, 98(3), 2008; Vicki Been and Francis Gupta, "Coming to the nuisance or going to the barrios?" *Ecology Law Quarterly*, 24(1), 1997; James K. Boyce, "Inequality and Environmental Protection," in Jean-Marie Baland, Pranab K. Bardhan, and Samuel Bowles, eds., *Inequality, Cooperation, and Environmental Sustainability* (Princeton University Press, 2007); James K. Boyce, *The Political Economy of the Environment* (Edward Elgar, 2002); Paul Mohai and Robin Saha, "Reassessing Racial and Socioeconomic Disparities in Environmental Justice Research," *Demography*, 43(2), 2006; Rachel Morello-Frosch, et al., "Environmental Justice and Regional Inequality in Southern California: Implications for Future Research," *Environmental Health Perspectives*, 110(S2), 2002; Manuel Pastor, Jim Sadd, and John Hipp, "Which Came First? Toxic Facilities, Minority Move-In, and Environmental Justice," *Journal of Urban Affairs*, 23(1), 2001; Evan J. Ringquist, "Assessing Evidence of Environmental Inequities: A Meta-Analysis," *Journal of Policy Analysis and Management*, 24(2), 2005; Klara Zwickl, Michael Ash, and James K. Boyce, "Regional Variation in Environmental Inequality: Industrial Air Toxics exposure in U.S. Cities," *Ecological Economics*, (107), 2014.

Chapter 7

LABOR MARKETS

INTRODUCTION

Mainstream economics textbooks emphasize the ways that labor markets are similar to other markets. In the standard model, labor suppliers (workers) decide how much to work in the same way that producers decide how much to supply, by weighing the revenues against the costs—in this case, the opportunity costs of foregone leisure, and other potential costs of having a job, like physical injury. Workers are paid their marginal product, the extra output the firm gets from employing one extra unit (e.g., hour) of labor. Workers earn different wages because they contribute different marginal products to output. Of course, economists of every stripe acknowledge that, in reality, many non-market factors, such as government assistance programs, unionization, and discrimination, affect labor markets. But in most economics textbooks, these produce only limited deviations from the basic laws of supply and demand.

In the first article, Alejandro Reuss addresses the reasons behind union decline in the United States (Article 7.1). While mainstream economists often attribute this trend to the inexorable forces of globalization, Reuss points out that unions have not declined to the same extent in other countries (including the United States' more globalized neighbor to the north). He emphasizes, instead, the differences between institutions and policies in different countries and their effects on the balance of power between workers and employers.

Zoe Sherman, in our second article, "The Fallout from Subcontracting" (Article 7.2), answers a reader's question as to the effect of subcontracting on a local community. Sherman finds that though cities, states, and institutions save money by outsourcing work from in-house employment to outside subcontractor, these benefits come at the expense of the employees. The resulting reduction in income and benefits aggravates the widening disparity of incomes and wealth within the very communities that they serve and undermines the power of these workers to bargain for better wages and working conditions.

Next, in "Working in the 'Sharing Economy'" (Article 7.3), Anders Fremstad sets his sights on Uber and explores how the ride-sharing service and related companies treat their workers. Fremstad argues that the "sharing economy" is fundamentally different for labor than for things such as power tools or apartments to rent. Even though the new technology have been more efficient on matching drivers to customers, the bottom line is that the resulting take-home pay after expenses is very low.

Gerald Friedman continues the discussion of insecure "contingent labor," or what he calls the "gig economy," in the United States. In "Dog Walking and College Teaching" (Article 7.4), Friedman shows how labor contracts with little job security have been on the rise in everything from construction and office work to higher education.

In her article, "What's Behind the Teachers' Strikes" (Article 7.5), labor organizer Ellen David Friedman explains the origins of the wildcat teacher strike wave, and its relationship to teaching's unique historic role in society and its recent cornering by resource cuts and the charter movement.

An interview with economist Nancy Folbre, "Household Labor, Caring Labor, Unpaid Labor" (Article 7.6), reveals that women's labor is often "invisible"—in this case to official government economic accounts—as unpaid household labor. As Folbre argues, the exclusion of this labor from government estimates of employment and output (GDP) is "pretty crazy, since we know that these services contribute to our living standards and also to the development of human capabilities."

In the next article, Arthur MacEwan addresses the question "Will Artificial Intelligence Mean Massive Job Loss?" (Article 7.7). This one is complicated! MacEwan is skeptical that technological innovations will mean mass unemployment now when it has not in previous eras. He argues, however, that the trend toward automation might aggravate an already skewed income and wealth distribution.

Finally, we have a timely piece by David Bacon, "Migration, Labor, and U.S. Policy" (Article 7.8). Bacon continues his chronicles of the Mexican working class with a review of the push and pull factors behind immigration, many of them easily seen in recent trade pacts like NAFTA. Bacon finds that these factors are strong enough to continue drawing workers despite the increased severity of migration laws, which instead increase the misery of the migrant work force and worsen conditions for workers across the board.

Discussion Questions

1. (Article 7.1) Why has the number of workers represented by unions fallen in the United States over the last few decades? Is globalization, by itself, a plausible explanation?

2. (Article 7.2) Zoe Sherman explores the effect of subcontracting on workers and communities. How does subcontracting "weaken" the relative power of workers? How does subcontracting affect employment and incomes in those very communities? How has the "traditional" employer/employee relationship broken down?

3. (Article 7.3) "The sharing economy has succeeded in making some people very rich, but it has not lived up to its full potential. By setting new rules, introducing fair-trade competitors, and democratizing monopolistic platforms, we can ensure that the sharing economy serves not just owners, but workers, consumers, and the planet." Evaluate Fremstad's conclusion. What is his "three-pronged approach" to advance labor's interests? Explore each suggestion.

4. (Article 7.4) Why have "contingent" labor arrangements increased so much in recent decades? How do employers benefit from these arrangements? If workers, on balance, are harmed by reduced job security, why do employers not have a hard time finding people willing to work under such contracts?

5. (Article 7.5) Describe the different origins of the wildcat teacher strikes of 2018 and the rise of "progressive" union locals like the Chicago Teachers Union.

6. (Article 7.6) In Folbre's view, how has the "invisibility" of household labor and production from official economic data had negative consequences, both on our economic understanding and economic policies?

7. (Article 7.7) What is it about artificial intelligence that has some observers so concerned about massive job loss with the current wave of automation? Why is MacEwan skeptical as to "massive job loss"? Why does MacEwan think, however, that artificial intelligence will probably aggravate inequality?

8. (Article 7.8) How have the trade effects of NAFTA added to the forces driving immigration from Mexico to the United States? What effect will more punitive immigration enforcement likely bring to these dynamics, according to Bacon?

Article 7.1

WHAT'S BEHIND UNION DECLINE?

It's not just globalization, as a U.S.-Canada comparison shows.

BY ALEJANDRO REUSS
May 2015

The total number of union members in the United States peaked between the late 1970s and early 1980s, at over 20 million. As of 2010, it remained near 15 million. The story of union decline in the United States, however, does not begin in the 1980s, nor is it as modest as these figures would suggest. Union density (or the "unionization rate"), the number of workers who are members of unions as a percentage of all employed workers, has been declining in the United States for over half a century. The share of U.S. workers in unions peaked in 1954, at just over 25%. For nonagricultural workers, the high-water mark—at more than one third of employed workers—came even earlier, in 1945. It would reach nearly the same percentage again in the early 1950s, before beginning a long and virtually uninterrupted decline.

By 2010, the U.S. unionization rate was less than 12%. It would be even lower were it not for the growth of public-sector unions since the 1960s. For private-sector workers, the unionization rate is now less than 7%.

There are multiple reasons for union decline, including shrinking employment in highly unionized industries, falling unionization rates within these traditional bastions of unionism, and failures to unionize in new, growing sectors.

Employers' determination to rid themselves of unions has certainly played a major role in declining unionization rates. Where employers could not break unions, they were determined to find ways around them—even during the period of the so-called "capital-labor accord," from the 1940s to the 1970s. In reality, this was less a friendly relationship than a transition, on the part of employers, to low-intensity warfare when a frontal assault was not possible. Unionized companies established parallel non-union operations, a practice sometimes known as "double breasting," gradually shifting production and employment away from their unionized facilities. Some employers began contracting out work formerly done by union employees to non-union subcontractors (the original meaning of "outsourcing"). Some established new operations far from their traditional production centers, especially in less unionized and lower-wage areas. Many companies based in the Northeast and Upper Midwest, for example, set up new production sites in the South and West, and eventually in other countries. Finally, new employers entering highly unionized sectors usually remained non-union. The auto industry is a good example. So-called "transplants" (factories owned by non-U.S. headquartered companies) have accounted for an increasing share of the industry's shrinking labor force, and have remained overwhelmingly non-union.

Historically, union growth has come primarily in short spurts when unions expand into new industries. Since the 1940s, however, U.S. unions have failed to organize in growing industries to compensate for the declines in employment and unionization rates in traditional union strongholds. The public sector represents the one major exception. Since the early 1970s, union density for public-sector workers has increased from about 20% to over 35%. This has not been nearly enough, however, to counteract the decline among private-sector workers. To maintain the overall unionization rates of the 1950s or 1960s, unions would have had to enlist millions more workers in the private sector, especially in services.

The Employers' Offensive

Since the 1970s, employers have fought unions and unionization drives with increasing aggressiveness, as part of what labor historian Michael Goldfield calls the "employer offensive." Many employers facing unionization drives fire vocal union supporters, both eliminating pro-union campaigners and spreading fear among the other workers. Researchers at the Center for Economic and Policy Research (CEPR) have found that, between 2001 and 2005, pro-union workers were illegally fired in around one-fourth of all union election campaigns. Meanwhile, during many unionization campaigns, employers threaten to shut down the facility (at least in part) if the union wins. Labor researcher Kate Bronfenbrenner reports, in a study from the mid 1990s, that employers threatened plant closings in more than half of all unionization campaigns, and that such threats cut the union victory rate (compared to those in which no such threat was made) by about 30%.

The employer offensive has unfolded, especially since the 1980s, against a backdrop of government hostility towards unions. The federal government has often turned a blind eye to illegal tactics (or "unfair labor practices") routinely used by employers to fight unionization drives. Employer retaliation against workers (by firing or otherwise) for union membership, union activity, or support for unionization is illegal. So is an employer threatening to close a specific plant in response to a unionization drive. However, since the 1980s, union supporters argue, the government agencies tasked with enforcing labor law have increasingly ignored such

FIGURE 1: UNION MEMBERS AS A PERCENTAGE OF EMPLOYED WORKERS UNITED STATES, 1930-2003

Source: Gerald Mayer, Union Membership Trends in the United States, CRS Report for Congress, August 31, 2004, Table A1, Union Membership in the United States, 1930-2003 (digitalcommons.ilr.cornell.edu/key_workplace/174).

FIGURE 2: WORK STOPPAGES INVOLVING 1,000 OR MORE WORKERS UNITED STATES, 1947-2010

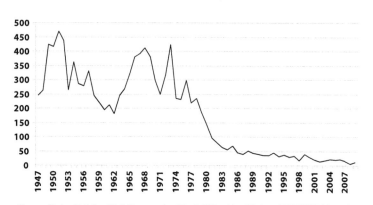

Source: Bureau of Labor Statistics, Work Stoppages Involving 1,000 or More Workers, 1947-2008 (bls.gov/news.release/wkstp.t01.htm).

practices, imposed only "slap on the wrist" punishments, or delayed judgment, sometimes for years, long after the unionization drive is over and done with.

Before the 1980s, it was relatively rare for employers to fire striking workers and hire "permanent replacements." (Sometimes, employers would bring in replacements during a strike, but striking workers would get their jobs back after a settlement was reached.) During the 1980s, private employers increasingly responded to strikes by firing the strikers and bringing in permanent replacements—a practice that is illegal in many countries, but not in the United States. Some labor historians point to the Reagan administration's mass firing of striking air-traffic controllers (members of the Professional Air Traffic Controllers Organization, or PATCO) in 1981 as a deliberate signal to private employers that the government approved their use of permanent replacements (as well as other union-busting tactics). The number of large strikes, already in sharp decline during the preceding few years (possibly due to the employers' offensive, rising unemployment, and other factors), has since declined to microscopic proportions. People do not go out on strike if they feel that they are not only likely to lose, but to lose their jobs in the bargain.

At this point, union density in the United States—less than a tenth of all private-sector workers—is almost back down to its level on the eve of the Great Depression. An optimistic union supporter might note that the 1930s turned out to be the greatest period of union growth in U.S. history, with substantial additional growth in the 1940s and 1950s largely an aftershock of that earlier explosion. There is no guarantee, however, that history will repeat itself, and that the weakness of organized labor today will give way to a new burst of energy. In the midst of a deep recession, and now more than five years of a feeble recovery, there have been few signs of a labor revival. Ironically, only the recent attacks on public-sector workers and unions have provoked a mass-movement fight-back. Labor supporters, however, should understand this, soberly, as coming from a very defensive position.

Is it Globalization?

Union size and strength have declined not only in the United States, but also in most other high-income countries. The reasons are complex, but globalization has surely played a role. Along with changing patterns of demand and increasing mechanization, global sourcing of production has contributed to employment declines in traditionally high-unionization industries. It has also provided employers with a stronger trump card when workers try to form new unions—the threat to relocate, especially to low-wage countries. To a greater or lesser extent, these effects are probably felt in all high-income countries.

Unionization rates, however, have declined in some countries much more than in others. According to data compiled by economist Gerald Friedman, the unionization rate for the United States peaked earlier, peaked at a lower percentage, and has declined to a lower percentage today, compared to those of most other high-income countries. Today, fourteen high-income countries (out of 15 listed by Friedman) currently have unionization rates higher than the United States' 14%. Ten have rates higher than the U.S. peak of about 26% (reached in 1956). Six have rates above 50%; three, above 80% (Gerald Friedman, "Is Labor Dead?" International Labor and Working Class History, Vol. 75, Issue 1, Table One: The Decline of the Labor Movement). (The declines in the unionization rates for ten of these countries, since each one's peak-unionization year, are shown in Figure 3.)

Let's compare, in more detail, the trajectories of unionization in the United States and its neighbor to the north, Canada (shown in Figure 4). Until the 1960s, the trends in the two countries were similar—declining in the 1920s, bottoming out in the early 1930s, growing dramatically through the rest of the 1930s, the 1940s, and into the 1950s. Since then, however, the two have diverged. The U.S. unionization rate has traced a long and nearly uninterrupted path of decline for the last half century. Meanwhile, the Canadian rate, which had gone into decline

FIGURE 3: PERCENTAGE DECLINE FROM PEAK UNIONZATION RATE, SELECTED COUNTRIES (PEAK YEAR IN PARENTHESES

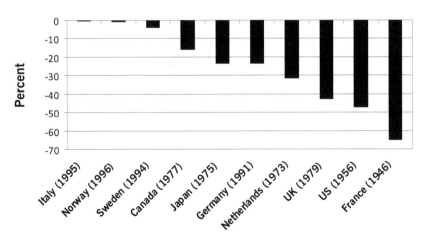

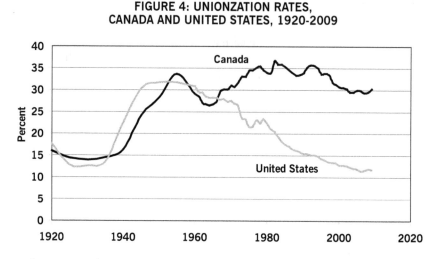

FIGURE 4: UNIONZATION RATES,
CANADA AND UNITED STATES, 1920-2009

in the 1950s and 1960s, recovered between the 1970s and 1990s. It has declined somewhat since then, but remains nearly three times the U.S. rate (almost 30%, compared to just over 10% for the United States). It would be difficult, even ignoring the Canadian data, to attribute U.S. union decline just to international factors, such as import competition (which became a major factor in the 1970s) or global sourcing (which has been a major factor since the 1990s). These factors simply come too late to fully explain trends going back to the 1950s. Looking at the comparison with Canada, however, drives the point home: "globalization" is simply not the irresistible tidal wave, wiping out unions across the globe, that many commentators claim.

There are a couple of possible explanations for the divergence of U.S. and Canadian unionization rates (or, more generally, the divergence of the unionization rates in any two capitalist economies in the era of globalization).

First, perhaps it is possible for a country to effectively insulate itself from the global economy. That is, it may use controls on international trade and investment to prevent its economy from becoming "globalized" or, more likely, to regulate the ways that it is integrated into the world capitalist economy. That is, however, definitely not what is going on with Canada. It is a member of NAFTA; its economy is highly integrated with that of the United States, both in terms of trade and investment; its imports and exports, as a percentage of GDP, are actually much larger than those of the United States. By any standard Canada has a more globalized economy than the United States.

Second, even if a country's economy is highly integrated into the world capitalist economy, the political and legal environments for labor relations—as well as the history and culture of its labor movement—have tremendous effects on the ability of unions to survive in the age of globalization. A recent report from the Center for Economic and Policy Research (CEPR) attributes the much sharper decline of U.S. unions primarily to "employer opposition to unions—together with relatively weak labor law" in the United States compared to Canada, rather than "structural changes to the economy ... related to globalization or technological progress."

The report, "Protecting Fundamental Labor Rights: Lessons from Canada for the United States," focuses in particular on two differences in labor law: In Canada, workers have card-check unionization, the right to form a union once most of the workers in a bargaining unit have signed a union card. This prevents employers from fighting unionization—including by firing union supporters or threatening shut downs, as are common in the United States—during a long, drawn-out period before a union election. (U.S. unions have proposed a similar legislation at the national level, but employers have so far prevented such a bill from passing.) Also, Canadian law requires, in the event that a union and employer cannot arrive at a first collective bargaining agreement, that the two parties enter arbitration. As the CEPR report put it, this "ensure[s] that workers who voted to unionize [are] able to negotiate a contract despite continued employer opposition." In the United States, in contrast, employers often stonewall in initial negotiations, and many new unions never actually achieve a signed union contract.

A third factor, not discussed in the CEPR report, is the difference between the United States and Canada in laws governing the right to strike. In the United States, it is legal for employers to fire striking workers and hire permanent replacements. Since the late 1970s, when U.S. employers started routinely using permanent replacements, strikes have become much harder for workers to win and, as a result, much less frequent. This has deprived U.S. workers of their main form of bargaining power, the ability to withdraw their labor and shut down production, cutting off the source of the employer's profits. In contrast, most Canadian provinces ban employers from using permanent replacements.

Finally, the CEPR report does note the possibility that weaknesses of the U.S. labor movement itself—especially the "lack of focus on organizing new members" —accounts for at least part of the divergence. Indeed, the labor movements in most capitalist countries have faced changes in employment patterns, and the relative decline of traditional high-unionization industries. As Friedman notes, however, some have been able to make up for declining employment in their traditional strongholds by organizing workers in growing-employment sectors (Friedman, Reigniting the Labor Movement (Routledge, 2008)). The U.S. labor movement—mostly, to be sure, due to the hostile environment for new organizing—has not been able to do so. The Canadian labor movement also differs from U.S. labor in having created an explicitly labor-oriented political party, the New Democratic Party. (Most western European countries also have strong labor, social democratic, or socialist parties with institutional and historical ties to unions.) In many countries, such parties have played an important role in gaining favorable labor legislation, and more generally blunting attacks on labor by employers and governments.

Global economic forces affecting all countries cannot, by themselves, explain the various patterns of union decline across different capitalist countries (or the patterns would be more similar). The differing political environments in different countries—such as the laws protecting workers' rights to form unions, to go on strike, and so on—likely explain most of the differences in the degree of union decline in different high-income countries. ❑

Sources: Michael Goldfield, "Labor in American Politics—Its Current Weakness," *The Journal of Politics*, Vol. 48, No. 1. (Feb., 1986), pp. 2-29; Kate Bronfenbrenner, "Final Report: The Effects of Plant Closing or Threat of Plant Closing on the Right of Workers to Organize," *International Publications,* Paper 1, 1996 (digitalcommons.ilr.cornell.edu/intl/1); Gerald Friedman, *Reigniting the Labor Movement: Restoring Means to Ends in a Democratic Labor Movement* (New York: Routledge, 2008); Gerald Mayer, "Union Membership Trends in the United States," CRS Report for Congress, August 31, 2004, Table A1, Union Membership in the United States, 1930-2003 (digitalcommons.ilr.cornell.edu/key_workplace/174); Bureau of Labor Statistics, "Work Stoppages Involving 1,000 or More Workers," 1947-2008 (www.bls.gov/news.release/wkstp.t01.htm); John Schmitt and Ben Zipperer, "Dropping the Ax: Illegal Firings During Union Election Campaigns," Center for Economic and Policy Research, January 2007 (www.cepr.net/documents/publications/unions_2007_01.pdf); Kris Warner, "Protecting Fundamental Labor Rights: Lessons from Canada for the United States," Center for Economic and Policy Research, August 2012 (http://cepr.net/documents/publications/canada-2012-08.pdf).

Article 7.2

THE FALLOUT FROM SUBCONTRACTING

BY ZOE SHERMAN
January/February 2017

Dear Dr. Dollar:
Has there ever been a study done on the economic impact of subcontracting on a local community? When, for example, a school district subs out its custodial work, with the obvious concomitant reduction of pay and benefits suffered by the employees involved, has anyone ever tried to determine the economic impact on the local community?
—Paul Gottlieb, Montgomeryville, Penn.

At a former workplace, I had some full-time, year-round, benefits-eligible coworkers on the janitorial and security staff. Over the years I was there, an increasing proportion of the cleaning and security work was transferred to sub-contracted cleaning and security companies.

My first impulse was to do the mental arithmetic this way: If the institution finds it more cost effective to subcontract the work rather than hire directly, they must pay the company supplying the services less than they pay their own employees. In addition, the subcontracting company must take a cut. (For example, a friend who was employed by a temp agency around the same time told me her agency took a one-third cut: If a client paid the agency $15/hour for her to show up and do some work, she herself would get paid $10/hour for that work.) So that means the people actually in the building doing the work as subcontractors must be getting paid a lot less than people who were hired directly.

In addition, subcontracting raises a host of other issues, beyond just pay and benefits questions. Under a subcontracting relationship, the people who do the work are not directly employed by the institution for which they perform the assigned work tasks. Instead, subcontracting inserts an intermediary between the worker and the ultimate employer. The intermediary can in principle, and even sometimes in practice, make the process of matching workers and employers more efficient: The employer can make one call and pay one invoice and have as many workers as needed, rather than dealing with recruitment and hiring and payroll. (The intermediary who does deal with all the recruitment, hiring, and payroll can enjoy economies of scale on those tasks.) Workers, meanwhile, can be matched to any number of jobs without having to take on the costs of searching and applying for many jobs.

This sounds great, except that subcontracting reshapes power relationships in ways that keep the rewards of efficiency gains beyond most workers' grasp. A common pattern identified by economist Ian Taplin in his study of the apparel industry is this: A "core" firm will subcontract out the most labor-intensive, lowest-profit-margin portions of the production process. The subcontractors are dependent on the core firm for sales and locked in intense price competition with one another. The flexibility gained by the core firm is "squarely predicated upon deskilling, wage depression, and labor intensification," often carried out within the subcontracted companies. In other words, whatever gains subcontracting brings too often come at the expense of workers' employment security and their ability to use their voice to affect working conditions at their workplace.

The labor-market intermediaries that match workers to jobs—for-profit temp agencies and the like—can make demands on workers' availability to work, but only pay them when they have a customer for that work. The intermediaries also increase the administrative distance between the workers and the people whose decisions most directly affect their working conditions. That distance weakens the social reciprocity that a direct, long-term employment relationship can sometimes foster and lessens the opportunity for collaborative problem solving. Subcontracted workers are more easily discarded and replaced, so subcontracting also weakens workers' ability to exercise voice in more combative ways, such as strikes. And subcontracting can sometimes be a cover for discriminatory employment practices, making it harder to enforce equal employment opportunity standards.

So subcontracting can be tough on the workers who are most directly affected. You asked, though, how it affects the larger community. That's a multi-headed hydra of a question.

In the example of a school district subcontracting custodial work, decent-paying employment opportunities disappear and lower-paying jobs appear in their places. Custodians' income goes down, so they buy less. Their reduction in spending means a loss of income for the people they buy things from. Now that *those* people's income is lower, *they* spend less too, and so on. This ripple effect multiplies the initial loss of income into a larger loss of aggregate income for the whole population.

In addition, many factors other than lower income for the workers cleaning the school are in play. Do the same individuals keep doing the work, but under worse conditions? Or are the subcontracted workers different people? And if the subcontracted workers are different people, what happens to the people who lost their jobs? What *does* the district do with the money it does not spend on decent pay, benefits, and working conditions for custodial workers? If budgeting in your school district looks like budgeting in my district, perhaps the district spends any money it squeezes out of the custodial services budget on maintaining comparable levels of health benefits paid to teachers in the face of rising insurance premiums. In that case the choice to subcontract custodial services reallocates income from workers who maintain school buildings to a few other recipients: to the owners and direct employees of the subcontracting company, to those who work at health insurance companies and, to the extent that teachers use their health insurance benefits to get care, to those who work in the medical sector. In the for-profit sector, subcontracting tends to concentrate economic rewards in the hands of the company at the top of the hierarchical production structure.

The intermediation and job insecurity associated with subcontracting, like the changes in income, can also have spillover effects on the community at large. There are two competing tendencies for how subcontracting and other types of what are called "flexible staffing arrangements" affect other workers. Employers could offer full-time, long-term employment to those employees they would find hardest to replace by concentrating the risk and desired flexibility on the temporary/contingent/subcontracted workers. A study of industries in Alabama in the 2000s found that this divergence within the workforce was significant: the greater an employer's use of flexible staffing arrangements to manage fluctuations in demand for their products, the greater the employment stability for a core of full-time workers. Job quality for some workers is maintained at the expense of other workers.

On the other hand, having an available employment arrangement that directly disempowers the workers who are caught in it can weaken the bargaining position of all workers. Sociologist Erin Hatton argues in her book *The Temp Economy* that the growth of the temp industry has culturally legitimated treatment of workers as disposable and shrinks the steady employment core. In other words, job quality for all workers is threatened; the interests of employers are protected at the expense of workers.

Macroeconomic data suggest that both things are happenings in the U.S. economy: overall, workers are in a weaker position and inequality between workers and owners is rising. Inequality is also rising *among* workers. A small group of well-compensated workers—often salaried professionals—occupy the rungs just below owners on the income distribution ladder while a widening swath of the population is confronted with stagnant or falling wages. There is a strong case that subcontracting and other "flexible staffing arrangements" contribute to both of those disparities. ❑

Sources: Cynthia L. Gramm and John F. Schnell, "The Use of Flexible Staffing Arrangements in Core Industrial Jobs," *Industrial and Labor Relations Review*, January 2001; Erin Hatton, *The Temp Economy: From Kelly Girls to Permatemps in Postwar America* (Temple University Press, 2011).

Article 7.3

WORKING IN THE "SHARING ECONOMY"
Labor is simply not as shareable as stuff.

BY ANDERS FREMSTAD
September/October 2016

The ride-sharing company Uber is now valued at $70 billion, far more than any taxi company and about as much as Daimler-Chrysler. But very little of this new wealth is trickling down to Uber's "driver partners." Although Uber claims that full-time drivers in New York City earn $90,000 a year, economists Jonathan Hall (Uber Technologies) and Alan Krueger (Princeton University) find that the average wage is actually about $17 an hour nationwide, and some drivers report taking home less than $10 an hour after they pay for gas, maintenance, and insurance. This raises two important questions. First, if "sharing-economy" companies like Uber are so successful, why do workers earn so little? Second, what is to be done to protect labor in the sharing economy?

Before the sharing economy became synonymous with firms like Uber, Lyft, and Airbnb, it referred to a wide range of initiatives to help people make better use of underutilized assets. In rich countries like the United States, material waste is astounding. The average power drill is used fifteen minutes over its entire lifetime. The average vehicle is driven 4% of the day. The average new home has over 1,000 square feet per person. The first sharing-economy platforms sought to match people wanting to use some asset with peers who had assets they weren't using. The most profitable example is Airbnb, which is now worth $30 billion. Airbnb makes some (but not most) of its money by connecting travelers with lodging that would otherwise go to waste: spare rooms and entire homes when their regular inhabitants are out of town. In most of these instances, the maximum the guest is willing to pay is far more than the minimum the host is willing to accept, so there is plenty of "surplus" (the difference between these two amounts) to split among the host, guest, and platform—so everyone wins.

Some argue that there are similar gains to be made by connecting people with labor services. In his new book *The Sharing Economy*, economist Arun Sundararajan argues that platforms can better match the supply and demand for labor. "Work was once relegated to work hours. Depending on the profession work happened during the 12-hour shift or the 8-hour workday. Today work can take place in increasingly microscopic units, in increments as short as a minute or two. The new marketplaces spawned by the sharing economy are allowing us to tap into labor supply in a much more granular and efficient way." But the fact is that people's time is not wasted to nearly the same degree as people's stuff. When I'm not using my car, it costs me very little for someone else to borrow it. When I'm not using my time to earn money, I am still using my time to do something that is necessary or enjoyable. It is interesting to imagine people earnestly solving tasks on Amazon Mechanical Turk's "marketplace for work" while they wait at the doctor's office, but most people will probably stick to reading the news, making small talk, or playing Candy Crush.

Moreover, the fact that people can now earn money with spare moments of time does not prove that they can earn a living in the sharing economy. Many of the people who do the work for these platforms have very onerous schedules, often with extended periods of unpaid time while still "on call" for work. Labor simply is not as shareable as stuff.

While the gains from "sharing" labor are smaller than the gains from sharing physical goods, there may still be some benefits to organizing work through online platforms. In the case of Uber, its algorithm for matching drivers with riders using GPS technology is probably more efficient that the traditional practice of hailing cabs from curbs and dispatching cabs by radio. In a recent paper, economists Judd Cramer and Alan Krueger find that drivers have a passenger in their car about 60% of miles driven on Uber, compared to about 40% of miles driven in a traditional cab. By placing riders headed along similar routes in a single vehicle, UberPool may generate even greater social surplus by boosting vehicle occupancy rates.

The problem for workers in the sharing economy, then, is that monopolistic platforms have no incentive to share the surplus generated by technological change. From Uber's perspective, it simply needs to ensure its drivers earn as much as they would earn working for traditional taxi companies, about $12 to $15 an hour according to Hall and Krueger. Uber currently keeps 20-30% of total fares, which makes the firm extremely profitable, considering that it does not purchase vehicles, maintain vehicles, insure vehicles, or acquire taxi medallions as regular taxi companies must. By passing almost none of the benefits of technological change on to its workers, Uber has made billions of dollars for its owners and investors.

What is to be done? I propose a three-pronged approach to advance labor's interests in the 21st century sharing economy.

First, we need public policies that protect sharing-economy workers. The Brookings Institute's "independent worker" proposal would provide workers with collective bargaining rights and require platforms like Uber to withhold taxes and make FICA contributions. Although Brookings argues that it is impractical to extend the minimum wage, overtime pay, or unemployment insurance to the sharing economy, these issues deserve more study. We must also redouble our efforts to build a safety net that protects labor under all kinds of work arrangements, especially those who work for multiple employers. In the 21st century, many workers will not receive health and retirement benefits from any job, which strengthens the argument for single-payer health insurance (like Medicare for All) and more generous Social Security benefits.

Second, we should expose exploitative platforms by promoting ethical alternatives or the kind of public option that economist Dean Baker has proposed. There are multiple ride-sharing apps that claim to provide workers with a fair shake, but without independent certification it is impossible for consumers to know which platforms to trust. Worker organizations could decide what constitute fair working conditions, and they could promote fair platforms with a digital equivalent of the 20th-century union label. Given Uber's massive scale, it will be difficult for upstarts to achieve its network economies. As long as it is easy for drivers to switch between Uber and other ride-sharing apps, though, platforms that offer drivers a better shake should be able to tap into Uber's massive labor force—including former drivers who quit after realizing they could not make a living at it. The greatest challenge will be convincing a critical mass of passengers to switch to using new, less-familiar platforms.

Third, we must recognize that, just like water and electrical utilities, sharing-economy platforms are essentially "natural monopolies" where it would be most efficient to have just one firm. In the short run, competitors can demonstrate that the behemoths have no monopoly on the technical know-how to build and manage platforms, but in the long run it does not make sense to have competing apps. Our ultimate goal must be to run monopolistic platforms to maximize public welfare instead of to maximize private profits. By socializing or democratizing the sharing economy, we can ensure that the gains from technological change are split fairly between workers and consumers. Just as importantly, a public platform could directly pursue the initial promise of the sharing economy—to reduce current levels of waste. While Airbnb makes money getting hosts to convert apartments into illicit hotels, which can drive up rental rates and undermine neighborhood stability, our social goal would be to put spare rooms and empty homes to better use. While Uber got rich by undercutting the traditional taxi industry, our goal must be to discourage private vehicle ownership and boost cycling, mass transit, and carpooling.

The sharing economy has succeeded in making some people very rich, but it has not lived up to its full potential. By setting new rules, introducing fair-trade competitors, and democratizing monopolistic platforms, we can ensure that the sharing economy serves not just owners, but workers, consumers, and the planet. ❏

Sources: Eric Auchard, "Now roughly equal in value, Uber and Daimler trade gentle blows," Reuters, June 8, 2016; Jonathan Hall and Alan Krueger, "An Analysis of the Labor Market for Uber's Driver-Partners in the United States," Jan. 22, 2015; Emily Guendelsberger, "I was an undercover Uber driver," *My City Paper:* New York, May 7, 2015; Arun Sundararajan, *The Sharing Economy: The End of Employment and the Rise of Crowd-Based Capitalism* (MIT Press, 2016); Mechanical Turk website; Judd Cramer and Alan B. Krueger, "Disruptive Change in the Taxi Business: The Case of Uber," *The American Economic Review*, Volume 106, Number 5, May 2016, pp. 177-182(6); Tom Slee, *What's Yours is Mine: Against the Sharing Economy* (OR Books, 2016); Alan B. Krueger and Seth D. Harris, "A proposal for modernizing labor laws for 21st century work: The 'independent worker'," Brookings Institution, Dec. 8, 2015; Dean Baker, "The sharing economy needs a public option," Al Jazeera America, March 30, 2015; Mike Konczal, "Socialize Uber: It's Easier Than You Think," *The Nation*, Dec. 10. 2014; Anders Fremstad, "Harvesting the Potential of the Sharing Economy," Center for Popular Economics, April 13, 2015 (populareconomics.org).

Article 7.4

DOG WALKING AND COLLEGE TEACHING
The Rise of the Gig Economy

BY GERALD FRIEDMAN
March/April 2014

Growing numbers of Americans no longer hold a regular "job" with a long-term connection to a particular business. Instead, they work "gigs" where they are employed on a particular task or for a defined time, with little more connection to their employer than a consumer has with a particular brand of chips. Borrowed from the music industry, the word "gig" has been applied to all sorts of flexible employment (otherwise referred to as "contingent labor," "temp labor," or the "precariat"). Some have praised the rise of the gig economy for freeing workers from the grip of employers' "internal labor markets," where career advancement is tied to a particular business instead of competitive bidding between employers. Rather than being driven by worker preferences, however, the rise of the gig economy comes from employers' drive to lower costs, especially during business downturns. Gig workers experience greater insecurity than workers in traditional jobs and suffer from lack of access to established systems of social insurance.

FIGURE 1: EMPLOYED WORKERS BY CONTRACT TYPE, 1999

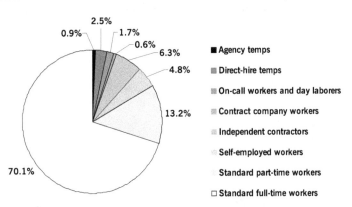

Special surveys by the Bureau of Labor Statistics in 1995, 2001, and 2005, and by the General Accounting Office in 1999, yielded widely varying estimates of the scale of the gig economy. The GAO estimated that as many as 30% of workers were on some type of contingent labor contract, including some categories of workers (self-employed and part-time workers) who are not counted as contingent workers by the BLS. According to BLS, 12% of workers were in "alternative work arrangements" (which includes independent contractors, temporary workers, on-call workers, and workers provided by contract firms) in 1999, similar to the number estimated from more recent surveys.

FIGURE 2: SHARE OF WORKERS IN ALTERNATIVE WORK ARRANGEMENTS, BY INDUSTRY, 2005

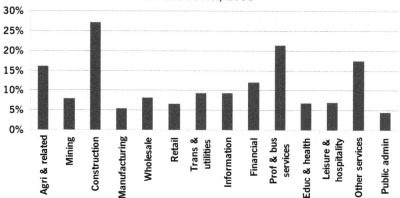

Contingent workers are employed throughout the economy, in all industries and in virtually all occupations. Workers in what the BLS terms "alternative work arrangements" made up over 11% of employed workers in 2005, according to BLS. Some workers in such arrangements do low-wage work in agriculture, construction, manufacturing, retail trade, and services; others are employed as highly paid financial analysts, lawyers, accountants, and physicians..

FIGURE 3: CONTINGENT LABOR, COLLEGE AND UNIVERSITY FACULTY

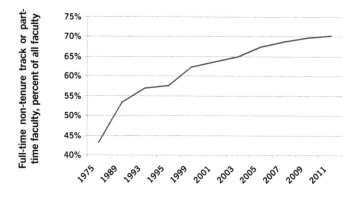

While many people may think of "day laborers" in construction or office "temps" when they think of contingent workers, few occupations have seen as sharp an increase in contingent labor as teaching in higher education. Full-time non-tenure track or part-time professors now account for the great majority of college faculty nationwide. Tenured and tenure-track faculty now comprise less than a third of the teaching staff, and teach barely half of all classes. Colleges and universities hire adjunct faculty because they make it possible to more precisely match faculty to the demand for classes, and because adjuncts are paid substantially less.

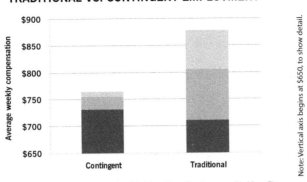

FIGURE 4: AVERAGE COMPENSATION,
TRADITIONAL VS. CONTINGENT EMPLOYMENT

Employers prefer contingent labor because it is more "flexible." Workers can be laid off at any time in response to a decline in sales. Employers can also pay contingent workers less by not offering benefits. By treating many contingent workers as independent contractors, employers avoid paying for government-mandated benefits (the employer's half of Social Security, unemployment insurance, workers' compensation, etc.). They also usually exclude contingent workers from employer-provided benefits such as health insurance and pensions. Counting wages and benefits, contingent workers are paid substantially less than workers in traditional jobs and are left much more vulnerable to illness or economic downturns.

FIGURE 5: NET JOB GROWTH, TRADITIONAL VS. CONTINGENT, 1995-2013

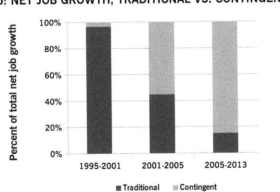

While a solid majority of workers is still employed under traditional arrangements, most new net job growth since 2001 has been under "alternative" arrangements. This is in sharp contrast to the late 1990s, when unemployment rates were low and employers had to offer workers more desirable long-term contracts. With the early 2000s recession, followed by the Great Recession and the anemic recovery (2007 to the present), however, employers have shunned long-term employment contracts and workers have had to settle. ❏

Sources: General Accounting Office (GAO), Contingent Workers: Incomes and Benefits Lag Behind Those of Rest of Workforce (gao.gov); Bureau of Labor Statistics (BLS), Contingent and Alternative Employment Arrangements, February 2005 and February 2001 (bls.gov); Sharon Cohany, "Workers in Alternative Employment Arrangements." *Monthly Labor Review* (October): 31–46; U.S. Department of Education, National Center for Education Statistics, National Study of Postsecondary Faculty; John Curtis, "Trends in Faculty Employment Status, 1975-2011" (aaup.org).

Article 7.5

WHAT'S BEHIND THE TEACHERS' STRIKES
The Labor-Movement Dynamic of Teacher Insurgencies

BY ELLEN DAVID FRIEDMAN
May/June 2018

As we watch—rapt—the unexpected teacher insurgencies in West Virginia, Oklahoma, Arizona, Kentucky, and Colorado, we're also grasping for understanding: Why is this stunning revolt occurring where unions are weak, where labor rights are thin, and where popular politics are considered to be on the right? To understand the insurgency, we need to look at economics, and at political economy specifically. But we especially need a labor-movement analysis.

A labor-movement analysis starts by understanding the political and economic conditions that shape the objective conditions of a particular group of workers (or labor market) at a given moment—prevailing wages, benefits, work processes, structures of employment, stability of work, market forces in the sector, etc. Then we look at how workers respond to those material factors and conditions: how they understand their interests, how they see their own power (or lack of it), how they understand the interests of the employers and what influences them, and how they develop tactics, strategies, and institutions to bring their power to bear against the power of employers. Finally, the self-directed activity of workers (including their ideas, ideologies, methods of organization, decision-making, and what actions they take) can be embedded in the larger context of other sectors of workers, other social movements, and historical labor movements. Such an analysis can help us interpret the teacher strike wave and, perhaps, gain insights that can help us rebuild capable, fighting unions.

Economics and Politics

The economic motivations of these insurgencies are clear: protracted and relentless constriction of wages and benefits have driven teachers to a condition of precarity normally reserved for workers who lack college degrees. Financial insecurity is matched by erosion of job security, as statutory probation periods are lengthened (three years of probation is now standard) and tenure is watered down. Facing severe job vacancies, many states lower—or eliminate—hiring standards and issue "emergency" waivers freely. In Arizona right now, there are more than 5,000 classrooms without a certified teacher. No wonder, then, that teachers feel they are being undervalued; they are.

The political economics of these insurgencies are also becoming more obvious. As tens of thousands of teachers—many of them newly politicized—rush to understand their states' tax structures, they discover a fiscal system engineered to starve public services and feed corporate portfolios. This transforms their sense of being undervalued into a comprehension that they have been betrayed by big business and the state itself.

Through years of frozen wages, cuts to student services, deteriorating buildings, and the hysterical drumbeat that public schools are failing and must be replaced with private charters, teachers have hunkered down and "made do." That is, they have accommodated themselves to a widely promoted "common sense" that argued that tax cuts serve the general good by creating jobs, and increasing individual's buying power. Starting with the infamous Prop 13 in California in 1978, which severely capped property taxes, and coincides with the rise of neoliberal ideology, the redistribution of wealth away from publicly held resources (notably, public schools) and into private hands has been relentless. But modern U.S. history reminds us that when inequalities become chronically damaging—as in the 1930s or the 1970s—the dominant narrative can crack and resistance can be kindled. This is when the paralysis of feeling disrespected and duped can transform into conviction and action.

A Labor-Movement Analysis

Challenging economic and political circumstances have certainly begun to foster a growing sense of commonality among teachers. But awareness alone does not automatically translate into action, much less the collective action we can legitimately call a labor movement. It's therefore helpful to build up a more nuanced analysis of teachers in their intertwined roles as workers, as unionists, and as members of civil society, to assess whether these insurgencies signal that teachers could emerge as leaders in a broader class movement.

As workers, teachers are in a unique structural position, for several reasons. Teaching is the only wholly "public profession" in the United States: a regulated category of work originally created to perform public service (this is still true, as teachers in private schools aren't required to hold teaching licenses). Teachers are employed and paid by public bodies and are subject to public governance. Moreover, it's a highly decentralized form of public employment, with both funding and governance historically centered in towns and cities. And it is a uniquely horizontal profession where, until fairly recently, schools were sites of little hierarchy and teachers were quite self-directing. These are all structural conditions reflecting, and reinforcing, radically democratic principles.

As unionists, teachers have a long history of organization. The National Education Association (NEA) was founded in 1857. Though it was not originally a labor union in function, it is now the largest union in the United States, with 3.2 million members. The American Federation of Teachers (AFT), founded in 1916, now has 1.7 million members. Teaching has the highest union density of any job category in the United States; union representation is essentially universal. Before collective bargaining was legally sanctioned at the state level for teachers, which happened first in 1959 in Wisconsin, there were traditions of consultation between teachers and their school boards. Even in states where collective bargaining is affirmatively banned, there are well-established standards—a unified salary schedule based on years of experience and education level, a comprehensive benefit package, pensions, specified length of work day and year, prep time, professional development subsidies, some kind of grievance procedure, and so on. More than any other sector of workers, teachers experience a union environment—or at least an associational and consultative environment—as the norm.

Teachers can be considered, in many ways, central to the project of U.S. civil society. Public education has been the main channel for incorporating "future citizens" into economic, social, and political engagement; and exclusion from adequate public education has been a device for exclusion from civil society more generally. And as tectonic upheavals occur—Reconstruction, the Jim Crow era, the build-up of industrial mass production, post-WWII consumer society, expansion of the liberal welfare state, and its deconstruction—the shifts and conflicts all play out in schools. Teachers are on the front line of interpreting every profound societal transformation, with all the tensions and challenges experienced personally in individual families. This places teachers in central positions in their communities. Because of their intimate and vital connections to parents, taxpayers, voters, providers of social services, higher education, and the job market into which students emerge, teachers can speak to, and amplify, the critical central needs of any community. The combination of these three intertwined roles has radical potential. The profession of teaching is shaped by public imperatives, grounded in democratic practices, present everywhere, and universally organized through job sites, and teachers hold the levers of social meaning and aspiration for our entire society. All the musculature of power is present—but, until now, largely unflexed.

Unflexed Musculature of Power

Explanations in traditional "industrial labor relations" theory—and in the practice of most U.S. unionists over the last half century—suggest that workers are strongest where there are comprehensive and enforceable labor laws that institutionalize freedom of association, protections against anti-union animus and retaliation, mechanisms to establish recognition of "exclusive bargaining representation" by a majority union, guarantees of collective bargaining, and of course the legally sanctioned right to strike. Our teacher unions have been considered strongest in those states where these rights existed, and where the most advanced forms of institutional practice could develop.

In many states where these conditions prevail, starting in the 1960s and continuing to the present day, the AFT and NEA affiliates often became known as the best damned service unions around. Teacher locals typically grew by training up rank-and-file members to bargain contracts, cost out proposals, and rep grievances—with all the rule-enforcing, technique-mastering power that these activities entail. Despite the very uneven quality of state teacher labor laws, the routine practice of formal labor relations—whether through "meet and confer," legislative lobbying, or strict collective bargaining—became nearly universal in the teaching sector. Reflecting the radically decentralized, bottom-up character of U.S. public education itself, every NEA or AFT local started at a school, or a school district, representing a discrete group of employees hired by a local school board. During the last half of the 20th century, the two national federations evolved as umbrellas for thousands and thousands of essentially autonomous local unions—all figuring out how to bargain and service their own contracts—reflecting the fact that no union could possibly afford to hire enough professional staff to centrally service them.

Under these objective conditions, innumerable rank-and-file teachers were elected, or drafted, or volunteered to learn the craft labor relations, and became a dense army of capable technicians. By the 1980s, as the numbers of unionized teachers swelled and dues revenue soared, the unions began to staff up and professionalize, precipitating a culture of negotiating instead of fighting, servicing instead of organizing, and relegating members to client status. As long as the economic tides were rising—as they generally did in the 1980s, '90s, and early 2000s—a complacent and increasingly bureaucratic system for maintaining the status quo seemed to make sense. This is consistent with the historically recognized tendency, articulated by Seymour Martin Lipset in 1956, as the "iron rule of oligarchy" through which bureaucracy supplants democracy.

But bureaucracy itself isn't the main problem. The arrival of neoliberalism—the driving political philosophy of the last 40 years—has also reshaped our unions. While we typically associate neoliberalism with market fundamentalism—deregulation of financial structures, regressive tax reform, privatization, weakening of the state role in labor and environmental protection—it is the rise of neoliberal organizational principles that proved toxic to union democracy. By the mid-90s, many unions, and non-profits of every stripe, took a turn toward corporate management methods. In AFT and NEA affiliates, leaders adopted key principles such as rule by experts, inflated executive salaries, limits on internal democracy, centralization of decision-making, and intolerance of dissent.

As the high-value operational aspects of the union—negotiating contracts and processing grievances—migrated upward into the hands of staff and top leaders, so too did power. Members were often treated paternalistically, with information and decision-making kept opaque, back-door deals struck between union leaders and politicians, and privileges accruing at the top. Salaries of top officers soared while average take-home pay of members stagnated, union halls were renovated into executive office suites while school buildings crumbled, and channels of union decision-making went from democratic to despotic, often reflecting the autocratic leadership of the employing school boards and administrators.

The demobilizing of millions of teachers within their own unions should not be understood as a problem of "apathetic members," though union staff and elected officers often describe it just this way. Rather, it is the logical result of unions adopting a corporate culture over the last few decades that degrades and excludes rank-and-file members. They were often grateful that someone was doing the arcane business of the union, but this was an institutional invitation to dependence and acquiescence. Many a naive newcomer goes to a union meeting and dares ask a question that is taken by leadership as a challenge; the newcomer is often patronized, ignored, disparaged, or actively marginalized. Bargaining teams disappear for months behind closed doors and then present a fully bargained tentative agreement to be ratified—take it or leave it. Membership meetings in many unions are dominated by one-way leadership reports or gripe sessions, where leaders are expected to take member concerns up the ladder of administration for them. It doesn't take too many of these cues before rank-and-file members stop coming around.

Concurrent with these trends has been the biggest failed strategy of all: substituting the power of rank-and-file members with dependence on the Democratic Party. Union members are not taught to analyze and fight collectively on issues that matter to them, but instead to docilely make PAC contributions, join campaign phone-banks, and support whichever candidate the union leaders endorsed. The results are pretty clear: Democrats have helped restructure the economy—in the interest of private wealth, at the expense of public good—as enthusiastically as Republicans. This has produced not only the well-documented upward redistribution of wealth, resulting in teacher poverty and starvation of school budgets, but also the travesty of "education reform"—where standardized curricula are tied to high-stakes testing, which produces failed schools, especially in communities of color, and allows for the entry of private charters, where the culture of teacher micro-management flourishes and bullying principals thrive. This set of policy imperatives has been brought to us by governors and legislatures of every party composition.

Between the financial hardship and professional affronts, the loss of voice and fear of retaliation by administrators, the degraded conditions and program losses for students, and the sense of being abandoned by the Democrats, many teachers have been teetering between shock, anxiety, and despair for years.

By the time the serious fiscal, political, and social crises really began bubbling in U.S. public education around the time of the 2008 financial crisis, the vast majority of teacher union members felt powerless. They were at best distant from, and at worst angrily resentful of, their unions. Most damningly, they saw the union as being the top officers and staff, not themselves. Even in states with relatively strong labor laws and well-resourced union structures, the norm was a hollowed-out organization, with low levels of knowledge and participation at the base, and little autonomous power. Rank-and-file members who did try to turn to their leaders for inspiration or guidance frequently found neither.

Re-energizing the Rank and File in Blue Cities and States

But out of this paralysis and isolation, a powerful counter-trend is emerging (not unknown in the history of our labor movement): Progressive rank-and-file teacher union caucuses—groups of union members formed to push their unions into action—are coalescing in cities and states, inspired by the stunning takeover of the Chicago Teachers Union by the Caucus of Rank-and-File Educators (CORE) in 2010, and their riveting, successful 2012 strike. This movement, an internal insurgency inside our biggest unions, possesses the authentic features of a social movement: it is bottom-up, scrappy, unfunded, rooted in a critical social analysis, and committed to radically democratic values. Their common program elements show up as union democracy, dignity of educators and students, and defense of public education, and often rally under the edict that "we should be the union we want our union to be."

These caucuses are now in elected leadership in Los Angeles, Boston, Chicago, and statewide in Hawai'i and Massachusetts. They are contending for—or sharing—leadership in Philadelphia, Baltimore, New York City, Minneapolis, Madison, Albuquerque, Seattle, and Oakland, and organizing at the state level in North

Carolina, New Jersey, and elsewhere. Through round upon round of trial and error, the caucuses are building a durable analytic framework and plan of action to guide them:

- Simply running to replace "bad union leaders" is rarely a solution to anything, if you haven't built a base among members who are joined by common values, deeply committed to making the union better and willing to work tirelessly.
- Learn how to survive the harsh charges from old guard leaders that they are divisive and even "anti-union" for daring to provoke debate.
- Fight to open up bargaining, to insist on transparency and accountability inside the union, to risk raising critical social issues—around racism, immigration, bullying, gentrification—and work through the resistance of fellow unionists.
- Reach out humbly and helpfully to parents, community groups, other unions, faith communities, and social issue organizations as a partner in the fight to rebalance power away from elites and toward the majority.
- Become confident in practices of inclusivity, debate, collaboration, and horizontal leadership.
- Learn how to fight the boss, the financial interests behind "education reform," and the state, directly and fearlessly.

Along the way these caucuses convened a national network—United Caucuses of Rank-and-File Educators (UCORE)—almost organically through Labor Notes, the project that has held down the "rank-and-file pole" of U.S. unionism through publications and conferences for 40 years.

Rank-and-File Insurgencies in Red States

Insurgents in WV, AZ, KY, OK, and CO thinking about how to consolidate rank-and-file power inside their unions have found their way onto the UCORE and Labor Notes platform, too, bringing together teacher activists from the red states and blue cities, union-weak and union-strong environments, to discover that they are all after the same thing: using collective power from the bottom-up to win social progress for the majority.

It is through this prism of labor-movement analysis that we can now start to understand the apparently paradoxical eruptions of teachers in states with the weakest institutional environment—regions with low union membership, weak infrastructure, no bargaining rights, and fiercely anti-union legislatures. When there is no effective access to meaningful channels for change, workers resort naturally to the only power no one can steal from them—the power to withhold their labor. This spontaneous chain of wildcat strikes may be the only recourse left for the teachers when the unions and the politicians fail them, but they are also facilitated by the very weakness of the union bureaucratic environment around them. By sharp contrast, the progressive teacher union caucuses have emerged in generally "strong" union environments in more progressive cities or regions, where they have had to spend more time fighting their own union bureaucracy and much less sparking the spontaneous and unified action showing up in the "weak" union environments.

But teacher unionists in both environments are moving. They are in a movement moment. If we keep in mind the immediate affinity felt by the insurgent teachers and the caucus teachers, their sense of shared purpose, their common hope for a democratic, activist, bottom-up union culture, their willingness to risk, and their refusal to be complacent, we can start to see the potential for teacher convergence. Coming from very disparate starting points, present in every corner of the country, connected by their fierce will to protect kids and public schools, increasingly cornered by the system of manufactured austerity and therefore ever-more identified with the majority of workers, teachers could give us a generative moment, a moment to be amplifed. ❏

Article 7.6

HOUSEHOLD LABOR, CARING LABOR, UNPAID LABOR

AN INTERVIEW with NANCY FOLBRE

September/October 2015

Nancy Folbre *is a professor emerita of economics at the University of Massachusetts-Amherst. She is the author of numerous books, including* Who Pays for the Kids? Gender and the Structures of Constraint *(1994),* The Invisible Heart: Economics and Family Values *(2001), and* Valuing Children: Rethinking the Economics of the Family *(2008), related to household and caring labor.*

Dollars & Sense: You've written about the tendency in economics to view household labor (and especially women's labor) as "unproductive." Can you explain how this is reflected in conventional macroeconomic measures?

Nancy Folbre: Non-market household services such as meal preparation and childcare are not considered part of what we call "the economy." This means they literally don't count as part of Gross Domestic Product, household income, or household consumption.

This is pretty crazy, since we know that these services contribute to our living standards and also to the development of human capabilities. They are all at least partially fungible: time and money may not be perfect substitutes, but there is clearly a tradeoff. You can, in principle, pay someone to prepare your meals (as you do in a restaurant), or to look after your kids.

If you or someone else in your household provides these services for no charge (even if they expect something in return, such as a share of household earnings) that leaves more earnings available to buy other things. In fact, you could think of household income after taxes and after needs for domestic services have been met as a more meaningful definition of "disposable income" than the conventional definition, which is simply market income after taxes.

D&S: What is the practical consequence of not measuring household labor and production? Are economic policies and institutions different, especially in their impact on women, than what they would be if household labor were fully reflected in statistics on total employment or output?

NF: One macroeconomic consequence is a tendency to overstate economic growth when activities shift from an arena in which they are unpaid to one in which they are paid (all else equal). When mothers of young children enter paid employment, for instance, they reduce the amount of time they engage in unpaid work, but that reduction goes unmeasured. All that is counted is the increase in earnings that results, along with the increase in expenditures on services such as paid childcare.

As a result, rapid increases in women's labor force participation, such as those typical in the United States between about 1960 and the mid-1990s, tend to boost the rate of growth of GDP. When women's labor force participation levels out, as it has in the United States since the mid 1990s, the rate of growth of GDP slows down. At least some part of the difference in growth rates over these two periods simply reflects the increased "countability" of women's work.

Consideration of the microeconomic consequences helps explain this phenomenon. When households collectively supply more labor hours to the market, their market incomes go up. But they have to use a substantial portion of those incomes to purchase substitutes for services they once provided on their own—spending more money on meals away from home (or pre-prepared foods), and child care. So, the increase in their money incomes overstates the improvement in their genuinely disposable income.

A disturbing example of policy relevance emerges from consideration of the changes in public assistance to single mothers implemented in the United States in 1996, which put increased pressure on these mothers to engage in paid employment. Many studies proclaimed the success because market income in many of these families went up. But much of that market income had to be spent paying for services such as child care, because public provision and subsidies fell short.

D&S: You've also written extensively about "caring labor"? What is caring labor? To what extent is this labor (and the output of services associated with it) directly or indirectly captured by conventional measures like GDP?

NF: Everything I've discussed above is about quantity. But quality is also important. I define caring labor as labor where the quality of the services provided is likely to be affected by concern for the well-being of the care recipient. Love, affection, and commitment almost always enhance the care of dependents, and this is a big reason why market-provided services are not always perfect substitutes for those provided by family members and friends.

On the other hand, many people—especially women—work in occupations like child care, elder care, education, medicine, or social services where they genuinely care about their clients or "consumers." The market value of this work is counted as part of Gross Domestic Product and household income. But in many cases, the wage paid is considerably less than the value of the services provided. Workers in these jobs often give more in the way of quality than they are actually paid for.

D&S: As a practical matter, how could one go about measuring the value of services currently provided by unpaid household labor? In your estimation, how would our picture of economic life change if we did?

NF: It is pretty easy to estimate a lower-bound for the value of unpaid work by counting the number of hours that people spend engaging in it (which in the United States adds up to almost exactly the same total as hours of market work), and multiplying those hours times the hourly wage one would pay for a replacement.

Measures of hours worked in different activities such as meal preparation, child care, cleaning, shopping, and so on are typically based on a nationally representative survey of individuals who report all of their activities on the preceding day. The American Time Use Survey, administered since 2003 on an annual basis as a supplement to the Current Population Survey, provides reliable, high-quality data on time use.

Several studies have used these data to assign a dollar value to non-market work in what is called a "satellite" national income account (because it revolves around, rather than replacing the conventional account). Obviously, including this value in a measure of "extended GDP" makes the economy look bigger. More importantly, it revises estimates of how the economy has grown over time—in the downward direction.

Counting the value of non-market work has an equalizing effect on measures of household income, not because low-income households do a lot more of it, but because most households of similar size and composition do about the same amount. Here again, the trends are more interesting than the levels: since the relative importance of non-market work has declined over time, its equalizing effect has probably also declined. ❑

Article 7.7

WHY ARE WAGES GROWING SO SLOWLY?

BY ARTHUR MacEWAN
September/October 2017

> Dear Dr. Dollar:
> *Wth unemployment so low these days, why are wages growing so slowly?*
> —Anonymous, via email

In June 1973, the average hourly wage of production and non-supervisory workers was $4.12. In terms of June 2017 purchasing power, this 1973 wage was $22.72. In June 2017, the actual average wage for this group of workers was $22.03. For no year in this 44 year period was the wage higher in terms of purchasing power (i.e., inflation adjusted) than in 1973. (For someone working full time, 2000 hours, for a whole year, $22.03 yields an annual income of $44,060, 66% above the poverty line for a family of four but about 20% below the median family income.)

In other words, on average, wages have stagnated for almost half a century. The slow growth of wages in recent years should, then, be viewed in this longer context.

Not So Good but Not So Bad

In recent years, as the unemployment rate has fallen, average wages have slowly increased, rising by 4.7% in the five years from June 2012 to June 2017. Not great. But compared to what happened to wages in similar periods following the three previous recessions, this is not so bad: following the recession of the early 1980s, wages simply did not rise; after

FIGURE 1: DISCONNECT BETWEEN PRODUCTIVITY AND TYPICAL WORKER'S COMPENSATION, 1948-2013

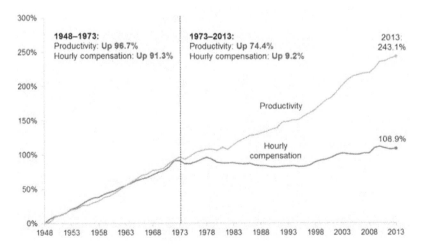

Source: Economic Policy Institute (EPI), *Raising America's Pay: Why It's Our Central Economic Policy Challenge*, Bureau of Labor Statistics (LCS) and Bureau or Economic Analysis (BEA) data; figure reproduced here courtesy of EPI.

FIGURE 2: CUMULATIVE CHANGE IN REAL HOURLY WAGE OF ALL WORKERS, BY WAGE PERCENTILE, 1979-2013

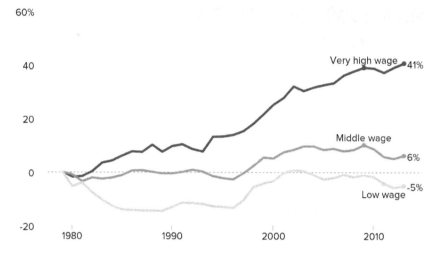

*Low wage is 10th percentile, middle wage is 50th percentile, very high wage is 95th percentile.

Source: Economic Policy Institute (EPI), *Why America's Workers Need Faster Wagre Growth And What We Can Do About It*; Current Population Survey (CPS) Outgoing Rotation Group microdata; figure reproduced here courtesy of EPI.

the early 1990s recession, the increase was also about 4.7%; and in the years following the early 2000s recession, the increase was only 2.5%.

There has been a connection between the unemployment rate and the wages in each of these periods. After the early 1980s recession, the unemployment rate never fell below 5%; after the early 2000s recession, the rate did fall below 5%, but not as low as after the early 1990s recession or after the Great Recession. So these experiences fit roughly with the pattern that low unemployment increases workers' bargaining power and makes it possible for them to push up their wages. When workers have more options, they have more power.

But bargaining power is not so simple—it does not depend on the unemployment rate alone—and wage increases do not follow automatically from a drop in the unemployment rate. First of all, there is a lag between the time unemployment drops and the time workers are able to push up their wages, and that lag time can be especially long following a severely disruptive recession, like the Great Recession. Also, there is a measurement problem: The official unemployment rate does not take into account the number of people who have given up looking for jobs during the downturn, but who would be ready to re-enter the labor force as things improve. (The official unemployment rate is defined as the number of people employed as a percentage of the labor force; the labor force, in turn, is defined as the number of people employed plus the number of people *actively* looking for jobs.)

Perhaps a better measure of the labor-market situation would be the labor force participation rate (LFPR, the percentage of people 16 and over employed working or actively looking for jobs). Leading into the Great Recession, in June 2008, the LFPR was 66.1%. In June of 2017, this rate was down to 62.8%. While part of this decline might be explained by the aging of the population (more people who have no intention of re-entering the labor force), part of it is surely a result of people giving up but who would be ready to take jobs again if more jobs were available. So the official unemployment rate makes it look as if the labor market is "tighter" than it really is. And a less-tight labor market tends to mean less power for workers.

The Important Reasons

There are, however, more important reasons that the relatively low unemployment rate does not readily translate into a strong upsurge of wages. These reasons are "more important" because they lie in long-term phenomena that help explain the several decades of wage stagnation. Foremost among these reasons is the decline of labor unions. Union membership in the private sector has fallen dramatically, from 24.2% in 1973 to 6.4% in 2016. (See table.) Bargaining on their own, workers are much less powerful and much less effective than when they bargain as a group—i.e., as a union. Furthermore, while workers have become less powerful, employers have become more powerful as business has become increasingly concentrated in a smaller number of firms. It is, for example, one thing to bargain with a local store, even a local chain, and quite another to bargain with a behemoth like Amazon or Walmart.

Explanations sometimes advanced for the decline of unions include global-ization and the smaller share of the workforce in large factories (e.g., auto and steel). These phenomena are not irrelevant, but much of the decline is explained by political factors. For one, Republic administrations have been able to shape the National Labor Relations Board (NLRB) in ways that make its rulings anti-union (and Democratic administrations have not wholly reversed the situation). For example, without effective NLRB protection during the Reagan adminis-tration, workers leading attempts to organize unions in their work places faced a 20% to 25% chance of being fired, and the odds were similar in the adminis-trations of George H.W. Bush and George W. Bush. Another factor weakening unions' and workers' ability to push up wages has been the erosion of the mini-mum wage as Washington has declined to increase the minimum to keep up with inflation. The current federal minimum wage of $7.25 is 18% below the 1973 minimum wage, in terms of real buying power. (The 1973 federal mini-mum wage was $1.60, which is equivalent to $8.84 in terms of 2017 prices—a July to July comparison.)

On top of government actions, employers have taken increasingly aggressive anti-union efforts in recent decades. A whole industry has arisen to guide employ-ers in preventing success of union-organizing campaigns. Anti-union consulting firms have certainly contributed to the union membership decline. On the other side, some established unions have been excessively timid in developing new orga-nizing drives.

And then there is globalization—but this too has been, in part, a political phe-nomenon. Global trade and investment agreements have been designed to bring about greater mobility for firms—to give them more options, which translates into greater power in their relations with workers. The mobility of firms has led to more movement of plants to low-wage sites outside the United States. As Kate

Brofenbrenner of Cornell University's School of Industrial and Labor Relations has pointed out in a study related to the North American Free Trade Agreement (NAFTA), the threat of plant movement has become increasingly credible, significantly weakening the effectiveness of union organizing drives. What is true in the context of NAFTA is also true with regard to the reduction of U.S. trade restrictions with other low-wage countries. It is only somewhat of an exaggeration to say the labor market has now become global, and the unemployment rate in the United States is only a minor indicator of the "tightness" of the labor market. It is hard for workers in the U.S. to push up their wages when they can be replaced by workers, in many parts of the world, who will accept much lower wages and who often face more severe repression of their right to unionize.

But what about workers in the public sector, where the percentage who are in unions has increased substantially over recent decades? (See Table.) They too have been affected by the larger economic and political situation, in spite of their higher rate of unionization. While union membership has helped, it is difficult for public-sector workers to improve their positions when private-sectors workers—the people who pay the taxes that provide the wages for the public-sector workers—are experiencing wage stagnation. Also, the anti-tax political climate, including of course the unwillingness of governments at all levels to raise taxes on the rich (quite the opposite, in fact), has put stress on public budgets. (On top of this, it appears likely that coming Supreme Court rulings will apply "right to work" regulations on public-sector workers, severely undermining their unions' operations.)

Measurement and Other Factors

Many other reasons have been offered in the media (just take a look on the web) as to why wages have been slow to rise in recent years as the unemployment rate has fallen. One explanation involves a measurement problem. As relatively high-wage workers (including many prime-age workers) retire or are pushed out, they are replaced with new, low-wage entrants to the labor market. Thus, even if the wages of all other workers remain the same, the average falls. This probably does make wage increases appear lower than they really are.

Another explanation for poor wage growth—put forth, for example, in a recent *New York Times* article—is that wage increases have been limited because productivity (output per worker) has grown so slowly since the Great Recession. The problem with this argument is that it assumes a link between productivity growth and wage growth. Clearly, however, that link has been broken since the 1970s; from then onward, wages have stagnated as productivity has risen right along.

When all is said and done, even under the best of circumstances, it takes time for a strong job market—i.e., low unemployment—to lead to significant wage increases. It is certainly possible that the coming years will see some more meaningful improvement. Don't hold your breath, but it might happen. ❑

Sources: All data used in this article, unless otherwise indicated are from the Bureau of Labor Statistics (BLS), either directly or via the Economic Report of the President, 2017, and the Census Bureau's American Community Survey. In some cases—e.g., to determine the buying power in

2017 of wages in earlier years—the BLS Consumer Price Index Calculator was used (bls.gov). Also: Neil Irwin, "The Question Isn't Why Wage Growth Is So Low. It's Why It's So High," *New York Times*, May 26, 2017; John Schmitt and Ben Zipperer, Dropping the Ax: Illegal Firings During Union Elections, 1951-2007, Center for Economic and Policy Research, Washington, DC, March 2009; Kate Brofenbrenner, "Organizing in the NAFTA Environment: How Companies Use 'Free Trade' to Stop Unions" (digitalcommons.ilr.cornell.edu).

Article 7.8

MIGRATION, LABOR, AND U.S. POLICY

BY DAVID BACON
September/October 2017

One winter morning in Los Angeles, group of healthcare activists set up a street-corner clinic for day laborers. One of the day laborers who lined up for medical tests was Omar Sierra. He got to the head of the line and then took his seat at the testing station. A nurse tied off his arm and inserted the needle to draw blood, when all of a sudden Migra agents came running from across the street. Everybody panicked and ran. Omar tore off the tourniquet, ripped out the needle, and ran as well. He was pretty lucky that day, because he escaped. But a lot of his friends didn't. So when he got home, disturbed about what had happened, he decided to write a song about it, which for a while actually became the anthem of the National Day Laborers Organizing Network.

> I'm going to sing you a story friends
> That will make you cry
> How one day in front of K-Mart
> The Migra came down on us
> Sent by the sheriff
> Of this very same place ...
>
> We don't understand why
> We don't know the reason
> Why there is so much
> Discrimination against us
> In the end we'll wind up all the same in the grave ...
>
> With this verse I leave you
> I'm tired of singing
> Hoping the Migra
> Won't come after us again
> Because in the end we all have to work.

Omar Sierra tells us the truth: We all have to work, at least if you're part of the working class. But today's reality is also that working has become a crime for millions of people. A few years ago, Immigration and Customs Enforcement (ICE) agents went to the Agriprocessors meat-packing plant in Postville, Iowa, and sent 388 young people from Guatemala to prison for six months for using bad Social Security numbers. Those folks were deported immediately afterwards. One of them—we know this because ICE told us in the affidavits they used to get the paperwork for the raid—was a young man who had been beaten with a meat hook on the line by his supervisor. He was picked up along with all the rest, imprisoned, and deported. His supervisor went on working.

Teresa Mina was a janitor in San Francisco, and she lived in San Francisco for six years. She couldn't see her kids grow up—even though it was for their sake that she came to San Francisco—because she couldn't go home and then pay the thousands of dollars it would have taken for her to re-cross the border and get back to her job. She says, "The woman in the office wouldn't pay me. She said the papers I had when I was hired were no good. I told her I didn't have any other papers. I felt really bad. After so many years of killing myself in that job, I needed to keep it so I could keep sending money home. This law is very unjust. We work day and night to help our children have a better life or just eat," she continues. "My kids won't have what they need now because I can't work."

ICE says on its website that "this kind of enforcement is targeting employers who pay illegal workers substandard wages or force them to endure illegal and intolerable working conditions." But curing intolerable conditions by firing workers certainly doesn't help the workers, and it doesn't change the conditions. Instead, ICE is punishing undocumented workers who earn too much or who demand higher wages or organize unions. Employers in these enforcement actions get rewarded, for cooperating with ICE, with immunity from prosecution, so the only people who get hurt by it are workers.

The Criminalization of Work

Michael Chertoff, who was the head of the Migra under Bush, said, "There is an obvious solution to the problem of illegal work, which is you open the front door and you shut the back door." He wants people to come as *braceros*, as contract workers recruited in Mexico. That's the front door. To make people do that, he would close the back door by picking people up at work or out on the sidewalk or crossing through the desert, because our government says all these things are a crime. That's the message of deporting 400,000 people a year. If you want to come, come as a guest worker, come as a *bracero*.

E-Verify is the same kind of solution, because it says that if you don't have papers, it is a crime to work. So you stand on a street corner and at truck stops and you get in. And then you work all day in the sun until you're so tired you can hardly make it back to your room. This is a crime. You do it to send money home to your family and the people who depend on you. That's a crime, too.

How many people are breaking the law in these ways? There are 11 million people living in the United States without papers. But this is a global phenomenon. People are going from Morocco to Spain, Turkey to Germany, and Jamaica to the U.K. The World Bank says more than 213 million people worldwide live outside the countries where they were born. Two decades earlier the number was under 156 million. That number increased by 58 million people in 20 years. The number of migrants in the world is going up, and it's going up very quickly.

The United States is home these days to about 43 million people born outside its borders, up from 23 million two decades earlier.

If working is a crime, then workers are criminals. And if workers are criminals and working becomes a crime, they will go home. That's one of the justifications for criminalization of migrants. But why don't we see people lined up at the border, paying coyotes thousands of dollars to get smuggled into Mexico? Because there are no jobs for people to go home to.

The Drivers of Migration

The increase in migration to the United States coincided, by no accident, with the period in which neoliberal economic reforms were implemented in those countries that are the main sources of migration to the United States.

In 1994, the year that NAFTA went into effect, there were about 4.5 million people born in Mexico living in the United States. In 2008, that number peaked at about 12.6 million. Of those people, about 5.7 million were able to get some kind of visa. But another 7 million people couldn't, and they came anyway. Fully 9% of the population of Mexico lives here on the north side of the border. People are coming now from the most remote areas of Mexico, where people are still speaking languages that were old when Columbus arrived—Mixteco, Zapoteco, Triqui, Purépecha, and others. The largest Salvadoran city in the world is what? San Salvador? No, it's Los Angeles. And remittances going back to El Salvador are 16.6% of Salvadoran GDP.

What produced the migration from Mexico is the same thing that closed factories here. NAFTA, for instance, let huge U.S. companies—Archer Daniels Midland, Cargill, Continental Grain Company—sell corn in Mexico for a price that was lower than what it cost farmers to grow it. Those companies are subsidized by the federal government. The last farm bill had $2 billion in subsidies for U.S. grain producers. Those companies took those subsidies and they sold corn in Mexico at 19% below the U.S. cost of production, according to Jonathan Fox and others who have studied the displacement of people that this has caused. Corn exports to Mexico went from 2 million to 10 million tons from 1992 to 2008.

It's not just corn. The price of pork in Mexico, because of pork exports to Mexico, went down 56%. That didn't mean that it got cheaper in supermarkets. It just meant that those people doing the business made more money. Mexico imported 30,000 tons of pork in 1995, and by 2010 it was 811,000 tons. One company, Smithfield Foods, now controls over 25% of the market for pork meat in Mexico, and as a result, Mexican pig farmers and slaughterhouse workers lost 120,000 jobs, according to the Mexican Pork Producers Association. The systems that helped rural farmers survive by buying corn, tobacco, or coffee at subsidized prices were all ruled illegal, a restraint of trade, under NAFTA. So displacement doesn't just hurt farmers; it hurts workers, too.

In Cananea, a small mining town in Sonora, just south of the U.S. border, miners went on strike in 2008 to stop a multinational corporation from eliminating their jobs and busting their union. When they lost their jobs, the border was there, only 50 miles north. The Mexican government dissolved the Mexican Power and Light Company, which provides electrical service in central Mexico, and fired 44,000 workers. This is a prelude to the privatization of the electrical system in Mexico. Where will those people go? The lack of labor rights, when it gets combined with economic reforms to benefit large corporations, is a source of migration as well.

And then there is environmental pollution. In Veracruz, Smithfield took a beautiful desert valley and turned it into an ecological disaster by building the world's largest pig farm complex. The story of Fausto Limón shows the consequences. On some warm nights, Fausto Limón's children wake up and vomit from the smell. He puts his wife, two sons, and a daughter into his beat-up pickup, and they drive away from his farm until they can breathe the air without getting sick. Then he parks, and they sleep there for the rest of the night. They all had kidney ailments, all of his family, until they stopped drinking from the well on the farm, because Smithfield had contaminated the whole aquifer under the valley there. Less than half a mile from his house is one of the 80 pig farms built by Smithfield. Each one has over 20,000 hogs. That's where the swine flu started.

Victoria Hernández, a teacher in one of the towns in the valley, La Gloria, said that her students would tell her that riding to school on the school bus was like riding in a toilet. She began writing leaflets about it and the ranchers in the valley began protesting about the expansion of these farms. That's when Smithfield had them arrested for defamation in order to stop those protests. Defamation meant telling the truth about what Smithfield was doing.

David Ceja left his home in Veracruz near the Perote Valley and he eventually went to work in a Smithfield plant, the slaughterhouse in Tar Heel, N.C. He says:

> The free trade agreement was the cause of our problems. They were just paying as little to farmers as they could. When the prices went up, no one had any money to pay. After the crisis, we couldn't pay for electricity, we just used candles at home. And when you see that your parents don't have any money, that's when you decide to come, to help them. In the ranches where we lived, the coyotes would come by offering to take us north. I was 18 years old when I left in 1999. My parents sold four cows and 10 hectares of land to get the money to get to the border. And then I walked across the river from Tamaulipas to Texas and walked through the mountains for two days and three nights. Some friends told me to go to North Carolina. And in Veracruz we had heard that there was a slaughterhouse there. So when I was hired, I saw people from the area near where I lived. Lots of people from Veracruz worked at Smithfield.

NAFTA and the U.S. and Mexican governments helped big companies get rich by keeping wages low and then giving them subsidies and letting them push farmers into bankruptcy. That's also why it's so hard for families to survive: because they can't farm and because of those low wages. They get laid off to cut costs, their workplaces are privatized, or their unions get busted. On the border, an economy of *maquiladoras* and low wages was promoted as a way to produce jobs. But in the last recession, in Matamoros or Juarez or Tijuana, hundreds of thousands of people lost their jobs instead. When U.S. consumers stopped buying what those factories were producing, people were laid off. When they were working, it took half a day's wages for a woman to buy a half-gallon of milk for her kids. People live in houses made out of materials cast off from the plants, in homes that often don't have any sewer system, on dirt roads, in terrible conditions. And that's when people are working.

So when people lose those jobs and the border is right there, where are they going to go? We all will do whatever it takes for our families to survive. If it's going north, that's what people do.

The DACA youth, the "dreamers" are the true children of NAFTA—those who, more than anyone, paid the price for the agreement. Their parents brought them with them when they crossed the border without papers, choosing survival over hunger, seeking to keep their families together and give them a future.

American Apartheid

Today's criminalization programs, the raids and the firings, are very tightly tied to the labor supply schemes, because fear and vulnerability make it harder for workers to organize and for unions to help and represent them. The displacement of people is an unspoken tool of that policy, because it produces workers.

This is an old story in the United States. It was a crime for decades, for instance, for Filipinos to marry women who were not Filipinas, because of anti-miscegenation laws. At the same time, our immigration laws kept women from coming from the Philippines, so for the farm workers of the 1930s and '40s it was a crime to have a family. Many men stayed single their whole lives, moving from labor camp to labor camp, contributing their labor wherever the growers needed it.

The *braceros* were "legal" because they had visas, the same thing employers say today about contract workers recruited in the H2-A and H2-B visa programs. But let's remember the true history. The *braceros* lived behind barbed wire in camps. If they went on strike, they were deported. They didn't get all the pay they were owed, and when their contract was over, they had to leave the country.

But the history of this abuse is also a history of resistance. Filipinos fought to stay, and just for the right to have a family. The *braceros* fought to stay, too. Some people just walked out of those labor camps, and kept on living and working without documents for 20 years, until the immigration amnesty of 1986. They are the grandparents of many, many families living in the United States today.

In 1964, people like Bert Corona, Cesar Chávez, Dolores Huerta, and Ernesto Galarza, trade unionists and leaders of the Chicano civil rights movement, fought to get Congress to end the *bracero* program. The next year Mexicans and Filipinos organized a union and they went out on strike in Coachella and Delano, and created the United Farm Workers of America. But they didn't stop there. In 1965, they went back to Congress and demanded a law that would not make workers into *braceros* for the growers. They demanded a law that prioritized families, and won the family preference system. Today, once you have a green card, you can get your mother or your father or your children to come and join you in the United States. The civil rights movement won that law.

They've starved that system of the visas it needs to function. Now the waiting line is 20 years long for people to bring family members from Mexico City or Manila. Corporate proposals for reforming immigration laws would pull that family preference system apart. Instead they propose systems in which visas are given based on skills that employers want. These ideas would push us backwards into the *bracero* era again.

Poverty and Profit

Migration is not an accident. Here in the United States, we have an economic system that depends on migration—and on migrants. If all the migrants went home tomorrow, would there be fruit and vegetables in the supermarkets? Who would be cutting up those pigs in Tar Heel? Who would clean the office buildings? Without the labor of today's migrants, the economic system in this country would stop. But do the companies that are using that labor, whether it's growers or the ones who own office buildings and hotels, pay for the needs of the workers' families in the towns that people are coming from? Who pays for the school in San Miguel Cuevas, a town that sends strawberry workers to the fields of California? Who builds the homes there? Who pays for the doctor? Growers and the employers here pay for nothing. They don't pay taxes in Mexico, and a lot of them don't pay taxes in the United States either.

Workers pay for everything. It's a very cheap system for employers. For employers, migration is a labor supply system, and for them it's not broken at all. In fact, it works very well. In the United States, it's cheap because workers without papers pay taxes and Social Security, but for them there are no unemployment benefits, no disability, no retirement. These are things that people fought for won in the New Deal. But if you don't have papers, the New Deal never happened.

We know that the wages of undocumented people are low and families can hardly live on them, but we also know that there's a big difference in wages between a day laborer and a longshoreman. If employers had to pay the same, people's lives would be a lot better. Before the longshoremen organized a union in the United States, they were like day laborers, hired every morning out on the docks. They were considered bums. You wouldn't want your daughter to marry one. Now they send their kids to the university. The union changed their lives. If employers had to raise the wages of immigrants just to the level of the average worker in this country, it would cost them billions of dollars. It's no wonder there's such fierce opposition when people organize unions or worker centers, or do anything to shake this system up.

But immigrants are fighters. It wasn't long ago when janitors sat down in the streets in Washington and across the country and won their right to a union, in a national campaign—Justice for Janitors. Immigrant workers have gone on strike in factories, in office buildings, laundries, hotels, fields. Some unions in this country are growing, and many of them are those that know that immigrant workers are often willing to fight to make things better. The battles fought by immigrant workers are helping to make our union stronger today.

We had a big change in our labor movement in 1999 in Los Angeles. At the AFL-CIO convention that year unions decided to fight to get rid of the law that makes work a crime, and to protect the rights of all workers to organize. With immigrants under attack today, it's important that unions live up to that promise, especially to oppose the firing of millions of workers, including their own members, because of mandatory E-Verify. Administration proposals to reinstate S-Com and 287(g) agreements, that mandate cooperation between the police and immigration authorities, in the past have led to the deportation of hundreds of thousands of people.

Divide and Rule

This kind of enforcement has an impact on the ability of people to advocate for social change. At Smithfield Foods, one of the world's biggest packinghouses in North Carolina, two raids and 300 firings scared workers so badly that their union drive stopped. But then Mexicans and African Americans found a way to make common cause, and together they won their union organizing drive. They said to each other, in effect, *We all need better wages and conditions, and we all have the right to work here and to fight for them.*

Immigration raids are used to prevent unity between immigrants and other workers. Immigration and Customs Enforcement agents made a huge raid on a factory belonging to Howard Industries in Laurel, Miss., and sent 481 workers to a privately run detention center. This raid occurred right before negotiations with the electrical workers unions, in one of the few unionized plants in Mississippi. Jim Evans, the president of the Mississippi Immigrant Rights Alliance and the AFL- CIO representative in Mississippi, says, "This was an attempt to drive a wedge between immigrants, African Americans, white people, and unions."

African Americans make up about 35% of the population in Mississippi. In ten years, immigrants will make up another 10%. The Mississippi Immigrant Rights Alliance and the Black Caucus in the Mississippi legislature believe they can combine those votes with the state's unions and with progressive white people, and get rid of the power structure that's governed Mississippi since the end of Reconstruction. Chokwe Lumumba, the lawyer for the Republic of New Africa, an Black liberation organization in Detroit, and later for the Mississippi Immigrant Rights Alliance, was elected mayor of Jackson, Miss., so this strategy works. Firings and this workplace enforcement are intended to drive a wedge into the heart of that political coalition to stop any possibility for change.

The Emerging Resistance

Last year teachers went on strike all over Mexico trying to defeat a kind of education reform that was invented here in the United States. All around Latin America, the U.S. Agency for International Development (USAID) has set up business groups that call for privatizing schools and firing teachers. In Mexico, teachers are upset, not just over their own job losses, but because there is so little alternative to migration for their students, for young people in Mexico.

Oaxaca is one of the states sending the largest number of migrants to the United States today. About three-quarters of the 3.4 million people who live in Oaxaca fit into the Mexican government's category of extreme poverty. The illiteracy rate in Oaxaca is over 20%, almost half of all students don't finish elementary school, 12% of homes don't have electricity, a quarter don't have running water, and 40% of the families living in Oaxaca live in a home that has a dirt floor.

But Oaxaca and Mexico are not so exceptional. In developing countries all over the world, people want an alternative: They want the right to a decent life in the communities where they live. Advocating for the right to stay home means that migration should be a choice, something voluntary, not forced. But advocating for policies to give life to this right usually means defying the government. Teachers and their supporters were shot and killed in Nochixtlan during that strike. The lack of human rights is itself a factor that contributes to migration from Oaxaca and Mexico, because it makes it so difficult for people to organize for change.

There are alternative proposals for changing this system to benefit workers and families instead. The American Friends Service Committee's document, called "A New Path," lays out principles for a humane immigration reform. So do proposals from the Binational Front of Indigenous Organizations and a network called The Dignity Campaign. They all start by asking not what Congress will vote for, but what will solve the problems of working people.

They propose legalization—green cards or permanent residence visas—that would let people live normal lives in families and communities. They advocate eliminating the criminalization of immigrants—no more deportations, no more detention centers, no more using the police as immigration agents, and no E-Verify database to target workers for firings. Instead, they propose a system based equality and rights, and oppose guest worker programs.

Families in Mexico, Guatemala, El Salvador, or the Philippines have a right to survive as well. Young people have a right to not migrate. And for that, people need jobs and productive farms and good schools and healthcare. Changing agreements like NAFTA should be part of any immigration reform proposal, and any process for renegotiating the treaty should look at its impact on the roots of migration.

It's not possible to win progressive changes in immigration law without fighting for jobs, education, healthcare, and justice. These demands unite people, and that unity can stop raids and create a more just society for everybody, immigrant and non-immigrant alike.

This is not just a dream of a remote or impossible future. In 1955, change for farm workers seemed impossible too. In the depth of the Cold War, growers had all the power and workers didn't have any. If you were Black and tried to vote in Mississippi, you could be lynched or your home or your church might be bombed. Yet, ten years later, the Civil Rights Act and the Voting Rights Act had passed, a new immigration law protected families, the *bracero* program was over, and a new union for farm workers had just gone out on strike in Delano.

Many of the same members of Congress who voted against these things in 1955 voted for them in 1965. What changed this country was the Civil Rights movement. Today a movement as strong and powerful, willing to fight for what we really need, can win an immigration system that respects human rights. It can stop deportations and provide a system of security for working families on both sides of the border. ❏

Chapter 8

THE DISTRIBUTION OF INCOME AND WEALTH

INTRODUCTION

For many mainstream economists, inequality in the distribution of income is a natural outcome of the functioning of markets. If workers get paid based on productivity, wage differences simply reflect underlying differences in productivity.

People who supply other inputs—investors or lenders supplying capital, landowners supplying land—are similarly rewarded according to the marginal products of those inputs. Even poverty is largely seen as a result of low productivity, which can be interpreted more compassionately as the consequence of a lack of education and training, or, at an extreme, as a result of shirking and a whole host of moral failings. President Ronald Reagan's deliberate use of the term "welfare queen" during the 1980s to cast poor, black women as undeserving of society's support is perhaps the most famous example of the latter. Indeed, in this view, a high degree of equality (or measures aimed at reducing inequality) would reduce the incentives for increasing productivity, slowing overall growth. Economists also argue that because the rich tend to save more (thus swelling the pool of resources available for investment), the larger the share of the economic pie that goes to them, the better the entire economy does. Trickle on down!

Chris Tilly, in his remarkable essay "Geese, Golden Eggs, and Traps" (Article 8.1), lays out the arguments for and against income equality and then takes down the rosy view of the economic benefits of inequality. His analysis shows how economies such as the United States' can end up in an "inequality trap" where high inequality leads to low growth, which in turn can lead to even higher inequality.

John Miller's "The Stock Market and Class Conflict" (Article 8.2) tempers the celebration of record-high stock prices with the reality of still stagnant wages and incomes for the vast majority of working people. If you own stocks, you are doing quite well, since returns on stocks have been exceptional after the market re-inflated since the Great Recession. But if you still rely on the mundane returns from your labor, you have likely noticed little growth in your nominal and real wages.

The next two articles look at patterns of inequality along lines of gender and race. In "'Equal Pay' Is Not So Equal" (Article 8.3), John Miller discusses unequal pay between men and women and responds to skeptics' claims that the pay gap is a statistical illusion. Meanwhile, Jeannette Wicks-Lim discusses how "It Pays to Be White" (Article 8.4)—whether we're talking about education, job opportunities, policing, or just about any other aspect of life in the United States today. Wicks-Lim argues that the "social environment in the United States, steeped in race-based haves and have-nots," causes deep-rooted racial biases throughout the society. She ends the article by discussing possible policies to uproot these biases.

The next two articles return to the underlying causes of income inequality. In "Unions and Income Inequality" (Article 8.5), Arthur MacEwan points out that the income share of the richest 1% declined when the share of workers who were union members rose, and has risen as union membership has fallen. To MacEwan, it seems clear that restoring union size and strength would go a long way toward reducing inequality. For anyone who wants to explore questions of inequality and fairness, Gar Alperovitz and Lew Daly's article "The Undeserving Rich" (Article 8.6) provides some fascinating grist for the mill. They argue that growth is built on a base of collectively produced knowledge that each generation inherits—not merely on the efforts of individuals. Therfore, they argue, those who appropriate a disproportionate share are "undeserving" of their fortunes.

Gerald Friedman (Article 8.7) describes one of the most extreme manifestations of inequality and poverty in the United States today, widespread food insecurity. He notes that government nutrition programs have positive impacts both in terms of short-term alleviation of hunger and long-term health and economic benefits for recipients—but are just not extensive enough.

Finally, in "What is U.S. Workers' Share of National Income?" (Article 8.8), Arthur MacEwan looks at the complexities involved in answering a seemingly simple question about workers' share of the national income. MacEwan notes that, using International Labour Organization statistics from 2013, the real workers' share of national income is masked through aggregation. When one accounts for and corrects the skew, we find that "[w]orkers in the United States do not fare so well in relation to workers in other countries in terms of shares of their nations' incomes."

Discussion Questions

1. (Article 8.1) According to Tilly, many of the mechanisms linking equality and growth are political. Should economic models incorporate political behavior as well as economic behavior? What are some ways they could do that?

2. (Article 8.1) Explain Tilly's metaphor about the "Goose That Laid the Golden Eggs." How is equality the goose?

3. (Article 8.2) Why, according to John Miller, have workers not benefited much from the re-inflation of stock prices since the Great Recession?

4. (Article 8.3) Why might someone think that the different industries and occupations men and women typically work in help explain away the gender pay gap? Why might someone think those differences can't explain it away?

5.   (Article 8.3) What policies might make the pay gap disappear, according to Miller?

6.   (Article 8.4) It is common for people to view racial disparities in society (like job discrimination or racial profiling) as a consequence of racial biases. Wicks-Lim argues that biases are a consequence of racial disparities. Explain.

7.   (Article 8.5) MacEwan shows that union strength and economic inequality are negatively associated (when one is high, the other is low). What possible explanations does MacEwan offer? Is there good reason to believe that higher unionization was the cause of greater equality in the past, and the decline of unions explains increased inequality in recent years?

8.   (Article 8.6) Consider the following quotation:

> "I think we've been through a period where too many people have been given to understand that if they have a problem, it's the government's job to cope with it. ... They're casting their problem on society. And, you know, there is no such thing as society. There are individual men and women, and there are families."
>
> —British Prime Minister Margaret Thatcher, talking to *Woman's Own* magazine, October 31, 1987

After reading Alperovitz and Daly's article "The Undeserving Rich," how do you think the authors would respond to Thatcher? How would you respond?

9.   (Article 8.7) If, as Friedman says, the United States is "wealthy enough that everyone could have enough to eat," why do people go hungry anyway? In your view, what could and should be done to remedy this situation?

10. (Article 8.8) "Workers in the United States do not fare so well in relation to workers in other countries in terms of shares of their nations' incomes." Why is this so?

GEESE, GOLDEN EGGS, AND TRAPS
Why inequality is bad for the economy.

BY CHRIS TILLY
July/August 2004

Whenever progressives propose ways to redistribute wealth from the rich to those with low and moderate incomes, conservative politicians and economists accuse them of trying to kill the goose that lays the golden egg. The advocates of unfettered capitalism proclaim that inequality is good for the economy because it promotes economic growth. Unequal incomes, they say, provide the incentives necessary to guide productive economic decisions by businesses and individuals. Try to reduce inequality, and you'll sap growth. Furthermore, the conservatives argue, growth actually promotes equality by boosting the have-nots more than the haves. So instead of fiddling with who gets how much, the best way to help those at the bottom is to pump up growth.

But these conservative prescriptions are absolutely, dangerously wrong. Instead of the goose-killer, equality turns out to be the goose. Inequality stifles growth; equality gooses it up. Moreover, economic expansion does not necessarily promote equality—instead, it is the types of jobs and the rules of the economic game that matter most.

Inequality: Goose or Goose-Killer?

The conservative argument may be wrong, but it's straightforward. Inequality is good for the economy, conservatives say, because it provides the right incentives for innovation and economic growth. First of all, people will only have the motivation to work hard, innovate, and invest wisely if the economic system rewards them for good economic choices and penalizes bad ones. Robin Hood-style policies that collect from the wealthy and help those who are worse off violate this principle. They reduce the payoff to smart decisions and lessen the sting of dumb ones. The result: people and companies are bound to make less efficient decisions. "We must allow [individuals] to fail, as well as succeed, and we must replace the nanny state with a regime of self-reliance and self-respect," writes conservative lawyer Stephen Kinsella in *The Freeman: Ideas on Liberty* (not clear how the free woman fits in). To prove their point, conservatives point to the former state socialist countries, whose economies had become stagnant and inefficient by the time they fell at the end of the 1980s.

If you don't buy this incentive story, there's always the well-worn trickle-down theory. To grow, the economy needs productive investments: new offices, factories, computers, and machines. To finance such investments takes a pool of savings. The rich save a larger fraction of their incomes than those less well-off. So to spur growth, give more to the well-heeled (or at least take less away from them in the form of taxes), and give less to the down-and-out. The rich will save their money and then invest it, promoting growth that's good for everyone.

Unfortunately for trickle-down, the brilliant economist John Maynard Keynes debunked the theory in his *General Theory of Employment, Interest, and*

Money in 1936. Keynes, whose precepts guided liberal U.S. economic policy from the 1940s through the 1970s, agreed that investments must be financed out of savings. But he showed that most often it's changes in investment that drive savings, rather than the other way around. When businesses are optimistic about the future and invest in building and retooling, the economy booms, all of us make more money, and we put some of it in banks, 401(k)s, stocks, and so on. That is, saving grows to match investment. When companies are glum, the process runs in reverse, and savings shrink to equal investment. This leads to the "paradox of thrift": if people try to save too much, businesses will see less consumer spending, will invest less, and total savings will end up diminishing rather than growing as the economy spirals downward. A number of Keynes's followers added the next logical step: shifting money from the high-saving rich to the high-spending rest of us, and not the other way around, will spur investment and growth.

Of the two conservative arguments in favor of inequality, the incentive argument is a little weightier. Keynes himself agreed that people needed financial consequences to steer their actions, but questioned whether the differences in pay-offs needed to be so huge. Certainly state socialist countries' attempts to replace material incentives with moral exhortation have often fallen short. In 1970, the Cuban government launched the Gran Zafra (Great Harvest), an attempt to reap 10 million tons of sugar cane with (strongly encouraged) volunteer labor. Originally inspired by Che Guevara's ideal of the New Socialist Man (not clear how the New Socialist Woman fit in), the effort ended with Fidel Castro tearfully apologizing to the Cuban people in a nationally broadcast speech for letting wishful thinking guide economic policy.

But before conceding this point to the conservatives, let's look at the evidence about the connection between equality and growth. Economists William Easterly of New York University and Gary Fields of Cornell University have recently summarized this evidence:

- Countries, and regions within countries, with more equal incomes grow faster. (These growth figures do not include environmental destruction or improvement. If they knocked off points for environmental destruction and added points for environmental improvement, the correlation between equality and growth would be even stronger, since desperation drives poor people to adopt environmentally destructive practices such as rapid deforestation.)
- Countries with more equally distributed land grow faster.
- Somewhat disturbingly, more ethnically homogeneous countries and regions grow faster—presumably because there are fewer ethnically based inequalities.
- In addition, more worker rights are associated with higher rates of economic growth, according to Josh Bivens and Christian Weller, economists at two Washington think tanks, the Economic Policy Institute and the Center for American Progress.

These patterns recommend a second look at the incentive question. In fact, more equality can actually strengthen incentives and opportunities to produce.

Equality as the Goose

Equality can boost growth in several ways. Perhaps the simplest is that study after study has shown that farmland is more productive when cultivated in small plots. So organizations promoting more equal distribution of land, like Brazil's Landless Workers' Movement, are not just helping the landless poor—they're contributing to agricultural productivity!

Another reason for the link between equality and growth is what Easterly calls "match effects," which have been highlighted in research by Stanford's Paul Roemer and others in recent years. One example of a match effect is the fact that well-educated people are most productive when working with others who have lots of schooling. Likewise, people working with computers are more productive when many others have computers (so that, for example, email communication is widespread, and know-how about computer repair and software is easy to come by). In very unequal societies, highly educated, computer-using elites are surrounded by majorities with little education and no computer access, dragging down their productivity. This decreases young people's incentive to get more education and businesses' incentive to invest in computers, since the payoff will be smaller.

Match effects can even matter at the level of a metropolitan area. Urban economist Larry Ledebur looked at income and employment growth in 85 U.S. cities and their neighboring suburbs. He found that where the income gap between those in the suburbs and those in the city was largest, income and job growth was slower for everyone.

"Pressure effects" also help explain why equality sparks growth. Policies that close off the low-road strategy of exploiting poor and working people create pressure effects, driving economic elites to search for investment opportunities that pay off by boosting productivity rather than squeezing the have-nots harder. For example, where workers have more rights, they will place greater demands on businesses. Business owners will respond by trying to increase productivity, both to remain profitable even after paying higher wages, and to find ways to produce with fewer workers. The CIO union drives in U.S. mass production industries in the 1930s and 1940s provide much of the explanation for the superb productivity growth of the 1950s and 1960s. (The absence of pressure effects may help explain why many past and present state socialist countries have seen slow growth, since they tend to offer numerous protections for workers but no right to organize independent unions.) Similarly, if a government buys out large land-holdings in order to break them up, wealthy families who simply kept their fortunes tied up in land for generations will look for new, productive investments. Industrialization in Asian "tigers" South Korea and Taiwan took off in the 1950s on the wings of funds freed up in exactly this way.

Inequality, Conflict, and Growth

Inequality hinders growth in another important way: it fuels social conflict. Stark inequality in countries such as Bolivia and Haiti has led to chronic conflict that hobbles economic growth. Moreover, inequality ties up resources in unproductive uses such as paying for large numbers of police and security guards—attempts to prevent individuals from redistributing resources through theft.

Ethnic variety is connected to slower growth because, on the average, more ethnically diverse countries are also more likely to be ethnically divided. In other words, the problem isn't ethnic variety itself, but racism and ethnic conflict that can exist among diverse populations. In nations like Guatemala, Congo, and Nigeria, ethnic strife has crippled growth—a problem alien to ethnically uniform Japan and South Korea. The reasons are similar to some of the reasons that large class divides hurt growth. Where ethnic divisions (which can take tribal, language, religious, racial, or regional forms) loom large, dominant ethnic groups seek to use government power to better themselves at the expense of other groups, rather than making broad-based investments in education and infrastructure. This can involve keeping down the underdogs—slower growth in the U.S. South for much of the country's history was linked to the Southern system of white supremacy. Or it can involve seizing the surplus of ethnic groups perceived as better off—in the extreme, Nazi Germany's expropriation and genocide of the Jews, who often held professional and commercial jobs.

Of course, the solution to such divisions is not "ethnic cleansing" so that each country has only one ethnic group—in addition to being morally abhorrent, this is simply impossible in a world with 191 countries and 5,000 ethnic groups. Rather, the solution is to diminish ethnic inequalities. Once the 1964 Civil Rights Act forced the South to drop racist laws, the New South's economic growth spurt began. Easterly reports that in countries with strong rule of law, professional bureaucracies, protection of contracts, and freedom from expropriation—all rules that make it harder for one ethnic group to economically oppress another—ethnic diversity has no negative impact on growth.

If more equality leads to faster growth so everybody benefits, why do the rich typically resist redistribution? Looking at the ways that equity seeds growth helps us understand why. The importance of pressure effects tells us that the wealthy often don't think about more productive ways to invest or reorganize their businesses until they are forced to. But also, if a country becomes very unequal, it can get stuck in an "inequality trap." Any redistribution involves a tradeoff for the rich. They lose by giving up part of their wealth, but they gain a share in increased economic growth. The bigger the disparity between the rich and the rest, the more the rich have to lose, and the less likely that the equal share of boosted growth they'll get will make up for their loss. Once the gap goes beyond a certain point, the wealthy have a strong incentive to restrict democracy, and to block spending on education which might lead the poor to challenge economic injustice—making reform that much harder.

Does Economic Growth Reduce Inequality?

If inequality isn't actually good for the economy, what about the second part of the conservatives' argument—that growth itself promotes equality? According to the conservatives, those who care about equality should simply pursue growth and wait for equality to follow.

"A rising tide lifts all boats," President John F. Kennedy famously declared. But he said nothing about which boats will rise fastest when the economic tide comes in. Growth does typically reduce poverty, according to studies reviewed by economist Gary Fields, though some "boats"—especially families with strong barriers to participating in the labor force—stay "stuck in the mud." But inequality can increase at the same time that poverty falls, if the rich gain even faster than the poor do. True, sustained periods of low unemployment, like that in the late 1990s United States, do tend to raise wages at the bottom even faster than salaries at the top. But growth after the recessions of 1991 and 2001 began with years of "jobless recoveries"—growth with inequality.

For decades the prevailing view about growth and inequality within countries was that expressed by Simon Kuznets in his 1955 presidential address to the American Economic Association. Kuznets argued that as countries grew, inequality would first increase, then decrease. The reason is that people will gradually move from the low-income agricultural sector to higher-income industrial jobs—with inequality peaking when the workforce is equally divided between low- and high-income sectors. For mature industrial economies, Kuznets's proposition counsels focusing on growth, assuming that it will bring equity. In developing countries, it calls for enduring current inequality for the sake of future equity and prosperity.

But economic growth doesn't automatically fuel equality. In 1998, economists Klaus Deininger and Lyn Squire traced inequality and growth over time in 48 countries. Five followed the Kuznets pattern, four followed the reverse pattern (decreasing inequality followed by an increase), and the rest showed no systematic pattern. In the United States, for example:

- incomes became more equal during the 1930s through 1940s New Deal period (a time that included economic decline followed by growth);
- from the 1950s through the 1970s, income gaps lessened during booms and expanded during slumps;
- from the late 1970s forward, income inequality worsened fairly consistently, whether the economy was stagnating or growing.

The reasons are not hard to guess. The New Deal introduced widespread unionization, a minimum wage, social security, unemployment insurance, and welfare. Since the late 1970s, unions have declined, the inflation-adjusted value of the minimum wage has fallen, and the social safety net has been shredded. In the United States, as elsewhere, growth only promotes equality if policies and institutions to support equity are in place.

Trapped?

Let's revisit the idea of an inequality trap. The notion is that as the gap between the rich and everybody else grows wider, the wealthy become more willing to give up overall growth in return for the larger share they're getting for themselves. The "haves" back policies to control the "have-nots," instead of devoting social resources to educating the poor so they'll be more productive.

Sound familiar? It should. After two decades of widening inequality, the last few years have brought us massive tax cuts that primarily benefit the wealthiest, at the expense of investment in infrastructure and the education, child care, and income supports that would help raise less well-off kids to be productive adults. Federal and state governments have cranked up expenditures on prisons, police, and "homeland security," and Republican campaign organizations have devoted major resources to keeping blacks and the poor away from the polls. If the economic patterns of the past are any indication, we're going to pay for these policies in slower growth and stagnation unless we can find our way out of this inequality trap. ❏

Article 8.2

THE STOCK MARKET AND CLASS CONFLICT
Trump's State of the Union Message and the Economy

BY JOHN MILLER
March/June 2018

> Since the election, we have created 2.4 million new jobs. After years of wage stagnation, we are finally seeing rising wages.
>
> Unemployment claims have hit a 45-year low. African-American unemployment stands at the lowest rate ever recorded.
>
> The stock market has smashed one record after another, gaining $8 trillion in value.
>
> —President Donald Trump's State of the Union address as prepared for delivery and released by the White House, January 30, 2018.

> Jay Powell started work as Federal Reserve chairman on Monday, and stocks promptly fell by the largest single-session point decline on record.
>
> The paradox of the equity-market correction is that it's taking place even as the real economy looks stronger than it's been since at least 2005 and maybe 1999.
>
> —"The Return to Normal Risk," by the Editorial Board, *Wall Street Journal*, February 5, 2018.

"**N**ever mind!" That's how Gilda Radner's character Emily Litella ended each of her error-filled commentaries on the Saturday Night Live news report. "Never mind!" would have been a fitting close to the economic news in President Trump's first State of the Union Message.

Just three days after his speech, volatility had returned to Trump's record-breaking stock market, at one point wiping out the euphoria-fueled gains made since the passage of the Republican tax cut for the wealthy in late December. And the Bureau of Labor Statistics reported that the record low African-American unemployment rate, which Trump's policies had done little to bring about, was a full percentage point higher in January 2018.

Nor was it the case that job growth had accelerated during Trump's first year in office. Counting from the first of the year, instead of from Trump's election, the economy added 2.1 million jobs during 2017, fewer jobs than the economy had added in any of Obama's last six years in office.

Wages and the Stock Market

The one bit of news that had staying power was Trump's claim that, "we are finally seeing rising wages." Average hourly wages for private-sector (nonfarm) employees rose 2.9% from January 2017 to January 2018, the highest rate since 2008. That was good news, a pick-up from the 2.3% rate during the second term of the Obama administration. But it was a far from a harbinger of the arrival of widespread economic prosperity in the ninth year of the long but slow economic expansion since the end of the Great Recession. To begin with, adjusted for inflation, average hourly earnings increased just 0.8%. What's more, the gains in earnings were concentrated among managerial workers, and were highest in the financial sector. Wages of non-supervisory workers, who hold about four-fifths of private sector jobs, rose just 2.4%, and only 0.1% after adjusting for inflation On top of that, without the increase in the minimum wage in 18 states that went into effect on the first of the year, those numbers would have been lower. Finally, 2.4% is well below the 3.8% increase in hourly wages of non-supervisory personnel during the last three years of the long economic expansion in the 1990s.

Nonetheless, the pick-up in wage growth was enough to send the stock market into paroxysms of volatility. In one way, the *Wall Street Journal* editors were right, the stock market volatility was a return to normal. The Standard & Poor's index of the price of 500 stocks, the benchmark used by most professional investors, had almost tripled in value from a low in March 2009 near the end of the Great Recession, with only four corrections, defined as a 10% or greater decline in stock prices. That track record, and 15 straight months without a market decline, fueled a growing sense that stock prices only went up. The 10.2% decline in stock prices (measured by the S&P 500) in early February was a harsh reminder of the risks inherent in stock investment, or what the editors call "normal risk."

In another way, however, the stock market has been operating in its normal way all along: Good news for investors on Wall Street came at the expense of bad news for workers on Main Street. As the stock market soared since March 2009, wage growth was kept in check. But when Wall Street was coming out on top, the conflict between wage growth and stock returns was of little concern to the editors. Only when the cumulative effects of over eight years of economic growth began to pay off in wage gains for workers and volatility returned to the stock market did the *WSJ* editors find it paradoxical that the interests of workers on Main Street and investors on Wall Street were not aligned.

It's No Paradox; It's Class Conflict.

But that conflict is hardly surprising. The stock market boom did little to make most workers better off. Stock returns go overwhelmingly to the wealthy. Economist Edward Wolff reports that in 2016 some 84% of stocks are owned by the wealthiest 10% of households. The richest 1% of households alone own two-fifths (40.3%) of stocks, more than twice the share of the bottom 90% of households. Fully one-half of households own no stock. Just 13.9% of households directly own stocks, and another 35.4% of households own stock indirectly (e.g., through retirement funds).

What wealth most workers have is in their homes. While national housing prices increased 43.7% from their December 2011 low to November 2017, that was just one-seventh of the threefold rise in stocks prices.

So it remains that most workers depend on wage growth, not the stock market gains or appreciating housing values, to improve their economic position. And contrary to most mainstream economics reporting, we are not all—workers and investors alike—on the same elevator, moving up or down in concert.

While the *WSJ* editors are rather puzzled by the adverse effects of wages increases on stock market returns, the conflict is not mysterious. Here's why.

Economic growth creates jobs, lowering unemployment. Low unemployment gives workers greater bargaining power to press for higher wages and benefits. Businesses can either absorb these higher labor costs by cutting profits, or pass them along by raising prices.

Either way, investors lose out. If their profits decline, corporations may pay their stockholders less in dividends and/or see their share prices fall. If prices rise, that inflation cuts into the real value of investor assets and may provoke the Federal Reserve to hike interest rates, dampening economic growth.

Concerns that the Fed might press harder on the economic brakes contributed to the February stock sell off. Higher interest rates make it harder to borrow, which would likely reduce the money going into the stock market. In addition, higher interest rates increase the rate of return on bonds, one of the chief alternatives to purchasing stocks. For instance, by mid-February the yield for holding a nearly risk-free ten-year Treasury bond had increased to 2.9% from its 2.3% interest rate a year earlier. Both these effects—higher costs of borrowing and higher yields on bonds—dampen the demand for stocks and lower stock prices.

On the other hand, when wage gains are kept in check and the Fed delivers rock-bottom interest rates, as was the case in the first eight years of the economic recovery, profits soar and Wall Street investors prosper, while those on Main Street flounder.

The Markets Protest Too Much

But are investors' fears of higher costs and inflation justified? Labor compensation does make up the largest chunk of business costs and rising labor costs can eat into business profits. And labor compensation (wages and benefits) as a share of the output of the non-farm sector did improve somewhat from its low point in 2011. But the labor share remains lower than any time before the 2008 onset of the Great Recession, and corporate profits as a share of national income continue at near record levels.

Also, "unit labor costs," which measure the actual dollar costs firms pay for employees to make a unit of output, have shown less upward pressure on costs than the wage increases that have rendered investors apoplectic. Despite a sizeable increase in the fourth quarter of 2017, unit labor costs remain below their levels in the second half of 2016.

These numbers reveal the unwillingness of the financial powers to share with workers the gains of economic growth even when increases in labor costs are modest and profit rates continue to outdistanced those of earlier periods.

But that's hardly new. In the midst of the Great Depression, Woody Guthrie said Wall Street was "the street that keeps the rest of us off Easy Street." It still is. ❏

Sources: "Employment Situation Summary," Bureau of Labor Statistics, Feb. 2, 2018 (bls.gov); "Productivity and Costs," Bureau of Labor Statistics, Feb. 1, 2018 (bls.gov); Chuck Jones, "Trump's Economic Scorecard: One Year Since Inauguration," *Forbes*, Jan. 18, 2018; Julien Ponthus and Ritvik Carvalho, "Explainer: Why higher wages are whacking global stock markets," Reuters, Feb. 5, 2018; Edward Wolff, "The Asset Price Meltdown and the Wealth of the Middle Class," National Bureau of Economic Research Working Paper, No.18559.

Article 8.3

"EQUAL PAY" IS NOT SO EQUAL

BY JOHN MILLER
September/October 2016

> The latest U.S. Department of Labor data show that women working full-time make 81 percent of full-time men's wages. But this figure is both inaccurate and misleading. This statistic looks only at raw averages and does not take into account factors such as education, skills, and hours worked. After controlling for other factors, the gender pay gap practically disappears. Legislation to close the gender "wage gap" is misguided: in reality, there is no gap to close.
>
> —Diana Furchgott-Roth, "Sorry, Elizabeth Warren, Women Already Have Equal Pay," Economics21, The Manhattan Institute for Policy Research, July 27, 2016

"We believe in equal pay for equal work." That was all Sen. Elizabeth Warren (D-Mass.) said about the gender pay gap during her keynote address to July's Democratic National Convention. But it was enough to provoke a response from economist Diana Furchgott-Roth, a senior fellow at the free-market Manhattan Institute.

That's hardly surprising. Furchgott-Roth has spent two decades issuing one version or another of one basic claim: "there is no gap to close between men's and women's wages."

Publishing article after article claiming that there is no gender pay gap, however, doesn't make it so. Here's why.

No Statistical Artifact

To begin with, the gender pay gap is no statistical artifact. The most common measure of the gender pay gap compares the median earnings (wages and salaries) of full-time working women over the year to the median earnings for men. That ratio does not compare the earnings of men and women doing the same job, but rather the earnings of all men and women who work full time.

In 2014, the latest year for which data are available, men's median earnings for the year were $50,383, while women's median earnings were $39,621, or 78.6% of men's. That's where the figure that women earn 79 cents for each dollar a man earns comes from. The National Committee on Pay Equity inaugurated the tradition of using this ratio to determine the date on which "Equal Pay Day" falls each year. This year, it fell on April 12, 2016, the date by which women would have earned enough to make up the $10,762 gap between their pay and men's in 2015. (Furchgott-Roth's figure for the gender pay gap, 81% in 2015, is calculated in the same way but compares the median weekly earnings of full-time wage and salary workers.)

Whether women earn 79 cents or 81 cents for every dollar a man earns, the gender pay gap is longstanding. In 1963, the year the Equal Pay Act became law, a full-time working woman (earning the median pay for women) got 59 cents for each dollar a full-time working man received (at the median pay for men). By the first Equal Pay Day in 1996, women earned 74 cents for a dollar of men's earnings; now the figure is up to 79 cents. The gender pay gap, however, is no longer narrowing as fast as it did earlier. During the 1980s, the gap declined by more than one-quarter (28.7%), as women's earnings improved from 60 cents for every dollar a man earned to 72 cents; during the 1990s, by just 6%, as women's earnings increased from 72 cents to 73 cents for every dollar of men's earnings; in the last ten years (2004-2014), by 7.4%, as women's earnings increased from 77 cents to 79 cents for every dollar of men's earnings.

The gender pay gap is also pervasive. Regardless of her education, her occupation, her race, or her age, a full-time working woman (getting the median wage for women of that group) is paid less than a full-time working man (getting the median wage for men of that group).

Women earn less than men at every educational level. In 2015, the median weekly earnings of women without a high school diploma were 80% of their male counterparts' earnings, 77% for women with (only) a high school diploma, 75% for women with some college, 75% for women who were college graduates, and 74% for women with an advanced degree.

Women earn less than men in all but five of the 800 detailed occupations tracked by the Bureau of Labor Statistics (for which there is comparable data). Women in female-dominated occupations—from maids to secretaries to registered nurses—earn less than men do in those same jobs, as do women in male-dominated jobs—from truck drivers to retail supervisors to janitors. The same is true for women in elite jobs such as physicians, surgeons, and financial managers.

Women of all racial/ethnic groups are paid less than white men and less than men of the same race/ethnicity. In 2015, the median weekly earnings of white women working full time were 80.8% of those for white men. The weekly earnings of black women were 89% of the earnings of black men; the earnings of Hispanic women, 90% of the earnings of Hispanic men. Meanwhile, the weekly earnings of black and Hispanic women were just 62% and 67%, respectively, of the weekly earnings of white men.

Women workers of all ages are paid less than their male counterparts. Older women, however, face the largest pay gap as they are penalized for leaving the workforce more often than men for childbirth, childcare, and eldercare. In 2014, the annual median wage of women ages 18–24 who worked full time was 88% of the median wage of full-time male workers of the same age group, but 81% for women ages 35–44, and just 68% for women over 55.

Making the Unequal Look Equal

But those differences, no matter how widespread or long lasting, don't impress economist Furchgott-Roth. In her version of reality, those differences disappear once the pay gap is adjusted for gender differences in hours worked, education, experience, and choice of industry and occupation. But each of these adjustments is problematic or makes less of a difference than Furchgott-Roth and other pay gap deniers suggest.

The deniers complain that earnings differentials calculated for full-time workers, including anyone who works 35 or more hours a week, mask the fact that men work more hours (in the money economy) than women. In fact, men are almost twice as likely as women work more than 40 hours a week. But that problem can be corrected by using hourly earnings to measure the gender pay gap. In 2014, hourly earnings of full- and part-time women wage-and-salary workers were 84.6% of men's. While smaller, that gap is still quite substantial and persists at all levels of education and for all racial/ethnic groups.

Nor will making adjustments for gender differences in education and experience, two traditional measures of labor-market skills, make the gender pay gap disappear. Adjustments for education explain much less of today's gender pay gap than they did in the early 1980s. Since then, more women have graduated from college than men, and by 1999 the average full-time working woman had more years of education than her male counterpart. Gender differences in years of experience are also far smaller than they were in the past. In 1981, men had, on average, 6.8 more years of full-time labor market experience than women, but the experience gap was just 1.4 years in 2011. In their detailed study of the sources of the gender pay gap, economists Francine Blau and Lawrence Kahn estimate that, taken together, differences in education (which favor women) and differences in experience (which favor men) explained 8.2% of the gender pay gap in 2011, or just 2 cents of the 23 cent gap.

There is little disagreement that differences between women and men in terms of the industries they work in and the jobs they hold have a profound effect on the gender pay gap. Blau and Kahn, for instance, estimate that industry and occupation accounted for fully one-half (49.5%) of the gender pay gap in 2010.

But just how women ended up in particular industries and occupations and not in others is a matter of sharp debate. For gender pay gap skeptics, this is a matter of individual choice. "Women gravitate toward jobs with fewer risks, more comfortable conditions, regular hours, more personal fulfillment, and greater flexibility," argues Carrie Lukas, executive director of the Independent Women's Forum. Women, she concludes, are "willing to trade higher pay for other desirable job characteristics." But the story Lukas tells is not the empirical reality faced by most women. To begin with, women's jobs do not possess the other desirable characteristics she says compensate women for accepting lower pay. In their study of the characteristics of men's and women's jobs in 27 countries including the United States, sociologists Haya Stier and Meir Yaish found that on average the jobs held by women offered less autonomy or time flexibility and that their working conditions were more stressful and exhausting than those of men, a condition that was surely exacerbated by women bearing an inordinate share of domestic labor. (Women's jobs did require less physical labor than men's jobs.)

If individual choices of women don't explain what crowds many women into lower paying jobs, then what is responsible for gender segregation by occupation and industry? Gender discrimination that disadvantages women in the labor market and devalues their work is the more plausible answer. If you doubt that women's work is undervalued, political scientist Ellen Frankel Paul would ask you to consider this example: zookeepers—a traditionally male job—earn more than workers caring for children—a traditionally female job. The evidence that the sorting of genders into industries and occupations is shaped "by discrimination, societal norms and other forces beyond women's control," as economists Jessica Schieder and Elisa Gould argue, is compelling. For instance, it is well documented that women in better-paying male-dominated jobs have faced hostile work environments. A 2008 study found that "52% of highly qualified females working for SET (science, technology, and engineering) companies quit their jobs, driven out by hostile work environments and extreme job pressures." And gender discrimination plays a role in who gets hired in the first place. In two studies, when participants reviewed resumes that were identical except for the names, the ones with male names were more likely to be offered a job. According to another study, after five top U.S. symphony orchestras switched to blind auditions, women were 50% more likely to get past the first round. But gender norms already direct women and men toward different jobs long before they enter in the labor market. For instance, Schieder and Gould report that women arrive at college far less likely than men are to major in engineering, computer sciences, or physics, even though those fields promise lucrative job opportunities.

Most low-paying jobs, on the other hand, are female dominated. In their 2009 study, sociologists Asaf Levanon, Paula England, and Paul Allison reported that occupations with a higher percentage of women workers generally paid less than those with a lower percentage of women, even when correcting for education and skill demands. On top of that, they found evidence that when more women enter a job category, employers start paying less. For example, as jobs in parks and camps went from being male-dominated to female-dominated, between 1950 and 2000, the median hourly wages (corrected for inflation) fell by more than half.

Finally, the adjustments favored by Furchgott-Roth and other gender-gap skeptics are not enough to statistically eliminate the gender pay gap. For instance, one research study, commissioned by the Department of Labor during the George W. Bush administration, estimated a wage gap between 4.8 and 7.1 percentage points after making adjustments for other gender differences. In the Blau and Kahn study the remaining gender gap in 2010 was 8.4 percentage points when fully adjusting for differences in education, experience, region, race, unionization, industry and occupation. Those gender pay gaps, which assume that differences in occupation and industry are not evidence of ongoing gender discrimination, are much smaller than the unadjusted gap, but still substantial.

For Blau and Kahn, the unexplained portion of the gender pay gap, "suggests, though it does not prove, that labor market discrimination continues to contribute to the gender wage gap." The unexplained gender pay gap (the portion still left over after statistically adjusting for occupation, industry, or worker qualifications) has actually worsened since the late 1980s (from 7.6 cents for each dollar a man made in 1989 to 8.4 cents in 2010). In 2010, over one-third (38%) of the gender pay gap remained unexplained. If we include the portion of the gap due to gender differences in occupation and industry, a whopping 87.5%, or 18 cents of the 21 cents of the unadjusted gender gap in their study, can be interpreted as a product of continued discrimination.

Truly Equal Pay

One important step to reduce continued labor market gender discrimination would be to pass the Paycheck Fairness Act. The law would require employers to show that wage differentials are based on factors other than gender, and would strike a blow against pay secrecy by banning retaliation against employees who reveal their own wages to other employees.

But much more needs to be done to combat workplace gender discrimination. More family-friendly policies are needed. The United States is the only advanced country that does not guarantee paid maternity leave. Comparable-worth policies are needed to promote pay equity. Those policies would ensure that jobs having the same value to employers would be paid the same whether performed by women or men. Also, in order to short-circuit historical gender pay discrimination, newly passed comparable-worth legislation in Massachusetts bars employers from asking job applicants how much they earned in previous jobs. In addition, raising the minimum wage would boost the earnings of workers in low-income jobs, the vast majority of which are female-dominated. Unionization in female-dominated occupations would also reduce the gender pay gap, as it has done among public employees.

For Furchgott-Roth and the gender-pay-gap skeptics, the pay gap disappears by statistical manipulation. These policies, on the other hand, are ways to make it go away for real. ❏

Sources: Francine Blau and Lawrence Kahn, "The Gender Wage Gap: Extent, and Explanations," IZA Research Network, Discussion Paper No. 9656, Jan. 2016; Jessica Schleder and Elise Gould, "'Women's work' and the gender pay gap," Economic Policy Institute, July 20, 2016; Asaf Levanon, Paula England, and Paul Allison, "Occupational Feminization and Pay," *Social Forces*, December 2009; Hava Stier and Meir Yaish, "Occupational segregation and gender inequality in job quality," *Work, Employment, and Society*, 28(2), 2014; Marlene Kim, "Policies to End the Gender Wage Gap in the United States," *Review of Radical Political Economics*, 45(3), 2013; Emily Liner, "The Wage Gap Over Time," "A Dollar Short: What's Holding Women Back form Equal Pay?" *Third Way Report*, March 18, 2016; "An Analysis of Reasons for the Disparity in Wages Between Men and Women," A Report by CONSAD Research Corp. for the Department of Labor, 2009; Ellen Frankel, ed., *Equity and Gender: The Comparable Worth Debate* (Transactions Publishers, 1989); Corrine Moss-Racusin et al, "Science faculty's subtle gender biases favor male students," *Proceedings of the National Academy of Sciences*, Oct. 9, 2012; Claudia Goldin and Cecilia Rouse, "Orchestrating Impartiality," National Bureau of Economic Research, Working Paper 5903, January 1997; Sylvia Ann Hewlett, et al., "The Athena Factor," *Harvard Business Review*, 2008; National Committee on Pay Equity, accessed August 2016; "The Gender Wage Gap by Occupation 2015 and by Race and Ethnicity," Institute For Women's Policy Research, Fact Sheet WPR #C440; April, 2016; Janet Adamy and Paul Overberg, "Women in Elite Jobs Face Stubborn Pay Gap," *Wall Street Journal*, May 17, 2016; Stacy Cowley, "Illegal in Massachusetts: Asking Your Salary in a Job Interview," *New York Times*, Aug. 2, 2016; Kaitlin Holmes and Danielle Corley, "The Top 10 Facts About the Gender Wage Gap," Center for American Progress, April 12, 2016.

Article 8.4

IT PAYS TO BE WHITE

Assessing how White people benefit from race-based economic inequality.

BY JEANNETTE WICKS-LIM
May/June 2016

By every major socioeconomic measure, there is an undeniable race-based hierarchy in the United States—with Black Americans sitting at or near the bot-tom. In 2014, the share of Black adults (at least 25 years old) with bachelor's or advanced degrees (22%) is notably lower than their White counterparts (32%). The official unemployment rate for Black workers is persistently double that of White workers: in 2015, 9.7% vs. 4.3%. Also in 2015, the African-American poverty rate (26.2%) stood at more than double that among White Americans (10.1%). Black Americans account for 38% of the prison population, nearly three times their share of the U.S. population. White Americans, in contrast, account for 59% of U.S. prisoners, under-representing their 77% population share.

These lopsided outcomes have, of course, two sides: by every major socioeconomic measure, White Americans sit at or near the top of the race-based hierarchy. This is an obvious point. Here's another one: if the economic odds are stacked against African Americans, the flipside is that White Americans have the odds stacked in their favor. We need to even these odds to achieve racial justice.

Current policy debates largely focus on reducing potential hurdles set in the way of African Americans. These same debates, however, overlook how race-based advantages put White Americans on an easier life path. To eliminate the United States' race-based hierarchy, we need to redirect economic resources that currently operate as a premium for being White into creating equal opportunities for African Americans and other communities of color.

Unfortunately, two policies specifically created to do so—affirmative action and reparations—only exist on the outer fringes of current policy debates.

It Pays to Be White at School

According to a 2012 study, about one-third of the nation's students attend hyper-segregated schools: schools that are 90% White or 90% non-White. Students in the nearly all-White schools benefit from $4,985 in local and state education spending per student (adjusted for regional differences in living costs), an $810 premium over the $4,176 spent on their counterparts in the nearly all-non-White schools. (All figures are inflation-adjusted to 2015 dollars.)

Over a 13-year K-12 public-school education, this White-school premium adds up to nearly $10,000 more spending on each student in nearly all-White schools compared to students in nearly all-non-White schools ($810 premium x 13 years of schooling = $10,530).

This White advantage is even more impressive when pooled together under one school's roof. Given the average school size of 500 students, this White premium scales up to an extra $2.8 million dollar investment into the elementary education in a nearly all-White school ($810 per student x 500 students x 7 years of elementary education = $2.8 million). This White school premium can translate into White students learning in better physical facilities, having access to more curriculum offerings with more and higher-quality materials, and served by greater numbers of teachers and support staff.

It Pays to Be White on the Streets

City police departments' pro-active "stop and frisk" policing techniques have come under scrutiny in recent years. The term "stop and frisk" refers to when a police officer stops and detains a person if the officer believes he or she has a reasonable suspicion that criminal activity is taking place. Controversy over "stop and frisk" policing is due to charges that officers apply the tactics unevenly—surveying and interrupting the daily routines of White Americans much less frequently than those of Black Americans.

Take, for example, the practices of the Boston Police Department (BPD). In 2010, the American Civil Liberties Union of Massachusetts and the BPD co-sponsored a study of the BPD's "Field Interrogating Observation Frisk and/or Search" (FIOS) practices. Researchers approved by both organizations examined the BPD's database of FIOS incidents from 2007–2010. The study, released in 2015, concluded that the BPD treated White neighborhoods more favorably—initiated fewer FIOS incidents, compared to Black neighborhoods, even after taking into account differences in neighborhood crime rates. In fact, the figures in the study indicate that White neighborhoods (defined here as 85% White) accumulated 2,500 fewer FIOS incidents annually compared to Boston neighborhoods with a high concentration of Black residents (85% Black).

This difference implies that if you're living in an 85% White neighborhood, chances are that you would be subject to police surveillance about once every decade. So, for example, by the age 30, such a resident might be surveyed, stopped and/or frisked twice: once at age 15 and then again at age 25. This resident's life is minimally disrupted by the BPD. If you're living in a Black neighborhood, chances are you'd have a FIOS incident every three years. In other words, by age 30, you can expect to have already had six unsolicited police encounters: at age 15, then at age 18, again at 21, again at 24, again at 27, and again at 30 years old. The situation for Whites is even better than these numbers suggest. If you're White, the police are 11% more likely to only stop and ask you questions, not frisk or search you and your belongings compared to if you're Black. This difference in frisking rates of Whites versus Blacks is the same as the BPD's differential frisking rate of non-gang members versus gang members.

What's it worth to be White on Boston's streets? It's hard to put a price tag on the ability to move around freely.

It Pays to Be White at Work

How much more do White workers benefit from paid employment than their Black counterparts? That is, what is the bonus for being White in the workplace? One way to get a handle on this is to calculate how much more the average White worker earns, over a working lifetime, compared to their Black counterpart. Note that in this exercise I do not "net out" differences in educational credentials, or any other type of possible measures of skill. This is in order to take account of how, for example, any White premium in schooling builds up into an additional White bonus at work in the form of job market preparation. In other words, the premium I calculate for being White at work includes the White bonus of better-funded educational opportunities, as well as increased access to better job opportunities, and higher rewards for work.

Take the situation of an average White male fulltime worker and compare his experience in the labor force to his Black counterpart: In 2014, the average White male full-time worker earned $10,900 more than his Black counterpart: $44,900 vs. $34,000. This average male White worker also has access to a paid job more consistently compared to his Black counterpart; the employment rate for White males is much higher than for Black males (95.7% vs. 90.3%). Their annual earnings equal $42,900 and $30,700, after accounting for their average unemployment spells. The gap is now $12,200. At this rate, this White worker could work three months less per year, and still earn more money.

What does this mean over their entire work careers? To keep things simple, let's say each continues to work until the end of his or her life. Because White men live longer than Black men, this means that the average male White worker could potentially work from 25 to 77 years old, or 52 years. Black men die, on average, five years sooner at 72 years, for a work career of 47 years. Therefore, over an entire working career, White workers get a work bonus of $790,000—$2.2 million vs. $1.4 million. It really does pay to be White at work.

It Pays to Be White When You Stumble

In 2011, the average White household held $23,000 in liquid wealth, like deposits in a checking account or a retirement account. This is more than 100 times the average amount of $200 held by African-American households. Considering all assets, including equity in a home, the average White American had more than ten times that of the average Black American, $111,740 vs. $7,113.

White people's access to wealth gives them a boost when they're down on their luck. Chances are much better that, if you're White, you can draw on some inherited asset or the assets of a family member when the proverbial chips are down. Hit with a large, unexpected medical bill? If you're White, your chances of managing this as just a bump in the road are much better than if you are Black.

Likewise, White people's greater access to wealth gives them a leg up when trying to get ahead. Starting a small business or trying to buy a house where there are good neighborhood schools? Trying to get a college degree without paying for tuition with your credit card? If you're White, your likelihood of being able to make that initial business investment, home down payment, or to cover that college bill, is far better than if you're Black. These, of course, are key steps to anyone's larger effort to enter and stay in America's middle class—by improving one's own educational and employment prospects, as well as those of one's children.

White households' outsized share of wealth is deeply tied to the country's history of racist social institutions. Public policy has built up wealth for White citizens, at the expense of any social group considered non-White, for nearly the United States' entire history. Exemplars of such public policies include, of course, enslaving Africans and African Americans and expropriating land from Native Americans.

But public policies that build up wealth for White citizens, at the expense of other social groups extend through to more recent times. Take Pres. Franklin Delano Roosevelt's New Deal programs starting in the 1930s, such as the Home Owners' Loan Corporation (HOLC) and the Federal Housing Administration (FHA), or the 1944 Servicemen's Readjustment Act (GI Bill) that provided aid to World War II veterans. These programs intervened massively in the housing market by providing federally subsidized home mortgages. From 1935 to 1953, FHA and the Veteran's Administration backed, on average, 45% of the mortgages for new construction. This support, however, focused specifically on subsidizing home ownership for Whites. White families benefited from the programs' use of restrictive covenants that required White homeowners to only sell to White buyers and from redlining that designated Black neighborhoods as undesirable areas for mortgage lending. These practices did not officially end until the 1968 passage of the Fair Housing Act. These policies effectively represented large-scale federal affirmative action programs for White Americans.

It Pays to Be White Nearly Everywhere

Growing evidence from the field of social psychology over roughly the past 20 years demonstrate how living and breathing in a world defined by an economic racial hierarchy appears to shape our most basic intuitions about the world—what is good or bad, what is dangerous or safe, what has value and what is valueless. This is the basic conclusion of social psychologists researching the phenomenon of implicit racial bias—a person's unconscious favorable or unfavorable action toward, or thoughts and feelings about, another person based on the person's race. Crucially, this bias occurs even in the absence of any consciously identified racial bias (see sidebar, next page).

Implicit racial bias helps to make sense of what economists Marianne Bertrand and Sendhil Mullainathan observed in their 2004 study, "Are Emily and Greg More Employable than Lakisha and Jamal?" They found that the answer is: yes, across a wide range of occupations and industries. For their study they sent out thousands of essentially identical resumes, with the exception of the name of the applicant. Those with stereotypically White names got callbacks for interviews 50% more frequently than resumes sent with stereotypically Black names.

Hard-pressed to find any economic rationale for this racial bias, the researchers speculate, "Employers receive so many resumes that they may use quick heuristics in reading these resumes. One such heuristic could be to simply read no further when they see an African-American name." Moreover, the shock expressed by human resource managers over Bertrand and Mullainathan's findings suggests that this heuristic operates through an implicit—rather than explicit—racial bias. That is, employers don't consciously discard resumes with Black-sounding names. More likely, employers' hold an implicit racial bias that causes them, at a glance, to consider more favorably resumes with White-sounding names.

The social environment in the United States, steeped in race-based haves and have-nots, appears to train people's gut feelings to turn positive towards White people and negative towards Black people, unconsciously and automatically. As a result, it pays to be White nearly everywhere.

Policy Implications of White Privilege

All this leads to the conclusion that if African Americans have the deck stacked against them in every major life activity, White Americans have the deck stacked in their favor. Current policy debates need to focus on the question of how to eliminate White privilege. Two examples of public policies designed to do this include affirmative action and reparations.

The explicit goal of affirmative action policies is to increase the number of people of socially stigmatized groups into positions of prestige. Affirmative action is not just a policy about diversifying the classroom or the workplace. These types of policies aim to change the make-up of who holds high-ranking positions by decreasing the over-representation of members of advantaged groups.

Reparations, in the U.S. context, typically refers to a policy of providing compensation to descendants of Africans and African Americans who were enslaved in the United States. It can also refer to compensation for the damage generated by any other systematically racist public policy. Whatever the form and amount of compensation, the basic aim of reparations is to use government funds to transfer wealth to African-American households in order to correct for past government practices that transferred wealth from Black households to White households.

How to Detect Implicit Racial Bias

Social psychologists have come up with clever experimental designs to detect implicit racial bias. They do this with what's called an "Implicit Association Test" (IAT). To detect implicit racial bias, the IAT measures whether a person associates, without conscious deliberation, the concept or feeling of "good" with a White person compared to a Black person.

One version of this test has a participant sit in front of a computer. Words and names alternately appear on the screen. First, the person is instructed to hit the "I" key with their right hand to indicate if a word is "good" (e.g., "joy") and the "E" key with their left hand if the word is "bad" (e.g., "pain"). When a name appears on the screen, the person is instructed to hit the "I" key if the name is typically White ("Brad") and the "E" key if the name is typically Black ("Jamal"). This set-up associates "good" with "White"—the "I" key is hit for both, and "bad" with "Black"—the "E" key is hit for both. Then the exercise is repeated but with the association reversed: the participant is instructed to hit the "I" key if the name is typically Black ("Lakisha") and the "E" key if the name is typically White ("Allison"), while the words are sorted in the same way as before. Now, the set-up associates "good" with "Black" and "bad" with "White."

Researchers have found that people sort with greater ease when the key for Black and negative are the same, and the key for White and positive words are the same— evidence of an implicit racial bias. Studies using an IAT test like this one have found evidence of implicit racial bias regardless of whether participants express any type of explicit racial bias.

Implicit racial bias, however, is a major pernicious obstacle to public policies aimed at correcting for White privilege. Implicit racial bias supports the existing racial hierarchy with a gut feeling that people get what they get because that's what they deserve—in particular, that White people tend to get more because they deserve more, while Black people get less because they deserve less. This is one factor explaining the often-vitriolic political resistance to calls for reparations. Even affirmative action is currently treated as a policy debate non-starter.

Policies that require White people to give something valuable up—privileged access to a well-funded neighborhood school, an apartment or house, admission to a university, a high-paying or high-status job, a seat in Congress—become politically toxic when combined with implicit racial bias. This is the ultimate upside of race-based inequality for White Americans: it encourages White Americans to feel entitled to rebuke the policies that would end their White privilege.

What about tackling the issue of economic inequality more broadly? A flatter social hierarchy would, at minimum, limit the size of race-based gaps. Take for example, raising the federal minimum from today's $7.25 to $15.00. This policy would result in raises to 54% of Black workers and 59% of Latino workers compared to 38% of White workers.

At the same time, to uphold the moral integrity of such a political movement, and its potential broad-based political appeal, depends on coming honestly to the unifying call that "we're all in this together." This requires explicitly addressing the reality that yes, we're all in this together, but even among the 99% some get—and feel entitled to—more than their fair share.

In other words, policies that address inequality more broadly must not be used as a way to sidestep the truth about the racial hierarchy that exists in the United States. To be sure, we need social policies that address inequality more generally to build a more just economy. The United States has about 20 million poor White Americans to show for that. Still, White people—up and down the economic scale—benefit from a race-based advantage that simply does not exist for African Americans.

Promoting race-based policies, such as affirmative action or reparations, does present a political risk: it could critically weaken class-based solidarity by exacerbating race-based tensions. Such racial division can thwart efforts to hold together the needed political coalitions to fight for a more broadly just economy. In a forceful critique against calls for reparations, Black American political scientist Adolph Reed states plainly that "there's nothing (less) solidaristic than demanding a designer type policy that will redistribute only to one's own group."

At the same time, the continuing success of Donald Trump's 2016 presidential bid (as of this writing) suggests that this view may be shortsighted. Trump's racist innuendos—his "dog-whistle" politics—clearly tap into deeply felt, race-based resentments among White workers frustrated by their four-decades-long experience of economic stagnation. His stump speeches might not have such an electrifying appeal if this country ever had an honest reckoning of past and existing racist policies and practices—an honest reckoning that would reasonably call for policies such as affirmative action and reparations.

Such a reconciliation process may represent the best chance of removing Black Americans from the go-to list of scapegoats for why America is no longer great, and must be made "great again," to paraphrase Trump's slogan. In the long run, challenging White privilege head-on may open the way to secure a cross-racial, class-based, political alliance resistant to cleaving under the pressure of economic hard times.

The sobering reality is that the odds that this type of reconciliation would lead to such a positive outcome, while greater than zero, are still slim, given the country's long-standing history of racial division. However, it could very well be the only path to building a solidarity movement among the 99% resilient enough to address inequality more broadly. ❑

Sources: Marianne Bertrand and Sendhil Mullainathan, "Are Emily and Greg More Employable than Lakisha and Jamal? A Field Experiment on Labor Market Discrimination," *The American Economic Review*, September 2004; Carmen DeNavas-Walt and Bernadette D. Proctor, "Income and Poverty in the United States: 2014," *Population Reports*, September 2015; Jeffrey Fagan, Anthony A. Braga, Rod K. Brunson, April Pattavina, "Final Report: An Analysis of Race and Ethnicity, Patterns in Boston Police Department Field Interrogation, Observation, Frisk, and/ or Search Reports," June 15, 2015; Federal Bureau of Prisons, March 26, 2016 (bop.gov); Leo Grebler, David M. Blank, and Louis Winnick, "The Role of Federal Aids in Mortgage Finance," in Leo Grebler, David M. Blank, and Louis Winnick, eds., *Capital Formation in Residential Real Estate: Trends and Prospects* (Princeton University Press, 1956); Anthony G. Greenwald, Debbie E. McGhee, and Jordan L. K. Schwartz, "Measuring Individual Differences in Implicit Cognition: The Implicit Association Test," *Journal of Personality and Social Psychology*, 1998; Anthony Greenwald and Mahzarin R. Banaji, "Implicit Social Cognition: Attitudes, Self-esteem, and Stereotypes," *Journal of Personality and Social Psychology*, 995; National Center for Education Statistics, "Numbers and Types of Public Elementary and Secondary Schools From the Common Core of Data: School Year 2009-10," September 2012 (nces. ed.gov); Adolph Reed, Jr., "The Case Against Reparations," *The Progressive*, December 2000; Ary Spatig-Amerikaner, "Unequal Education: Federal Loophole Enables Lower Spending on Students of Color," Center for American Progress, August 2012; Rebecca Tippett, Avis Jones-DeWeever, May Rockeymoore, Darrick Hamilton, and William Darity, "Beyond Broke: Why Closing the Racial Wealth Gap is a Priority for National Economic Security," Center for Global Policy Solutions, 2014; United States Bureau of Labor Statistics, "Labor Force Characteristics by Race and Ethnicity," November 2015 (bls.gov); United States Census Bureau, "QuickFacts," 2015 (census. gov); United States Census Bureau, "Educational Attainment in the United States: 2014," 2015 (census.gov); Jeannette Wicks-Lim, "A $15 Federal Minimum Wage: Who Would Benefit?" PERI Research Brief, March 2016; Jiaquan Xu, Sherry L. Murphy, Kenneth D. Kochanek and Brigham A. Bastian, "Deaths: Final Data for 2013," Division of Vital Statistics, Feb. 6, 2016

Article 8.5

UNIONS AND INCOME INEQUALITY

BY ARTHUR MacEWAN
November/December 2011

Dear Dr. Dollar:
I know unions have shrunk in the United States, but by how much? And how best to respond to my right-wing friends who claim that unions are bad for the economy?
—Rich Sanford, Hardwick, Mass.

Take a look at the graph below. The two lines on the graph show for the period 1917 through 2007 (1) labor union membership as a percentage of the total U.S. work force and (2) the percentage of all income obtained by the highest 1% of income recipients. So the lines show, roughly, the strength of unions and the distribution of income for the past century. (John Miller and I developed this graph for our book *Economic Collapse, Economic Change.*)

The picture is pretty clear. In periods when unions have been strong, income distribution has been less unequal. In periods when unions have been weak, income distribution has been more unequal. In the post-World War II era, union members were about 25% of the labor force; today the figure is about 10%. In those postwar years, the highest-income 1% got 10% to 12% of all income; today they get about 25%.

UNION MEMBERSHIP AND INCOME INEQUALITY, 1917-2007

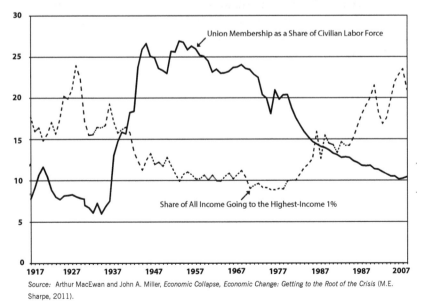

Source: Arthur MacEwan and John A. Miller, *Economic Collapse, Economic Change: Getting to the Root of the Crisis* (M.E. Sharpe, 2011).

The causation between union strength and income distribution is not simple. Nonetheless, there are some fairly direct connections. For example, when unions are strong, they can push for higher wages and thus we see a more equal distribution of income. Also, strong unions can have an impact on the political process, bringing about policies that are more favorable to workers.

But causation can work in the other direction as well. Great income inequality puts more power in the hands of the rich, and they can use that power to get policies put in place that weaken unions—for example, getting people who are hostile to unions appointed to the National Labor Relations Board.

And then there are other factors that affect both union strength and income distribution—for example, the changing structure of the global economy, which places U.S. workers in competition with poorly paid workers elsewhere. Yet the structure of the global economy is itself affected by the distribution of political power. For example, the "free trade" agreements that the United States has established with other countries generally ignore workers' rights (to say nothing of the environment) and go to great lengths to protect the rights of corporations. So, again, causation works in complex ways, and there are certainly other factors that need to be taken account of to explain the relationship shown in the graph.

However one explains the relationship, it is hard to imagine that we can return to a more equal distribution of income while unions remain weak. This means, at the very least, that the interests of unions and of people at the bottom of the income distribution are bound up with one another. Building stronger unions is an important part of fighting poverty—and the hunger and homelessness that are the clear manifestations of poverty.

One important thing to notice in the graph: In the post–World War II years, economic growth was the best we have seen. Certainly no one can claim that it is impossible for strong unions and a more equal distribution of income to co-exist with fairly rapid economic growth. Indeed, we might even argue that strong unions and a more equal distribution of income create favorable conditions for economic growth!

Stronger unions, it turns out, could be good preventive medicine for much of what ails our economy. ❏

Article 8.6

THE UNDESERVING RICH
Collectively produced and inherited knowledge and the (re)distribution of income and wealth.

BY GAR ALPEROVITZ AND LEW DALY
March/April 2010

Warren Buffett, one of the wealthiest men in the nation, is worth nearly $50 billion. Does he "deserve" all this money? Why? Did he work so much harder than everyone else? Did he create something so extraordinary that no one else could have created it? Ask Buffett himself and he will tell you that he thinks "society is responsible for a very significant percentage of what I've earned." But if that's true, doesn't society deserve a very significant share of what he has earned?

When asked why he is so successful, Buffett commonly replies that this is the wrong question. The more important question, he stresses, is why he has *so much to work with* compared to other people in the world, or compared to previous generations of Americans. Buffett asks: how much money would he have if he had been born in Bangladesh, or in the United States in 1700?

Buffett may or may not deserve something more than another person working with what a given historical or collective context provides. As he observes, however, it is simply not possible to argue in any serious way that he deserves *all* of the benefits that are clearly attributable to living in a highly developed society.

Buffett has put his finger on one of the most explosive issues developing just beneath the surface of public awareness. Over the last several decades, economic research has done a great deal of solid work pinpointing much more precisely than in the past what share of what we call "wealth" society creates versus what share any individual can be said to have earned and thus deserved. This research raises profound moral—and ultimately political—questions.

Through No Effort of Our Own

Recent estimates suggest that U.S. economic output per capita has increased more than twenty-fold since 1800. Output per hour worked has increased an estimated 15-fold since 1870 alone. Yet the average modern person likely works with no greater commitment, risk, or intelligence than his or her counterpart from the past. What is the primary cause of such vast gains if individuals do not really "improve"? Clearly, it is largely that the scientific, technical, and cultural knowledge available to us, and the efficiency of our means of storing and retrieving this knowledge, have grown at a scale and pace that far outstrip any other factor in the nation's economic development.

A half century ago, in 1957, economist Robert Solow calculated that nearly 90% of productivity growth in the first half of the 20th century (from 1909 to 1949) could only be attributed to "technical change in the broadest sense." The supply of labor and capital—what workers and employers contribute—appeared almost incidental to this massive technological "residual." Subsequent research inspired by

Solow and others continued to point to "advances in knowledge" as the main source of growth. Economist William Baumol calculates that "nearly 90 percent . . . of current GDP was contributed by innovation carried out since 1870." Baumol judges that his estimate, in fact, understates the cumulative influence of past advances: Even "the steam engine, the railroad, and many other inventions of an earlier era, still add to today's GDP."

Related research on the sources of invention bolsters the new view, posing a powerful challenge to conventional, heroic views of technology that characterize progress as a sequence of extraordinary contributions by "Great Men" (occasionally "Great Women") and their "Great Inventions." In contrast to this popular view, historians of technology have carefully delineated the incremental and cumulative way most technologies actually develop. In general, a specific field of knowledge builds up slowly through diverse contributions over time until—at a particular moment when enough has been established—the next so-called "breakthrough" becomes all but inevitable.

Often many people reach the same point at virtually the same time, for the simple reason that they all are working from the same developing information and research base. The next step commonly becomes obvious (or if not obvious, very likely to be taken within a few months or years). We tend to give credit to the person who gets there first—or rather, who gets the first public attention, since often the real originator is not as good at public relations as the one who jumps to the front of the line and claims credit. Thus, we remember Alexander Graham Bell as the inventor of the telephone even though, among others, Elisha Gray and Antonio Meucci got there at the same time or even before him. Newton and Leibniz hit upon the calculus at roughly the same time in the 1670s; Darwin and Alfred Russel Wallace produced essentially the same theory of evolution at roughly the same time in the late 1850s.

Less important than who gets the credit is the simple fact that most breakthroughs occur not so much thanks to one "genius," but because of the longer historical unfolding of knowledge. All of this knowledge—the overwhelming source of all modern wealth—comes to us today *through no effort of our own*. It is the generous and unearned gift of the past. In the words of Northwestern economist Joel Mokyr, it is a "free lunch."

Collective knowledge is often created by formal public efforts as well, a point progressives often stress. Many of the advances which propelled our high-tech economy in the early 1990s grew directly out of research programs and technical systems financed and often collaboratively developed by the federal government. The Internet, to take the most obvious example, began as a government defense project, the ARPANET, in the early 1960s. Up through the 1980s there was little private investment or interest in developing computer networks. Today's vast software industry also rests on a foundation of computer language and operating hardware developed in large part with public support. The Bill Gateses of the world—the heroes of the "New Economy"—might still be working with vacuum tubes and punch cards were it not for critical research and technology programs created or financed by the federal government after World War II. Other illustrations range from jet airplanes and radar to the basic life science research undergirding many pharmaceutical industry advances. Yet the truth is that the role of collectively inherited knowledge is far, far greater than just the contributions made by direct public support, important as they are.

Earned Income?

A straightforward but rarely confronted question arises from these facts: If most of what we have today is attributable to advances we inherit in common, then why should this gift of our collective history not more generously benefit all members of society?

The top 1% of U.S. households now receives more income than the bottom 120 million Americans combined. The richest 1% of households owns nearly half of all investment assets (stocks and mutual funds, financial securities, business equity, trusts, non-home real estate). The bottom 90% of the population owns less than 15%; the bottom half—150 million Americans—owns less than 1%. If America's vast wealth is mainly a gift of our common past, what justifies such disparities?

Robert Dahl, one of America's leading political scientists—and one of the few to have confronted these facts—put it this way after reading economist Edward Denison's pioneering work on growth accounting: "It is immediately obvious that little growth in the American economy can be attributed to the actions of particular individuals." He concluded straightforwardly that, accordingly, "the control and ownership of the economy rightfully belongs to 'society.'"

Contrast Dahl's view with that of Joe the Plumber, who famously inserted himself into the 2008 presidential campaign with his repeated claim that he has "earned" everything he gets and so any attempt to tax his earnings is totally unjustified. Likewise, "we didn't rely on somebody else to build what we built," banking titan Sanford Weill tells us in a *New York Times* front-page story on the "New Gilded Age." "I think there are people," another executive tells the *Times*, "who because of their uniqueness warrant whatever the market will bear."

A direct confrontation with the role of knowledge—and especially inherited knowledge—goes to the root of a profound challenge to such arguments. One way to think about all this is by focusing on the concept of "earned" versus "unearned" income. Today this distinction can be found in conservative attacks on welfare "cheats" who refuse to work to earn their keep, as well as in calls even by some Republican senators to tax the windfall oil-company profits occasioned by the Iraq war and Hurricane Katrina.

The concept of unearned income first came into clear focus during the era of rapidly rising land values caused by grain shortages in early 19th-century England. Wealth derived *simply* from owning land whose price was escalating appeared illegitimate because no individual truly "earned" such wealth. Land values—and especially explosively high values—were largely the product of factors such as fertility, location, and population pressures. The huge profits (unearned "rents," in the technical language of economics) landowners reaped when there were food shortages were viewed as particularly egregious. David Ricardo's influential theory of "differential rent"—i.e., that land values are determined by differences in fertility and location between different plots of land—along with religious perspectives reaching back to the Book of Genesis played a central role in sharpening this critical moral distinction.

John Stuart Mill, among others, developed the distinction between "earned" and "unearned" in the middle decades of the 19th century and applied it to other forms of "external wealth," or what he called "wealth created by circumstances." Mill's approach fed into a growing sense of the importance of societal inputs which produce economic gains beyond what can be ascribed to one person working alone in nature without benefit of civilization's many contributions. Here a second element of what appears, historically, as a slowly evolving understanding also becomes clear: If contribution is important in determining rewards, then, Mill and others urged, since society at large makes major contributions to economic achievement, it too has "earned" and deserves a share of what has been created. Mill believed strongly in personal contribution and individual reward, but he held that in principle wealth "created by circumstances" should be reclaimed for social purposes. Karl Marx, of course, tapped the distinction between earned and unearned in his much broader attack on capitalism and its exploitation of workers' labor.

The American republican writer Thomas Paine was among the first to articulate a societal theory of wealth based directly on the earned/unearned distinction. Paine argued that everything "beyond what a man's own hands produce" was a gift which came to him simply by living in society, and hence "he owes on every principle of justice, of gratitude, and of civilization, a part of that accumulation back again to society from whence the whole came." A later American reformer, Henry George, focused on urban land rather than the agricultural land at the heart of Ricardo's concern. George challenged what he called "the unearned increment" which is created when population growth and other societal factors increase land values. In Britain, J. A. Hobson argued that the unearned value created by the industrial system in general was much larger than just the part which accrued to landowners, and that it should be treated in a similar (if not more radical and comprehensive) fashion. In a similar vein, Hobson's early 20th-century contemporary Leonard Trelawny Hobhouse declared that the "prosperous business man" should consider "what single step he could have taken" without the "sum of intelligence which civilization has placed at his disposal." More recently, the famed American social scientist Herbert Simon judged that if "we are very generous with ourselves, I suppose we might claim that we 'earned' as much as one fifth of [our income]."

The distinction between earned and unearned gains is central to most of these thinkers, as is the notion that societal contributions—including everything an industrial economy requires, from the creation of laws, police, and courts to the development of schools, trade restrictions, and patents—must be recognized and rewarded. The understanding that such societal contributions are both contemporary and have made a huge and cumulative contribution over all of history is also widely accepted. Much of the income they permit and confer now appears broadly analogous to the unearned rent a landlord claims. What is new and significant here is the further clarification that by far the most important element in all this is the accumulated *knowledge* which society contributes over time.

All of this, as sociologist Daniel Bell has suggested, requires a new "knowledge theory of value"—especially as we move deeper into the high-tech era through computerization, the Internet, cybernetics, and cutting-edge fields such as gene therapy and nanotechnology. One way to grasp what is at stake is the following: A person today working the same number of hours as a similar person in 1870—working just as hard but no harder—will produce perhaps 15 times as much economic output. It is clear that the contemporary person can hardly be said to have "earned" his much greater productivity.

Consider further that if we project forward the past century's rate of growth, a person working a century from now would be able to produce—and potentially receive as "income"—up to seven times today's average income. By far the greatest part of this gain will also come to this person as a free gift of the past—the gift of the new knowledge created, passed on, and inherited from our own time forward.

She and her descendents, in fact, will inevitably contribute less, relative to the huge and now expanded contribution of the past, than we do today. The obvious question, again, is simply this: to what degree is it meaningful to say that this person will have "earned" all that may come her way? These and other realities suggest that the quiet revolution in our understanding of how wealth is created has ramifications for a much more profound and far-reaching challenge to today's untenable distribution of income and wealth. ❑

Article 8.7

HUNGER IN AFFLUENT AMERICA

BY GERALD FRIEDMAN
March/April 2015

The United States is wealthy enough that everyone could have enough to eat. Nonetheless, millions of Americans go hungry each day, subsist on an unhealthy diet because they cannot afford healthier foods, or would go hungry except for social assistance, notably the Food Stamp program, now known as the Supplemental Nutritional Assistance Program (SNAP). Rising average income has done little to reduce the problem of food insecurity, and cutbacks in effective social welfare programs have added to the problems of hunger and malnutrition. SNAP and other safety-net programs are far too small to end hunger in America.

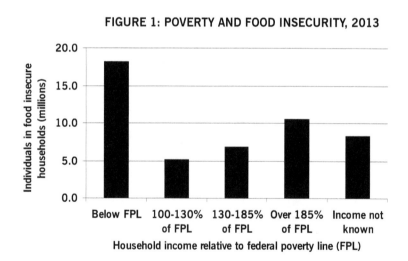

FIGURE 1: POVERTY AND FOOD INSECURITY, 2013

Millions of Americans cannot afford adequate nutrition. Nearly 50 million Americans are in "food insecure" households, which lack access to enough food for an active, healthy life for all household members. Food insecurity is most common in households under the federal poverty line. Insecurity is also more common in households with many children. While the urban poor dominate our images of hunger, rural residents actually have a slightly higher rate of food insecurity. (Data on food insecurity are based on an annual survey by the Current Population Survey. U.S. Department of Agriculture studies based on these data distinguish between low food security households ("reduced quality, variety, or desirability of diet") andvery low food security households ("disrupted eating patterns and reduced food intake").

FIGURE 2: ECONOMIC GROWTH AND FOOD INSECURITY

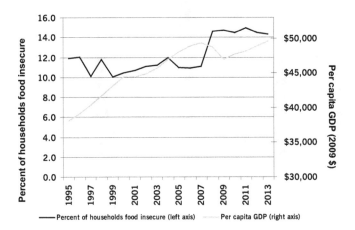

Percent of households food insecure (left axis) — Per capita GDP (right axis)

Economic growth does not solve the problem of food insecurity. Food insecurity has increased since the 1990s despite rising average income. A small decline in food insecurity during the boom of the late 1990s was largely reversed even before the Great Recession. Insecurity then soared with the economic crisis, beginning in 2007. High unemployment rates and stagnant or falling wages for working Americans have left illions hungry; cutbacks in social welfare programs have added to the burden of poverty. A dramatic increase in the size of the SNAP program, however, has helped prevent the problem from growing worse since 2009.

FIGURE 3: PEOPLE IN FOOD INSECURE HOUSEHOLDS, 2013

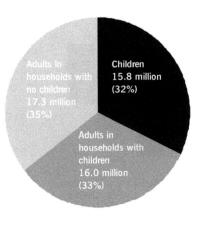

Children and their care-givers account for the majority of people in food-insecure households. Of the 49 million people in food-insecure households, nearly 16 million are children. Another 16 million are their caregivers, including 4 million single mothers. The remaining 17 million people in food-insecure households—adults in households without children—include not only many who are unemployed or working sporadically, but also many full-time workers whose wages are too low for them to afford adequate food.

FIGURE 4: VERY LOW FOOD SECURITY HOUSEHOLDS, 2013

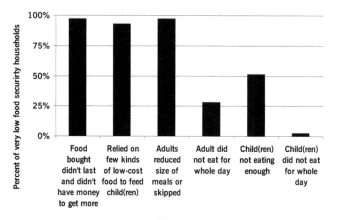

Food-insecure people go hungry, eat badly, and try to save food for their children. Food insecurity means anxiety, stress, sacrifice, and real hunger for millions of Americans. Almost all "very low food security households"—including more than 17 million people—run out of food sometimes, even though they rely on low-cost foods, skimp on portion size, or skip meals. Adults in these households sacrifice so their children can eat. Almost all reported skipping meals, and over a quarter skipped eating for a whole day. Despite these sacrifices, children in over half the households at least sometimes did not get enough to eat. In over 400,000 very low food security households, at least one child did not eat at all for at least one day in the previous month.

FIGURE 5: DIFFERENCES IN ADULT OUTCOMES, CHILDREN WHO RECEIVED SNAP COMPARED TO THOSE WHO DID NOT

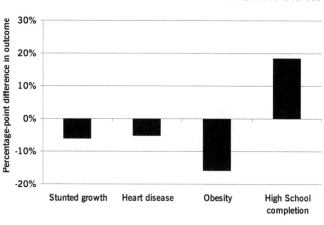

Note: From sample of individuals born 1956-1981 into "disadvantaged families" (household head had less than a high-school education).

SNAP (Food Stamps) increases food security and has lasting beneficial effects. While 26% of food-insecure households report using food pantries and 3% use soup kitchens, the federal Supplemental Nutrition Assistance Program (SNAP) is the largest source of food assistance. Even SNAP's $70 billion is only enough to provide $125 in food assistance per person per month, barely $1.30 per meal. SNAP reduces the incidence of food insecurity, but it still leaves 49 million people in food-insecure households. Despite these limitations, SNAP has both immediate and lasting benefits. Households that receive SNAP benefits eat better and have better health than similar households that do not. When aid is provided to households with young children, these benefits persist throughout the lifetimes of recipients. Those who receive assistance are healthier as adults and are more likely to finish high school, compared to those who do not. ❑

Sources: United States Department of Agriculture, Household Food Security in the United States (ers.usda.gov); Bureau of Economic Analysis (bea.gov); Federal Reserve Bank of St. Louis (FRED) (research.stlouisfed.org); Hilary W. Hoynes, Diane Whitmore Schanzenbach, and Douglas Almond, "Long Run Impacts of Childhood Access to the Safety Net," National Bureau for Economic Research (NBER), November 2012.

Article 8.8

WHAT IS U.S. WORKERS' SHARE OF NATIONAL INCOME?

BY ARTHUR MacEWAN

November/December 2017

Dear Dr. Dollar:

How well do U.S. workers fare in relation to workers in other countries when you compare workers' shares of national income?

—Martin Voelker, Golden, Colo.

Not so well. That's the answer that we can readily obtain from what is now well known about income inequality in the United States and other countries. Among high-income countries, the United States is one of the most unequal, if not *the* most unequal. Under these circumstances, it is pretty clear that workers are getting a smaller share of national income in this country than in most other high-income countries.

We do, in addition, have some other information that helps in answering this question. The International Labour Organization provides data on "labor's share" of national income for several countries. These data are shown in Table 1 for 2013. (More recent data were not available.) The United States does not do so well, falling about in the middle of the countries shown in Table 1 (below).

There are, however, problems with these standard "labor's share" data. The data include the wages and salaries of everyone from Walmart clerks to the president of Citibank. So the data in Table 1 overstate what we want to know—that is the share of income going to those most of us think of as "working people," a concept that does not include executives.

The overstatement, however, is not the same for all countries in the table. Because the salaries of executives in the United States are generally a good deal higher than those in other countries, the labor's share for this country is overstated more than for most other countries. If we could correct the data to show the share going to those we think of as "working people," the U.S. position in Table 1 would be lower.

Some other useful data give us the same general picture with some detail. Consider Table 2 (opposite page), showing for 2015 average hourly compensation costs in manufacturing and per capita income in U.S. dollars for nineteen relatively high income countries. (Each country in the table has a per capita income above $25,000 and a population greater than five million.) Compensation costs include direct pay,

TABLE 1: "LABOR'S SHARE" OF NATIONAL INCOME, SELECTED COUNTRIES, 2013

United Kingdom	62.3%
Japan	59.6%
France	59.0%
Germany	57.9%
United States	56.4%
Canada	56.0%
Italy	55.4%
Australia	54.8%

Source: International Labour Organization, www.ilo.org/gwr-figures.

social insurance expenditures, and labor-related taxes. While it is not clear if the pay of high-level executives is included in these figures, the fact that they are presented on a per hour basis suggests that the data are for "working people."

In Frame One of Table 2, countries are ranked by hourly compensation costs, and the United States falls right about in the middle. However, to a large extent (though by no means entirely) the higher hourly compensation is associated with a higher per capita income. Insofar as this is the case, we see simply that countries with high per capita incomes also have higher wages in manufacturing. No surprise. There's Norway, right at the top in terms of both hourly costs and per capita income.

TABLE 2: AVERAGE HOURLY COMPENSATION COSTS IN MANUFACTURING, AVERAGE NATIONAL INCOME, AND HOURS IN MANUFACTURING NEEDED TO EARN AVERAGE NATIONAL INCOME, SELECTED COUNTRIES, 2015

Frame One			Frame Two	
Country	Hourly Compensation Costs	Per capita Income	Country	Hours needed to earn per capita annual income
Norway	$49.67	$74,505	Belgium	867
Belgium	$46.56	$40,357	Italy	955
Denmark	$44.44	$53,014	German	971
Germany	$42.42	$41,177	France	972
Sweden	$41.68	$50,585	Spain	1,086
Austria	$39.19	$43,665	Finland	1,103
Australia	$38.75	$56,554	Austria	1,114
Finland	$38.46	$42,405	Denmark	1,193
United States	$37.71	$56,207	South Korea	1,195
France	$37.59	$36,527	Sweden	1,214
Netherlands	$36.53	$44,493	Netherlands	1,218
Italy	$31.48	$30,049	United Kingdom	1,397
United Kingdom	$31.44	$43,930	Canada	1,400
Canada	$30.94	$43,316	Australia	1,459
Spain	$23.65	$25,684	Japan	1,461
Japan	$23.60	$34,474	United States	1,491
Singapore	$25.41	$53,628	Norway	1,500
South Korea	$22.68	$27,105	Israel	1,647
Israel	$21.69	$35,729	Singapore	2,111

Notes: Selected countries are all countries with per capita income greater than $25,000 and population greater than five million. Compensation costs include direct pay, social insurance expenditures, and labor-related taxes.

Sources: For hourly compensation costs, The Conference Board (conference-board.org/ilcprogram/). For per capita income, The World Bank, (data.worldbank.org/indicator/NY.GDP.PCAP.CD).

But if we are interested in how workers do in the contexts of their own countries, we need to adjust for per capita income. One way to do this is to use the figures in Frame One of the table to calculate the number of hours a person receiving the average wage in manufacturing would have to work to earn the per capita annual income in the country. Things change, as shown in Frame Two of Table 2. The United States is no longer near the middle, but now ranks near the bottom. Norway falls just below the United States, along with only Israel and Singapore.

So, within the context of their own countries, manufacturing workers in all the other fifteen countries fare better than manufacturing workers in the United States. Belgium, with a per capita income of 75% of that in the United States, has moved to the top of the list.

The figures in Table 2 should be viewed as very rough indicators of the actual situation. The value of wages in different countries in dollar terms can change substantially from year to year as exchange rates change. Also, manufacturing plays very different roles in different countries, and in all of the countries in the table manufacturing accounts for less than about 20% of the workforce. So the manufacturing experience is not necessarily typical for the whole economies of these countries. Nonetheless, the general implication of the table regarding the comparison of U.S. workers and workers in other countries seems reasonable and is consistent with other data—for example, data on income inequality.

The conclusion: Workers in the United States do not fare so well in relation to workers in other countries in terms of shares of their nations' incomes. ❑

Chapter 9

TAXATION

INTRODUCTION

"Only the little people pay taxes." —Leona Helmsley
"Taxes are the price we pay for civilization." —Oliver Wendell Holmes, Jr.

Taxation is a fascinating subject. It is perhaps the clearest manifestation of class struggle one can find. How a modern government funds itself in order to provide services is an elaborate study in power. The contentious tango of taxes and their inverse, subsidies, plays out daily at all three levels of government—federal, state, and local. Who pays taxes and at what rates? What is taxed? Who bears the burden of taxation? And how are tax revenues collected? These are questions that this chapter will address.

In the Reagan era, "supply-side" economist Arthur Laffer famously claimed that high marginal tax rates discourage work and saving, and that cutting tax rates on the rich would spur investment and economic growth. We start the chapter with two articles on the subject: In "Can Tax Cuts Really Increase Government Revenue?" (Article 9.1), economist Ellen Frank reviews the basic arguments made by Laffer and the other supply-siders, and why there is reason to be skeptical. Gerald Friedman puts these arguments to the test, and finds that cutting taxes on the very rich, as the U.S. government has been doing for decades, has not led to the promised investment or economic growth (Article 9.2).

Next, John Miller evaluates the provisions of the Trump tax bill, including its enormous reductions in the tax bill of the 1%, along with its time-limited cuts for lower incomes (Article 9.3).

Gerald Friedman's "Progressives Need a Tax-Reform Agenda" (Article 9.4) outlines a streamlined three-part tax policy revamp that would create the resources needed to fund the programs supported by progressive leaders like Senator Bernie Sanders.

Gerald Friedman (Article 9.5) argues that a focus on federal taxes creates the mistaken impression that the U.S. tax system is quite progressive, falling more heavily on high-income people than low-income people. In fact, he notes, the heavy reliance of state and local governments on regressive taxes and fees greatly reduces this progressivity.

Steven Pressman (Article 9.6) analyzes the celebrated work of French economist Thomas Piketty on the growth of income inequality over the history of capitalism.

Pressman summarizes Piketty's arguments that rising inequality is not a short-term anomaly, but a deep long-term trend in capitalist societies, then turns to a thoughtful discussion of Piketty's proposed policy responses.

Discussion Questions

1. (Articles 9.1 and 9.2) What is the basis of supply-siders' claim that lowering the highest marginal tax rate will generate more tax revenue? What are the main arguments against this view?

2. (Article 9.2) In what way have tax policies contributed to growing inequality in the United States? How does U.S. tax policy compare to other developed countries, and how has that related to productivity growth?

3. (Article 9.3) According to John Miller, how do the gains for high-income tax filers compare to those with small or modest incomes? What leads to the difference in outcomes?

4. (Article 9.3) Can the upper-income tax cuts be expected to lead to an increase in economic growth, as advertised? What evidence from recent history suggests big companies may not invest their tax savings?

5. (Article 9.4) Gerald Friedman proposes a progressive tax plan in three parts. Broadly speaking, who would win and lose form such a tax policy?

6. (Article 9.5) Are state and local tax systems inherently more regressive than the federal system? Could state and local governments raise revenue in more progressive ways?

7. (Article 9.6) Economist Thomas Piketty proposes a global tax on wealth as a response to rising inequality. Do you think that his solution is feasible? Is it desirable?

Article 9.1

CAN TAX CUTS REALLY INCREASE GOVERNMENT REVENUE?

BY ELLEN FRANK
November/December 2003

> Dear Dr. Dollar:
> *A Republican friend tells me that the huge new tax cuts will actually produce more revenue than the government would have collected before the cut, because once rich beneficiaries invest the money, they will pay taxes on every transaction. He suggested that the increase could be as much as 50% more than the originally scheduled revenues. Is this possible?*
> —Judith Walker, New York, N.Y.

Back in the 1970s, conservative economist Arthur Laffer proposed that high marginal tax rates discouraged people from earning additional income. By cutting taxes, especially on those with the highest incomes, Laffer argued, governments would spur individuals to work harder and invest more, stoking economic growth. Though the government would get a smaller bite from every dollar the economy generated, there would be so many more dollars to tax that government revenues would actually rise. Ronald Reagan invoked the "Laffer curve" in the 1980s, insisting he could cut taxes, hike defense spending, and still balance the budget.

Bush's 2001 and 2003 tax packages are eerily reminiscent of the Reagan cuts. They reduce rates levied on ordinary income, with the largest rate cut going to the wealthiest taxpayers. They extend business tax write-offs and increase the child tax credit (though only for two years and only for families who earn enough to pay federal income taxes). They cut the tax on capital gains from 28% to 15%; dividend income, previously taxed at the same rate as ordinary income, now faces a top rate of 15%.

Citizens for Tax Justice estimates that two-thirds of the 2003 tax cut will accrue to the richest 10% of taxpayers. By 2006, the increased child credit will be phased out and nine out of ten taxpayers will find their taxes cut by less than $100. The top 1%, in contrast, will save an average $24,000 annually over the next four years, thanks to the 2003 cut alone.

Though inspired by the same "supply-side" vision that guided Reagan, Bush officials have not explicitly cited Laffer's arguments in defense of their tax packages. Probably, they wish to avoid ridicule. After the Reagan tax cut, the U.S. economy sank into recession and federal tax collections dropped nearly 10%. The deficit soared and economic growth was tepid through much of Reagan's presidency, despite sharp hikes in military spending. Some of the Republican faithful continue to argue that tax cuts will unleash enough growth to pay for themselves, but most are embarrassed to raise the now discredited Laffer curve.

The problem with your friend's assertion is fairly simple. If the government cuts projected taxes by $1.5 trillion over the next decade, those dollars will recirculate through the economy. The $1.5 trillion tax cut becomes $1.5 trillion in taxable income and is itself taxed, as your friend suggests. But this would be just as true if, instead of cutting taxes, the government spent $1.5 trillion on highways or national defense or schools or, for that matter, if it trimmed $1.5 trillion from the tax liability of low- and middle-income households. All tax cuts become income, are re-spent, and taxed. That reality is already factored into everyone's economic projections. But the new income, taxed at a lower rate, will generate lower overall tax collections.

To conclude that revenues will rise rather than fall following a tax cut, one must maintain that the tax cut causes the economy to grow faster than it would have otherwise—that cutting taxes on the upper crust stimulates enough additional growth to offset the lower tax rates, more growth than would be propelled by, say, building roads or reducing payroll taxes. Free-marketeers insist that this is indeed the case. Spend $1.5 trillion on highways and you get $1.5 trillion worth of highways. Give it to Wall Street and investors will develop new technologies, improve productivity, and spur the economy to new heights.

Critics of the Bush cuts contend, however, that faster growth arises from robust demand for goods and from solid, well-maintained public infrastructure. Give $1.5 to Wall Street and you get inflated stock prices and real estate bubbles. Give it to working families or state governments and you get crowded malls, ringing cash registers, and businesses busily investing to keep up with their customers.

Who is right? Die-hard supply-siders insist that the Reagan tax cuts worked as planned—the payoff just didn't arrive until the mid-1990s! But the Bush administration's own budget office is predicting sizable deficits for the next several years. Maybe, like your friend, they believe the tax cuts will pay for themselves—but they're not banking on it. ❏

Article 9.2

THE GREAT TAX-CUT EXPERIMENT
Has cutting tax rates for the rich helped the economy?

BY GERALD FRIEDMAN
January/February 2013

Since the late 1970s, during the Carter Administration, conservative economists have been warning that high taxes retard economic growth by discouraging productive work and investment. These arguments have resonated with politicians, who have steadily cut income taxes, especially those borne by the richest Americans. The highest marginal tax rate, which stood at 70% by the end of the 1970s, was cut to less than 30% in less than a decade. (The "marginal" rate for a person is the one applied to his or her last dollar of income. A marginal rate that applies to, say, the bracket above $250,000, then, is paid only on that portion of income. The portion of a person's income below that threshold is taxed at the lower rates applying to lower tax brackets.) Despite increases in the early 1990s, the top marginal rate remained below 40%, when it was cut further during the administration of George W. Bush. These dramatic cuts in tax rates, however, have not led to an acceleration in economic growth, investment, or productivity.

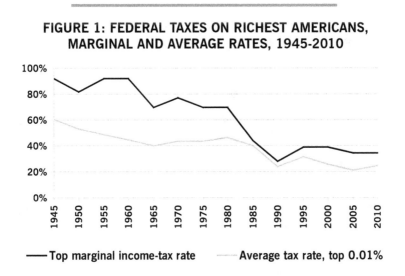

FIGURE 1: FEDERAL TAXES ON RICHEST AMERICANS, MARGINAL AND AVERAGE RATES, 1945-2010

—— Top marginal income-tax rate ⋯⋯ Average tax rate, top 0.01%

The federal government has been cutting taxes on the richest Americans since the end of World War II. The average tax paid by the richest taxpayers, as a percentage of income, is typically less than the top marginal rate. Some of their income (the portion below the threshold for the top marginal rate, any capital-gains income, etc.) is taxed at lower rates. Some is not subject to federal income tax because of deductions for state and local taxes, healthcare costs, and other expenses. The decline in the average tax rate for the richest, however, does follow the cuts in the top marginal income-tax rate.

FIGURE 2: TAX REVENUE AS A PERCENTAGE OF GDP, 2008

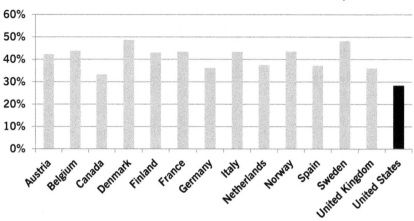

Americans pay a smaller proportion of total income in taxes than do people in any other advanced capitalist economy. As recently as the late 1960s, taxes accounted for as high a share of national income in the United States as in Western European countries. After decades of tax cuts, however, the United States now stands out for its low taxes and small government sector.

FIGURE 3: AVERAGE TAX RATES ON RICHEST AND REAL GDP GROWTH, BY PRESIDENT, 1947-2010

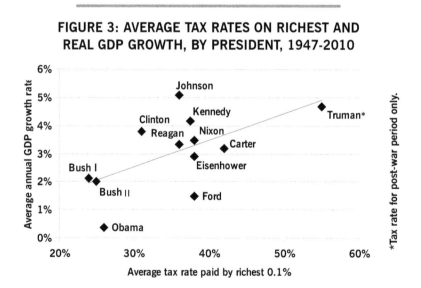

On average, the economy has grown faster during presidential administrations with higher tax rates on the richest Americans. Growth was unusually slow during George W. Bush's two terms (Bush II) and during Obama's first term, when the Bush tax cuts remained in effect. On average, every 10 percentage-point rise in the average tax rate on the richest has been associated with an increase in annual GDP growth of almost one percentage point.

FIGURE 4: TOP MARGINAL TAX RATE AND INVESTMENT, 1963-2011

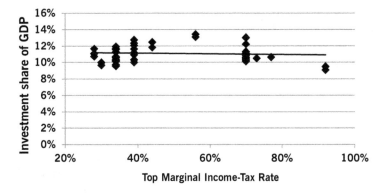

Cutting taxes on the richest Americans has not led them to invest more in plant and equipment. Over the past 50 years, as tax rates have declined, there has been no increase in investment spending as a percentage of GDP. (The flat trend line shows that changes in the highest marginal income-tax rate have not affected investment much, one way or the other.) Instead, the investment share of the economy has been determined by other factors, such as aggregate demand, rather than tax policy.

FIGURE 5: TAX SHARE OF GDP AND PRODUCTIVITY GROWTH

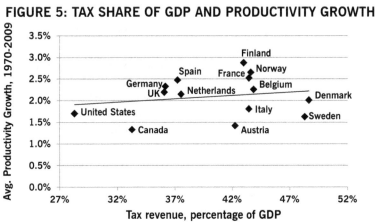

Despite lower and declining tax rates, especially on the rich, the United States has had slower productivity growth over the last several decades than other advanced economies. Overall, lower taxes are associated with slower growth in GDP per hour worked. A 10 percentage point increase in taxes as a share of GDP is associated with an increase in the productivity growth rate of 0.2 percentage points. ❑

Sources: Tom Petska and Mike Strudler, "Income, Taxes, and Tax Progressivity: An Examination of Recent Trends in the Distribution of Individual Income and Taxes" (Statistics of Income Division, Internal Revenue Service, 1997); Thomas Hungerford, "Taxes and the Economy: An Economic Analysis of the Top Tax Rates Since 1945" (Congressional Research Service, 2012); Economic Report of the President, 2012; Bureau of Economic Analysis (bea.gov); Organization of Economic Cooperation and Development, OECD STAT.

Article 9.3

THE TRUMP/GOP TAX ACT
Update on the Massive Giveaway to the Rich

BY JOHN MILLER
January 2018, Labor Notes

Judging by what's in the Tax Cut and Jobs Act, Donald Trump and the Republicans who pushed this disastrous bill through Congress in December must have thought American inequality wasn't severe enough.

As anticipated their act showers benefits on the best-off taxpayers. For the rest of us, it offers only meager tax reductions written in disappearing ink.

In 2018, the Tax Policy Center estimates, taxpayers with incomes of $1 million or more will get an average tax cut of $69,660, while those under $75,000 will get an average cut of $353. By 2027, 81% of the tax cuts will go to those taking in more than $1 million, while taxes on those making less than $75,000 will go up.

Bonanza for the Rich

The final version of tax act did not repeal the estate tax and the Alternative Minimum Tax (AMT) as some earlier versions had, but it nonetheless lavished tax cuts on the wealthy.

First, the act lowers the top income tax rate from 39.6% to 37%, benefiting taxpayers whose income exceeds $426,700.

Second, it increases the exemption for the alternative minimum income tax, which benefits nearly exclusively taxpayers with over $200,000 of income.

Third, it doubles the exemption for the estate tax to $11.2 million. This overwhelmingly benefits the top 10% of income earners, and especially the richest 0.1%—those with annual incomes in excess of $3.9 million.

The act does put a $10,000 cap on the state and local taxes you can deduct from your federal income tax, a provision that will hit wealthier taxpayers in high-tax states. Residents of those high-tax states often vote Democratic.

Business owners and corporate stockholders will be especially rewarded. The act slashes taxes on corporate profits from 35% to 21%. Most studies find that more than three-quarters of the benefits of lower corporate tax rates go to owners of capital, rather than their employees, and close to half of the benefits go to the richest 1% of taxpayers.

In the name of providing tax relief to small businesses, the act allows one-fifth of the first $315,000 of profits of pass-through businesses (which pay personal income taxes instead of corporate income taxes) to go untaxed. Over 80% of the benefits of this provision will go to the top 5% of taxpayers, including the Trump family, which owns more than 500 pass-through businesses.

Effects Cancel Out

Republicans were far stingier when it came to taxpayers with modest incomes, and most of tax cuts that will benefit lower and middle income people are set to expire in 2025.

The act did double the standard deduction—used by most low- and middle-income taxpayers—to $12,000 for individuals and $24,000 for married couples. But at the same time, it eliminates the $4,500 exemption for each taxpayer and each dependent. For a family of three, these lost exemptions will cancel out the doubling of the standard deduction.

The act doubles the child tax credit to $2,000. A family with two children and $100,000 of income will get the full $2,000 credit per child. But because the credit is only partially refundable, a family with two children and $24,000 of income will get a credit of just $1,400 per child, and families with lower incomes will receive even less—as little as $75 per child.

The bill also ends the itemized deduction for an employee's unreimbursed job expenses, including union dues.

On top of all that, the bill scraps the Affordable Care Act mandate for individuals to buy health insurance or pay a fine. As a result, a projected 13 million fewer people will have health insurance. Premiums will rise, for non-group plans, by "about 10 percent in most years" in the next decade, according to the Congressional Budget Office.

Expect No Boom

Tax cut supporters insist that this lopsided pro-rich law will create an explosion of economic growth that will create jobs and enrich us all. It's not happening.

Cutting taxes on the rich is not an engine of economic growth, as even the Congressional Research Service attests to. For Congressional Research Service economists Jane Gravelle and Donald Marples report that, "past changes in tax rates have had no large clear effects on economic growth,"

Cutting taxes on corporate profits is similarly unlikely to trickle down. After-tax corporate profits, when compared to gross domestic product, are already nearing record highs. In addition, corporations are unlikely to use their windfall to make the investments that will jump-start economic growth, create jobs, and raise wages. After all, if they're not investing now, it's not because of lack of funds. In 2016, according to Standard and Poor's, U.S. firms were already holding in the country $800 billion in cash and liquid assets, which they were unwilling to invest in long-term projects.

Seemingly intoxicated by their coming tax windfall, some corporations are handing out bonuses to their workers. Most prominently Walmart announced a one-time $1,000 bonus to its employees—but buried the fact that only workers who have been with the company for 20 years will get the full $1,000. The average Walmart worker is expected to get under $200. The bonuses will cost Walmart only 2.2% of the $18 billion it's likely to save over the next decade from the tax cut, leaving plenty to hand over to shareholders.

Hours later, Walmart revealed it was closing more than 60 of its Sam's Club stores and laying off thousands of workers.

Watch Out

On top of all that, this tax giveaway to the rich adds a whopping $1.8 trillion to the federal budget deficit, according to the Congressional Budget Office. Republican lawmakers are already bemoaning the ballooning deficit they've created and saying they'll have to cut Social Security, Medicare, Medicaid, and public services to close the budget gap.

That's a one-two punch that we need to make sure doesn't connect. ❏

Article 9.4

PROGRESSIVES NEED A TAX-REFORM AGENDA

BY GERALD FRIEDMAN
January/February 2018

While slashing taxes for some of the country's most privileged, including Donald Trump and his family, the GOP's new tax act fails to address America's most pressing problems: rising inequality, the climate crisis, macroeconomic instability, and declining resources for needed public services in urban and rural America alike. But progressives should resist the temptation to simply attack the GOP giveaway to the ultra-rich. Instead, they should articulate their own tax plan, one that would fund needed services, promote stable growth, and compensate the unlucky, including the victims of globalization. We can have a tax system founded on coherent economic theory, a system that promotes fairness and economic efficiency by following three reasonable principles: all forms of income should be taxed equally, dangerous and destructive activities should be discouraged, and the distribution of income should reflect work rather than luck.

Ensure Fair Taxation of All Forms of Income

- *Tax all corporate profits regardless of where they are earned.* While keeping the corporate tax rate at 35%, eliminate the deferral of taxes on profits earned outside the United States. According to the Institute on Taxation and Economic Policy, corporations currently owe $700 billion in taxes on $2.6 trillion worth of profits, parked abroad in tax havens like the Cayman Islands.
- *Eliminate preference for unearned over earned income.* Since 1990, capital gains and some dividends are taxed at a lower rate than is earned income and wages. While workers pay payroll taxes for Social Security and Medicare, 25% income taxes on earnings above $37,651, and more on wage and sakary income above $91,150, capital gains income is taxed at 15% for most Americans, and no more than 20% for higher incomes. Eliminating this preferential treatment and taxing unearned income at the same rate as earned income would raise more than $100 billion a year in additional revenues.
- *Eliminate the tax preference for high-wage income.* The 12.4% retirement payroll tax that funds Social Security only applies to the first $118,500 of income, so about 6% of wage and salary earners only pay the tax on part of their earnings. Restoring the Social Security payroll tax for the richest 1%, those with wages and salaries above $300,000, would raise over $50 billion.

Promote Economic Efficiency

- *Restore the Financial Transactions Tax and implement a financial excise tax.* Until 1966, the United States, like 30 other countries including the United Kingdom, Singapore, and Switzerland, taxed financial transactions to discourage speculative financial activities that would distract from businesses' productive work. Taxing the giant banks would restore the economic balance, favoring the productive activities of Main Street over the financial shenanigans of Wall Street. A tax like this would raise more than $100 billion while increasing economic efficiency.

- *Reduce the deductibility of low wages and strengthen the penalty for companies that do not provide health insurance or pension benefits.* The public safety net, including SNAP and Medicaid, bear much of the burden when profitable companies pay low wages. *Forbes* estimated that in 2014 low-wage workers at Walmart received more than $6 billion in public assistance; Connecticut taxpayers in 2015 paid nearly $500 million in public assistance to employees of profitable businesses. Taxing low-wage employers would encourage higher wages while raising more than $14 billion in revenue.

- *Tax carbon emissions at $25/ton, to begin with, rising by $10/ton every year.* The build-up of carbon dioxide in the atmosphere from the burning of fossil fuels is already transforming the environment with devastating effects on crops, forests, and seaside communities. Charging for the damage done by burning carbon would slow global climate change and encourage the growth of energy-efficient and green industries. It would also raise nearly $100 billion a year at $25/ton and more at higher rates.

Reward Work Not Luck

- *Restore the 1980 estate tax (adjusted for inflation).* In 1980, the estate tax rate was 70% with an exemption (for gifts and estates) of about $1,000,000 in 2017 dollars. At this level of exemption, more than 97% of estates would go untaxed because the great majority of Americans are not fortunate enough to be born into families with such large estates. Revenue would increase by more than $50 billion, the great majority paid by a very small number of very lucky people.

While promoting healthy and stable economic growth, this program would generate more than $500 billion a year in additional revenue. If $400 billion of this revenue was devoted to eliminating income and payroll taxes for households with family income of under $75,000, then that would still leave $100 billion to spend on priorities like infrastructure and education. Instead of the Republicans' proposals designed to enrich a few, opponents can present a coherent program founded on principles of fairness. That is the tax reform that working Americans deserve.❑

Sources: "Fortune 500 Companies Hold a Record $2.6 Trillion Offshore," Institute on Taxation and Economic Policy, March 28, 2017 (itep.org); "The Tax Break-Down: Preferential Rates on Capital Gains," Committee for a Responsible Federal Budget, August 27, 2013 (crfb.org); Kathleen Romig, "Increasing Payroll Taxes Would Strengthen Social Security," Center on Budget and Policy Priorities, September 27, 2016 (cbpp.org); "The 2016 Annual Report of the Board of Trustees of the Federal Old-Age and Survivors Insurance and Federal Disability Insurance Trust Funds," Social Security Administration (ssa.gov); "Walmart on Tax Day: How Taxpayers Subsidize America's Biggest Employer and Richest Family," Americans for Tax Fairness, April 2014 (americansfortaxfairness.org); Daniel Kennedy, Stan McMillen, and Louise Simmons, "The Economic and Fiscal Impact of Connecticut's Proposed Statute to Recoup Costs Attributable to Low-Wage Employers," UCONN School of Social Work, May 18, 2015 (ssw.uconn.edu); "Options for Reducing the Deficit, 2017 to 2026," Congressional Budget Office, December 8, 2016 (cbo.gov); "Federal Estate and Gift Tax Rates, Exemptions, and Exclusions, 1916-2014," Tax Foundation, February 4, 2014 (taxfoundation.org); "The Distribution of Household Income and Federal Taxes, 2013," Congressional Budget Office (cbo.gov).

Article 9.5

THE BURDENS OF AMERICAN FEDERALISM
Income Redistribution Through Taxation

BY GERALD FRIEDMAN
September/October 2015

Because of increasing economic inequality, many scholars and activists have looked at tax policy both for changes that may explain widening income gaps and for reforms that might reduce inequality of market incomes. While it is appropriate to study the role of federal taxes, state and local governments take in nearly half of all government revenue. Non-tax revenues from fees and service charges account for nearly 15% of government revenue (all levels).

Americans are accustomed to thinking of the tax system as progressive, requiring higher-income people to pay a higher percentage of their incomes in taxes than lower-income people. Because the burden of state and local taxes and non-tax revenues is much heavier on poor people and the working class than it is on the rich, however, the fiscal system as a whole is much less progressive than it seems from looking only at federal-level taxation. While all states have regressive tax systems, requiring lower-income people to pay a higher percentage of their incomes than higher-income people, some states are more regressive than others. States that rely on sales taxes and user fees impose a heavier burden on poor and working people; states that rely more on income taxes do less to widen the income gap.

FIGURE 1: TOTAL GOVERNMENT REVENUE BY LEVEL, 2012

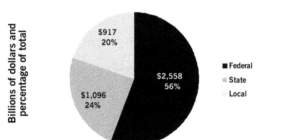

The federal government collects only a little more than half of government revenues. The federal government and its taxes—totaling just over $2.5 trillion (or 56% of government revenue)—have often been the focus of political attention and controversy. State and local governments, however, collect nearly $2 trillion in taxes and other types of revenue. (Non-tax revenue includes charges for services (such as water, the lottery, or college tuition) as well as fees (such as motor vehicle registration or licenses).) States and localities collect 44% of total government revenues. Therefore, to understand the distributional impact of government revenue policies in the United States, we have to consider all levels of government, not just the federal.

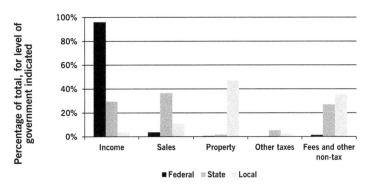

FIGURE 2: GOVERNMENT REVENUE BY SOURCE, 2012

Federal revenues are collected largely from income and payroll taxes; states and localities collect sales and property taxes, and charge fees. There are three distinct tax systems in the United States, corresponding to the three levels of government. The federal government draws the vast majority of its revenue from taxes on income, including corporate and personal income taxes as well as Social Security and Medicare payroll taxes. In contrast, income taxes account for less than 30% of state tax revenue and virtually no local tax revenue. States are more likely to collect revenue from fees and from sales taxes, especially on material goods. (Business and consumer services usually go untaxed.) For their part, local governments rely little on sales taxes but draw most of their revenue from fees and from property taxes, mostly on real estate.

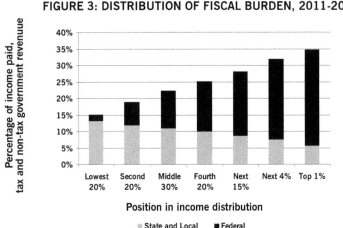

FIGURE 3: DISTRIBUTION OF FISCAL BURDEN, 2011-2012

The economic burden of state and local government falls most heavily on poor and working people. Most Americans pay more in state and local government taxes and fees than they do in federal taxes. Because federal taxes fall more heavily on the rich than on the poor, they redistribute income "downwards." In contrast, state and local taxes and fees fall more heavily on the poor and the working class, while the richest Americans pay relatively little. (Property taxes, significant at the local level, are actually *regressive* on balance: While it depends somewhat on how one apportions the burden of property taxes between landlords and renters, the Intstitute for Taxation and Economic Policy calculates the bottom 20% pay 3.7% of their incomes in property taxes while the richest 1% pay only 1.6%.) The balance between state and local revenues, on the one hand, and federal revenues, on the other, is therefore important for understanding the impact of taxation on income distribution. The larger the share of state and local taxes and fees—apart from state and local income taxes—the less government redistributes income downward; and the larger the share of national taxation, the more the government does to equalize after-tax incomes.

FIGURE 4A: DISTRIBUTION OF INCOME TAX BURDEN, 2011-2012

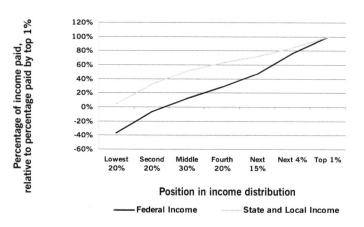

FIGURE 4B: DISTRIBUTION OF SALES TAX BURDEN, 2011-2012

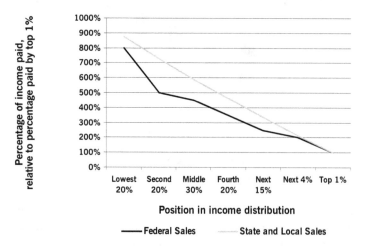

Differences in the burdens of taxation between the federal government and states and localities result from the type of tax assessed. Whether assessed on the state or on the national level, income taxes fall more heavily on the rich than on the poor. Because of federal and state earned-income tax credits (tax exemptions on labor income that favor low-income people) and progressive income-tax rates, high-income people pay a much higher percentage of their incomes in income taxes than do lower-income people. This is true on both the state and federal levels. By contrast, sales taxes fall more heavily on lower-income people. This is because poor and working people spend higher proportions of their incomes on consumption than rich people do, and are more likely to consume material goods subject to sales taxes. Rich people spend more of their incomes on sales-tax-exempt services, such as legal services and personal care.

FIGURE 5: PROGRESSIVITY OF STATE TAX SYSTEMS, 2012

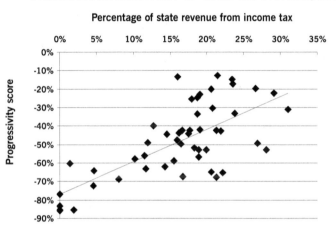

Note: Progressivity score = (percentage of income paid by top 1% - percentage of income paid by bottom 20%)/(percentage of income paid by bottom 20%). Only for state taxes (excludes local taxes and all fees).

States that rely on income taxes have more equitable tax systems; those that rely on sales taxes and fees widen the gap between rich and poor. While every state has a regressive tax system, some states are much more regressive than others. Regionally, southern states have more regressive tax systems, with the richest 1% paying only half as much of their incomes (in percentage terms) as do the poorest 20%; in northeastern states, by contrast, the richest 1% pay two-thirds as much as do the poor. The regressive effect of state and local revenue collection is not just a matter of region, but of policy. As with the federal government, progressivity in state and local taxation comes from reliance on income taxes. Whether in the North or the South, states without an income tax, like Texas, Washington, and Wyoming, or states where relatively little revenue comes from the income tax, have the most regressive revenue systems. By contrast, the states with the least regressive systems tend to rely more on income taxation and draw less of their revenue from sales taxes and fees. ❑

Sources: Internal Revenue Service (irs.gov); The White House, Budget for Fiscal Year 2016 (whitehouse. gov); U.S. Bureau of the Census (census.gov); Institute for Taxation and Economic Policy (itep.org); Congressional Budget Office, The Distribution of Household Income and Federal Taxes(cbo.gov).

Article 9.6

WEALTH INEQUALITY AND WEALTH TAXATION
A Primer on Piketty

BY STEVEN PRESSMAN
May 2014

Great works in economics address important issues head-on, adopt a broad per-spective, and change our views regarding how economies work. Make no mis-take about it: Thomas Piketty's *Capital in the Twenty-First Century* is a great work. As an added bonus, it is extremely well written (and translated).

Given decades of rising inequality and its negative consequences and public concern about a disappearing middle class, this book is particularly timely. It relies on a wide array of data, collected by the author, showing long-term trends in income and wealth distribution. It explains the causes of these trends and ends by setting forth some bold policy solutions.

Still, the most important aspect of *Capital in the Twenty-First Century* is that it changes how we view the world. The following parallel might provide some histori-cal perspective on the book, and help understand its importance and the emotional reaction it has elicited.

Thomas Malthus became one of the most controversial figures in economics fol-lowing the publication of his *Essay on Population* in 1798. Despite much optimism at the time that ordinary people's lives could be improved, for Malthus poverty was inevitable due to the relationship between population growth and the growth of the food supply. His *Essay* argued (based on some empirical data) that population growth would outstrip food supply growth, resulting in famine and misery.

Piketty can best be understood as a sort of modern-day Malthus. Both doubt-ing Thomases sought to refute popular beliefs that life could easily be improved for most people, both used simple growth rates to do this, and both were criticized for their pessimistic conclusions.

Optimism regarding the future distribution of income stems from the work of Nobel laureate Simon Kuznets. In the 1950s, Kuznets examined U.S. income-tax data and saw income inequality improving over several decades. According to the standard interpretation of his work, he hypothesized that as capitalist economies developed, inequality first increases and then decreases. This message fit America's economic experience during the post-war years and its geo-political needs during the Cold War. Most economists came to accept this message of hope.

But times have changed. Inequality is rising in the United States and other high-income capitalist countries. Piketty explains why economists got it wrong. He argues that greater equality between World War I and the 1960s was not part of some positive long-term trend; rather, it stemmed from a unique set of factors—two wars (that destroyed much wealth), the very high marginal tax rates implemented to pay for these wars, plus a stock-market crash and Great Depression. Starting in the 1970s or 1980s (dates differ by country) the moneyed class revolted and began to influence policy. Top income-tax rates fell; income and wealth inequality rose rapidly. As a result, we seem headed toward another Gilded Age, similar to the late 19th century, where the fabulously wealthy live charmed lives and everyone else struggles to survive.

Piketty, like Malthus, draws his dismal conclusion from the relationship between two growth rates. In Piketty's case, they are the rate of return to wealth or capital (r) and the growth rate of the economy (g). When r exceeds g, more money flows to those at the top and inequality increases; when r is less than g, more benefits of economic growth flow to workers, making income and wealth distribution more equal.

One great virtue of Piketty's book is that it explains why income inequality has grown of late. First, the ratio of wealth to GDP declined in Europe from 6:1 or 7:1 around World War I to 2:1 in the 1960s. It has since rebounded to nearly 6:1. The United States experienced a smaller decline, since its factories were not destroyed by the two wars, but has also experienced a growing wealth-to-GDP ratio of late. Second, r has averaged around 5% over long periods of time in many different countries, while g cannot be expected to grow by much more than 1%.

Together these results create a distribution problem, which may be easiest to comprehend in personal terms.

Suppose you receive a $200,000 inheritance (your wealth) and you make $100,000 a year. If your wealth grows at 5% per year and your wages grow by 1%, after 35 years (a typical working life) your wages would be around $140,000 and your wealth (assuming no spending down of this wealth) over $1 million. After several generations, around 100 years, your great grandchild would have labor income of $268,000 and have $25 million in capital assets. With a 5% return, their capital income ($1.25 million) would dwarf their labor income. If some income from wealth gets consumed, which is likely, this process just takes a little longer to work out. At some point income from wealth will far exceed income from labor.

The problem is that we don't all begin with equal amounts of capital. Some start with large inheritances; most people begin with nothing. As a result, the incomes of the haves grow much more rapidly than those of the have-nots and wealth inequality soars.

Piketty's story is far superior to standard economic explanations of rising inequality, such as technological change and globalization. He rightly rejects these theories because they cannot explain national differences in rising inequality—technological change and globalization should have similar impacts on all developed nations.

Compiling the data to make this case has been a heroic endeavor. Piketty uses income tax returns to get data on the share of national income going to the top 10%, the top 1%, and the top 0.1% of households. Estate tax returns enable him to estimate wealth inequality. Substantial evidence supports Piketty's conclusion that income and wealth inequality have risen in the United States and elsewhere since the late 20th century.

Similar to Malthus's *Essay*, Piketty's *Capital* contains virtually no economic theory. It does not address what determines economic growth or the return to wealth. Its dismal conclusion stems from historic trends and Piketty's explanation of why high rates of return to wealth increase inequality.

So Where Do We Go From Here?

The last part of Piketty's book discusses how to deal with rising inequality. Piketty is skeptical that institutional policies such as raising the minimum wage, or more generous government spending programs, will help much. It is not that he opposes such efforts. Rather, he thinks they are inadequate when wealth is so unevenly distributed and grows so rapidly. Government spending programs can help, but they cannot increase labor income by 5% annually over the long run.

Tax policy is all that is left (no pun intended). Piketty favors a more progressive individual income tax, with a 70% top rate. Corporations, he argues, also need to be taxed based on where they pay wages so they cannot book profits to subsidiaries in low-tax countries.

These policies would reduce income inequality and slow down, but not reverse, the more pressing issue of greater wealth inequality. To deal with this latter problem, Piketty advocates an annual wealth tax, imposed at very low rates—one or two percent on wealth in excess of 1 million euros (nearly $1.4 million). And it must be a global tax, so that it cannot be escaped by moving wealth abroad.

Those on the right objected to the tax rates that Piketty proposes as excessively high. The worst of these objections engaged in name-calling, deeming anyone a socialist who proposes higher taxes for whatever reason. Almost as bad have been the objections that higher taxes would give the government more money to waste—as if businesses never, ever wasted money and consumers always spent their money cautiously and rationally (e.g., they would never buy homes or be able to obtain mortgages that they couldn't possibly afford to repay). The more thoughtful and reasonable objections from the right have focused on the bad incentives to work hard, earn money, accumulate wealth, and provide for one's children and grandchildren as a result of higher taxes.

Those on the left and toward the center of the political spectrum have been fairly consistent in maintaining that the main policy proposal of Piketty was impractical because a global wealth tax would never get enacted. After making this point, the next sentence of these critiques typically push other policies (invariably the personal favorites of those criticizing Piketty), which are just as unlikely to get enacted given the current political situation in the United States and elsewhere.

I find all these criticisms both disturbing and a little bit off the mark. But before looking at his wealth tax proposals in greater detail, it is worth examining what Piketty has to say regarding monetary policy and fiscal policy, something which was not discussed in most of the prominent reviews of his book. Piketty downplays monetary policy in favor of fiscal policy. Monetary policy, he contends, cannot deal with the problem of rising inequality. In fact, he contends that we cannot know the impact of monetary policy on income and wealth distribution, although there is no argument for this. My gut instinct is that this is true, but I would have liked to see some data that supports this contention—say, looking at how income and wealth distribution vary based on interest rates. Such a study would make for a great thesis or doctoral dissertation, to say nothing about a nice professional paper.

Regarding fiscal policy, Piketty is fairly critical of government deficits. He spends a good deal of time focusing on the need to tax wealth so that we can repay existing government debt, but he fails to address the issue of whether government deficits and debt may be necessary at times. He also doesn't address the issue of whether government debt does any actual harm to overall macroeconomic performance. Rather, the focus is mainly (Surprise! Surprise!) on the impact of debt on income distribution. Piketty's main point is that the large majority of government bonds created when the government goes into debt is owned by the very wealthy. They benefit greatly from government debt. With little risk, they receive positive returns on their money. This income generates part of their 5% rate of return on wealth or capital.

Unfortunately, the passages on fiscal policy and distribution are too brief. There are two key reasons I wish Piketty had written a good deal more on the relationship between fiscal policy and inequality. First, he argues throughout Capital that one main reason inequality declined from World War I through the 1950s was that there were high marginal tax rates on top incomes. This reduced the after-tax gains from owning wealth. Second, fiscal policy is central to Piketty's major policy proposals.

Writing more on fiscal policy and distribution would not have been all that difficult to do. Moreover, his entire case for changes in tax policy would have been considerably stronger had Piketty spent more time on this topic and then related it to the beginnings of the revolt of the rentiers in the United Kingdom and the United States when Margaret Thatcher and Ronald Reagan were elected heads of government.

The story in both cases is rather similar and involved several policy changes. There was a sharp cut in government spending (that hurt the poor and middle class more than wealthy households, which can provide their own benefits) and a sharp cut in taxes focused at the top of the income distribution. Overall, the cuts in government expenditures were less than the tax cuts, and the government had to borrow money by selling bonds. Abstracting a little from the overall process, the Reagan and Thatcher governments gave large tax breaks to the wealthy, and then borrowed the money back from them to pay for the tax cuts. Everyone else got small tax cuts that were funded by cutting the government benefits they received. Or in slightly bolder and simpler terms, the Reagan and Thatcher governments decided to fund a good deal of government spending by borrowing money from the wealthy rather than taxing the wealthy.

As Piketty's data demonstrate, these changes led to sharply rising inequality in the UK and the United States over the past several decades. And it is no wonder why this occurred. Those earning high incomes got to keep a lot more of their income. Yet they had to do something with all this additional money. It could not be kept under the mattress, earning nothing. Bank deposits were insured, but not for balances of the sort that the very wealthy possessed. The result could only be that all this additional disposable income fueled rising asset prices, which also primarily benefited the wealthy.

According to the gospel of "supply-side" economics, which was used to justify these policy changes, the whole process should have resulted in much greater economic growth and enormous tax collections by the government so that there would be no deficit. However, this claim ignored the "balanced-budget multiplier" described by the great 20th-century U.S. economist Paul Samuelson. Samuelson showed that an equal cut in taxes and in government spending would slow economic growth or reduce GDP by an amount equal to the tax cut (or cut in government spending). The reason for this is very simple. A dollar less in government spending is a dollar less spending while a dollar tax cut was not an additional dollar in spending since some of the spending will be saved. Overall, this will reduce spending and economic growth. Yet ideology triumphed over economic knowledge. The U.S. government and the UK government gave huge tax cuts to the wealthy, and then borrowed the money back from them in order to fund the tax cut. Economic growth slowed as the balanced budget multiplier predicted it would. This made distributional matters even worse because it increased the gap between r and g by lowering g.

One last thing is worth some additional comments before getting to the issue of income and wealth taxes, especially since this has been one of the most frequent criticisms of Piketty. Many commentators complained that Piketty ignored alternative policies such as supporting unions and raising the minimum wage—but Piketty actually does discuss these policies. Chapter 9 of the book includes an extensive discussion of the minimum wage. The data Piketty presents and the written text both make it very clear that the distribution of wages has remained relatively equal in France because the French have continually increased the minimum wage and that the French minimum wage is rather high compared to average wages. Piketty even discusses why this happened—French President Charles de Gaulle (in office 1958–1969) was worried about the crisis of May 1968 and used higher minimum wages to deal with a problem that was more cultural and social than economic. Moreover, Piketty clearly supports raising the minimum wage and even provides several justifications for raising the minimum wage. So it is puzzling that so many people would criticize Piketty for not supporting higher minimum wages.

The real problem Piketty has with raising the minimum wage is not that it won't help equalize wage income, but that it won't deal with the problem of rising capital income in the long run. He is also skeptical that the minimum wage can be increased enough (5% per year in real terms) over the long haul without generating substantial unemployment. To try to make Piketty's point as simple and clear as possible, even if wages (and we can add rising union power here) were made completely equal across the board, inequality would be high and would continue to increase because of the immense wealth that is possessed by a few people.

It is wealth inequality for Piketty that is the main force driving inequality to rise under capitalism. A higher minimum wage can slow the process down. So too can stronger unions. So too can government spending policies that equalize after-tax incomes, such as paid parental leave, child allowances, generous unemployment insurance programs, and a large and sturdy social safety net. These are all policies that Piketty, I imagine, would support. But the key insight of Capital is this: the driving force of inequality is that we start with great wealth inequality and the high returns to wealth make things worse over time. Policies that equalize income distribution will help a little, but they ignore the main problem.

Still, Piketty does focus on tax policy to reduce the distribution of wage income. He argues first for a progressive income tax because this (along with inheritance taxes) is the only progressive form of taxation that governments have. Sales or indirect taxes are regressive in nature and social-insurance taxes (for retirement and for unemployment) tend to be proportional or regressive. Again, Piketty does not make either a strong or forceful case for this policy. I wish he had put a little more emphasis on the fact that high marginal tax rates during the war years and in the decade or so after World War II contributed to the falling inequality in this era. Historically, he contends that high marginal income tax rates have led to lower (before-tax) inequality. It is in the data; it should have been stressed more in the policy section of the book.

On the other hand, Piketty does worry about current trends in individual income taxation. In particular, by exempting capital income from the income tax (or taxing it at lower rates) the income tax becomes regressive at the very top (because that is where they get most of their income) and tends to make the entire tax system regressive in developed countries. But, again, the big issue for Piketty is that progressive income taxes cannot solve the wealth inequality problem. Like progressive spending programs, a progressive income tax would help reduce income inequality, but it does not solve the problem that wealth inequality tends to rise because of the high returns to wealth—much of it, such as stocks and homes that are not sold, are not taxed at all.

In a couple of pages that were pretty much ignored in the reviews of Capital, Piketty calls for a reform of corporate taxation. He proposes that corporate income taxes be assessed based on wages paid in different countries rather than on where in the world the multi-national firm declares its profits to come from (typically the country that has the lowest corporate income tax rate). This is not headline grabbing, and tax reform is never as exciting as proposing a new type of tax (this is why there are so many articles on the flat tax and the Tobin Tax and why reviews of this book focused on the global wealth tax), but it is something that needs to receive serious consideration and should be pushed more.

Again, the fact that Piketty does not focus a lot of attention on this proposal probably stems from the fact that (like higher marginal income tax rates) it will affect income distribution but not wealth distribution. When corporations pay higher taxes to governments there is less profit to distribute to the owners as dividends. This will reduce current incomes. However, higher corporate income taxes also reduce future profits after-taxes, which should affect the value of corporate stock. This will lower the price of shares of stock. Since it is mainly the very wealthy who own large amounts of stock, and whose wealth portfolio contains a higher percentage of stock compared to middle-income households, this policy should have significant and substantial effect on wealth inequality.

Piketty and the Global Tax on Wealth

At last, we come to Piketty's main policy conclusion, his claim that the way to keep more and more income from going to those at the very top of the distribution is a global wealth tax. The tax needs to be global in order to keep wealth from moving to tax havens where it is not subject to the tax. Piketty also wants to keep the tax rate low (1–2%) in order to mitigate negative disincentives. His particular plan is that net assets worth between 1 million Euros ($1.35 million) and 5 million Euros

($6.75 million) be taxed at 1% and net assets worth more than 5 million Euros be taxed at 2%. The goal in all this, Piketty makes clear, is not to raise money for social programs but to tame the inequality that inevitably results under capitalism.

Piketty provides several different arguments for his progressive and global wealth tax.

First, he resorts to an appeal to authority. He invokes the 1918 American Economic Association Presidential address by Irving Fisher, in which Fisher worries about the fact that only 2% of the U.S. population owned more than 50% of the nation's wealth while two-thirds of the population had no net wealth. Fisher then went on to suggest a steeply progressive wealth tax to remedy this situation.

Second, Piketty argues that the rewards going to the very top are not justified by traditional economic arguments (that they depend on the marginal productivity of the worker). Instead, Piketty makes the case that CEO pay is due to luck to a large degree and that a bargaining model fits the data better than marginal productivity theory. He argues that when the government takes a very large chunk of any extra income, it is not worth it for a CEO to bargain with a compensation committee or shareholders to get higher pay. And he points to empirical evidence that high marginal tax rates keep down CEO pay while not hurting the economic performance of the firm.

Finally there is the main argument—that a global wealth tax is the only way to limit the growth of wealth accumulation and a return to 19th-century levels of inequality. Or, this is the only way we can avoid all the negative economic, social, and political consequences of great inequality. A tax on income will not achieve this end because much income is tied up in stocks and bonds and real estate that generally do not get taxed. The gains from these investments are taxed when assets are sold. This allows the gains to accumulate at the top and to keep doing so. Only a wealth tax can stop this process.

Finally, while his many critics fault Piketty for making such an unrealistic proposal, Piketty himself recognizes that a global wealth tax (or even higher taxes on income from capital in the United States) is not likely to happen anytime soon and perhaps will never happen. He has no unrealistic illusions about this policy being passed in the United States or Europe.

The alternative policy proposals made by critics of Piketty, as noted above, are probably as unrealistic as a global wealth tax. But the strong case against them, as Piketty points out, is that only a progressive wealth tax deals with the problem of rising inequality in income and wealth under capitalism. A higher minimum wage and greater support for labor unions cannot reduce the concentration of capital. Nor can progressive government programs such as paid parental leave and generous unemployment insurance. Even reforming individual and corporate income taxes will be of limited help (although, as I argue above, global corporate tax reform can do a lot of good). We are left with few options if we want to halt a return to the Gilded Age. ❏

Chapter 10

TRADE AND DEVELOPMENT

INTRODUCTION

Given the economic turmoil of the last decade in high-income countries, it is ironic that the developing world is still being urged to adopt free markets and increased privatization as the keys to catching up with the West. These neoliberal policy prescriptions have been applied across the developing world, over the last few decades, as a one-size-fits-all solution to problems such as poverty, malnutrition, and political conflict. While spiking unemployment in the United States led to a (temporary) surge in government spending, developing countries with double-digit unemployment were routinely told that macroeconomic crises could only be dealt with by "tightening their belts." And while the West, having experienced a financial crisis, now embraced some new financial regulations, similar calls for more regulation from developing countries have been dismissed as misguided.

The contributors to this section take on different aspects of the neoliberal (or "free market") policy mix, raising questions that recur through this entire volume. Where do the limits of the market lie? At what point do we decide that markets are no longer serving the general public, whose well-being economists claim to champion? And to what extent should communities, via politically representative bodies of all kinds, be able to regulate and control markets?

The first tenet of the neoliberal faith is the belief that openness to international trade is the key to growth and development. Ramaa Vasudevan, in her primer "Comparative Advantage" (Article 10.1), starts off this chapter with a critique of the Ricardian theory of comparative advantage that is central to the neoclassical argument for free trade.

Next, in "Beyond Trump's Tariffs and Trade War" (Article 10.2), John Miller provides a welcome primer on the current status of trade and the economic theory behind it. Miller explores the previous neoliberal regime of global trade and Trump's "economic nationalist" reaction against it. Miller suggests an alternative to both that attempts to address the needs of working people globally.

Then, in "After Horror, Change?" (Article 10.3), Miller looks at the worker-safety accord put in place in Bangladesh in the wake of the 2013 Rana Plaza disaster, a factory collapse that killed over 1,100 workers. Miller argues that the legal liability of major clothing companies (who outsource clothing production to subcontractor companies) is a major positive step for worker safety. He also notes, however, that most major U.S. clothing companies have so far refused to sign onto the accord.

The next article turns to the current debt crisis in Puerto Rico. In "Puerto Rico's Colonial Debt" (Article 10.4), José A. Laguarta Ramírez puts the recent Puerto Rico Oversight, Management, and Economic Stability Act (PROMESA) in the context of Puerto Rico's history as a U.S. colony. The island's government is saddled with what should be considered "odious debt"—debt that was incurred neither with the people's consent nor to their benefit. But PROMESA forecloses recognizing or discharging it as such, and Puerto Ricans must face austerity so creditors can be paid.

Ellen Frank's "Should Developing Countries Embrace Protectionism?" (Article 10.5) points out that, contrary to the claims of globalization advocates and the theory of comparative advantage, the historical record suggests that protectionism may be a better strategy for economic development. In fact, it is hard to provide an example of successful economic growth and development from countries that "got prices right" as opposed to those that "got prices wrong"—but to their trading advantage.

Finally, Jawied Nawabi's "Whatever Happened to Development?" (Article 10.6) provides a primer on development economics. Nawabi begins with a simple observation: "…why have so few countries—out of about 120 newly independent countries that have emerged since World War II—achieved successful development?" To answer that question, he walks us through the history of development economics up through the present and introduces us to the "role of the state in economic development," or RSED, a school of thought which challenges the dominant neoliberal orthodoxy.

Discussion Questions

1. (Article 10.1) Under what conditions might the mainstream argument about the advantages of specialization based on comparative advantage break down?

2. (Article 10.2) Why does imposition of tariffs risk causing a trade war? What is a trade war? Can a trade war be won?

5. (Article 10.2) What kinds of trade policies would help workers in the United States and around the world?

6. (Article 10.3) Opponents of international labor standards argue that workers in very low-income countries just need jobs, and will only be hurt by well-intentioned efforts to raise wages or improve working conditions. How do such arguments hold up to the experience in Bangladesh since the Rana Plaza disaster?

7. (Article 10.4) Explain the two examples from U.S. history that Laguarta Ramírez says should show a different way of dealing with Puerto Rico's debt than the one the recent PROMESA legislation provides.

8. (Article 10.5) What is the basic argument made by mainstream economists in favor of free trade? Frank argues that free trade can prevent poorer countries

from developing, rather than helping them do so. (The same argument applies to poorer regions within richer countries like the United States.) What is her reasoning? How do you think a pro-free-trade economist would respond?

9. (Article 10.6) Nawabi presents the RSED school of thought as an emerging alternative to the current orthodox neoliberalism within development economics. Explain what the RSED school is and why it is critical of neoliberalism and the "Washington Consensus."

Article 10.1

COMPARATIVE ADVANTAGE

BY RAMAA VASUDEVAN

July/August 2007

Dear Dr. Dollar:

When economists argue that the outsourcing of jobs might be a plus for the U.S. economy, they often mention the idea of comparative advantage. So free trade would allow the United States to specialize in higher-end service-sector businesses, creating higher-paying jobs than the ones that would be outsourced. But is it really true that free trade leads to universal benefits?
—David Goodman, Boston, Mass.

You're right: The purveyors of the free trade gospel do invoke the doctrine of comparative advantage to dismiss widespread concerns about the export of jobs. Attributed to 19th-century British political-economist David Ricardo, the doctrine says that a nation always stands to gain if it exports the goods it produces *relatively* more cheaply in exchange for goods that it can get *comparatively* more cheaply from abroad. Free trade would lead to each country specializing in the products it can produce at *relatively* lower costs. Such specialization allows both trading partners to gain from trade, the theory goes, even if in one of the countries production of *both* goods costs more in absolute terms.

For instance, suppose that in the United States the cost to produce one car equals the cost to produce 10 bags of cotton, while in the Philippines the cost to produce one car equals the cost to produce 100 bags of cotton. The Philippines would then have a comparative advantage in the production of cotton, producing one bag at a cost equal to the production cost of 1/100 of a car, versus 1/10 of a car in the United States; likewise, the United States would hold a comparative advantage in the production of cars. Whatever the prices of cars and cotton in the global market, the theory goes, the Philippines would be better off producing only cotton and importing all its cars from the United States, and the United States would be better off producing only cars and importing all of its cotton from the Philippines. If the international terms of trade—the relative price—is one car for 50 bags, then the United States will take in 50 bags of cotton for each car it exports, 40 more than the 10 bags it forgoes by putting its productive resources into making the car rather than growing cotton. The Philippines is also better off: it can import a car in exchange for the export of 50 bags of cotton, whereas it would have had to forgo the production of 100 bags of cotton in order to produce that car domestically. If the price of cars goes up in the global marketplace, the Philippines will lose out in relative terms—but will still be better off than if it tried to produce its own cars.

The real world, unfortunately, does not always conform to the assumptions underlying comparative-advantage theory. One assumption is that trade is balanced. But many countries are running persistent deficits, notably the United States, whose trade deficit is now at nearly 7% of its GDP. A second premise, that there is full employment within the trading nations, is also patently unrealistic. As global trade intensifies, jobs created in the export sector do not necessarily compensate for the jobs lost in the sectors wiped out by foreign competition.

The comparative advantage story faces more direct empirical challenges as well. Nearly 70% of U.S. trade is trade in similar goods, known as *intra-industry trade*: for example, exporting Fords and importing BMWs. And about one third of U.S. trade as of the late 1990s was trade between branches of a single corporation located in different countries (*intra-firm trade*). Comparative advantage cannot explain these patterns.

Comparative advantage is a static concept that identifies immediate gains from trade but is a poor guide to economic development, a process of structural change over time which is by definition dynamic. Thus the comparative advantage tale is particularly pernicious when preached to developing countries, consigning many to "specialize" in agricultural goods or be forced into a race to the bottom where cheap sweatshop labor is their sole source of competitiveness.

The irony, of course, is that none of the rich countries got that way by following the maxim that they now preach. These countries historically relied on tariff walls and other forms of protectionism to build their industrial base. And even now, they continue to protect sectors like agriculture with subsidies. The countries now touted as new models of the benefits of free trade—South Korea and the other "Asian tigers," for instance—actually flouted this economic wisdom, nurturing their technological capabilities in specific manufacturing sectors and taking advantage of their lower wage costs to *gradually* become effective competitors of the United States and Europe in manufacturing.

The fundamental point is this: contrary to the comparative-advantage claim that trade is universally beneficial, nations as a whole do not prosper from free trade. Free trade creates winners and losers, both within and between countries. In today's context it is the global corporate giants that are propelling and profiting from "free trade": not only outsourcing white-collar jobs, but creating global commodity chains linking sweatshop labor in the developing countries of Latin America and Asia (Africa being largely left out of the game aside from the export of natural resources such as oil) with ever-more insecure consumers in the developed world. Promoting "free trade" as a political cause enables this process to continue.

It is a process with real human costs in terms of both wages and work. People in developing countries across the globe continue to face these costs as trade liberalization measures are enforced; and the working class in the United States is also being forced to bear the brunt of the relentless logic of competition. ❑

Sources: Arthur MacEwan, "The Gospel of Free Trade: The New Evangelists," *Dollars & Sense*, July/August 2002; Ha-Joon Chang, *Kicking away the Ladder: The Real History of Fair Trade*, Foreign Policy in Focus, 2003; Anwar Shaikh, "Globalization and the Myths of Free Trade," in *Globalization and the Myths of Free Trade: History, Theory, and Empirical Evidence*, ed. Anwar Shaikh, Routledge 2007.

Article 10.2

BEYOND TRUMP'S TARIFFS AND TRADE WAR

BY JOHN MILLER
May/June 2018

> Mr. Trump raised the stakes late Thursday in his tariff showdown with Beijing, vowing to impose another $100 billion in tariffs on Chinese goods in light of its "unfair retaliation" after his initial $50 billion in tariffs. ...
>
> Then China popped off in return, saying it was ready to "forcefully" strike back if the new tariffs are imposed
>
> The basic economic problem with trade protectionism is that it is a political intervention that distorts markets. One political intervention leads to another, and the cumulative consequence is higher prices, less investment, and slower economic growth.
>
> —"Punishing America First" by the Editorial Board, *Wall Street Journal*, April 7, 2018.

The *Wall Street Journal* editors are right that President Trump's tariffs will undoubtedly harm the U.S. economy. Just how much will depend on whether his tariffs and trade bluster ignite a trade war. Not that it much worries Trump, who insists that trade wars "are easy to win." (See the box on the next page for an account of Trump's tariffs and trade threats.)

But that doesn't make the non-interventionist, free-market policies the *Wall Street Journal* editors are peddling a desirable alternative. Their hyper-globalization policies have not brought and will not bring economic relief to those who have been left behind and will instead continue to shower gains on financial elites.

The Trump Tariffs and the Triumph of Economic Illiteracy

The *Wall Street Journal* editors have complained that it is hard to discern the overall strategy to Trump trade policy, which seems to be backed up by little other than "nonsense trade economics." Economists of all stripes, advocates and critics of market-led globalization, agree.

To begin with, there's Trump's fixation with the U.S. trade deficit with China ($337 billion in 2017), when the United States trades with many other countries, too. Martin Wolf, the pro-globalization columnist at the *Financial Times*, the leading British business daily, likens worrying about running a trade deficit with one country to worrying about running a consistent trade deficit with your local supermarket (where you buy without selling). Your supermarket deficit is of no concern to you (or the supermarket) as long as you continue to pay your bills. Economist Joseph Stiglitz, a leading critic of corporate globalization, adds that even if tariffs reduced Chinese imports, they would not create jobs in the United States. Those tariffs would just increase prices for U.S. consumers and create jobs in Bangladesh, Vietnam, or any other country that steps in to replace the imports that had come from China.

> **The Trump Tariff Saga in a Nutshell**
>
> In February, the Trump administration imposed a 30% tariff on solar imports, an industry dominated by China. A month later, the Trump administration added a 30% tariff on steel and a 10% tariff on aluminum. After a multitude of country exemptions, several Asian countries and Russia are likely to be the only major importers subject to the tariffs. In April, China retaliated with tariffs on 128 U.S. products. Trump then announced 25% tariffs on another 1,300 Chinese products, about $50 billion of China's exports into the United States. In response, China threatened a 25% tariff on 106 U.S. exports (including soybeans, cars, and airplanes), to go in effect whenever the U.S. tariffs do. Then Trump vowed to impose another $100 billion in tariffs on Chinese goods because of China's "unfair retaliation" to his initial $50 billion in tariffs. That's when the *Wall Street Journal* editors chimed in with the editorial above.
>
> Since then, Trump has angered Mexico and U.S. allies Canada and Europe by adding them to list of countries on which he will impose his steel and aluminum tariffs set to go into effect of July 1.
>
> Each country has promised to retaliate by imposing tariffs of U.S. goods. Canada announced a list tariffs it would impose on steel imports from the United States as well as 84 other U.S. products from yogurt to lawnmowers (both made in the swing state Wisconsin) to beer kegs to hair lacquers. The European Union would impose $3.4 billion of tariffs on U.S. imports including Harley Davidson motorcycles (manufactured in Wisconsin), bourbon whiskey (from Mitch McConnell's Kentucky), Levi's jeans and a host of other U.S. imports. Mexico promises "dollar for dollar" tariffs on U.S. imports, targeting steel, pork, bourbon, motorboats, apples, potatoes, cranberries, and many other U.S. imports.
>
> Finally, when the conference of G-7 nations held in early June ended in conflict, the threat of a trade war was yet closer to becoming a reality.

Then there's Trump's exports-only approach to trade policy. "Selling stuff [made in the United States] to foreigners is good, and buying stuff [that could have been made in the United States] from foreigners is bad," is conservative economist Robert Barro's best guess as to what constitutes Trump's theory of international trade. For Barro, Trump has things backward: "Imports are things we want," and "exports are the price we have to pay to get the imports." One doesn't have to accept Barro's vision of trade to acknowledge that any coherent trade theory needs to take into account the benefits of imports to consumers and producers as well as the production and employment effect of exports, and to recognize that running a trade deficit (imports that exceed exports) is not in and of itself a sign of a failed trade policy.

On top of that, Trump's tariffs are likely to cost U.S. manufacturers jobs, even without considering the debilitating effects of Chinese retaliatory tariffs. Take the 25% tariff that Trump imposed on imported steel. Steel tariffs might protect the jobs of workers in the steel industry, but they will damage industries and cost jobs in the many industries that use steel as an input. That includes the automobile sector, aerospace, heavy equipment, and construction, all of which will have to pay higher prices for steel. And the industries that use steel employ 80 times as many people as steel-producing industries, according to the estimates of economists Lydia Cox and Kadee Russ. While the United States might not get punished first, as the editors maintain, Trump's tariff policy does amount to a "stop or I'll shoot our economy in the foot strategy," as former Clinton Administration Treasury Secretary and Obama Administration economic advisor, Lawrence Summers, has put it.

Free-Trade Free Fall

The free-trade policies favored by the *Wall Street Journal* editors and traditional trade economists might be more disciplined than Trump's hodgepodge of tariffs, but they would do no less to serve the rich and do no more to improve the lot of those who have been left behind by globalization. In fact, a populist backlash against those policies helped to elect Trump president.

Honestly presented trade theory never promised a "win-win for everyone," as economist Paul Krugman puts it. Rather, traditional trade theory suggests that trade, rather than increase or decrease the number of jobs in a country, instead changes the mix of jobs. That in turn causes massive dislocation that leaves many behind, especially when they get little or no support from government. In his book *The Globalization Paradox*, economist Dani Rodrik finds that the primary effect of reducing tariffs in the United States would be to shift income from some groups to others, typically from those already hurt by globalization to those who are already benefitting. Rodrik calculates that in the case of the United States, for every $1 of overall gains, $50 of income gets shifted from one group to another. For typical working families, the $1 of overall gains is likely to be swamped by the fact that they are on the losing end of the $50 income shift.

On top of that, much of the gains from trade are diffuse, going to millions of consumers in the form of lower prices for cheap imports, while losses are highly concentrated, materializing in the form of lost jobs and the economic decline of towns and regions. An honest case for freer trade would require government to compensate those losers to ensure that everyone wins. But in the United States that compensation seldom, if ever, happens.

Even the net gains from free trade have been called into question. In their exhaustive empirical study of the major studies of trade policy and economic growth, Rodrik and fellow economist Francisco Rodriguez found "little evidence that open trade policies…are significantly associated with economic growth."

Historical evidence also casts doubt on the benefits of free trade. *New York Times* columnist Thomas Friedman once challenged the critics of globalization to name "a single country that has flourished, or upgraded its living or worker standards, without free trade and integration." The accurate answer is that every one of today's developed countries relied heavily on government policies that managed and controlled its involvement in international commerce during its rise to prowess. The world's first industrial power, Great Britain, advocated free trade only after protectionist policies helped 18th-century industries become well established. In the half century following the Civil War, the United States imposed tariffs on imports that averaged around 40%, a level higher than those imposed in virtually all of today's developing economies. During the second half of the 20th century, both Germany and Japan relied on managed trade, not free trade, to propel their rapid economic growth, as did South Korea and Taiwan during the 1960s and 1970s.

What Would Be Better?

A progressive policy would not turn away from trade but would engage the global economy with rules and policies that are more democratic and serve the interests of people across the globe. To begin with, a global commitment to sustained full employment would help workers escape jobs with dangerous working conditions that pay rock-bottom wages. It would also go a long way toward limiting transnational corporations' ability to pit the workers in one country against their employees in another country.

Nor should a progressive policy sweep away all tariffs. In his column last year ("What Would a Progressive Trade Policy Look Like?" *D&S*, July/August 2017), Arthur MacEwan made the case for two changes in U.S. international agreements that would use tariffs to reduce inequality and insecurity. First, goods produced under conditions where workers' basic rights to organize and to reasonable health and safety conditions are denied would not be given unfettered access to global markets. Second, goods whose production or use is environmentally destructive would likewise face trade restrictions.

Beyond those changes, with increased international trade comes the need for increased government intervention. Government must support people displaced by changes due to trade, from employment insurance funds to well-funded retraining programs to provisions for continuing medical care and pensions.

Those sorts of trade policies would help the majority of the world's people flourish economically. ❑

Sources: "Trump's China Tariffs," *Wall Street Journal* editorial, March 22, 2018; Joseph Stiglitz, "Trump's Trade Confusion," Project Syndicate, April 5, 2018; Martin Wolf, "The Folly of Donald Trump's Bilateralism in Global Trade," *Financial Times*, March 14, 2017; Robert Barro, "Trump and China Share a Bad Idea on Trade," *Wall Street Journal*, April 10, 2018; Bob Davis and Lingling Wei, "U.S. Set to Boost Pressure on China," *Wall Street Journal*, April 12, 2018; Lydia Cox and Kadee Russ, "Will Steel Tariffs put U.S. Jobs at Risk?" Econofact, February 26, 2018; Paul Krugman, "Oh, What a Trumpy Trade War!" *New York Times*, March 8, 2018; Larry Summers, "Tariffs Are a 'Stop or I'll Shoot Myself in the Foot' Policy," CNBC, April 6, 2018; Dani Rodrik, *The Globalization Paradox* (W.W. Norton, New York: 2011); John Miller, "The Misleading Case for Unmanaged Global Free Trade," Scholars Strategy Network, January 13, 2015.

Article 10.3

AFTER HORROR, CHANGE?
Taking Stock of Conditions in Bangladesh's Garment Factories

BY JOHN MILLER
September/October 2014

On April 24, 2013, the Rana Plaza factory building, just outside of Bangladesh's capital city of Dhaka, collapsed—killing 1,138 workers and inflicting serious long-term injuries on at least 1,000 others.

While the collapse of Rana Plaza was in one sense an accident, the policies that led to it surely were not. Bangladesh's garment industry grew to be the world's second largest exporter, behind only China's, by endangering and exploiting workers. Bangladesh's 5,000 garment factories paid rock-bottom wages, much lower than those in China, and just half of those in Vietnam. One foreign buyer told The Economist magazine, "There are no rules whatsoever that can not be bent." Cost-saving measures included the widespread use of retail buildings as factories—including at Rana Plaza—adding weight that sometimes exceeded the load-bearing capacity of the structures.

As Scott Nova, executive director of the Worker Rights Consortium, testified before Congress, "the danger to workers in Bangladesh has been apparent for many years." The first documented mass-fatality incident in the country's export garment sector occurred in December 1990. In addition to those killed at Rana Plaza, more than 600 garment workers have died in factory fires in Bangladesh since 2005. After Rana Plaza, however, Bangladesh finally reached a crossroads. The policies that had led to the stunning growth of its garment industry had so tarnished the "Made in Bangladesh" label that they were no longer sustainable.

But just how much change has taken place since Rana Plaza? That was the focus of an International Conference at Harvard this June, bringing together government officials from Bangladesh and the United States, representatives of the Bangladesh garment industry, the international brands, women's groups, trade unions, the International Labor Organization (ILO), and monitoring groups working in Bangladesh.

How Much Change On the Ground?

Srinivas B. Reddy of the ILO spoke favorably of an "unprecedented level of ... practical action" toward workplace safety in Bangladesh.

The "practical action" on the ground, however, has been much more of a mixed bag than Reddy suggests. In the wake of massive protests and mounting international pressure, Bangladesh amended its labor laws to remove some obstacles to workers forming unions. Most importantly, the new law bars the country's labor ministry from giving factory owners lists of workers who want to organize.

But formidable obstacles to unionization still remain. At least 30% of the workers at an entire company are required to join a union before the government will grant recognition. This is a higher hurdle than workers face even in the not-so-union-friendly United States, where recognition is based at the level of the workplace, not the company. Workers in special export-processing zones (the source of about 16% of Bangladesh's exports), moreover, remain ineligible to form unions.

The Bangladesh government did register 160 new garment unions in 2013 and the first half of this year, compared to just two between 2010 and 2012. Nonetheless, collective bargaining happens in only 3% of garment plants. And employers have responded with firings and violence to workers registering for union recognition or making bargaining demands. Union organizers have been kidnapped, brutally beaten, and killed.

After protests that shut down over 400 factories last fall, the Bangladesh government raised the minimum wage for garment workers from the equivalent of $38 a month to $68. The higher minimum wage, however, fell short of the $103 demanded by workers.

The government and the garment brands have also set up the Rana Plaza Donor Trust Fund to compensate victims and their families for their losses and injuries. But according to the fund's website, it stood at just $17.9 million at the beginning of August, well below its $40 million target. Only about half of the 29 international brands that had their clothes sewn at Rana Plaza have made contributions. Ineke Zeldenrust of the Amsterdam-based labor-rights group Clean Clothes Campaign estimates that those 29 brands are being asked to contribute less than 0.2% of their $22 billion in total profits for 2013.

The Accord and the Alliance

Following Rana Plaza, a group of mostly European retail chains turned away from the business-as-usual approach of company codes that had failed to ensure safe working conditions in the factories that made their clothes. Some 151 apparel brands and retailers doing business in Bangladesh, including 16 U.S.-based retailers, signed the Accord on Fire and Building Safety in Bangladesh. Together the signatories of this five-year agreement contracted with 1,639 of the 3,498 Bangladesh factories making garments for export.

The Accord broke important new ground. Unlike earlier efforts:

It was negotiated with two global unions, UndustriALL and UNI (Global).

It sets up a governing board with equal numbers of labor and retail representatives, and a chair chosen by the ILO.

Independent inspectors will conduct audits of factory hazards and make their results public on the Accord website, including the name of the factory, detailed information about the hazard, and recommended repairs.

The retailers will provide direct funding for repairs (up to a maximum of $2.5 million per company) and assume responsibility for ensuring that all needed renovations and repairs are paid for.

Most importantly, the Accord is legally binding. Disputes between retailers and union representatives are subject to arbitration, with decisions enforceable by a court of law in the retailer's home country.

But most U.S. retailers doing business in Bangladesh—including giants like Wal-Mart, JCPenney, The Gap, and Sears—refused to sign. They objected to the Accord's open-ended financial commitment and to its legally binding provisions.

Those companies, along with 21 other North American retailers and brands, developed an alternative five-year agreement, called the Alliance For Bangladesh Worker Safety. Some 770 factories in Bangladesh produce garments for these 26 companies.

Unlike the Accord, the Alliance is not legally binding and lacks labor- organization representatives. Moreover, retailers contribute a maximum of $1 million per retailer (less than half the $2.5 million under the Accord) to implement their safety plan and needed repairs, and face no binding commitment to pay for needed improvements beyond that. The responsibility to comply with safety standards falls to factory owners, although the Alliance does offer up to $100 million in loans for these expenses.

Kalpona Akter, executive director of the Bangladesh Center for Worker Solidarity, told the U.S. Senate Foreign Relations Committee, "There is no meaningful difference between the Alliance and the corporate-controlled 'corporate social responsibility' programs that have failed Bangladeshi garment workers in the past, and have left behind thousands of dead and injured workers."

Historic and Unprecedented?

Dan Mozena, U.S. Ambassador to Bangladesh, believes that, despite facing significant obstacles, "Bangladesh is making history as it creates new standards for the apparel industry globally."

While the Accord may be without contemporary precedent, joint liability agreements that make retailers responsible for the safety conditions of their subcontractor's factories do have historical antecedents. As political scientist Mark Anner has documented, beginning in the 1920s the International Ladies Garment Workers Union (ILGWU) began negotiating "jobber agreements" in the United States that held the buyer (or "jobber") for an apparel brand "jointly liable" for wages and working conditions in the contractor's factories. Jobber agreements played a central role in the near-eradication of sweatshops in the United States by the late 1950s. In today's global economy, however, international buyers are once again able to escape responsibility for conditions in the far-flung factories of their subcontractors.

Like jobber agreements, the Accord holds apparel manufacturers and retailers legally accountable for the safety conditions in the factories that make their clothes through agreements negotiated between workers or unions and buyers or brands. The next steps for the Accord model, as Anner has argued, are to address working conditions other than building safety (as jobber agreements had), to get more brands to sign on to the Accord, and to negotiate similar agreements in other countries.

That will be no easy task. But, according to Arnold Zack, who helped to negotiate the Better Factories program that brought ILO monitoring of Cambodian garment factories, "Bangladesh is the lynch pin that can bring an end to the bottom feeding shopping the brands practice." ❑

Sources: Arnold M. Zack, "In an Era of Accelerating Attention to Workplace Equity: What Place for Bangladesh," Boston Global Forum, July 8, 2014; Testimony of Kalpona Akter, Testimony of Scott Nova, Senate Committee on Foreign Relations, Feb. 11, 2014; Mark Anner, Jennifer Bair, and Jeremy Blasi, "Toward Joint Liability in Global Supply Chains," *Comparative Labor Law & Policy Journal*, Vol. 35:1, Fall 2013; Prepared Remarks for Rep. George Miller (D-Calif.), Keynote Remarks by U.S. Ambassador to Bangladesh Dan Mozena, Remarks by Country Director ILO Bangladesh Srinivas B. Reddy, International Conference on Globalization and Sustainability of the Bangladesh Garment Sector, June 14, 2014; "Rags in the ruins," *The Economist*, May 4, 2013; "Bangladesh: Amended Labor Law Falls Short," Human Rights Watch, July 18, 2013; Rana Plaza Donor Trust Fund (ranaplaza-arrangement.org/fund).

Article 10.4

PUERTO RICO'S COLONIAL DEBT

"Compromise" protects vulture funds, not Puerto Rico.

BY JOSÉ A. LAGUARTA RAMÍREZ
JULY/AUGUST 2016

At least 23 of the 49 people killed in the mass shooting that took place at Pulse nightclub in Orlando on June 12 were born in Puerto Rico. While the horrendous hate crime targeted LGBT people of all ethnicities, the large proportion of island-born casualties is not surprising, as the central Florida city has become a preferred destination of Puerto Rican migrants over the past two decades. Steadily growing since the onset of the island's current "fiscal" crisis in 2006, yearly out-migration from Puerto Rico now surpasses that of the 1950s. The island's total population has begun to decline for the first time in its history.

Nearly a third of the island-born victims of the Orlando massacre were 25 or younger, most of them students employed in services or retail. This is the population group that will be hit hardest when the ironically named Puerto Rico Oversight, Management, and Economic Stability Act (PROMESA) comes into effect. Among its other "promises" for working-class Puerto Ricans, PROMESA will cut the minimum wage in Puerto Rico for those under 25, from the current federally mandated $7.25 to $4.25 per hour, and scale back the federal nutritional assistance program on the island. Purportedly aimed at "job-creation," these measures will likely intensify the outflow of able-bodied "low-skilled" workers. Ongoing out-migration has already decimated the number of available healthcare and other professionals on the island. Puerto Rico's 2013 median household income of $19,183 was barely half that of Mississippi, the poorest U.S. state (at $37,479), despite a cost of living that rivals that of most major cities in the United States. Inequality on the island is also greater than in any of the states.

The U.S. House of Representatives approved PROMESA on the evening of June 9, following a strong endorsement by President Barack Obama. The bill, which would also impose an unelected and unaccountable federal oversight board and allow court-supervised restructuring of part of the island's $73 billion debt, now awaits consideration by the Senate. Its advocates hope the president can sign PROMESA into law before July 1, when $1.9 billion's worth of Puerto Rico general obligation bonds will come due. Unlike those issued by public utility corporations and certain autonomous agencies, general obligation bonds, under Puerto Rico's colonial constitution, must be repaid before any further public spending for the following fiscal year is authorized. Puerto Rico's government has partially defaulted three times within the past year, but not on general obligation bonds. Puerto Rico is not the only place, under the global regime of austerity capitalism, to face predatory creditors and the imposition of unelected rulers—as illustrated by cases like Argentina, Greece, and post-industrial U.S. cities such as Flint, Mich.—but its century-old colonial status has made it particularly vulnerable and defenseless.

The House vote followed a concerted, carefully timed media push by the Democratic establishment, on the premise that "despite its flaws" PROMESA represents a bipartisan compromise that is, in Obama's words, "far superior to the status quo." Among similar statements, a *New York Times* editorial on May 31 claimed that PROMESA "offers the island its best chance of survival." However, following the bill's approval, Republican House Speaker Paul Ryan tweeted in almost identical terms that PROMESA is "the best chance," but for something quite different—"for American taxpayers to be protected from a bailout of Puerto Rico." The threat of a taxpayer-funded "bailout" (which has never been on the table) has been deployed in anonymous scare ads, probably financed by high-risk/yield-seeking "vulture funds" that hold Puerto Rican bonds and so oppose PROMESA's mild restructuring provisions.

PROMESA's oversight board, which will be staffed by San Juan and Washington insiders with the bondholders' best interests at heart, is sure to continue to impose draconian austerity measures that have already slashed much-needed social services. (Former Puerto Rico governor Luis Fortuño, a Republican who enacted legislation laying off up to 30,000 public employees in order to appease credit rating agencies, has been mentioned as a likely appointee.) Democratic support for the bill was forthcoming despite the fact that neither the oversight provisions nor those reducing the minimum wage were removed.

Most U.S. observers reduce Puerto Rico's debt crisis to a result of "mismanagement" by its local administrators. (A Google search of the terms "Puerto Rico," "debt," and "mismanagement" yields pieces articulating this narrative from Bloomberg, CNN, *USA Today*, the *National Review*, and the Huffington Post, among others, within the top 10 hits.) This view conveniently erases the historical and structural roots of the crisis.

U.S. troops occupied Puerto Rico in 1898 and the Supreme Court quickly declared it an "unincorporated territory" subject to the authority of the U.S. Congress and federal courts system, without voting representation in Congress. Although U.S. citizenship was extended to individuals in 1917, and a local constitution was authorized and adopted in 1952 (not without significant amendments by Congress), the juridical fact of colonialism has remained unaltered, as reiterated by the Court on the very day of the House vote on PROMESA. (See Puerto Rico v. Sánchez Valle, a criminal case on double jeopardy, in which the Court reminds Puerto Rico's local government that unlike states, it is not legally considered a "sovereign" separate from Congress.) In the mid-1970s, Puerto Rico's comparative advantage as the only low-wage tax haven with direct access to the U.S. market waned. Washington's solution to the colony's economic stagnation was Section 936 of the Internal Revenue Code, which granted federal tax exemptions to U.S. corporations on products made in Puerto Rico, in addition to local tax breaks in place since the 1940s. The local government, in turn, pursued massive debt-fueled investment in infrastructure, whose use by these corporations it heavily subsidized. The resulting debt addiction spiraled out of control in the 1990s, fed by easy credit, and exacerbated after Congress began a ten-year phase out of Section 936 in 1996. Meanwhile, profits continue to leave the island to the tune of $30 billion annually.

In international law, the term for debt incurred by colonial, corrupt, or authoritarian regimes is "odious debt." A prominent example of its application was the cancellation of Cuba's colonial debt when that country achieved its independence from Spain, following the so-called Spanish-American War of 1898. The U.S. government's argument at the time, which Spain never formally accepted but most of Cuba's creditors eventually did, was that the debt was incurred neither with the consent of the Cuban people nor to their benefit. Although odious debt is a grey area of international law, with sufficient political resolve Puerto Rico's leadership could use it to bolster a claim to refuse payment. In 2008, Ecuador invoked the doctrine as part of a largely successful audit and partial default. Such a course would necessarily put Puerto Rico on a collision course with colonialism, as it would need to refuse to recognize any resulting lawsuits in U.S. courts.

This is precisely the type of outcome that PROMESA is designed to prevent. It is one which Puerto Rico's current administrators have proven entirely unwilling to pursue. Yet it is a path that is not alien to U.S. political history: one of the grievances that led to the thirteen colonies' Declaration of Independence was the imposition of new taxes—largely to pay debts incurred by Britain in the Seven Years' War. An independent Puerto Rico, released of an illegitimate debt burden incurred to profit U.S. corporations, could better focus on serving the needs of its poor and working-class majority. A movement capable of leading such a process has yet to materialize, but with U.S. statehood farther away than ever and housing and labor markets in migrant destinations becoming increasingly saturated, the matter is far from decided.

As living conditions on the island continue to deteriorate under PROMESA (and they surely will), young Puerto Rican students and workers will continue to flood those places where family connections, climate, the price of airfare, and job opportunities pull them. Not all will be targeted for physical violence because of their multiple identities, as the Orlando victims were. Their fate, however, will continue to be a haunting reminder of the ways in which invisible forces pattern seemingly random events in the lives of individuals and communities. ❑

Article 10.5

SHOULD DEVELOPING COUNTRIES EMBRACE PROTECTIONISM?

BY ELLEN FRANK
July 2004

> Dear Dr. Dollar:
> *Supposedly, countries should produce what they are best at. If the United States makes computers and China produces rice, then the theory of free trade says China should trade its rice for computers. But if China puts tariffs on U.S.-made computers and builds up its own computer industry, then it will become best at making them and can buy rice from Vietnam. Isn't it advantageous for poor countries to practice protectionism and become industrial powers themselves, rather than simply producing mono-crop commodities? I'm asking because local alternative currencies like Ithaca Hours benefit local businesses, though they restrict consumers to local goods that may be more expensive than goods from further away.*
> —Matt Cary, Hollywood, Fla.

The modern theory of free trade argues that countries are "endowed" with certain quantities of labor, capital, and natural resources. A country with lots of labor but little capital should specialize in the production of labor-intensive goods, like hand-woven rugs, hand-sewn garments, or hand-picked fruit. By ramping up produc-tion of these goods, a developing country can trade on world markets, earning the foreign exchange to purchase capital-intensive products like computers and cars. Free trade thus permits poor countries (or, to be more precise, their most well-off citizens) to *consume* high-tech goods that they lack the ability to *produce* and so obtain higher living standards. "Capital-rich" countries like the United States benefit from relatively cheap fruit and garments, freeing up their workforce to focus on high-tech goods. Free trade, according to this story, is a win-win game for everyone.

The flaw in this tale, which you have hit upon exactly, is that being "capital-rich" or "capital-poor" is not a natural phenomenon like having lots of oil. Capital is created—typically with plenty of government assistance and protection.

Developing countries can create industrial capacity and train their citizens to manufacture high-tech goods. But doing so takes time. Building up the capacity to manufacture computers, for example, at prices that are competitive with firms in developed countries may take several years. To buy this time, a government needs to keep foreign-made computers from flooding its market and undercutting less-established local producers. It also needs to limit inflows of foreign capital. Studies show that when foreign firms set up production facilities in developing countries, they are unlikely to share their latest techniques, so such foreign investment does not typically build local expertise or benefit local entrepreneurs.

The United States and other rich countries employed these protectionist strategies. In the 1800s, American entrepreneurs traveled to England and France to learn the latest manufacturing techniques and freely appropriated designs for cutting-edge industrial equipment. The U.S. government protected its nascent industries with high tariff walls until they could compete with European manufacturers.

After World War II, Japan effectively froze out foreign goods while building up world-class auto, computer, and electronics industries. Korea later followed Japan's strategy; in recent years, so has China. There, "infant industries" are heavily protected by tariffs, quotas, and other trade barriers. Foreign producers are welcome only if they establish high-tech facilities in which Chinese engineers and production workers can garner the most modern skills.

Development economists like Alice Amsden and Dani Rodrik are increasingly reaching the conclusion that carefully designed industrial policies, combined with protections for infant industries, are most effective in promoting internal development in poor countries. "Free-trade" policies, on the other hand, seem to lock poor countries into producing low-tech goods like garments and agricultural commodities, whose prices tend to decline on world markets due to intense competition with other poor countries.

In the contemporary global economy, however, there are three difficulties with implementing a local development strategy. First, some countries have bargained away their right to protect local firms by entering into free-trade agreements. Second, protectionism means that local consumers are denied the benefits of cheap manufactured goods from abroad, at least in the short run.

Finally, in many parts of the world the floodgates of foreign-made goods have already been opened and, with the middle and upper classes enjoying their computers and cell phones, it may be impossible to build the political consensus to close them. This last concern bears on the prospects for local alternative currencies. Since it is impos-sible to "close off" the local economy, the success of local currencies in bolstering hometown businesses depends on the willingness of local residents to deny themselves the benefits of cheaper nonlocal goods. Like national protectionist polices, local currencies restrict consumer choice.

Ultimately, the success or failure of such ventures rests on the degree of public support for local business. With local currencies, participation is voluntary and attitudes toward local producers often favorable. National protectionist polices, however, entail coerced public participation and generally fail when governments are corrupt and unable to command public support. ❏

Article 10.6

WHATEVER HAPPENED TO DEVELOPMENT?

BY JAWIED NAWABI
January/February 2018

Since World War II, if we count the number of countries that can be considered to have moved from being "Third World" (or "developing") countries to being developed countries, how many make the list? By my count it would be five: South Korea, Taiwan, Singapore, Hong Kong, and Qatar. China is on its way and certain regions of China are already fit to be termed "developed." In Africa, out of the 54 countries, we cannot confidently tally any to have attained developed status (South Africa is termed an "emerging market economy"). Latin America has had several more decades since independence to build an industrial base. (Most of Latin America, not including the Caribbean, nominally gained independence between the 1820s and 1880s, 80-150 years before most of Africa, the Caribbean (outside of Haiti), and most of Asia.) However, the region's industry has not reached globally competitive levels compared to the Asian "Tigers." Latin America and the Caribbean's share of world income grew from about 5.8% in 1985 to about 7.2% in 2010. Meanwhile, East Asia and Pacific's (excluding Japan) grew from 4.1% in 1985 to 11.6% in 2010.

An increasing share of total world income has been going to the developing part of the world. In 1995, about 17.5% of world income went to 83% of the world population (developing countries); by 2010, the figure had increased to about 30.3% (mostly because of East Asia). But that means that about 70% of the income still went to the richest 17% of the world population (the developed world) down from about 83%. This distribution is still starkly uneven: About 3 billion people, out of a world population of 7 billion, live on less than $2.50 a day, and about half of them (1.5 billion) live on less than $1.25, experiencing what international development agencies call "extreme poverty." Out of those living in extreme poverty, 800-900 million (depending on how we count) experience hunger or what the UN terms "chronic undernourishment." Out of these hundreds of millions of hungry people, one million children die yearly from malnourishment. So why have so few countries—out of about 120 newly independent countries that have emerged since World War II—achieved successful development?

The Optimism of Decolonization and Hope of Development

This question poses a challenge to mainstream economics, which has theorized that less-developed countries enjoy certain "advantages of backwardness" (like being able to copy technologies already developed elsewhere). If they simply have high rates of saving and investment in physical capital, within one to two generations they should be able to reach income parity with the developed world. So why haven't they?

After World War II, with the struggles of de-colonization movements, the concept of "growth and development" for Third World countries became an ideological battle ground. The industrialized capitalist countries, engaged in postwar reconstruction, experienced an economic boom that is today considered "the Golden Age of Capitalism." Meanwhile, the Third World countries that had gained political independence remained mired in poverty and destitution. And because of the fear for the spread of the socialist system, the governments of the advanced capitalist West constantly pushed Third World governments, even to the point of using covert and overt physical force, to adopt to the laws of the "free market" and "free trade." The capitalist market system, they assured the Third World leaders, would surely move their countries out of poverty and towards prosperity and progress.

What had to happen, according to probably the most influential and famous modernist theorist, Walt Whitman Rostow, was for so-called backward countries to emulate Western ways. Rostow believed that development was a linear path through five stages along which all countries travel. The five stages were traditional society, the preconditions for take-off, the take-off, the drive to maturity, and the age of high consumption. Of course, the West had traveled these paths and reached the ultimate destination, which is the mature capitalist economic system and high-mass consumption. All that had to happen now was for the West to share its technology, capital, educational systems, forms of government, and most especially their value system, with those traditional countries. Then the latter, too, would be able to achieve the preconditions that would propel them into economic takeoff. This assumes the advantage to the newly independent countries of not having to "reinvent the wheel" of how to develop.

Keynesian policies—especially government management of total demand, with the aim of maintaining economic growth and high employment—were used in the West to help reconstruct their economies after World War II. So the core Western international institutions and mainstream economics field, between the 1950s and 1960s, tolerated or even encouraged a more central role for the state in the economic development for the newly independent countries. However, the modernist theories and the mainstream economic theories did not have a sophisticated understanding

---

What Is the "Third World"?

The term "Third World" refers to a wide array of countries which have wide living standard differences today but that share a common colonial historical background. They are predominately countries of Asia, Africa, and Latin America/Caribbean that have gained formal political independence since World War II and that were part of a non-aligned movement during the Cold War. The non-alignment movement originated with the intention to chart a third path of political and economic development for the newly independent countries, different from either the U.S. model of capitalism or the Soviet model of communism. (Since they were not part of the "Western World" or the "Eastern World" in the previous "two world" division of the globe, the term "Third World" was coined.) In that spirit, they struggled to protect their political sovereignty and formulate approaches to development which would not be dominated by the leading powers. Today, these same countries (about 125 of them) are struggling against the onslaught of neoliberalism. Thus, "Third World" is not just a geographic designation of countries of the Global South nor an economic category but rather a conceptual project of newly independent countries who have struggled to develop their own economic and political systems without being dominated by the big colonial/neo-colonial powers.

of the legacies of colonialism and their role in the Third World countries' impoverished economies and lack of proper developmental institutions. Their equations assumed all states to be the same (just like the dominant model of economic growth assumed that all countries had access to the same level of technology). Thus, they did not differentiate between the newly independent countries and the developed Western states in terms of state effectiveness.

Unfortunately, colonialism had forcefully incorporated the Third World countries as subordinate economies, solely producing primary (raw materials) commodities for advanced capitalist markets. The diversity, scope, and technological sophistication of local industry was suppressed. In the years following independence, these asymmetric trade relations resulted in further disadvantages for Third World countries, in the form of deteriorating "terms of trade" of their primary commodities for the manufactured goods of the developed economies. Raul Prebisch and Hans Singer's empirical studies showed how the prices of the Third World countries' primary products steadily declined relative to those of the manufactured products they purchased from the advanced developed countries—a pattern that continued from the 1950s to the late 1990s.

It takes more and more cocoa, rubber, coffee, tea, bananas, tin or copper to buy an automobile, a truck or a piece of heavy equipment. When an index of the prices of non-fuel primary commodities is divided by an index of the unit value of manufactured goods constructed so their ratio is 100 in 1960, this ratio is found to have fallen from 131 in 1900, and it continues falling to reach 67 in 1986.

By the early 1970s it had become clear that this was leading the developing countries into balance of payments problems: They were importing much more than exporting, which left little capital for investing into the advancement of their economies, kept them dependent on manufactured parts and goods from the developed world, and resulted in a major debt crisis. Data from the World Bank show the continuing falling prices of non-fuel commodities up to 1999.

On the political level, most of the new independent countries—mostly in Africa and Asia, the majority in Latin America and the Caribbean—lacked state institutions which were linked to and dependent on the population for the majority of their revenues. Instead, these countries were saddled with colonial state institutions which were designed by the colonizing powers to extract resources through despotic power. The term "despotic power," as used by sociologist Michael Mann, means having coercive power over society. In states with "despotic power" policing and military capabilities are emphasized, but administrative capacity for complex projects (like building rural roads, electrical power grids, public housing and transportation, public education, etc.) remains limited. Postcolonial states, with only very rare exceptions, did not have built-in professionalized bureaucracies which were accountable to the masses of the people. The postcolonial state was not open to the influence of civil society institutions—like labor unions that advocate for safer work conditions, rural farmers who want local rural roads, or a legal system independent from the coercive powers of the state. Since the postcolonial states were forcefully grafted onto indigenous societies, the governing elites were not challenged to build what Mann terms infrastructural power—power through society instead of over society.

The states which emerged from the post-World War II independence struggles exhibited the characteristics of either predatory or intermediate states. Governing elites were mainly from the landed class, part of the oligarchy which controlled the resources of the country. Alternately, if there emerged a political elite ideologically committed to the country's national development, it was not able to gain sufficient autonomy from the oligarchy to direct an independent course for the country's economy on behalf of the majority of its population. Instead, the states that emerged were dependent upon international sources for financial and military support and not sufficiently embedded with their own populations.

Neoliberalism: From State-Led to Market-Led Development

By the 1970s, the economies of the Third World had not shown significant results in converging towards the economies of the developed countries. Meanwhile, inside the United States and other developed economies, there was a counter-reaction to Keynesian policies, which business and government elites blamed for slow growth and high inflation (known as "stagflation"). This created the intellectual and political climate for a backlash against the role of the state in the economy. The argument was that "government is too big," stifling private entrepreneurship and investment—thus, there was a need to privatize state services and deregulate private industries. The state was viewed as creating opportunities for corruption and distorting the market's efficient allocation of resources. This was the start of so-called "free market" (or "neoliberal") policies, which were pushed on the Third World by international financial institutions like the World Bank and International Monetary Fund. Starting in the 1970s, they started placing policy conditions on loans and other forms of assistance for developing countries much more explicitly than previous decades.

Preventing states from intervening in the economy and unleashing the disciplining pressures of market competition, the argument went, would make the developing countries' economies perform more efficiently and productively. According to neoliberal theory (or the "Washington Consensus") the behavior of individuals in the market, due to self-interested motivations, was also capable of explaining public official malfeasance. As economist Ha-Joon Chang described the Washington Consensus in his article "The Economic Theory of the Developmental State":

Its contention was that the universally valid assumption of self-seeking motives by individuals should also be applied to politics as well as to economics and that it is therefore wrong to believe that the objective of the state, which is ultimately determined by certain individuals, will be commensurate with what is good for society. On this premise, various models of neo-liberal political economy characterized the state as an organization controlled by interest group, politicians or bureaucrats who utilize it for their own self-interest, producing socially undesirable outcomes. The possibility that at least some state may be run and influenced by groups whose objectives are not mere self-enrichment or personal aggrandizement but less personal things such as welfare statism or economic modernization was not even seriously contemplated on the grounds of the alleged self-seeking motives behind all human actions.

For the neoliberals, the solution was to deregulate private industries and privatize industries owned by Third World governments. Both government regulation and government ownership, it was believed, allowed officials to enrich themselves—demanding kick-backs and engaging in other "rent-seeking" behavior. Privatization would force these inefficient and subsidized industries to become disciplined, to adopt reforms and boost efficiency or else be punished by the competitive pressures of the market system. Competition would determine whether any particular industry or firm would swim or sink, depending on whether the proper reforms were made or not, and hence, indirectly benefit society with cheaper and higher-quality goods and services, and higher tax revenues.

The problem with the neoliberal theory of the state is that it does not distinguish between the various types of states that have existed in the capitalist world. Clearly, during the 1970s, the states of the developed world could not be considered to be as corrupt or inept as the newly independent states of the Third World. Neoliberal theory assumes that the minimalist state in an automatic evolution of state institutions in all capitalist societies. However, it is in these very basic bureaucratic functions that many developing nations have a critical shortage. It would have made sense to help the latter states become more institutionally effective, to build their infrastructural power so that they could perform at least the minimal state functions that neoliberalism delegated to the state. Instead, the World Bank/IMF complex, with their neoliberal policies, further weakened the already institutionally limited developmental aspects of these states, while helping to strengthen some of their policing powers. The developing countries were nudged, cajoled, even strong-armed to abandon the state-led model of development and adopt the market-led development model.

Listing the various roles of the state and the state's degree of involvement in the economy, moving from the most basic functions to the most extensive interventions:

- Legal protection of private property, contract enforcement, and regulation
- Defense of the state's sovereignty and territorial integrity (essentially policing the workers and the population at large)
- Provision of public goods and services (schools, infrastructure, health, clean water, sanitation, rural and urban services)
- Counter-cyclical policies (monetary and fiscal) due to the instability of the market system
- Welfare services: unemployment, retirement, poverty programs
- Coordination of development projects (indicative planning thru public-private cooperation)

The neoliberal advice to governments was and is basically to focus on functions 1-2, while delegating functions 3-6 as much as possible to a private sector exposed to the disciplinary pressures of competitive markets. The prediction was that private firms would do a much better job than the state in providing affordable private schools, clean water, health clinics, infrastructure like roads and bridges (with tolls), and private financial services for everyone from small farmers in the villages to large firms in the cities.

One would assume that, if the World Bank/IMF complex was advising the developing countries to downsize the state role in the economy, the total government expenditure (federal, state, and local) as the share of the economy would shrink in the advanced capitalist economies as well. In fact, as political economist Atilio Boron argues, the developed countries do not practice what they preach to the developing world. Between 1970 and 1995, Boron shows, the core capitalist countries' average government expenditures grew from about 35% to 49%). Furthermore, in the 1990s "the proportion of public employees over the total population was 7.2% in the United States, 8.3% in Germany, 8.5% in England, 9.7% in France." Comparatively, in Latin America, public employees represented 3.5% of the population in Brazil and 2.8% in Chile and Argentina. Despite these numbers, Boron observes, the "pundits at the World Bank or the IMF have successfully insisted that Latin American states are 'too big' and should be downsized."

Even when we look at the financial press, we don't find much evidence that the economies with the least state involvement are the best performing economies for businesses to invest in. On the contrary, *Forbes* magazine, today one of the foremost publications in defense of the "free market" and "free enterprise," in 2016 ranked Sweden number one on its list of the top countries in which to do business. If we scroll down the same list, the top ten countries include Denmark, Holland, Finland, Norway, Ireland, England, and Canada. On average, their states account for 30-45% of GDP. Ironically, the very countries that are bastions of so-called welfare states (derogatorily called "nanny states") are considered by the pro-capitalist press to be the best places for business investors.

In almost all developing countries (in Latin America and the Caribbean, Africa, the Middle East, and South East Asia) the state contribution to GDP is much lower. For example, Mexico's is about 15% and Chile's is a little more than 20%. They are examples of the developing countries which arguably have insufficient government involvement as a percentage of their economies GDPs. Furthermore, these states rely overwhelmingly on indirect taxation like sales taxes and value added taxes (VAT), so their tax structures tend to be regressive (the poor and middle-class pay more). In contrast, the developed countries tend to rely on income and property taxes (direct taxes), and so have more progressive taxation (the higher income classes pay more).

While neoliberalism was able to push the developing world away from state-led development toward more market-oriented policies, these latter policies have not shown positive results either. Economists Mark Weisbrot and Rebecca Ray have surveyed the scorecard on development between 1960 and 2010: The developing countries had higher growth rates during the years of government-led development, from 1960 to 1980, averaging about 2.5% per year, compared to 1.1% between 1980 and 2000—the high years of neoliberal policy. Latin America's average annual real GDP per capita growth rate in the era of "too big" government, 1960-1980, was 3.3%; during the height of the neoliberal era, 1980-2000, just 0.3%.

Bringing the State Back into Economic Development

During the 1980s, while the majority of the developing world (and even the developed world) was experiencing declining growth rates, the East Asian countries were experiencing high growth. The institutions of the World Bank/IMF complex attempted to credit the East Asian economies' high growth rates to their adoptions of market policies. Scholars such as Chalmers Johnson, Alice Amsden, Robert Wade, Peter Evans, and others (together, I term them the Role of the State in Economic Development, or RSED, school) critically responded to the neoliberal assumptions of efficient markets and government malfeasance as too simplistic and without sufficient historical depth. They were able to empirically establish that state intervention in rapidly industrializing countries of East Asia was, "characterized by market-reinforcing behavior, understood in the sense of supporting profitability for private investors .... The state versus market mind-set thus is simply not very helpful for understanding how the interaction of states and markets has served to produce a range of economic outcomes." So, instead of blanket generalizations—whether they come from the left, which views the state as nothing more than the executive committee of the bourgeoisie, or from the right, which argues that state intervention necessarily hinders economic growth and development—the real question is what kind of administrative structure do states need in order to enable growth and development within a market economy?

To the RSED school, this question required detailed study of each state. Why did some states perform as developmental states—guiding their economies to high living standards—while other states became predatory and impoverished their people? The fundamental characteristics of a developmental state are a determined elite which seeks their country's rapid development; relative autonomy of the state from powerful landed and industrial elites; a rational bureaucracy which is competent, powerful, and insulated from political swings; a somewhat authoritarian character which ensures that competing interests are subordinated to states' developmental goals of industrialization; and the capacity to manage effectively the economic sector through a broad range of policies. (The most important economic policies include tariffs, financial credit controls, technological promotion, human capital training, and competency in selecting which market signals to deliberately distort. Yes, states can promote development by deliberately altering market signals and incentives, for example, by using subsidies to help infant industries become competitive in the international market. The developmental state, in short, is the highest authority committed to economic development through growth, productivity, and competitiveness.

The relationship between the state and market need not be a zero-sum relationship, but rather can be one of synergy. The argument of the RSED school was that market society could not be what it is without the role of the state. The active role of the state has been clear at least as far back as economic historian Karl Polanyi's masterpiece, *The Great Transformation: The Political and Economic Origins of Our Time* (1944). In the words of economist and Noble laureate Joseph Stilitz, Polanyi's analysis "exposes the myth of the free market: there never was a truly free, self-regulating market system. In their transformations, the governments of today's industrialized countries took an active role, not only in protecting their industries through tariffs, but also in promoting new technologies."

Theories of development have two axes around which they revolve: state-led development versus market-led development. Economic theories can be distinguished conceptually by the centrality of the state's role in "governing the market." Some theories envision a limited and passive role for the state because they view the market as an efficient mechanism for allocating resources to meet society's developmental needs. Government intervention, in this view, distorts prices and throws the market system into disequilibrium. In contrast, developmental economists like Ragnar Nurske, Paul Rosentein-Rodan, Albert Hirschman, Gunnar Myrdal, and Arthur Lewis—whose influence within academia and international institutions was at its height from the 1940s to late 1960s—viewed the state the one institution that could lead the "big-push" out of the poverty traps that ensnared the Third World. Unfortunately, by the 1970s, neoliberal/neoclassical economists rejected the theories of state-led development economists and excluded them from the policy calculations of the World Bank/IMF complex as well as the United Nations Development Program (UNDP). After about twenty years of neoliberal dominance in academia and international institutions (from 1980 to 2000), the RSED school and their state-led theories of development made a comeback. They undermined the intellectual hegemony of the neoliberal paradigm, demonstrating in their own original works the administrative and regulatory importance of the developmental state. They showed that economic development requires a state that is effective in managing the monetary system, protecting private property laws, setting taxes, funding public goods such as infrastructure and education, coordinating between industries, and promoting long-term investment—that is, in all six functions of the state listed above.

Return to the 1950s Spirit of Development

If we are serious about solving the problem of development, we must bring back mass development projects through the developmental state. In the last 30 or 40 years, parallel to the downsizing of the states in the Third World, there has been a shift towards micro-oriented development projects. Such projects give non-governmental organizations (NGOs) and other charity aid organizations a central role, supported by the international institutions as well as mainstream economic theory. We have to make the case to returning international institutions to developmental policies—to what political scientist Eric Helleiner calls the "Forgotten Legacy of Bretton Woods"—infant industry tariffs protections, commodity price stabilization, international debt restructuring, short-term capital movement restrictions, and long-term development lending. In the spirit of the 1950s and 1960s, we must bring back the socially transforming aims of development policy—which include building the institutional capacity of states to collect taxes on a progressive basis, redistributing wealth through policies like radical land reforms, etc. Last but not least, the Third World needs to revive the planning and execution of their own regionally based and environmentally sustainable industrial policies. For these projects to be realized, we need to build the developmental capacity of the Third World states. ❑

Sources: Nina Bandelj and Elizabeth Sowers, *Economy and State: A Sociological Perspective* (Polity Press, 2010); Nancy Birdsall, Augusto De La Torre, and Rachel Menezes, *Fair Growth: Economic Policies for Latin America's Poor and Middle-Income Majority* (Center for Global Development and Inter-American Dialogue, 2008); A. Atilio Boron, "Latin American Thinking on the State and Development: From Statelessness to Statelessness," in Sam Moyo and Paris Yeros (eds), *Reclaiming the Nation: The Return of the National Question in Africa, Asia and Latin America* (Pluto Press, 2011); Fred Block, "The Roles of the State in the Economy," in Neil J. Smelser and Richard Swedberg ; Ana Corbacho, Vicente Fretes Cibils, and Eduardo Lora (eds.), *More Than Revenue: Taxation as a Developmental Tool* (Palgrave Macmillan, 2013); Ha-Joon Chang, "The Economic Theory of the Developmental State," in Meredith Woo-Cumings (ed.), *The Developmental State* (Cornell University Press, 1999); James Cypher, *The Process of Economic Development* (Routledge, 2014); Robert Chernomas and Ian Hudson, *Economics in the Twenty-First Century: A Critical Perspective* (University of Toronto Press, 2016); Peter Evans, *Embedded Autonomy: States & Industrial Transformation* (Princeton University Press, 1995); Stephan Haggard, *Pathways From the Periphery: The Politics of Growth in the Newly Industrializing Countries* (Cornell University Press, 1990); Eric Helleiner, "International Policy Coordination for Development: The Forgotten Legacy of Bretton Woods" United Nations Conference on Trade and Development (UNCTAD Discussion Papers, No. 221), May 2015; Chalmers Johnson, *MITI and The Japanese Miracle: The Growth of Industrial Policy, 1925-1975* (Stanford University Press, 1982); Atul Kohli, *State-Directed Development: Political Power and Industrialization in the Global Periphery* (Cambridge University Press, 2004); Jonathan Krieckahaus, *Dictating Development: How Europe Shaped the Global Periphery* (University of Pittsburgh Press, 2006); Matthew Lange and Dietrich Rueschemeyer, "States and Development," in Lange, Matthew and Dietrich Rueschemeyer, *States and Development: Historical Antecedents of Stagnation and Advance* (Palgrave, Macmillan, 2005); Adrian Leftwich, *States of Development: On the Primacy of Politics in Development* (Polity Press, 2000); Michael Mann, *The Sources of Social Power: The Rise of Classes and Nation States, 1760-1914* (Vol.2) (Cambridge University Press, 1993); S.V.R. Nasr, "European Colonialism and The Emergence of Modern Muslim States," in John L. Esposito (ed.), *The Oxford History of Islam* (Oxford University Press, 1999); Ziya Onis, "The Logic of the Developmental State," *Comparative Politics*, Vol. 24, No. 1 (pp. 109-126), Oct. 1991; James Petras, "Imperialism and NGOs in Latin America," *Monthly Review*, Vol. 49, Issue 7, December 1997; Prashant Prakash, "Property Taxes Across G20 Countries: Can India Get It Right?" Oxfam India Working Papers, January 2013; Vijay Prashad, *The Darker Nations: A People's History of the Third World* (New Press, 2007); Louis Putterman, *Dollars and Change: Economics in Context* (Yale University Press, 2001); Revenue Statistics 2016: Tax Revenue Trends in OECD (oecd.org); Joseph Stiglitz, "Foreword," in Karl Polanyi, *The Great Transformation: The Political and Economic Origins of Our Time* (Beacon Press, 2001); Bob Sutcliffe, *100 Ways of Seeing an Unequal World* (Zed Books, 2001); David Waldner, *State Building and Late Development* (Cornell University Press, 1999); Mark Weisbrot and Rebecca Ray, "The Scorecard on Development, 1960-2010: Closing the Gap?" United Nations Department of Economic and Social Affairs (UN DESA Working Paper No. 106), June 2011.

Chapter 11

POLICY SPOTLIGHT: DEINDUSTRIALIZATION

INTRODUCTION

Finally we turn to the hot topic of job losses in manufacturing. The Trump Administration is only the most recent manifestation of anxiety and anger about the loss of jobs to global trade shifts, most often in the form of trade deals like NAFTA or the Trans-Pacific Partnership. But misunderstandings of trade abound, and careful thinking is needed to make sense of the record. The authors in this chapter address whether automation is to blame for job loss, and examine the case that trade deficits are responsible instead. A two-part case study of deindustrialization in New Hampshire drills down to look at the role that financialization, monetary policy, and asset bubbles have played in creating job losses.

Thomas Palley offers a concise and useful metaphor for the effects of globalization and outsourcing on productive industry in the United States. "The Globalization Clock" (Article 11.1) describes how globalization and outsourcing pick off domestic industries one by one, based on the relative exportability of the goods or services and the skill level of the workers. This metaphor also illustrates why, at any given period of time, there has not been a majority consensus against outsourcing: The majority of consumers benefit through lower prices from the outsourced industry; only those acutely affected through the loss of their jobs are against it. But as the clock ticks forward, more and more industries at higher and higher levels of skill become outsourced.

Dean Baker in "Trade Denialism Continues" (Article 11.2) discusses trade deficits, using data on U.S. industrial employment to find flaws in the common argument that "automation" is responsible for manufacturing job losses. Patterns in job levels relative to industrial output suggest that this common pro-trade argument can't be sustained in light of the data. The tendency of the national news media to cover trade in the most shallow and often misleading way also comes up.

Then economist Marie Duggan takes the spotlight to a pair of detailed case studies, to show that international competition is far from the only contributor to major shifts like the decline of U.S. industry. In Article 11.3, focusing on machine-tool manufacturers in the Connecticut River Valley, Duggan explains the role of shifting economic policies regarding interest rates and exchange rates in creating a background hostile to industry in the 1980s. Then in Article 11.4, Duggan examines the huge loss of manufacturing jobs in the 2000s. Focusing on another New Hampshire firm producing miniature ball bearings, she shows how the financial chicanery of Wall Street and its warped incentives bear on the trajectory of small New England manufacturing in the globalized economy.

Discussion Questions

1. (Article 11.1) Describe the different "times" on Palley's "globalization clock." What time is it in the United States today according to this clock?

2. (Article 11.2) Describe the common argument that automation is responsible for the decline of manufacturing jobs, rather than trade deals.

3. (Article 11.2) How does Baker use employment data to show that shifts in the trade balance, rather than automation, are responsible for the decline in U.S. manufacturing employment?

4. (Article 11.3) Duggan's first article suggests that rather than foreign competition, "financialization" was the driving force. What are some of the examples Duggan gives of this process?

5. (Article 11.3) Duggan also suggests that economic policy may have played a role in the decline of U.S. industry. Describe this argument, including the role of interest rates and exchange rates.

6. (Article 11.4) Describe how the changes in the stock market of the 1980s and 1990s altered small manufacturers' priorities regarding investment in industrial equipment.

7. (Article 11.4) Explain the concept of a stock buyback. How does a buyback program affect the value of a company's stock? How does it affect its investments in capital? How might this ultimately affect jobs?

8. (Articles 11.1, 11.2, 11.3, and 11.4) This chapter's articles on the decline of U.S. manufacturing employment focus on different reasons—Baker and Palley on the drawbacks of global trade, Duggan on the rise of automation and evaluating companies based on stock performance instead of community importance or even profitability. Are these views irreconcilable? What market characteristics make one reason or another more or less likely?

Article 11.1

THE GLOBALIZATION CLOCK
Why corporations are winning and workers are losing.

BY THOMAS PALLEY
May/June 2006

Political economy has historically been constructed around the divide between capital and labor, with firms and workers at odds over the division of the economic pie. Within this construct, labor is usually represented as a monolithic interest, yet the reality is that labor has always suffered from internal divisions—by race, by occupational status, and along many other fault lines. Neoliberal globalization has in many ways sharpened these divisions, which helps to explain why corporations have been winning and workers losing.

One of these fault lines divides workers from themselves: since workers are also consumers, they face a divide between the desire for higher wages and the desire for lower prices. Historically, this identity split has been exploited to divide union from nonunion workers, with anti-labor advocates accusing union workers of causing higher prices. Today, globalization is amplifying the divide between people's interests as workers and their interests as consumers through its promise of ever-lower prices.

Consider the debate over Wal-Mart's low-road labor policies. While Wal-Mart's low wages and skimpy benefits have recently faced scrutiny, even some liberal commentators argue that Wal-Mart is actually good for low-wage workers because they gain more as consumers from its "low, low prices" than they lose as workers from its low wages. But this static, snapshot analysis fails to capture the full impact of globalization, past and future.

Globalization affects the economy unevenly, hitting some sectors first and others later. The process can be understood in terms of the hands of a clock. At one o'clock is the apparel sector; at two o'clock the textile sector; at three the steel sector; at six the auto sector. Workers in the apparel sector are the first to have their jobs shifted to lower-wage venues; at the same time, though, all other workers get price reductions. Next, the process picks off textile sector workers at two o'clock. Meanwhile, workers from three o'clock onward get price cuts, as do the apparel workers at one o'clock. Each time the hands of the clock move, the workers taking the hit are isolated. In this fashion globalization moves around the clock, with labor perennially divided.

Manufacturing was first to experience this process, but technological innovations associated with the Internet are putting service and knowledge workers in the firing line as well. Online business models are making even retail workers vulnerable—consider Amazon.com, for example, which has opened a customer support center and two technology development centers in India. Public sector wages are also in play, at least indirectly, since falling wages mean falling tax revenues. The problem is that each time the hands on the globalization clock move forward, workers are divided: the majority is made slightly better off while the few are made much worse off.

Globalization also alters the historical divisions within capital, creating a new split between bigger internationalized firms and smaller firms that remain nationally centered. This division has been brought into sharp focus with the debate over the trade deficit and the overvalued dollar. In previous decades, manufacturing as a whole opposed running trade deficits and maintaining an overvalued dollar because of the adverse impact of increased imports. The one major business sector with a different view was retailing, which benefited from cheap imports.

However, the spread of multinational production and outsourcing has divided manufacturing in wealthy countries into two camps. In one camp are larger multinational corporations that have gone global and benefit from cheap imports; in the other are smaller businesses that remain nationally centered in terms of sales, production and input sourcing. Multinational corporations tend to support an overvalued dollar since this makes imports produced in their foreign factories cheaper. Conversely, domestic manufacturers are hurt by an overvalued dollar, which advantages import competition.

This division opens the possibility of a new alliance between labor and those manufacturers and businesses that remain nationally based—potentially a potent one, since there are approximately seven million enterprises with sales of less than $10 million in the United States, versus only 200,000 with sales greater than $10 million. However, such an alliance will always be unstable as the inherent labor-capital conflict over income distribution can always reassert itself. Indeed, this pattern is already evident in the internal politics of the National Association of Manufacturers, whose members have been significantly divided regarding the overvalued dollar. As one way to address this division, the group is promoting a domestic "competitiveness" agenda aimed at weakening regulation, reducing corporate legal liability, and lowering employee benefit costs—an agenda designed to appeal to both camps, but at the expense of workers.

Solidarity has always been key to political and economic advance by working families, and it is key to mastering the politics of globalization. Developing a coherent story about the economics of neoliberal globalization around which working families can coalesce is a key ingredient for solidarity. So too is understanding how globalization divides labor. These narratives and analyses can help counter deep cultural proclivities to individualism, as well as other historic divides such as racism. However, as if this were not difficult enough, globalization creates additional challenges. National political solutions that worked in the past are not adequate to the task of controlling international competition. That means the solidarity bar is further raised, calling for international solidarity that supports new forms of international economic regulation. ❏

Article 11.2

TRADE DENIALISM CONTINUES
Trade really did kill manufacturing jobs.

BY DEAN BAKER
March 2017; Center for Economic and Policy Research

There have been a flood of opinion pieces and news stories recently wrongly telling people that it was not trade that led to the loss of manufacturing jobs in recent years, but rather automation. This would mean that all of those people who are worried about trade deficits costing jobs are simply being silly. The promulgators of the automation story want everyone to stop talking about trade and instead focus on education, technology or whatever other item they can throw out as a distraction.

This "automation rather than trade" story is the equivalent of global warming denialism for the well-educated. And its proponents deserve at least as much contempt as global warming deniers.

The basic story on automation, trade, and jobs is fairly straightforward. "Automation" is also known as "productivity growth," and it is not new. We have been seeing gains in productivity in manufacturing ever since we started manufacturing things.

Productivity gains mean that we can produce more output with the same amount of work. Before the trade deficit exploded in the last decade, increases in productivity were largely offset by increases in output, making it so the total jobs in manufacturing did not change much.

Imagine that productivity increased by 20% over the course of a decade, roughly its average rate of growth. If manufacturing output also increases by 20%, then we have the same number of jobs at the end of the decade as at the beginning. This is pretty much what happened before the trade deficit exploded.

This is easy to see in the data. In December of 1970 the US had 17.3 million manufacturing jobs. Thirty years later, in December of 2000, it had 17.2 million manufacturing jobs. We had enormous growth in manufacturing productivity over this period, yet we had very little change in total employment.

To be clear, manufacturing did decline as a share of total employment. Total employment nearly doubled from 1970 to 2000, which means that the share of manufacturing employment in total employment fell by almost half. People were increasingly spending their money on services rather than manufactured goods.

However what we saw in the years after 2000 was qualitatively different. The number of manufacturing jobs fell by 3.4 million, more than 20%, between December 2000 and December of 2007. Note that this is before the collapse of the housing bubbled caused the recession. Manufacturing employment dropped by an additional 2.3 million in the recession, although it has since regained roughly half of these jobs.

The extraordinary plunge in manufacturing jobs in the years 2000 to 2007 was due to the explosion of the trade deficit, which peaked at just under 6% of GDP

($1.2 trillion in today's economy) in 2005 and 2006. This was first and foremost due to the growth of imports from China during these years, although we ran large trade deficits with other countries as well.

There really is very little ambiguity in this story. Does anyone believe that if we had balanced trade it wouldn't mean more manufacturing jobs? Do they think we could produce another $1.2 trillion in manufacturing output without employing any workers?

It is incredible how acceptable it is for our elites to lie about trade rather than deal with the issue candidly. The most blatant example of this dishonesty is a December, 2007 *Washington Post* editorial that praised NAFTA and, incidentally, criticized the Democratic presidential candidate for calling for renegotiating the trade deal.

The editorial absurdly asserted: "Mexico's gross domestic product, now more than $875 billion, has more than quadrupled since 1987."

For GDP to quadruple over the course of two decades, it would have to sustain a 7% average annual rate of growth. China has managed to do this and almost no one else, certainly not Mexico. According to the IMF, Mexico's GDP grew by 83% over this period.

While it is striking that the *Washington Post*'s editorial board would have been so ill-informed as to make such a huge mistake in their original editorial, the really incredible part of the story is that they still have not corrected the online version almost a decade later. After all, a reader could stumble on the GDP quadrupling claim and think that it is actually true.

This level of dishonesty separates trade out from most other areas of public debate. There can be grounds for honest people to differ on many issues, but there is less of a basis for asserting Mexico's GDP quadrupled during this period than there is for denying global warming. It is unfortunate that the proponents of recent trade deals feel they have to be this dishonest to push their agenda. ❑

Sources: "Trade Distortions," Washington Post, December 3, 2007 (washingtonpost.com); International Monetary Fund, World Economic Outlook Database (imf.org).

Article 11.3

MONETARY POLICY, FINANCIALIZATION, AND THE LOSS OF U.S. MANUFACTURING JOBS

Part One of a Series on Deindustrialization in the Granite State

BY MARIE DUGGAN
November/December 2017

The central room is 65,000 square feet with a high ceiling. This room is noisy, with large machines emitting loud hums and whirrs. The machinists are dwarfed within the canyons between the rows of equipment. Many of the machines have plastic housings, so that each looks like a giant photocopier. There is a window on the side of each one. Inside, the drilling/lathing/milling operation is performed on the metal. However, someone peering in through the window doesn't actually see a metal tool hitting the material. The surprising sight of water gushing furiously meets the eye. The tools themselves operate at tremendously high speeds (2,000 inches per minute, or 20,000-50,000 rpm). The water pushes metal debris away, as human hands or air flow did on the previous generation of machines. But water also acts as a coolant to put out sparks and to counteract the tremendous heat created by the friction of metal tool on metal part.

This scene is not from Germany or South Korea, but rather from the southwest corner of New Hampshire, only 15 miles from the borders with Massachusetts and Vermont. The high-tech machine shop described was Knappe and Koester—in 2011, before it was sold to GS Precision, which has since expanded the operation. Manufacturing industry in Keene specializes in the production of capital-goods— products used as parts or machines at other businesses in other production processes: ball bearings, diamond turning machines, lens producers, lubricants for machinery, and inks and date-stamp printers for food and pharmaceutical plants around the globe. These factories are so clean and relatively small (employing about a hundred people) that newcomers to New Hampshire, like myself, tend to notice the cows at the dairy farms and the fresh ice cream stands, not the manufacturing plants tucked behind real estate offices or next to hardware stores.

I contacted some local managing owners to ask if my undergraduates could tour the plants. The industrialists were excited that someone at "the college" showed interest in what they did. We saw a high-tech machine shop unloading the latest computerized five-axis machines from Japan in 2011. We watched young machinists assemble diamond turning machines by hand, and saw a demonstration of how the machines drill plastic molds for producing touchscreens in factories around the globe.

Keene lies in the Connecticut River Valley, which in the mid-19th century witnessed the birth of the machines that make replaceable metal parts. Machinists from Hartford, Conn., to Lebanon, N.H., drove up global productivity during the industrial revolution, and since that time the machinists' skills had been passed down from father to son (and occasionally to daughter). This chain was damaged with the layoffs and plant closings between 1980 and 1990. In those years, few fathers told their eighteen-year-old children to become machinists. As a result, there is now a shortage of computer-savvy machinists, so local firms donated funds to build a computerized machine tools laboratory at Keene State and have offered a $1,000 scholarship to train at the local community college, which shares the lab.

The economic forces impacting the machining jobs that continue to sustain local families are hard to see using standard economic datasets. Most databases provide information only on publicly held firms—those that issue shares that are traded on the stock exchange. Ownership transitions between 1998 and 2012 shifted some of the local plants into the hands of large, publicly held corporations. Yet some of the local manufacturing firms, including some of the most dynamic in the United States, remain smaller in scale and independently owned. My students and I began conducting oral histories of owners and workers in order to learn more about the private firms that do not appear in the data.

The Elephant in the Room

In November 2016, Trump started to pick up a surprising amount of support in many parts of the nation. As it turned out, even though Clinton won the popular vote, 2,026 counties went for Trump, while 447 went for Clinton. As I began to pull together my research about deindustrialization in my new hometown, the Trump phenomenon was getting hard to ignore. It suddenly dawned on me: *Keene, N.H., wasn't the only place to have experienced an attack on its export-competitive industrial base between 2000 and 2012. Was it all of New Hampshire? Or was it just about every-where but San Francisco, Boston, and New York City?*

The crushing loss of manufacturing jobs between 1980 and 1985 is a vivid memory for me, because I graduated from California's Berkeley High School in 1981, where 90% of my peers were not going on to four-year college. When I arrived at Tufts University in Medford, Mass., I saw storefronts boarded up and watched people in line at the convenience store pay with food stamps. The baleful glares at us privileged college students only got worse as the unemployment rate reached 10.9% in November 1982. When I moved to Brooklyn in 1990, I often drove by the empty industrial buildings along the waterfront.

So, when I saw the graph in Figure 1 (see next page) and learned that the manufacturing job loss of 2001–2009 was triple that of 1979–1985, my jaw dropped. Why didn't I know this? I read the *New York Times*, the *New Yorker*, the *Financial Times*. I hang out with heterodox economists, for goodness sake! I now suspect that industry left our intellectual centers between 1979 and 1985—out of sight, and so out of mind—but remained a powerhouse in so-called "rural" areas until 2001, only to suddenly and precipitously decline. I realized how lucky I was to be living in a place that is like a good bit of the United States.

Many economists have been focusing on macroeconomics—the ups and downs of the entire national economy, measured in "aggregate" data—for the past twenty-five years. The instability of the financial sector and rising income inequality could both be analyzed through economy-wide data, so we all rightly got our heads in that game by 2007. If one takes manufacturing jobs as a percentage of total employment, there has been a continuous decline since the late 1960s, and

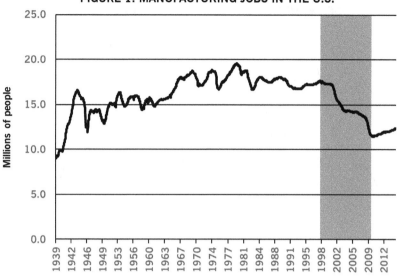

FIGURE 1. MANUFACTURING JOBS IN THE U.S.

Source: Federal Reserve Bank of St. Louis (Fred II)

one would therefore see little new between 2001 and 2009. Some people point to China's accession to the WTO in 2001 as the cause of the U.S. decline in manufacturing. However, my own research inside firms suggests that competition from China is not the main story.

Keene's capital goods producers do not compete with producers in low-wage nations, but rather with firms in Europe and Japan, and unit labor costs have generally been higher in those places than in the United States since 1990. The decline in U.S. jobs has less to do with external forces than Americans seem to think, and more to do with the policies taken (or not taken) inside the United States itself. If a firm was going to collapse in the face of cheap labor overseas, it would have happened in 1982 (as in shoes and textiles). The manufacturers who survived until 2000 were made of sterner stuff. Monetary policy that promoted financial bubbles turns out to be another ingredient in the decline of manufacturing jobs between 1978 and 2012.

The Connecticut River Valley Machine Tool Sector, 1980–90

Hank Frechette purchased Kingsbury Machine Tool from his father-in-law, E.J. Kingsbury, in 1963. That year, Frechette hired the entire graduating class of Wentworth Tech in Boston. "I had never heard of Keene," relates Donegan, an electrical engineer in that class. But it would become his home and his life for the next forty-odd years. Machinists from Vermont and New Hampshire considered Kingsbury to be one of the most exciting places to work in New England. Their work ethic and skills, plus the innovations of the young electrical and mechanical engineers and the management by Frechette and Charlie Hanrahan—a co-owner who was also a member of the founding family—grew the company threefold between 1963 and 1976, so that it employed around 1,000 people. Many machinists commented that, in those days,

FIGURE 2. PROFITS IN MACHINE TOOL SECTOR
OF THE UNITED STATES IN MILLIONS OF DOLLARS

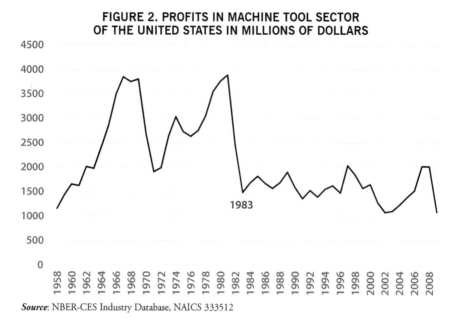

Source: NBER-CES Industry Database, NAICS 333512

Kingsbury was like a family. Hanrahan worked hard to keep it that way. He had a notebook in which he wrote down every man's name and the names of his wife and children, with their ages. (Yes, all the workers at Kingsbury—indeed, all the machinists in Keene—were men. That is no longer the case.) He trained new supervisors to make similar efforts to know each member of the shop personally. Once a man got a job at Kingsbury, he was set for life—until 1984.

Frechette made a name for himself nationally and became a leader in the National Association of Manufacturers. There he met another rising executive, Jim Koontz, who was based in Detroit. When Frechette died suddenly in 1976, his astute widow Sally Kingsbury asked Koontz to come to Keene and take the helm of the business. Koontz's wife had doubts about leaving the community of executives in Ann Arbor for remote Keene, N.H., but the couple made the move with their four children. Between 1978 and 1982, Kingsbury was employing three shifts of workers to keep up with continuous orders as Detroit auto companies tried to retool to compete with small cars from Japan. Koontz became CEO in 1983.

In 1984, Kingsbury had its first layoff: over 200 people. This was a shock to the community, and many blamed Koontz as an outsider with no local ties—Hanrahan, by contrast, had gone to grade school with many of the men. But this wasn't just a personality issue. There were larger economic forces at work. In 2012, Jim Koontz related to me that it felt in 1983 as if the company had gone off a cliff, one minute producing three shifts a day with paychecks chock full of overtime and bonuses—to suddenly a period of six months with no orders. Figure 2 shows that machine tool industry profits for the nation as a whole dropped in 1983 from nearly $4 billion to $1.5 billion. What was causing that massive decline in industry-wide profits in U.S. machine tools? One factor was a dramatic technological shift from mass production to flexible production. Jim Koontz explained it:

Kingsbury made machines that could produce one million to two million parts for the Big Three auto manufacturers….At one point, those three automakers produced all the autos in the world. By 1980, there were 30 companies producing for the world, but by now [2012], there are 300 auto companies worldwide. Each automobile has 30,000 parts, and 80% of them today are produced by suppliers, so there must be tens of thousands of suppliers globally. Because of this, the volumes that automakers needed their machines to produce went down from one million to 100,000. This changed the style of the technology that the manufacturers needed.

Few businesses today need a machine that can produce millions of identical parts, like Kingsbury produced back in the 1970s. Instead, they need machines that can be reprogrammed to produce different parts. The name for such machines is "CNC"—computer numerical control, which means that the computerized machines are run by software. The machinist enters the dimensions of the parts to be produced, and then listens as the machine chooses the tools and goes about making the parts. Kingsbury had purchased such a machine by 1987. Machinist Phil Hilliker thought it was the finest piece of equipment he had ever worked with. The gossip among owners of plants in and around Keene is that Koontz never adopted CNC technology, and this is why it failed to make profits after 1983. As one financial wizard told me, the reason U.S. machine tool makers did not survive until the 21st century is that they were "fat, lazy, and stupid." But this judgement is far too hasty.

For one thing, Kingsbury acquired the machine tool firm Hillyer, which did make CNC machines. Secondly, the CNC machine Hilliker used was made by Jones and Lamson. J&L was a machine tool maker in Springfield, Vt., a town about 15 miles from Keene. The company filed for bankruptcy in 1986, so the "can't adapt" argument had been applied to them, too. But J&L had produced a computerized lathe by 1986, and Hilliker said he was using it by 1987, and it was the finest machine he had ever worked with. Thirdly, the machine shop next door to J&L in Springfield, Bryant Grinding, was in decline by 1990. Yet at a recent lecture a computer scientist told me he had applied for a job as a computer programmer at Bryant in 1981, and they were using what he considered a "nifty" program for machine tools. These are three hints that the Connecticut River Valley machine tool sector was adapting.

Financial changes were a second factor exacerbating the pressure inherent in a period of technological change and low profits. It was not until 1983 that Jim Koontz became managing owner of the company. He did so by means of an internal leveraged buyout (LBO). Koontz did not have the personal wealth necessary to purchase the company. However, Sally Kingsbury and the rest of the board felt that he had demonstrated the managerial skill in 1978–1982 to take over, and they wanted the manager of the firm to have an ownership stake to tie him to the community. In an LBO, a consortium of banks puts the money up to purchase the company. They put the money into a fund that purchases the company. The profits that the firm makes are then earmarked to pay off the banks. Once the bank loan has been paid off, the fund is owned by management. In this case, Koontz was not the only one "in on" the fund. Some of the engineers wound up being part-owners of the fund, as did members of the Kingsbury family.

The use of an "inside LBO" to transfer ownership of Kingsbury from one generation/owner to the next was not new. Frechette had done the same thing when he purchased Kingsbury from his father-in-law. Yet it seems that something went wrong with this second LBO. LBOs were more common by the 1980s, and it is likely that the leverage was higher—meaning a smaller down payment, and a larger amount lent. Everyone who was in on the LBO considers Koontz to have been an outstanding executive who did his best in difficult times. The workers on the shop floor and the supervisors who were not part of the LBO, however, consider him to have been their worst nightmare.

As an educated guess, I would say there were two problems: First, paying off an LBO with profits from the firm would be difficult when the profits of the entire industry suddenly fell by 60%. Second, the stock market rose continuously from 1987 to 1999. Between 1969 and 1982, an investor in the stock market would not have made capital gains, but only dividends. Those ambitious for more dramatic returns put their money into physical plant and talented labor, and made profits by expanding market share through quality products. After 1982, industrial profits were hard to come by, while Federal Reserve chairman Alan Greenspan kept interest rates relatively low between 1987 to 1999, which made capital gains in the stock market the new normal. At Kingsbury, managers "in on" the fund initially used to pay off the LBO profits out of production, and invested them into the rising stock market where they must have reaped consistent capital gains—while workers on the shop floor lost their bonuses because the profits made from producing and selling machine tools were meager. At the time, gains made in shares of other companies on the stock market may not have seemed to come at the expense of the workers inside Kingsbury. But a wedge had emerged between the interests of owners and the workers on the shop floor. Supervisor Kenny Johnson described "a change in how [Koontz] handles his people."

> It was his way and no other way. There was a period of time where he managed by fear, in the sense that if people didn't go along with his idea he would put fear into them and he wanted to make them into a "yes" person.… For instance, when the union was being introduced at Kingsbury's…he thought I was being too easy on some of my employees, but my philosophy hasn't changed…you treat people how you like to be treated. I'm not a "yes" person. So I told him how I felt.…He said I had too much compassion for my employees.…He almost fired me on the spot.

Putting his job on the line to stand up for the employees in the late 1980s was a turning point in Johnson's life, a moment that took great courage and won him the lasting respect of the workers. He had been trained by Hanrahan to know and care for his employees and their families. Johnson was not a fan of unions, arguing that "you don't need a union if you treat your people right." However, Koontz was not, in Johnson's opinion, treating the shop floor right. Koontz hired Jeff Toner as vice president, who was viewed as a hatchet man to fire pro-union workers. Still, the machinists voted for a union in 1991.

The union got workers access to the gains from the stock market by means of their pension plan. As one retired machinist put it recently, "I have been retired for eight years, I am getting a pension from that place, and it's going to keep on going.

I mean, the guy who set up the 401(k) plan…the guys knew what they were doing." The trick was to keep your job. The industry's profits were down, so only half the machinists kept their jobs into the 21st century.

The layoffs at places like Kingsbury in 1984 broke a social compact between owners and workers, and from 1983 to 1991, the Connecticut River Valley felt like a war zone. Workers lost confidence in management's ability to look out for product quality and the labor force, and the ratio of owner compensation to worker compensation grew. When the workers at Kingsbury mobilized for a union, they were publicly demonstrating that they had lost confidence in Jim Koontz. At stake was really who owned the plant: the legal owners, or the men whose skill gave the machines their reputation? Machinist Hilliker was one of the first to wear a union shirt. He related to my students in 2015 the pressure he was under:

> They would send my work out to have it done somewhere else. "I've got no work for you Hilly, got to lay you off." They didn't have to lay me off, I had so many things I could do around there. I was their whipping boy. They wanted to break me down because I was an older one. But it couldn't be done. I said, If B-52s didn't kill me during the Korean thing, when they bombed me, you sure as hell ain't gonna be able to do it.

Most of the male workers had served in war, so the comparison was not made lightly.

Divisions That Wore People Down

The 1980s were a time of intense technological change, as Kingsbury began to use computerized machine tools, and then acquired Hillyer Machine Tool to have their own line of computerized products. The loyalty that supervisors like Johnson exhibited to older workers meant the young were fired first, even though they might have young children to support at home. One of the men laid off in 1984 had lost a finger at Kingsbury's. Yet, as a young man, he had never favored the union, because unions supported seniority rights. He felt that the younger cohort to which he belonged was better able than the old timers to learn new technology and turn the firm's prospects around. This younger man hates unions, and blames Kingsbury management for acting like a unionized shop in 1984, though no union was voted in until 1991.

The changes weren't just felt on the shop floor. Hanrahan, who had run the company after Frechette's death and taught Koontz the ropes before retiring, gave the speech of his life trying to prevent the vote for a union. He had a heart attack during this period, and his children believe it was caused by his divided loyalties. He respected Koontz, but he developed close ties to the shop-floor workers. That was his way of inspiring people to give their best effort. Though Hanrahan passionately believed a union was the wrong way to go, every machinist I have spoken to goes out of his way to explain the confidence, affection, and appreciation they had for him. Hanrahan was caught between a manufacturing world that viewed the workers' skills as the source of profits and a new era when the source of wealth was capital gains on the stock market, which could be harvested best by laying workers off from time to time.

The tragedy of the tensions in the 1980s is that both managing owners and machinists cared deeply about the future of the firm. For all the flaws that the workers saw in Koontz, he had virtues also, especially compared with his successor. Koontz was trained to work with machines—he did not have an MBA. He lived in Keene. He maintained the workers' pension with utmost regularity. As auto production went global, he traveled the world from South Africa to Brazil to sell Kingsbury products. He used Kingsbury retained earnings to acquire Hillyer to keep up with technological change.

The Volcker Shock Makes Imports Cheap

Technological change does not seem adequate to explain the number of firms that closed in the Connecticut River Valley between 1980 and 1990. What else was going on between 1979 and 1984 that could explain the massive drop in U.S. machine tool profits of 1983?

During the 1979 to 1983 time period highlighted in Figure 3, the base U.S. nominal rate of interest rose from 9% to 19%. The Federal Funds Rate is what banks pay to borrow from each other for overnight loans, and banks pop a markup on top of that before they lend to consumers, so the interest rate for a credit card to a person of sound credit was probably 29% when the Federal Funds Rate was 19%. The reason Fed chair Paul Volcker raised the interest rate so high was to kill off inflation, which was about 10% per year in the late seventies. He did reduce inflation, but using the interest rate to fight inflation is like using chemo to fight cancer: It killed off a lot more than inflation.

Everyone knew that a high rate of interest would reduce business investment in fixed capital equipment like machine tools. Such spending is financed largely by debt. When interest rates are high, the cost of borrowing rises. U.S. firms made the rational decision to delay new capital spending in the hope that the interest rate would come down.

FIGURE 3. U.S. FEDERAL FUNDS INTEREST RATE

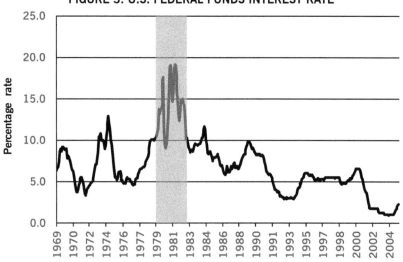

Source: Federal Reserve Bank of St. Louis (FRED II).

Figure 4 illustrates unit labor costs—the cost of wages and benefits employers incurred in the making a hypothetical widget in various countries. While U.S. unit labor costs (the black line) had long been higher than German (light gray) or Japanese (medium gray), that gap widened precisely between 1979 and 1984. This was due to two factors:

First, U.S. manufacturers may have delayed purchasing new equipment until after interest rates came down, while their Japanese and German counterparts did not. Instead, they invested in new machinery that meant workers could produce more units in the same amount of time.

Second, what U.S. policymakers may not have realized is how much the exchange rate for the U.S. dollar would appreciate in response to the rising rate of interest. Exchange rates had been flexible only since 1971. A rising interest rate pulled wealth from around the globe into U.S. bank accounts and this drove up the value of the U.S. dollar relative to every other currency in the world. The dollar appreciated relative to the German deutsche mark and the Japanese yen, and competitors using those currencies were the ones that the machine tool sector faced. Suddenly, the prices of U.S.-made products went up when converted to deutsche marks or yen, and the prices of German and Japanese products went down when converted to dollars.

This drop in relative unit labor costs gave the Germans and the newly industrializing Japanese an opening they needed into the U.S. market for machine tools. To see how this worked, consider a hypothetical tool such a CNC lathe, produced by a U.S. company. It is 1979, and the tool costs $100,000 in the United States. A customer been buying from the U.S. company for 50 years, so they stick with the U.S.-made machine, even though the Japanese or German import costs the same.

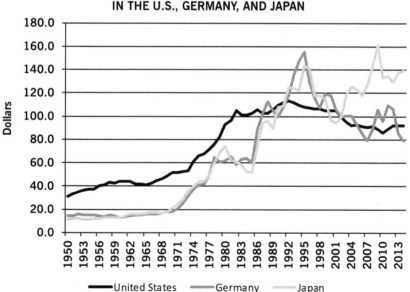

FIGURE 4. INDEX OF UNIT LABOR COSTS IN THE U.S., GERMANY, AND JAPAN

Source: The Conference Board (conference-board.org). ULC is labor cost per unit of output. Labor cost is evaluated using nominal exchange rates, and output is evaluated using purchasing power parity exchange rates.

However, by December 1984, U.S. machine tools experience inflation of 36%, so the U.S. machine costs $136,000. Meanwhile back in Japan, rising productivity reduces costs by 12%. If productivity rises more slowly in United States than Japan, then the U.S. dollar should depreciate, which would hold steady the price that U.S. buyers pay for a Japanese machine. However, Volcker tries to control inflation by raising U.S. interest rates to 19% in 1981, and the high interest rate drives up the value of the dollar, and the import is now "on sale" for only $85,500. That is $51,000 in savings! Under these circumstances some firms decide to try out the import. In short, the U.S. Federal Reserve gave imports an opening into the U.S. market by creating a discount on the price of an import relative to a U.S.-made machine tool in 1984.

By 1986, Volcker had realized his mistake and depreciated the dollar by around 38%, so that the Japanese import would cost the same as the American machine. By then 400 people had already been laid off from Kingsbury, and Jones & Lamson sold out in 1986.

Financial Engineers Finished the Job

By 1988, the Goldman Industrial Group had purchased J&L out of bankruptcy, and began applying "financial engineering" techniques to extract value from the firm. Financial engineering is used to make profits from dying companies by taking them apart. (Of course, many times it's not clear that the firm was going to die if the financial predator had not attacked.) By 1990, Goldman had purchased another once-fine firm, next door to J&L, Bryant Grinding. And in 1998, Goldman protégé Iris Mitropoulis purchased Keene's Kingsbury from Koontz. Mitropoulis owned Ventura Industries, a separate company that owned only one thing, Kingsbury Machine Tool. By 2001, it was clear that she was not investing the retained earnings she had acquired along with the plant into new equipment.

**FIGURE 5. HYPOTHETICAL COMPETITION BETWEEN
U.S. AND IMPORTED MACHINE TOOL, 1979-84**

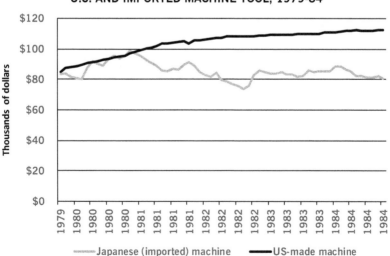

Source: Author's calculations.

Half of the pension fund went missing as well. In 2016, I submitted a Freedom of Information Act request to the Federal Pension Benefit Guarantee Corporation, and there was a very fat file on Kingsbury. Up to 1998, Jim Koontz ran the company and the accountant Tom Cookson filed nice neat forms verifying the financial health of the workers' pension fund. He made it through ups and downs of the stock market with only a few bumps, so that $45 million was in the fund by 1998 when Koontz sold it. Mitropoulis, on the other hand, filed messy and incomplete pension documents, and by 2007 the fund had only $26 million in it. In addition, she went out tirelessly asking the federal government to lend the company money earmarked for woman-owned businesses. It appears that all the money that was ever granted to Kingsbury by its previous owners, its employees, or lenders was transferred to Ventura Industries, so that Kingsbury declared bankruptcy in 2012.

When Keene looks at Mitropoulis's actions 1999–2012, the reign of Koontz appears in a more nuanced light. Mitropoulis was easy to get along with, and so friendly to the union men, that she disarmed them while transferring value to Ventura Industries. She never traveled overseas to find any customers, she did not invest the retained earnings in the company, half the pension fund vanished on her watch, and she borrowed money at subsidized interest rates and then declared bankruptcy so she wouldn't have to pay it back. If we step back to see what Kingsbury's story tells us about U.S. deindustrialization, it's not only that Volcker's high interest rates tilted the scale toward imports. There is a second, more insidious aspect: The easy money provided by Greenspan after 1987 created a rising stock market that rewarded people who took value out of industrial production. Koontz and people of his era stumbled upon those capital gains, while financial engineers such as Mitropoulis actively extracted value from industry to shift the wealth into other assets. Class struggle was nothing new to factories, but between 1980 and 1990, unstable monetary policy was a new pressure hard for either owners or workers to see. They wound up turning on each other. The influence of changing monetary policy has been hard for left economists to see. We are only now beginning to understand what a sea change in the institutional context for industry was taking place. ❑

Sources: On the machine tool firms of the Connecticut River Valley, see Robert Forrant, *Metal Fatigue: The Rise and Precipitous Decline of the Connecticut River Valley Industrial Corridor*, Baywood Publishers, 2009. On financial engineering, see Eileen Applebaum and Rosemary Batt, *Private Equity at Work*, Russell Sage (2014). On how an independent firm is affected by rise of stock market, see John Hacket, *Race to the Bottom*. Author House, 2004. This is a novel, but the author was a PhD economist and chief financial officer at Cummins Engine for decades, so his insights are worth reading. On pensions, the following is still a good overview: Theresa Ghilarducci, *Labor's Capital*, MIT Press (1992).

Article 11.4

RISING ASSET BUBBLES DISTORT THE INDUSTRIAL BASE
Part Two of a Series on Deindustrialization in the Granite State

BY MARIE DUGGAN
March/April 2018

Why did one third of U.S manufacturing jobs disappear between 2001 and 2009? And more generally, why did the U.S. industrial base go into decline after 1980? Conventional wisdom has it that job loss was due to competition from low-wage labor overseas, and as such was inevitable. However, by walking into plants in Keene, N.H., my students and I have learned of homemade causes of industrial decline. Below, I tell the story of Miniature Precision Bearings (MPB), a firm whose competitors lie in high-wage nations such as Denmark, Sweden, Germany, and Japan. If MPB is indicative, the debt-fueled rise of the stock market between the eighties and the year 2000 put the firm into the hands of owners who used the profits to manipulate share price, while sidelining local managers whose focus had been product quality and worker skill. When the asset values of company shares became managers' priority, workers lost the one asset that meant the most to them: secure jobs that produced a stream of income for 20 years with benefits that made savings unnecessary.

Some jobs remain but, without security and benefits, the same positions are a ticket to debt and stress. The shareholder-value revolution turns out to be the economic backstory to the unraveling of rural America.

Ownership Changes

Miniature bearings were developed by Winslow Pierce in the 1920s at Lebanon, N.H. He initially created them to repair his own watch. He sent his associate Horace Gilbert to Keene to open a facility to produce them. Bearings include three metal components: the outer races (a "race" is a ring with a groove in which the ball bearings move), the inner races, and the tiny balls themselves, which are sealed into the races with grease to lubricate them. Bob Rooney, a human resources executive from 1974 to 2003, explains the production process: "The inner and outer [races], the retainers and the balls would be issued to our assembly department, where they would be hand assembled, mostly by women, because women seem to have better fine motor dexterity then men….After the bearings were assembled they would enter into what we call the 'clean room'…some of the bearings—which are tiny—a small particle of dirt or dust could cause a catastrophic failure."

During World War II, demand for miniature bearings increased exponentially due to their use in the gyroscopes of the Norden bombsight of military jets. By 1956, the smallest bearing measured 0.078 inches in outside diameter. By 1959, 500 of them would fit into a thimble. Gilbert had a state-of-the-art plant, attracting top talent to engineer tiny round things that reduced friction. He also attracted national attention by sponsoring a contest for engineers in miniaturization. By the sixties, MPB was developing bearings for the lunar rovers of the Apollo mission.

After Gilbert's death in 1976, MPB fell into the hands of the conglomerate Allied Signal, which then sold it to speculator Harold Geneen in 1987. Geneen was one of the first investors to put very little down to purchase companies by means of issuing junk bonds, and though he expanded operations at MPB, his goal was to make payments on his debt and then get out so that banks would finance his future buyout activity. (See box for an explanation of how junk bonds work.)

MPB's local executives were glad to see him sell the company to Timken Bearing and Steel of Ohio in 1990, which had a reputation for quality and prudence. More recently, Keene's specialty became producing silver-coated bearings that go inside glass X-ray tubes. As CT scans became common, need for these ingenious little bearings grew. By the early 2000s, rumor had it that Timken's Keene plant controlled 80% of the market. Yet during the first decade of the 21st century, the plant fell into decline. Where MPB once employed close to 1,000, as Timken Superprecision the Keene facility now employs perhaps 200. An engineer who toured the facility around 2003 was shocked at the deterioration in the plant's equipment, declaring, "Horace Gilbert would never have let that happen!"

Like many producers of U.S. metal products, Timken was founded in the late 19th century by German immigrants. The company made its own steel because vertical integration permitted control over quality. Specializing in tapered roller bearings that went into vehicle wheels gained Timken a reputation for reliability and quality. Why did the prudent Timkens expand in 1990 away from the niche in which they had a secure reputation, and why were they willing to pay Geneen's high asking price to do so? The answer lies outside the firm, in the go-go financial world of the late eighties and the wild stock market of the nineties.

Junk Bonds Come to Keene in 1987

The first sign that U.S. asset prices had lost touch with gravity was not the stock market but rather the wave of highly leveraged buyouts (LBOs) in the 1980s. Geneen bought MPB in 1987 by putting little money down and borrowing at high interest rates more money than the firm was worth from a bank, Donaldson, Lufkin & Jenrette (DLJ). Geneen got the loan from DLJ with the promise to make a big installment payment by June 1990 by growing little MPB into a powerhouse. Why did DLJ lend Geneen so much? First, Geneen had already grown a company with sales of $700 million into a conglomerate with sales of $22 billion in 17 years. So when Geneen said that he could grow MPB bigger fast, the claim was credible. Second, DLJ was not going to wait for Geneen to pay them back; rather they would sell Geneen's debt off in the form of junk bonds at 15% interest to third parties. If Geneen failed to make his loan payment in 1990, buyers would see the capital value of their bonds decline. If Geneen did make his first fat installment, everybody holding pieces of his debt would see the asset value of the junk bonds soar.

Geneen flew into sleepy Keene in his private jet, and showered young executives with eye-popping salaries, with the proviso that they grow the firm by 50% in three years. With his loan, Geneen also bought brand new equipment and hired new people. His management philosophy was the following: "I wanted the people... to reach for goals that they might think were beyond them...And I wanted them to

How Junk Bonds Work

If Geneen made his balloon payment in 1990 successfully, holders of the high-interest bonds which DLJ had issued would appreciate quickly: for example, a $1,000 bond paying $150 per year (15%) might be snapped up by a secondary buyer for $2,000. Why? Investors would no longer demand an interest rate as high as 15%, because the risk of bankruptcy would have declined. The way that bond interest rates come down is for the market to bid up the price of the bond until its coupon (the $150 in this case) divided by that price results in a lower interest rate; for example, $150 coupon divided by a $2,000 bond value would yield 7.5% interest.

do it not only for the company and their careers, but also for the fun of it." To hear the executives of MPB tell it, there was excitement working for Geneen, but there was also a lot of pressure. Geneen believed, "The most difficult task of all is firing a man who is working hard, doing the best he can, but whose confidence in himself outstrips his abilities. He's in over his head. It breaks your heart to tell such a man he is incompetent. After all...it was you who put him in deep water over his head." In other words, Geneen placed large speculative bets using other people's money and portions of the U.S. industrial base. If a bet failed to pay off, Geneen blamed others, and abandoned the company. The black magic of LBOs meant the debt would stay with the company, not with Geneen.

The Keene crew did grow the firm by as much as 20% in one year, but Geneen had saddled MPB with debt payments that the firm could not make, so in 1990 MPB was in financial distress despite rapid expansion into profitable markets. He could have renegotiated the loan on easier terms with longer repayment. But neither DLJ nor Geneen wanted that to happen; they wanted the junk bonds to appreciate. A bankruptcy would have had the opposite effect. Geneen had to make the payment if he wanted to ever do business with DLJ again—and he planned to do a lot of debt-financed acquisitions. Geneen knew that Timken wanted MPB badly, because Timken had come in second in the 1987 bidding, with Swedish firm SKF in third. Geneen intimated to Timken in 1990 that the Europeans were still interested—though in reality their response to Geneen's asking price had been, "Are you kidding?" He convinced Timken to pay $185 million for the company in 1990, although Timken valued MPB at only $93 million. With cash from the sale, Geneen made his balloon payment to DLJ. Since the only part of his own money that he had risked was the down payment in 1987, he could net very little and still make a high return. For example, if Geneen (hypothetically) had put down $8 million to purchase MPB, and sold MPB for $4 million more than necessary to repay DLJ, then Geneen would have made a 50% return on equity in three years.

By 1990 the profits a firm could produce from products were no longer at the forefront of the mind of the firm's owner. Rather, what interested Geneen was the increase in the firm's asset value. And for the bank that essentially co-owned the firm, what mattered was the increase in the asset value of the firm's debt. Geneen valued his relationship with his bank more than his relationship with the firm's managers. As for the workers of the shop floor, Geneen never met them. This change from viewing the stream of profits that a firm produces to looking at the potential to grow the firm's asset value in a very short period was fundamental between 1987 and 2003.

Focus Shifts from Production Toward the Stock Market

Timken's wealth was tied up in shares of firm stock, of which the family owned 30%. Since Timken bearings went into wheels, the firm was an "automotive supplier." That label was the kiss of death for Timken's share price in the eighties, given the troubles of the U.S. auto industry. Failure of stock price to rise was typical prior to 1980 (see Figure 1). But after 1987, the laws of gravity no longer applied to the stock market. The Timkens wanted in on the bonanza. Purchasing MPB was the cornerstone of a strategy to remake Timken as a diversified bearings supplier. MPB's customer base was aerospace, and in the late eighties, aerospace was booming. Ronald Reagan was building cruise missiles and each one had $3,000 of MPB product in its guidance system. When Timken purchased MPB in 1990, then-CEO Joe Toot told executives in Ohio to let Keene-based management continue to run the plant because they were profitable.

But Timken began to measure success not by the old-fashioned rate of profit, but rather using the five-year return on shareholder value. This distinction is the key to understanding the decline of MPB in the 1990s. As Figure 2 illustrates, with Timken shares, the five-year return on shareholder value is vastly more volatile than the rate of profit. The five-year return on shareholder value answers the question, if someone invests in a share of Timken stock and holds it for five years, how much money will he or she make? There are two sources of gain: dividends and capital gains. The dividend is a portion of company profits paid out to shareholders. If the company experiences no profits, it has the option to issue no dividend. If dividends are 3% of share price, then someone who invests a million dollars in Timken shares, will receive $30,000 per year in dividend income. Dividends are not the source of big bucks, but, given a large enough investment, they can permit the wealthy to live without working.

The stock market gains of the nineties originate with the other factor, capital gains, which are the difference between the share price when the stock is purchased, and price when it is sold later. To calculate the five-year return, the five-year capital gain is added to the sum of five years of dividends, and then this sum is divided by the initial price paid for the share. If somebody purchased a share of Timken stock in 1991 for $24.81, and sold it in 1995 for $34.31, she made a capital gain of $9.50. The share also issued dividends in 1991, 1992, 1993, and 1994 of $1 each year, and $1.11 in 1995, for total dividends of $5.11. Her five-year return on a share of Timken stock was ($9.50+$5.11)/24.81, which comes to 59%. She would get back her initial investment of $24.81, and she would make an additional $14.61. If we assume she purchased 100 shares with $2,482, then she not only got her money back but also obtained an additional $1,461, which is a good return for five years.

What Is Rate of Profit?

Profits are sales less costs of production, commonly known as earnings before interest and taxation (EBIT). To compute the rate of profit, divide EBIT by working capital. Working capital is made up of gross property, plant, and equipment; total current assets; and costs of doing business. Current assets include inventories, and costs of doing business include payroll. According to the 1996 annual report, Timken's EBIT was $257,257,000. Working capital was $5,096,551,000. The rate of profit was therefore 5%.

FIGURE 1. THE INFLATION-ADJUSTED VALUE OF THE S&P 500 STOCK INDEX

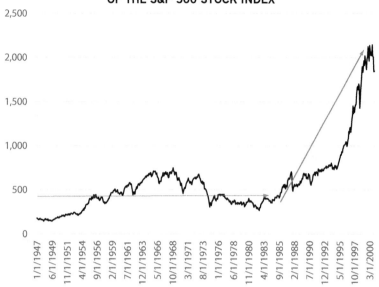

Source: Macrotrends (macrotrends.net).

FIGURE 2. FIVE-YEAR RETURN ON SHAREHOLDER VALUE VS. RATE OF PROFIT AT TIMKEN

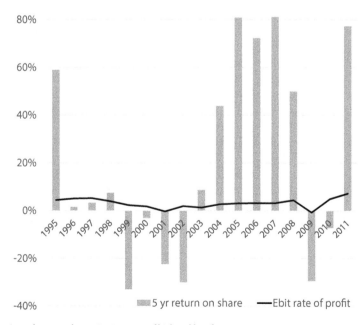

Source: Annual reports; share price is average of high and low first quarter.

Ebit rate of profit excludes one-time accounting changes.

Remember that prior to 1980, the stock market was flat (see Figure 1), which means that capital gains tended to be negligible. If our investor had received dividends alone, her five-year return would have been only 21%, or about 4% a year. That is why, prior to 1980, firms were content to maximize the rate of profit instead of maximizing shareholder value.

MPB was Timken's first acquisition in the new era, but not the last. In 1993, Timken acquired a Connecticut facility that made bearings for helicopters. In 1994, Timken started making bearings for computer disk drives in Singapore, and it opened plants in Asheboro, N.C., and another in Virginia. In 1995, Timken acquired the U.S. firm Rail Bearing Services. In 1996 and 1997, Timken purchased plants in Poland, Romania, Italy, and China. The plant in China would make giant bearings for wind turbines, a product that Asheboro made for the U.S. market by the early 2000s. By 1998, Timken was also refurbishing rail bearings in Indiana and South Africa.

We usually suppose that U.S. corporations purchase plants overseas because the labor is cheaper. Yet Timken's acquisitions occurred in countries at all levels of the wage scale. The goal was diversification, and to break into markets around the world rather than rely upon the U.S. domestic market. Timken diversified products and markets to cushion gyrations in shareholder value. If the firm produced multiple products for multiple markets, then bad news in any one market wouldn't harm the stock price much. Yet diversifying caused a growing disconnect between Timken headquarters and production workers at plants around the world.

When asked in 2012 why he was building new plants in Asia, Timken CEO Griffith explained: "[Timken bearings] make machines more reliable...Where the

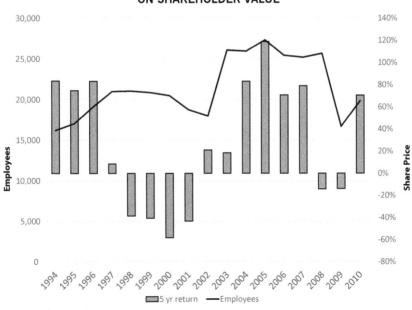

FIGURE 3. JOBS AT TIMKEN AND FIVE-YEAR RETURN ON SHAREHOLDER VALUE

Source: Timken annual reports.

applications were the hardest, the dirtiest, and the most challenging, those were the industrial markets, those were the infrastructure markets. And interestingly, where did the infrastructure get developed in the last decade?" In 2012, the answer to his question was Asia, while in the 1995–2000 period, infrastructure was being developed in Eastern Europe (after the Berlin Wall came down) and in South Africa (apartheid ended in 1990)—precisely where Timken made acquisitions. Timken was buying plants in other nations because the people buying bearings were in those nations. In contrast to the expansion of infrastructure in Eastern Europe and China, U.S. investment in infrastructure declined between 1990 and 2000 from 3% of GDP to 2%.

How did Timken's strategy of reducing new capital investment in favor of acquisitions work out? When Timken purchased MPB in 1990, its share price experienced a 15% capital gain, though the firm experienced a 1% loss on operations. Yet despite diversifying away from U.S. auto, Timken's five-year return on shareholder value was a 60% loss in 2000 (see Figure 3). Timken had expanded into Asia and Eastern Europe, and the 1997 financial crisis caused GDP to contract in both locations. The setback only increased Timken's determination to loosen ties to communities so that it could rapidly contract where sales were in decline. With the U.S. recession in 2001, Timken closed a legacy plant in Ohio and expanded in China, Romania, and North Carolina. Figure 3 illustrates that after 2001 layoffs followed the five-year return on shareholder value closely. By 2010, CEO Jim Griffith must have been regarded by his peers as a genius when, despite global recession, the five-year return to Timken shareholders fell only 10%. The fall in the one-year return was far more drastic, but Timken laid employees off so rapidly that the company's share price was protected.

By the late eighties the stock market was taking more money from business than it was providing to business. Firms raise money from the stock market only when they issue new shares. After that first issue, any resale of the shares does not benefit the company, but rather benefits the owners of the shares. Thus, most of the capital gains in the stock market did not finance U.S. business activity, but financed instead U.S. households. On a personal level, executives held shares of stock, and workers sometimes held pensions that were invested in shares of company stock.

Few people caught on to the fact that the rising stock market of the 1987 to 1999 period might erode incentives to invest in new equipment for the industrial base. To understand how the capital gains in shares could curtail new capital spending, it is necessary to understand dividends, stock buybacks, and acquisitions.

Stock Options and Change at the Top

By 1985, Timken executives were getting paid in stock options, giving them an incentive to spend cash in such a way that share price would rise. A "stock option" is a certificate that gives the bearer the right to purchase shares at a specified price, say $20 per share. If the share price never rises to that level, the options are worthless. But if the share price rises higher—for example to $30—then the holder of options can purchase them at the locked-in price of $20 and sell them the next day for $30. Paying executives by stock option permitted them to increase their wealth substantially and rapidly, but caused them to devote attention to managerial actions that would have an immediate effect on share price. Working people were won over to this strategy when their pensions were invested into the company's stock, as was the case at Timken.

In 1992, Robert Mahoney was brought on the board of Timken. Wall Street loved him because he was laying off workers and distributing dividends. By 1994, Timken's board included J. Clayburn La Force, retired Dean of UCLA's business school. He believed that removing the social safety net would make people work harder, and that firms should not be in the business of community philanthropy. The 1994 annual report noted that Timken would now "emphasize initiatives and investment that are more likely to create short-term impact"—code for using cash from operations to make the share price rise.

In 1993, the Timken board in Ohio was split, with the old school represented by W.R. Timken, Jr., whose family's reputation was staked on the quality of the product, and new people such as La Force and Mahoney seeking to divert funds to stock market strategy. The new ideology had not completely taken hold. But in early 1995, W.R. Timken, Sr. died. Joe Toot retired in 1997. Jim Griffith, with a Stanford MBA, would rise to Chief Operating Officer in 1999, and to CEO in 2002.

Managing Industry to Raise Share Price

At Timken between 1991 and 2000, 88% of cash came from existing operations, and 12% from debt (no funds were raised from the stock market). These funds financed five activities: acquisitions, dividends, stock buybacks, debt reduction, and new capital spending. That last is the purchase of new equipment to keep up with technological change. Economist William Lazonick was one of the first to notice that firms were diverting money away from investing in new capital equipment toward the stock market, through two channels: higher and more consistent dividends, and the practice of buying back shares of their own stock, which has only been legal since 1983.

The share of cash that Timken used to pay out dividends and stock buybacks increased from 15% of the cash in 1990 to 22% in one year, and settled at 20% by 2000. The dividend remained constant even in years when the firm made little profit or suffered a loss. The logic behind the dividend is that if it is typically a percentage of the share price, one can also conclude that the share price is typically some multiple of the dividend. Hence, if the dividend is held steady during a period of low profits, the value of shares should hold as well. Raising the dividend as a method of raising stock price does not always work, but it is a strategy to which corporate executives have easy access.

Timken also undertook stock buybacks (see Figure 4). Timken's share price was suffering a decline between 1996 and 1998. The company purchased $80 million of its own shares, presumably to reverse that decline. This is similar to a poker player bluffing by betting large amounts of money on her own hand in an attempt to get the other players to assume she has been dealt a good set of cards. Did Timken's $80 million bluff

FIGURE 4. TIMKEN SHARE PRICE VS. STOCK BUYBACKS, 1990 TO 2000

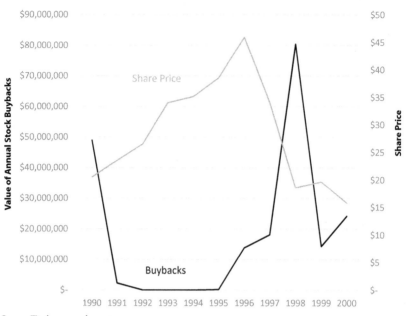

Source: Timken annual reports.

work? The stock price does not seem to have reversed course by much. In a card game, when a bluff does not work, the one who made it simply loses the money. However, in the case of a buyback, even if the maneuver doesn't raise share price directly, simply buying back some shares reduces the number of shares outstanding. A critical measure of success in the age of the stock market is earnings per share (EPS). The firm with low earnings can buy back some shares, and then the denominator of EPS is smaller, so that EPS rises. A rising EPS is a second method to push up stock price.

At 7%, acquisitions used more cash than dividends (5%). The tradeoff between capital spending and acquisitions is direct: a firm can either invest in in-house capacity to innovate and stay competitive, or the firm can let existing capacity dwindle, and use the funds to purchase other plants that are innovative and competitive. Over the course of the nineties, Timken was choosing more and more to acquire: new capital absorbed 79% of Timken cash 1991 to 1995, but fell to 61% from 1996 to 2000. Acquisitions rose from a negligible share of spending for 1991 to 1995, to 14% between 1996 and 2000. From the perspective of the firm's profits, whether the management invests in new equipment or acquires another firm is not important. But if every firm begins to acquire instead of investing, the industrial base will cease to expand. Acquisition simply transfers ownership, rather than adding productive capacity to the economy. Furthermore, acquisition often breaks down the human ties that are the yeast of innovation. Finally, the price paid for an acquisition may well be higher than fair market value. Timken paid twice as much as MPB was worth. How did Timken's acquisition of MPB affect the little plant's reputation for offering attractive employment and manufacturing a product reliable and precise enough to be incorporated into the Hubble Telescope?

Human Ties in Keene

People connected with industry in Keene make a distinction between managers who live in a community and know the shop floor, versus managers who live in another state or never walk into the plant. For executives who live in a community, the purpose of the plant is to provide them with a decent income and reputation in the location where they reside, while also keeping that location pleasant through philanthropic activity. Positive relations with the shop floor mean that when the executives walk down Main Street, the community says, "Look, there goes so and so. He runs the place." Making a quality product is also a source of public satisfaction; that MPB made components of the Mars Rover is part of local lore. It is easy to discount this community pressure and pride, yet it is an important part of the social fabric that makes small towns thrive, and is a reason that acquisition of independent firms by larger corporations tends to lead plants in small towns into gradual decline.

Tom Uhlig, the president of MPB in 1990, was determined to make the transition from Geneen to Timken work. Timken's reputation in 1990 rested on the decision to build a state-of-the-art steel plant in Ohio in 1982, in the depths of recession. That showed prudent focus on quality for the long-term—and the use of Japanese methods at the steel plant was evidence of intelligence. To Uhlig, Timken seemed a lot better basis for MPB's future than Harold Geneen's debt-fueled dreams. But Uhlig was aware of something that may have eluded Timken executives in Ohio. MPB had relied heavily on military sales, especially during the Reagan years. With the end of the Cold War in 1989, that market shrank severely. Worse yet: GPS technology was about to make miniature bearings in guidance systems obsolete. The aerospace instruments were about to switch from mechanics to solid-state technology.

Uhlig and chief engineer Don Leroy had the motivation and capacity to adapt the plant as it faced obsolescence. They had spent decades at MPB, directing where Geneen should invest his cash and protecting the shop floor from the extreme pressure he was putting on the executives. Louise Clark, an employee who inspected bearings for quality at MPB, said that Uhlig would "be right in the shipping room helping us out. No matter where there was a need for help, he didn't mind getting dirty." As manager of a business, Uhlig controlled costs and invested in new equipment, but most importantly between 1989 and 1992, he developed new product lines. It turned out that rising healthcare costs had a positive side: increasing demand for miniature bearings in CT scans and dental drills. The Keene-based salesforce identified opportunities, and engineers at the Keene research lab developed new products. The strong human ties between Uhlig, Leroy, the salesforce, the machinists, and the bearings inspectors were critical in making such a dramatic shift.

The success the Keene crew had at adapting miniature bearings to new markets won Uhlig promotion to oversee Timken manufacturing for all of North and South America. Leaving his home in New England was the last thing that Uhlig wanted to do. In Ohio he found that Timken's management wanted him to focus solely on cutting costs by 1992; he had little room to bring in new equipment or to develop new product lines. Timken pitted each production facility against the others in competition for the annual capital expenditure budget. Only those plants that could demonstrate that they expected a return of more than 8% on the capital invested received new equipment. Another Keene-based executive believed Geneen had purchased more new equipment for Keene's plant between 1987 and 1990 than Timken did in the next 15 years. Though Uhlig's new title and the relocation to corporate headquarters both implied that the promotion gave him authority, he had held greater room to maneuver when he ran the miniature bearing plant in Keene because there he had both a salesforce and an engineering staff to help him adapt to markets. He didn't want to simply cut costs, so he quit within a year.

Uhlig came back to MPB in 1998 in a slot reporting to the plant manager, and Clark was hopeful that he would bring back the old ethos, but he resigned in 2001. In 2003, a local inventor was in negotiations to sell the plant new diamond-tipped grinding machines. Instead, Timken diverted resources to the acquisition of Torrington Bearings in Connecticut. The giant merger captured the stock market's attention, and loaded the company with debt, which is perhaps why Timken sold half of the facilities acquired to a European competitor only four years later. Back in Keene in 2003, Timken cut costs by removing the salesforce, and relocating the engineers to headquarters in Ohio. The idea was to save money, and yet corporate headquarters charged Keene's facility $5 million dollars a year for their share of Canton's facility, so it really would have been in the Keene facility's best interest to keep the engineers in New Hampshire.

Another person who left was machinist Reggie Clark. Where he had once supervised 26 people, there were by 2003 only three, because most of the machining had been outsourced to local shops. So the company proposed cutting his pay. Such vertical disintegration means product quality is not as high a priority as cutting costs. In a surprisingly bright turn of events, Mr. Clark was recruited by a precision lens manufacturer down the street where he was considerably happier for his last decade of employment. Today Timken's Keene plant employs fewer than 200 people, and production of bearings for X-ray tubes was snapped up by a regional competitor. The implication from this analysis of Timken and MPB is that acquisitions by outside owners who have an eye on shareholder value reduce the role of staff who have the commitment and ability to adapt plants to changing market conditions. This could explain why firms that had survived for 70 or 80 years suddenly went into decline at the end of the 20th century.

Benefits and Shareholder Value.

With the advent of Timken's control, Clark started to notice the change in management philosophy that was rippling through board rooms, executive suites, and shop floors throughout the United States between 1987 and 2003. "All of a sudden they are making us push, push, push....[W]e were never in the red, they just wanted more out of us, but for less." This was a change from her experience at New Hampshire factories between 1974 and 1989: "The companies really cared for the employees, especially if you were a good employee...I mean, we had 100% Blue Cross and Blue Shield, my two boys cost nothing. But as I was working at Timken, every year from 1989 we'd have a corporate meeting in the cafeteria, and it was the same old, same old: we went from 90/10, 80/20, and then before I left [in 2009] it was 60/40. And then you see the premiums of what we have to pay!" Union organizers met with workers off site. Though nothing came of it, even to consider a union was a dramatic step for Keene people.

In national economic news, wages take center stage more than benefits, and yet when the people who worked at MPB recounted their story, they said it was the loss of benefits that hurt them the most. Benefits were one reason that Clark and her husband Reggie (a machinist at MPB) had been attracted to industrial employment in the first place. Mr. Clark recounted: "Back in the fifties and sixties ... I remember my father and my uncle that owned the farm. We didn't have any insurance, we didn't have any holidays. We didn't have any vacation." The powerful magnet of a job with benefits pulled him off the farm into the life of a machinist at Sanders Associates in Nashua (now BAE Systems). At Sanders, he met Louise working on sonar and radar for submarines. In 1974, they moved back to 156 acres of hardscrabble farm in Alstead, but their source of income would remain industrial employment down in the valley of Keene.

An example of how pro-shareholder thinking affected the way firms handled rising healthcare costs is illustrated by Financial Accounting Standards Board Ruling No. 106. FASB 106 mandated that employers set aside more funds for retiree healthcare costs, given the aging population and rising health costs. The ruling went into effect in 1993, requiring Timken to set aside $254 million immediately. It was already a very bad year for Timken, which anticipated a 0.43% loss. FASB 106 pushed Timken's 1993 loss to -7%. The company responded by cutting healthcare benefits, including retiree benefits. Bob Rooney negotiated benefits for the Keene facility until he retired in 2003, and he says with rising costs, it just wasn't feasible for the company to cover 100% anymore. His new goal became 80%, and he held onto that until in 2003. One reason he retired early was that Timken planned on removing the ability of Keene-based executives to negotiate benefits contracts for the local plant. Indeed, the 60/40 split that so outraged Clark emerged after Rooney left. Other employers also responded to the increased requirements in FASB 106 by reducing healthcare benefits. The business press reported that the stock market was pleased by the reductions in benefits. Despite the 7% loss, Timken's stock price rose between 1993 and 1994.

Inflating Stock Market Returns Eroded Investment in People and Equipment

The spectacular rise of the stock market between 1987 and 2000 gave influence to the kind of management that did not promote the health of the industrial base. Figure 5 illustrates the near-inverse relationship that developed between the stock market and capital investments at bearing plants nationwide between 1987 and 2009.

The rising stock market coupled with stock options and buybacks created incentives for a company such as Timken to acquire multiple plants making related products for multiple markets. This diverted attention from the human relationships and technology that created quality product and innovation at any one plant. Diversification gave executives the power to reallocate resources to avoid those terrifying drops in shareholder value—but it also put distance between top executives

FIGURE 5. NATIONWIDE CAPITAL INVESTMENT IN BEARINGS COMPARED TO REAL S&P STOCK MARKET INDEX

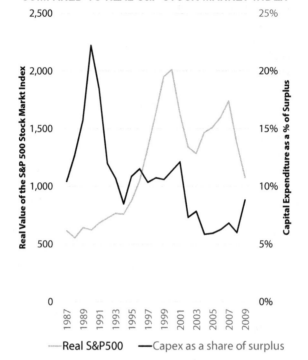

——Real S&P500   —Capex as a share of surplus

Sources: North American Industry Classification System (NAICS), Bureau of Economic Analysis.

FIGURE 6. STOCK MARKET AND INTEREST RATE

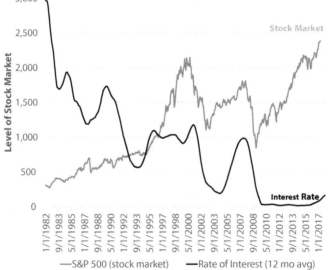

——S&P 500 (stock market)   —Rate of Interest (12 mo avg)

Sources: Macrotrends (inflation-adjusted S&P); St. Louis Federal Reserve (Federal Funds Rate of Interest).

and local management where production took place. If wealth is tied to share price, executives are rewarded for abandoning communities in order to make capital gains. In contrast, executives and managers whose own place in the world is tied to the community—people motivated to dig in and find a path forward—get sidelined from authority.

Whose job is it to stabilize the stock market to prevent bubbles that funnel funds out of the industrial base? The rate of interest set by the U.S. Federal Reserve and the stock market are inversely correlated, as Figure 6 shows. Making stock buybacks legal in 1983 may be one reason that the stock market began to rise beyond its historical range. The repair for that is obvious. Alan Greenspan came into office in 1987, just as the stock market lost touch with gravity. A more systemic cause of the stock market bubble 1987 to 1999 may be the steady influx of wealth into the U.S. financial markets as restrictions on international financial flows were lifted. It was Greenspan's job to manage that inflow.

Yet in 2002 his successor Ben Bernanke stated, "The Fed cannot reliably identify bubbles in asset prices....Even if it could identify bubbles, monetary policy is far too blunt a tool for effective use against them." My introductory macroeconomics class identified a bubble in the stock market two weeks ago, and then the S&P 500 slid 6%. Identifying bubbles is not rocket science. A larger problem is that controlling bubbles means raising interest rates preemptively. Most heterodox economists argue that the Fed's job is to keep interest rates low to promote investment in equipment that creates jobs. However, if rising asset markets pull money out of the production process, and if low interest rates promote rising asset markets, then this conclusion requires modification. Economist Thomas Palley suggested in 2005 that the Fed could require more collateral for the types of loans used to invest in certain assets—a second way the Fed could reduce asset bubbles that would not rely upon the "blunt instrument" of interest rates. There will be many who do not want to imagine that a stock market bubble can do harm to the real economy. However, the rate at which America's social fabric is tearing is too rapid for putting our heads in the sand. At least that's the view from Keene, N.H. ❑

Sources: Brian Alexander, *Glass House: The 1% Economy and the Shattering of the All-American Town* (St. Martin's Press, 2017); German Gutierrez and Thomas Philippon, "Investment-less Growth: An Empirical Investigation," Brookings Papers for Economic Activity (2017); Thomas Palley, "The Questionable Legacy of Allan Greenspan," *Challenge* (2005); William Lazonick, *Sustainable Prosperity in the New Economy?* (Upjohn Institute, 2009);Rana Foroohar, *The Rise of Finance and the Fall of American Business* (Crown Publishing, 2016); Jane D'Arista and Korkut Erturk, "The Monetary Explanation of the Crisis and the Ongoing Threat to the Global Economy," *Challenge* (2010).

CONTRIBUTORS

Frank Ackerman is an economist with Synapse Energy Economics and a founder of *Dollars & Sense*.

Gar Alperovitz is a professor of political economy at the University of Maryland and co-author, with Lew Daly, of *Unjust Deserts: How the Rich Are Taking Our Common Inheritance and Why We Should Take It Back* (New Press, 2009).

Eileen Appelbaum is a senior economist at the Center for Economic and Policy Research and a visiting professor at the University of Leicester, UK

Michael Ash is an associate professor of economics at the University of Massachusetts-Amherst.

David Bacon is a journalist and photographer covering labor, immigration, and the impact of the global economy on workers. He is author of several books, including *Illegal People: How Globalization Creates Migration and Criminalizes Immigrants* (Beacon Press, 2009).

Dean Baker is co-director of the Center for Economic and Policy Research.

Peter Barnes, co-founder of Working Assets, is a senior fellow at the Tomales Bay Institute.

Rosemary Batt is the Alice Hanson Cook Professor of Women and Work at the Industrial and Labor Relations School, Cornell University, and a *Dollars & Sense* Associate.

Sarah Blaskey is a student at the University of Wisconsin-Madison and a member of the Student Labor Action Coalition.

James K. Boyce is a professor of economics at the University of Massachusetts-Amherst and co-director of the Political Economy Research Institute (PERI) Program on Development, Peacebuilding, and the Environment.

Jeremy Brecher is author of *Strike!* (revised, expanded, and updated edition 2015) and *Climate Insurgency: A Strategy for Survival* (2015), and co-founder of the Labor Network for Sustainability (www.labor4sustainabiconlity.org).

Sasha Breger Bush is a lecturer at the Josef Korbel School of International Studies at the University of Denver and author of *Derivatives and Development: A Political Economy of Global Finance, Farming, and Poverty* (Palgrave Macmillan, 2012).

Marc Breslow is co-chair of the Massachusetts Climate Action Network and a former *Dollars & Sense* collective member.

Lew Daly is a senior fellow at Demos and co-author, with Gar Alperovitz, of *Unjust Deserts: How the Rich Are Taking Our Common Inheritance and Why We Should Take It Back* (New Press, 2009).

Marie Duggan is a professor of economics at Keene State College in Keene, N.H.

Deborah M. Figart is a professor or education and economics at the Richard Stockton College of New Jersey.

Nancy Folbre is a professor emerita of economics at the University of Massachusetts-Amherst. She contributes regularly to the *New York Times* Economix blog.

Ellen Frank teaches economics at the University of Massachusetts-Boston and is a *Dollars & Sense* Associate.

Anders Fremstad is an assistant professor of economics at Colorado State University.

Ellen David Friedman is a long-time organizer with the National Education Association in Vermont. She facilitates the United Caucuses of Rank-and-File Educators (UCORE), the national network of progressive teacher union caucuses.

Gerald Friedman is a professor of economics at the University of Massachusetts-Amherst.

Phil Gasper teaches at Madison College and writes the "Critical Thinking" column for *International Socialist Review.*

Lisa Heinzerling is a professor of law at Georgetown University Law School, specializing in environmental law.

Edward Herman is an economist and co-author of *The Global Media: The New Missionaries of Corporate Capitalism.*

José A. Laguarta Ramírez is a scholar-activist and educator born in San Juan, Puerto Rico and trained in anthropology, law, and comparative politics.

Rob Larson is a professor of economics at Tacoma Community College and author of *Capitalism vs. Freedom: The Toll Road to Serfdom* (Zero Books).

Arthur MacEwan, a *Dollars & Sense* Associate, is professor emeritus of economics at the University of Massachusetts-Boston.

John Miller, a *Dollars & Sense* collective member, teaches economics at Wheaton College.

Jawied Nawabi is a professor of economics and sociology at CUNY Bronx Community College and a member of the *Dollars & Sense* collective.

Martin Oppenheimer is professor emeritus of sociology, Rutgers University, where he was a union grievance counselor. He is the author of White Collar Politics (Monthly Review, 1985) and other works on social movements.

Thomas Palley is an economist who has held positions at the AFL-CIO, Open Society Institute, and the U.S./China Economic and Security Review Commission.

Sam Pizzigati is a veteran labor journalist and an Institute for Policy Studies associate fellow.

Robert Pollin teaches economics and is co-director of the Political Economy Research Institute at the University of Massachusetts-Amherst.

Steven Pressman is a professor of economics at Colorado State University and the author of *Fifty Major Economists*.

Alejandro Reuss is a historian and economist and the former co-editor of *Dollars & Sense*.

Helen Scharber is an assistant professor of economics at Hampshire College in Amherst, Mass.

Geoff Schneider is a professor of economics at Bucknell University.

Juliet Schor is a professor of sociology at Boston College and the author of *The Overworked American*, *The Overspent American*, and *True Wealth*.

Zoe Sherman is an assistant professor at Merrimack College and a member of the *Dollars & Sense* collective.

Bryan Snyder (co-editor of this volume) is a senior lecturer in economics at Bentley University.

Chris Sturr (co-editor of this volume) is co-editor of *Dollars & Sense* and a lecturer on Social Studies at Harvard University.

Chris Tilly is a *Dollars & Sense* Associate and director of UCLA's Institute for Research on Labor and Employment and professor in the Urban Planning Department.

Ramaa Vasudevan teaches economics at Colorado State University and is a *Dollars & Sense* Associate.

Craig Watts is a chicken producer for Perdue in Fairmont, N.C.

Jeannette Wicks-Lim is an economist and research fellow at the Political Economy Research Institute at the University of Massachusetts-Amherst.

Marty Wolfson is a professor of economics at the University of Notre Dame.

Klara Zwickl is a post-doctoral researcher at the Vienna University of Economics and Business.